I0138955

A

DICTIONARY

OF THE

Norman or Old French Language;

COLLECTED FROM SUCH

ACTS OF PARLIAMENT,
PARLIAMENT ROLLS,
JOURNALS,
ACTS OF STATE,
RECORDS,
LAW BOOKS,
ANTIENT HISTORIANS,
AND MANUSCRIPTS,

AS RELATE TO THIS NATION.

CALCULATED

To illuſtrate the Rights and Cuſtoms of former Ages, the Forms of Laws and Juriſprudence, the Names of Dignities and Offices, of Perſons and Places; and to render the Reading of thoſe Records, Books, and Manuſcripts, which are written in that Language, more eaſy; as well as to reſtore the true Senſe and Meaning of many Words, hitherto deemed quite obſcure or miſtranſlated.

TO WHICH ARE ADDED

THE LAWS

OF

WILLIAM THE CONQUEROR,

WITH NOTES AND REFERENCES.

By ROBERT KELHAM,
OF LINCOLNS-INN.

Multa ignoramus quæ non laterent, ſi veterum Lectio nobis eſſet familiaris.
MACROBIUS.

THE LAWBOOK EXCHANGE, LTD.
Clark, New Jersey

ISBN 978-1-58477-719-9

Lawbook Exchange edition 2007, 2018

The quality of this reprint is equivalent to the quality of the original work.

THE LAWBOOK EXCHANGE, LTD.
33 Terminal Avenue
Clark, New Jersey 07066-1321

Please see our website for a selection of our other publications and fine facsimile reprints of classic works of legal history:
www.lawbookexchange.com

Library of Congress Cataloging-in-Publication Data

Kelham, Robert, 1717-1808.
A dictionary of the Norman or Old French language : collected from such acts of parliament, parliament rolls, journals, acts of state, records, law books, ... the names of dignities and offices, of persons and places; and to render the reading of those records, more easy ... true sense and meaning of many words ... to which are added the laws of William the Conqueror, with notes and references / Robert Kelham.
p. cm.
Originally published: London : E. Brooke, 1779.
Includes bibliographical references.
ISBN-13: 978-1-58477-719-9 (cloth : alk. paper)
ISBN-10: 1-58477-719-2 (cloth : alk. paper)
1. Law--Great Britain--Dictionaries. 2. Law--Great Britain--Terminology. 3. Anglo-Norman dialect--Dictionaries. 4. Law, Medieval--Dictionaries. I. Title.
KD313.K44 2007
349.4203--dc22 2007002476

Printed in the United States of America on acid-free paper

A

DICTIONARY

OF THE

Norman or Old French Language;

COLLECTED FROM SUCH

ACTS OF PARLIAMENT,
PARLIAMENT ROLLS,
JOURNALS,
ACTS OF STATE,
RECORDS.
LAW BOOKS,
ANTIENT HISTORIANS,
AND MANUSCRIPTS,

AS RELATE TO THIS NATION.

CALCULATED

To illuftrate the Rights and Cuftoms of former Ages, the Forms of Laws and Jurifprudence, the Names of Dignities and Offices, of Perfons and Places; and to render the Reading of thofe Records, Books, and Manufcripts, which are written in that Language, more eafy; as well as to reftore the true Senfe and Meaning of many Words, hitherto deemed quite obfcure or miftranflated.

TO WHICH ARE ADDED

THE LAWS

OF

WILLIAM THE CONQUEROR,

WITH NOTES AND REFERENCES.

By ROBERT KELHAM,
OF LINCOLNS-INN.

Multa ignoramus quæ non laterent, fi veterum Lectio nobis effet familiaris.
MACROBIUS.

LONDON:
Printed for EDWARD BROOKE,
Succeffor to Meff. WORRALL and TOVEY,
in BELL-YARD, near TEMPLE-BAR.
MDCCLXXIX.

PREFACE

TO THE

DICTIONARY.

SO many Statutes, Acts of State, Records, Law Books, and MSS. are extant in the Norman and old French Language, that a Dictionary is become neceſſary to enable the Reader to underſtand ſuch difficult Words as occur therein in that Language; whether ſuch Difficulty ariſes from the Words being merely idiomatical, or from the Inorthography of them.

There is indeed a Book called the Law French Dictionary; but it is ſo trifling a Performance, and ſo incorrect, that it greatly miſleads the Reader, as will evidently appear to any one who will compare ſeveral of the Words in that Dictionary [a] with their Origi-

[a] *As Oeptaz*—Nov. Nar. 6, b.—until the Octaves—tranſlated *they have wiſhed.*
Deins—ibid—11. b.—Teeth—*the Eyes.*
Un longayne—No. Nar. 16. a. b.—a Houſe of Office, a Jakes—*a Sheep walk.*
Pereſoys—Nov. Nar. 17. a. b.—by Turns—*the Agreement or Covenant.*
Deſyra—Nov. Nar. 47. b.—tore—*took away, ſpoiled.*
Geſta—Ibid.—carried away—*put, caſt in.*
Ent grand pren—2. In. 506—great Profit therefrom—*in great Fear.*
Remints—Brit. 49. a.—fined—*reſts, remains.*
Ramis—ibid. 66. a.—replaced, fixed on again—*torn.*
Reys—ibid. 83. a.—Kings—*Faults.*
Enteſſaunt—ibid. 242. a.—Tacitly, by being ſilent—*in witneſſing.*
Suppletions—Preamble, Stat. Glou. 2 In. 277.—Helps, Amendments—*Petition.*

 nals

nals in the Authors from whence they are taken. Mr. Hughes (whoſe Merit in tranſlating ſo antient an Author, as the Mirroir, was not inconſiderable) has yet frequently miſtaken the Senſe of the Text, as I preſume will be manifeſt from the Paſſages here cited [b].

[b] *Inviergoigne*—p. 4—to the Reproach—tranſlated *in condemnation.*
Fiſſend les vienes—13—make their Views—*make their Viſnes.*
La Neece, le Ante le Heire, le Roy—22—the Niece being the Heir of the King—*the Nurſe, the Aunt, Heir to the King.*
Tache de lour arte—23—infected with their Art—*taken with their Art.*
En volles Chautes et gargaus dr Oiſeaux—23—In the Flight, ſinging and chattering of Birds—*In the Intrails and Bowels of Birds.*
Garniſhant—33—warning—*defending.*
Moirent de diſette—34—die for Want—*die in the Deſerts.*
Per noyer—47—by being drowned—*by hurt.*
Appreſter—49—to pray, to be prepared—*to take an Oath.*
Oiſel—50—Bird—*Cat.*
En pure ſacote—53—in his Coat only—*in pure Sackloth.*
Gardaſſent—102—ſupport—*defend.*
N'eſt atteintable—113—is not to be attainted—*is not atteſtable.*
Son peir—116—his equal—*his ſuperior.*
A moneſter—117—to admoniſh—*to ſhew.*
Eins ceux que—p. 308.—before that—*after that.*
Quantum vene viſe Naam—158—when one forbids the replevying a live Diſtreſs—*when a Man leads away a live Diſtreſs.*
Garrantizables—176—are to be warranted, or to be proved—*are to appear.*
Ou containes—178—or far off—*or contain.*
Enemies diſcries—178—proclaimed, notorious Enemies—*Enemies diſcovered.*
Si Clerke ordeine—188—if a Clerk ordained—*if a Clerk be ordered.*
A chever—201—to perform, to attourn—*to come to.*
D'maine un gule—212—from Hand to Mouth—*of his own Hand.*
Eſt fief des tailles—212—is ſeiſed of the Tallies—*by Tallies.*
De quire—218—with Leather—*with Iron.*
Eſcu du cuyre—a Shield of Leather—*a Shield of Iron.*
Per le reſoil de la mer—222—by the Ebbing of the Sea—*by the Waves of the Sea.*
Sons—223—payment—*a Releaſe.*
Sil ferniſt ſa ley—241—if he performs his Law—*if he wage his Law.*

If the Word *defends* made ufe of in a Defendant's Plea had been confidered as derived from the Norman French Word *defender*, and to fignify to *oppofe* or *deny*, and not to juftify; Mr. Booth in his accurate Treatife of Real Actions would not have acknowledged himfelf fo much at a Lofs to explain the Entry of the Defendant's Defence in a Writ of Right. Booth xciv. 112.—3 Blackftone 296.

Nor furely, if the Idiom of this Language had been underftood, would this Paffage in Britton, "Si lefglife "demoerge defcounfeille outre vi. moys, adonques "folonc le Counceil de Lions par l'defcord d's "parties, le fra levefque del lieu counfeiller & dorra "lefglife a afcun clerke d'son office, fauve chefcun "droit," been rendered, by fo elaborate and judicious an Abridger as Mr. Viner, in the following Manner.

"*If the Church remains difcouncilled beyond fix "Months, then, according to the Council of Lyons, "by the Difcord of the Parties, the Bifhop fhall be "in the Place of a Counfellor, and fhall give the "Church to any Clerk, faving every one's Right;*" inftead of (as with great Deference I think it ought to be tranflated) "If the Church remains unprovided beyond fix Months, then, according to the Council of Lyons, by Reafon of the Difagreement of the Parties, the Bifhop of the Diocefe fhall provide for it, and fhall, *ex officio*, collate fome Clerk to the Church, faving every one's Right." Britton 225. a. 17. Viner 377.

Per vift enfaver—248—by burying alive—*by burning alive.*
Per urur de eux—261—by plucking out the Eyes—*by burning them over the Eyes.*
Que ne noirent—271—who do not fend—*hurted not.*
Afforcement de la ley—282—a forcing, or ftraining of the Law, *erring from the Law.*
Ou avoient vee—300—or had denyed—*or had fent.*
Eins ceo que—308—before that—*inafmuch as.*

Nor if the Norman Law French had been properly underſtood by the Profeſſors of our Law, would a Frenchman, on a late remarkable Trial, have been called in to read and explain ſome Norman French Charters produced in a Britiſh Court of Judicature.

Even the Statutes themſelves, as found in our Books, are, I am afraid, in many Places too liable to the ſame Cenſure; a Specimen from the ſhort Statute of Fines *, and from the Statute of Acton † Burnell, will ſhew this;

lieu la pees ſur la pie	tranſlated	*delivered* *the Peace* *by the County*	inſtead of	read the Concord on the Foot.

The Mention therefore of theſe Paſſages, thus erroneouſly tranſlated, may be of ſome Uſe, I truſt, to incite young Students to attain to a more perfect Knowledge of the antient Norman Law French; for Juſtice Forteſcue, in his learned Preface prefixed to his Reports, and to the Treatiſe of Abſolute and Limited Monarchy wrote by Sir John Forteſcue, Lord Chief Juſtice of England under Henry VI. ſays, that without being acquainted with this Language, wherein ſo much of our Laws yet in force is written, a Man cannot pretend to the Name of a Lawyer; and as many of the Public Acts which are in Latin in Rymer's Fœdera are not, in the Judgment of Rapin, to be underſtood without the Aſſiſtance of Ducange or Spelman; I may venture to ſay, that great Numbers of the ſame Kind of Inſtruments found there in the old French Language are not leſs difficult for want of ſome Dictionary of that Language. Even ſo late as the Time of Queen Elizabeth, when one would have thought that almoſt all Barbariſms had been aboliſhed,

* 18 Edward I.

† *Priſtes lour avers,* borrowed their *Cattle,* inſtead of *Money,*

we find Treaties drawn up, and Secretaries of State, Ambaſſadors, and Kings in her Reign, correſponding in a very uncouth Stile; for I believe there are very few Readers, who, *tout d'un coup*, will underſtand ſuch Words as "*de repes—arrablez, plieur—panures—* "*rovenereray—truerant—leuryauxi—unglos—ſyny-* "*uemant—auplieies—delleanſes—l'adutent—ſainte-* "*mant—avabler—oiſuir—ſans anviſer—j'eſcrine—* "*acharuez—au oult*;" with many others equally obſolete, and which are not explained in any Dictionary. Yet this Collection, extenſive as I have endeavoured to make it, does not, I muſt confeſs, take in every difficult or obſolete Norman French Word; ſeveral of this Kind are purpoſely omitted, on account of the Senſe of them not readily occurring, and are left for ſome more able Hand to inveſtigate; others alſo will, without Doubt, be met with in ſome Books and Manuſcripts which have eſcaped my Reading: though I perſuade myſelf the Number will not be very conſiderable; and that it may with Truth be ſaid, that very few of the antient Norman French Words which occur in this Work, are to be met with elſewhere.

This Compilation, the Reader will pleaſe to obſerve, is confined to ſuch Words of the old French Language as occur chiefly in Rymer's Fœdera, our Statutes, Parliament Rolls, Journals, Records, Law Books, and, Hiſtorians; for as to thoſe which are to be met with in ancient Writers of the French Nation, and in the Provençal Poets and Romances, they are foreign to our Purpoſe; and may be found in the Dictionary lately compiled by the learned M. La Combe *, in 2 Volumes: Nor have I traced the Norman French Language up to its Origin, this being alſo already done by

* Dictionnaire du Vieux Langage François, par M. La Combe. à Paris, 1766.

the

the above Author, and ſeveral others who have profeſſedly written on that Subject.

It would probably likewiſe not have been unentertaining, and at the ſame Time more ſatisfactory to ſome Readers, to have given, as *Menage* and others have done, the Paſſages and Sentences at length, from thoſe Records, Books, and Manuſcripts, from which moſt of the Words in this Collection are taken; this indeed would have helped to point out the different Epochs when ſuch and ſuch Words firſt aſſumed ſuch a Senſe, as well as given the Reader an Opportunity of comparing the Words themſelves with the Context; but this Parade would have rendered the Work much larger, and I am afraid too expenſive. My only View, in making this Compilation, is to promote Hiſtorical Knowlege, and enable the Studious to read with Satisfaction, and underſtand, thoſe many intereſting and curious Records diſperſed in our Acts of State; and particularly in the Parliament Rolls (which under the Sanction of the Legiſlature have been lately publiſhed), Law Books, and Hiſtorians, and which, for want of ſome Aſſiſtance of this Kind, loſe much of their Force: if this End is anſwered without making thoſe numerous Quotations which the obſerving the above Order would have occaſioned, I hope, the Want of it will be readily excuſed.

A

DICTIONARY

OF THE

NORMAN AND OLD FRENCH

LANGUAGE.

A, *at, and, with, from, for, by.*

A causa de cy, *for this reason.*

A ce, *for this purpose.*

A cestuy, *from him.*

A la facon, *in the fashion.*

A la presence, *in the presence.*

A peu perd, *with small loss.*

A sont, *and are.*

A tort, *by wrong.*

Aage, *age.*

Aagiee etant, *being of the age.*

Aan, ā, *year.*

Abaiesse, *an abbess.*

Abaiez, *afraid, intimidated.*

Abaiez du peril, *put in peril.*

Abaiser, *to appease.*

Abaisse, *deprived.*

Abaissiees (si), *so impoverished.*

Abaizance, abbaiaunce, *in abeyance, in expectation.*

Abatist, *abated, beat down, pulled down, threw down, quashed, defeated, interposed.*

s'Abaty, *entered by abatement, interposed.*

Abatu (Bois), *wood cut or fallen.*

Abaudissent (sei), *embolden themselves, give themselves up to.*

Abbassement, *abatement.*

Abbeissant, *obedient.*

Abbessed, *cast down.*

Abbessement, *lessening, lowering.*

Abbessent, *abate, lower.*

Abbrevoir, *a watering place.*

Abbs, *an abbey.*

Abbeuver, *to give water to.*
Abeissant, *obedient.*
Abeisse, abesse, *abated, lessened, abased.*
Abeissement, *lowering.*
Abeissez, *oppressed.*
Aber, *abetting.*
Abesilie, *abated.*
Abetir, *to render stupid.*
Abette, *abetment.*
Abetuz, *abating, allowing for.*
Abeyė, abit, *habit.*
Ablessement (en), *to the scandal, injury.*
Ablez, *able, fit.*
Abogen, *bowed.*
Aboilage, *honey.*
Aborder, *to apply to, arrive at.*
Aboutir, *to draw to, to abut.*
Aboutissants, aboutissements, *limits or boundaries.*
Ab Owein, *ap Owen.*
Abreeu, *April.*
Abroceurs, *brokers.*
Abruver, *to water.*
Absoile, absoller, absouldre, absodre, *to absolve, forgive, pardon.*
Abstiegner, *to abstain.*
Abstinence, *cessation.*
Abusshementz, *concealments.*
Abutrements, *ornaments.*
Aca, ca, *then.*
Acat, *buying.*
Acate (p vois d'), *by way of bargain.*
Acaterie (Sergeaunt de l'), *serjeant of the catery.*
Accepsant (en), *in accepting, objecting.*
Accessement, *addition.*
Accesser, *to assess.*
Accion, accyoun, *action.*
Accoitant (en), *in bording up.*
Accoinct, *very necessary or familiar.*
Accointance, *aid, favour, association.*
Accoller, *to embrace.*
Accollee (donner l'), *to dub a knight.*
Accomptablez, comptable pesson, *countable, small fish.*
Accord (d'), *the concord.*
Accoritez, *agreed to it.*
Accort, *ready, wary.*
Accoster, *to prop, or hold up.*
Accoursement, *the taking away.*
Accouter, *to hearken.*
Accresser, accrester, *to increase, to accrew, to happen.*
Accressent, *arise from.*
Accresser (qui droit ad a), *who has a right to the profits.*

Accreve,

Accreve, *increased.*

Accreaunt, *gathering, obtaining, accroaching.*

Accrocher, *accroach, usurp, attempt to exercise.*

Acrois, *increase, accession, improvement.*

Accuserez, *reproach, accuse.*

Accusement, *accusation.*

Acensement, *a letting to harm.*

Acenseur, *a farmer.*

Aceres, *maple-trees.*

Acertener, *ascertained, being well assured of.*

Acertez, *certified, get intelligence of, in good earnest.*

Acessent, *assess.*

Achampart (garder les), *to keep them separate, safe.*

Acharuez, *incensed, cruelly bent against.*

Achat, *buying.*

Acheter, *to buy.*

Achatur, acatour, *buyer.*

Achatre, *to ransom.*

Achemine, *directed.*

Acheson, achaysson, *reason, occasion, cause, hurt.*

Achesonez de bel p̃leder, *called in question for beaupleder.*

Acheve (ne se), *does not attourn.*

Achever, achiver, *to perform.*

Acheu, *attourned.*

Achioer, *to finish.*

Achoisoner, achessoner, *to accuse.*

Aci, *here.*

Acier, *steel.*

Aco, *that.*

Acoigne, *favour, association.*

Acone fei, *sometimes.*

Acons, *sore.*

Aconvenu, *covenanted, agreed upon.*

Acort, *agreement, accord, consent.*

Acoudre, *to join.*

Acoulper, *to accuse.*

Acounte, aconte, *to be reckoned, deemed, accounted.*

Acoupes, *accused, guilty.*

Acouter, *deemed, accounted.*

Acovyegnent, *agree, settle.*

Acqueister, *to pacify.*

Acquisser, *to receive, gather.*

Acre, *an acre, a measure of land.*

q̃ ne fuist unques acree ne vergee, *which was never surveyed, measured, or laid out into acres, rods, &c.*

Acres, *increased.*

Acresce, *increase.*

Acrestre, acresser, acresere, *to multiply, to increase, advance, rise, accrew.*

Acrestant a lui, *taking upon himself.*

Acrire, *to write.*

d'Acrocher, *to assume, incroach, increase.*

Acroire, *to lend.*

Acruist, *accrewed.*

Act, *action.*

Actines, actons, *cloaks.*

Actuel, *ready, speedy.*

Actualment, actuelment, *presently.*

Acunement, *in any other manner.*

Acunte, *account.*

Acunt (deit), *owes any thing.*

Acuse, *excuses.*

Adaerains, *at last.*

Adavaunt ale, *so far gone.*

Adayer, *to provoke.*

Adeiz, *already.*

Adenc, *now.*

Adeprimes, *first, at first, for the first time.*

Adept, *obtained.*

Aderere, *behind, in arrear, strayed from.*

Aderener, *to appraise.*

Ades, *by and by.*

Adesoure, *underneath, below.*

Adesouth lui, *under him.*

Adesseement, *constantly.*

Adetteres, *sincerely.*

Adevant, *before.*

Adevenir, *to become.*

Adgares (ne), *lately.*

Adgisantz, *adjacent.*

Addculeir, *to mitigate, to asswage.*

Addone, *given to.*

Addoubers, *see adoubers.*

Addoubeur, *a promoter, or setter-up of causes.*

Addresse, *directed to, sent; also redress.*

Addresseroient en haut lour maynes dextres, *should hold up on high their right hands.*

Adherdantz, *adherents.*

A dieu commandez, *gone to God, departed this life.*

Adjeuster, *to adjust, contrive, dispose of.*

Adjouster foy, *to give faith.*

Adire, *by saying.*

Adire, *that is to say.*

Adire, *to abandon, forsake.*

Aditerent, *should summon to the eyre.*

Adjure, *abjured, abandoned.*

Admenestres, *admonished, brought.*

Administres, *the administrators.*

Adnates, *the first fruits.*

Adnerer, *to ſet a price.*
Adoler, *to lament.*
Adonques, adonges, *then.*
Adouler, *to repair.*
Adoubers de viels draps, *patchers, botchers, or menders of apparel.*
Adoun, *then.*
Adrecans, adroiſſans, *addreſſed, directed to.*
Adreciez, adreitees, *redreſſed.*
Adrein, *until.*
Adreitament, *with addreſs,* alſo *directly, forthwith, readily.*
Adres, *readily, conveniently.*
Adreſcer, *to redreſs.*
Adreſcer a nous, *behave to us.*
l'Adreſcement, *the management, improvement, reformation, reform, repairing.*
Adreſſer ſes reſons, *to make out, to prepare his defence.*
Adreſſes, *going, proceeding on, continuing along.*
Qu'ils adreſſaſſent, *that they ſhould prepare themſelves.*
Nous nous adreſſeoms, *we are getting ready.*
Adreſſez, *erect.*
Adreſſez, *ornamented, gilded.*
Chaſer adreſſez, *drive them ſtrait along.*
Adreſtement, *directly, forthwith.*
Adrier, *in arrear.*
Adtret, *drawn.*
Adveigne, *happens, becomes.*
En adventure ſi, *in caſe.*
Adveu (ſoubz l'), *with the approbation.*
Advitailles, *victualled.*
Advocaſſie, *office of advocate.*
Advoue, advoes, *advocates, perſons ſkilled in the law.*
Advover, *to avow.*
Adueinent, *ariſe.*
Adunque, *then.*
l'Adutent, *making uſe of.*
Adyre, *to ſay.*
Aé, *the age of a man.*
Aele, *grandmother.*
Aem perlir, *peril of our ſoul.*
Aerdanz, aordanz, *adherents.*
Aerder, *to accrew.*
Aererer, *to plough.*
Aerin, *braſs.*
Aernovel, *Auguſt.*
Aerres, *earneſt.*
Aery, *neſt of hawks.*
Aes, *eaſe.*
Aeues, *waters.*
Aez, *has.*

Afeore, *affeered.*

Affaire, *to make.*

Affaires, affairez, *to be made.*

Affaironτ, *affeer.*

Affaitier, *to render learned.*

Affame, *famiſhed.*

Affectate, *wilful.*

Affectes, *beſtowed on.*

Affectuous, *deſirous.*

Affecteuſment, *affectionately.*

Afferre (nus eqoms), *we have occaſion for.*

Afferaunt (ſolonc ſon), *according to his ſhare, proportion, or what belongs to him.*

Afferont (en lor), *in their proportion.*

Afferme, *contract.*

Afferment, *lodge, lay.*

Affermer, *to let to farm.*

Affermes, afermees *granted, limited, confirmed.*

Affer, affri, affra, *cattle, or beaſts.*

Affers des carads, *beaſts of the plow.*

Affere, *to do.*

Afferer, *to tax, aſſeſs, moderate.*

Afferrit, afferoit, *belonged.*

Affert, *it behoveth.*

Affiaunce, *confidence.*

Affiauntz, *by the affirmance, oath.*

Affie (nul ſe), *let none preſume.*

Affiert, *it belongs, is meet.*

Affinage, *refining of metal.*

Affins, *kindred by marriage, friends.*

Pur affiner, *to put an end to it.*

Affiont, affiantz, affie, *truſting, confiding in.*

Affirmacōns, *confirmations.*

Affirmaſſoms, *had affirmed.*

Suit affirme, *ſuit affirmed.*

Pur default d'affirmure, *for want of confirming.*

Affirez, *affeered.*

Affoire, *to do.*

Que mien y ſoit affoire, *what is beſt to be done.*

Afforcer, *to ſtrengthen.*

Afforce, *increaſed, ſtrengthened.*

s'Afforcent, *aim at, attempt.*

Si ſe afforce, *if he ſhould attempt.*

Afforcement de femme, *forcing a woman.*

Afforcement de la ley, *a forcing or ſtraining of the law.*

Afforcement, *effectually.*

Afforer, *to eſtimate, to tax.*

Affortement, *ſtrength, aid, aſſiſtance.*

Afforterez, *will enforce.*

Affrai, affrei, *terror.*

En

En affrai de la pees, *in breach of the peace.*
Affraíetz, *terrified.*
Affranchir, *to set free.*
Affretter (d'), *to freight.*
Affublez des manteau, *habited with the mantle.*
Affyereit, *trust to.*
Afolee, *cripled.*
Aforce, *strengthened.*
Aforcer, *to endeavour, to compel, to inforce.*
Aforcent, *tend to, endeavour.*
Aforesters, *aforested.*
A for prendre, *to be forprized.*
Afouement (si), *as soon as, as fast as.*
Afoula, *damaged, wasted.*
Ag̅, *wait, keep, observe.*
Agactz, *assaults.*
Agager nule ley, *wage any law.*
Agagez, *pledged.*
Agaitz, *lie in wait.*
Agaites (les), *the watch.*
Agardant, *regarding.*
Agardetz; agard, *awarded; keep, observe, attend.*
En vos agardetz, *in your judgement, determination.*
En vos agard, *in your own delay.*
Agayte, agait (en), *by await.*
Agatere (pur male), *of expecting mischief.*
Age, *water.*
Agenuz, *on their knees.*
Agglue, *joined, congealed.*
Aggreaunt (en), *in aggrevation.*
Aggreggez, *enumerated, specified.*
Agilte, *acted.*
Agisant environ, *lying near, adjacent.*
Agiser, *to be levant and couchant.*
Agneler, *to yean or bring forth lambs.*
Agniser, *to acknowledge.*
Agrea (ele s'), *she agreed.*
Agreation, *agreement.*
Agrestical, *clownish.*
Aguet a pansé, *malice prepense.*
Aguet, aquet (par), *by ambuscade.*
A guey, *near.*
Aguir, *to guide.*
Aguiser, *to sharpen.*
Agules pur saccs, *pack needles.*
Aguyen, *Acquitain.*
Aherdanntz, *adhering.*
Aheritez, *heir, inheritor.*
Ahontir, *to abash, or make one ashamed.*
Ajants, *having.*
Aice, *thereto.*
Aie, *aid, relief.*
Aient, *are.*
Aienz, *having.*

Aier, *ſteel.*

Aiet, *he ſhall have.*

Aile, *a wing.*

Ailefs, *a grandmother.*

Ailors, *elſewhere, beſides, then.*

Aimans, *diamonds.*

Aimant, *a loadſtone.*

Aimer (l'), *the love.*

Ain, *a book.*

Ainceis, *but.*

Ainneeſche, *elderſhip, birthright.*

Ains, *his.*

Ains, *oppoſed, obſtructed.*

Ains, d'ams, (par quintal d'), *for a quintal of almonds.*

Ainſi come (per), *in the ſame manner as.*

Aintz, *but.*

Ainz, einz qe, *before that.*

Ainznez, *eldeſt.*

Aion, aiomz, *have.*

Ajourner ceus, *remove them.*

Ajouſtre (ſanz), *without adding.*

Ajoyni, *joined.*

Airaine, *braſs.*

Aire, *neſt of the hawk.*

Aireau, *a plough.*

Airens en pourpos, *intend.*

Aires, *eared, ploughed.*

Airignante, *adjoining.*

Ais, *a board.*

l'Aiſe, *the eaſe.*

Aiſement, *eaſement.*

Aiſne filz, *eldeſt ſon.*

Aiſnee fille, *eldeſt daughter.*

Aiſt, *aided.*

Aiſtre, *exiſtence, life.*

Aitre, *a houſe, an apartment, a room.*

Aive, *water.*

Ajudar, *to aſſiſt.*

Ajuge, *adjudged.*

Ajuſtement, ajouſtances, *addition.*

Aketon, hoketon de plate, *coat of plate, metal.*

Akune, *ſome.*

Al, *to, from.*

Al, *went to.*

Ala devie a treſpaſs, *departed this life.*

Alaier, *alledge.*

Alant, alantes, *going.*

Al armes, *with armes.*

Alaſſent quere hors, *they ſhould go and take them out.*

Alaſtes, *gone.*

Allaceaulx, *collateral.*

Allancz al roy, *going to the king.*

Alcome, *alchymy.*

Alcons, *any one.*

Alcunz e alcun, *one or more.*

Alee, *allay.*

Alees, *paſſages abroad.*

Aletoitz, *ſometimes.*

Alegannce, *allowance, redreſs.*

Aleger

Aleger (lui), *to relieve himself.*

Alegge, *eased, redressed, relieved.*

Alegerez, *will alleviate.*

Alencontre, *to the contrary, against.*

Aler (le), *the bringing.*

Aler (lour), *their departure.*

Ales de gales (en fees), *in his journey into France.*

Alettes, *little eagles.*

Aletz adieu, *go quit.*

Aleur (a grant), *in great haste.*

Aleviance, *ease.*

Ali, *to another.*

Aliance, *allegiance.*

Aliaunces, alience, *confederacies, allegations, suggestions.*

Alias, *heretofore.*

Alienacan, *kindred.*

Aliennee, *an alien.*

Alienee, *the buyer.*

Alier, *at large, to go at large.*

Alier hors, *to go out of.*

Aliez (lour), *their relations, friends.*

Alisaundre, *Alexander.*

Alissir, aleisser, *at going out.*

Alkemine, *alchemy.*

Alleage, allegag, *alledged.*

Allec, *herring.*

Alledgie, *bought in, made satisfaction.*

Allees (si), *so far proceeded in.*

Alleger, *to lessen.*

Allegier, *to alleviate, remove.*

Alleggeance (en), *for redress, in ease of.*

Allegeaunce (sans), *without alledging.*

Allegies, *imprisoned.*

Allegiance (forsque), *only an alleviation, exemption.*

Allegiez, *alleviated, redressed.*

Alleguez, *cited.*

Alleient avant, *may proceed.*

Alleie, *allay.*

Alleques, *alledged.*

Alleront, *went.*

Alles, *allies.*

Alleu, allieu, aleu, alieu, *a possession free from all subjection, allodial.*

Alleve, *levyed.*

Alleyn, *an alien.*

Alliance, aliance, alience, aleyngnanse, *confederacy, protestation, allegiance.*

Alliance (faux), *by false allegations.*

Alliantz, *aliens.*

Allieger, *alledge.*

Allient (sen), *may depart.*
Allies, alliez, *kindred, confederates.*
Alliours lieux, *other places.*
Alloee, *allowed.*
Alloigne, alligne, *put off or delayed, carried away, conveyed from.*
Alloigner le terme, *inlarge the time.*
Allopee, *eloped.*
Des allopers de nunns, *of those who elope with nuns.*
Allowables, *genuine.*
Allower (ne poet), *cannot let.*
Allowent, *hire.*
Alloycanche, alloyance, *alliance.*
Alloynes, *stolen, alienated, removed, carried off, drove away.*
Alloynours, alleynours, *those who conceal, steal, or carry a thing off privately.*
Alluer, *to allow.*
Alluminor, *a limner or gilder of letters in old manuscripts.*
Alm, *soul.*
Lendemayn des almes, *on the morrow of souls.*
Al menne people, *to inferior people.*
Almoignes, *alms, almonds.*
Alns, *a wood of elders.*
Alnyours, *aulnagers.*
Aloigner, *to enlarge.*
Aloine, *ousted.*
Aloinent, *eloign.*
Alongerent (se), *withdrew themselves.*
Alors, *there, at that time, in that place.*
Aloft, *go.*
Alote, *allotted.*
Aloues, *worthy of praise.*
Alquons, *any one.*
Alre-siee, *at another time, afore time.*
Alt, *high.*
Alt al ewe, *let him go to water Ordeal.*
Alterquer, *to wrangle.*
Altres IIII (les), *the other 4.*
Altres (per), *by others.*
Altresi, *in like manner.*
Alye, *fastened, fixed.*
Alyenont le judgement, *they defer the judgement.*
Alvey, *alderground.*
Aluable, *allowable.*
Aluer (li), *allow him.*
Alun, *allom.*
Alz, az, *they, them.*
Am, *I love.*
Amans, *diamonds.*
Amaroit, *should love.*
Amat, *beloved.*
Amatistre, *an amethist.*
Ambassiatt, *embassage.*
Ambaxeurs, *ambassadors.*

Ambodeux,

Ambodeux, amdeus, ambedoi, amb. *both.*

Amorey, *a cupboard.*

Ame, *friend.*

Ame çosyn, *beloved cousin.*

AmF, *amen.*

Amedeus les pties, *both parties.*

Amee, *desired, coveted.*

Ameis, ametz gentieux hommes, *beloved gentlemen.*

Ameinise, *diminishes.*

Amene, *seduced, forced.*

Amenez, amegnez, *produced, brought.*

Amenuser, *to abridge, abate, decrease, diminish, lessen, annihilate, to fall.*

Amenusoit, *brought.*

Amenisse, *amended.*

Amendement, *for the amendment, improvement.*

En amendement, *in amends.*

Ament, *let him make amends.*

Amentineez, *maintain.*

Les amends de assyse enfreynte, *the correction of the breach of assyse.*

Amenrir, *to diminish.*

Amenistrez, *administered.*

Amer, *bitter.*

Amer (ne de), *nor to love.*

Ames, *mercy.*

Ames et foyables, *beloved and faithful.*

Ames (es), *on the souls.*

Amesner, *to bring, convey.*

Amesnauncez, *carrying away.*

Amesnaunce, ameìgnaunce, *bringing in.*

Amesure, *moderated.*

Amez, *friends.*

Amiable, *friendly.*

Amiablement, *amicably.*

Amice, *beloved.*

Amiraudes, *emeralds.*

Amisours (ses), *those who are prejudiced against him.*

Amittee, *friendship.*

Amistre, *annuity.*

Amnasse, *threaten.*

Amoindrir, *to make thin or lean.*

Amoinorissant, *wasting, diminishing.*

Amoler, *to melt.*

Amolir, amollir, *to soften.*

Amonestoms, *admonish.*

Amonestment, *warning, notice.*

Amont, *a mount, upwards, against, above.*

Amort, amorti, *dead.*

Amorte, *allured, won.*

Amortir, amortizer, amorteyser, *to amortise, to purchase in mortmain.*

Amountaunt, *ascending.*

d'Amour jour, *day of grace; a day alſo given to compromiſe the ſuit.*
Amous, *very.*
Amoyneric, *almonry.*
Ampiere, *an empire.*
Amplier, *to increaſe, enlarge.*
Amprendre, *to undertake.*
Ampres, *after.*
En ampres, *hereafter.*
d'Ams quintal, *a quintal of almonds.*
Amue, *friends.*
Amur, *love.*
Amuue, *moves, grieves.*
Amuzer aſcun, *to put one in a ſtudy.*
Amyes concubines, *beloved concubines.*
Amyte, *friendſhip.*
l'An, *the one.*
Ana, *without.*
Analeſſent, *going, went.*
Anamalez, *enamelled.*
Anchiſors, *anceſtors.*
Ancelle, *a maid ſervant.*
Anceſtre en court, *ſummoned to appear in court.*
Ancoys, *but.*
Ancuſer, *to accuſe.*
Ande, *mother in law.*
l'Andemain, *the morrow.*
Aneals, aneus, *rings.*
Anel, *a ring.*
A l'anell, *on delivery of the nuptial ring, on ſolemnization of the marriage.*
Anel, *an angel.*
l'Anel, *the handle.*
Anelyng de tewles, *anealing of tiles.*
Anemis, *enemies.*
Anenent, *happen, ariſe.*
Angeine, *the feaſt of the Holy Virgin.*
Anginees, *engine, devices.*
Anguites, *anguiſh.*
Anguſſes, *ſtraights.*
Angutez, *ſtraightened.*
Anichilée, *annihilated.*
Anienter, anientir, *to take away, to defeat, make void, to annul.*
Anient, anientie, *void, diſannulled.*
Tot anientie, *entirely ruined.*
En anientiſement, *to the deſtruction, waſte, ruin, diſannulling, leſſening, impoveriſhment, waſting.*
An il enuſt (l'), *from whence there follows.*
Aniſancz, ayniſans, *annoyance.*
Aniz, *friend.*
Ankes, *geeſe.*
Ankes, *preſently.*
Ankes avant (que), *that before.*
Anne, *year.*

Annealing, *a burning or hardening by fire.*

Annel, annuel, *a ring.*

Anuels, anuels livres, *the year books.*

Annez, *years.*

l'Anoiture, *the nurture.*

Anoye, *injured, damaged.*

Anoya, *hurt.*

Anquare, *yet, ſtill, again.*

Anques, *but, very.*

A ans, *for a time.*

Anſement auſement (tout), *entirely in the ſame manner.*

Anſois, *but, although.*

Ant (le), *being.*

Antandre, *to inform.*

Anten (de), *of the laſt year.*

Antic, *old.*

Antor le tour, *round the tower.*

Antyer tout, *entirely.*

Anuales chauntantz, *ſinging annuals, or maſſes every day.*

Anuelx, *rings.*

Anui, *to day, this night.*

Anulterie (en), *in adultry.*

Anures mals, *evil works.*

Anuſance, anuſantz, *annoyance.*

Anute, *annuity.*

Anuyt, *vexes.*

Anviſer (ſans), *without waiting.*

Anyentiſſent, *annul.*

Anyntier, *to annul.*

Anz, *years.*

Anzoiz, anſois, *but.*

Aordaunce, *confederacy.*

Aore, *now.*

Aour, *gold.*

Aourer, *to pray to, worſhip.*

Aournemens, *ornaments.*

Aouſt, *Auguſt.*

Apandy, *belongs.*

Apara, *will appear.*

Aparelle, aparaile, apparellie, *ready.*

Aparille (de tot), *with all readineſs.*

Aparceyver, *to perceive.*

A par luy, *on his part.*

Aparmenes, ore aparmenns, *at this preſent.*

Aparte, *open, full.*

Apartement, *plainly.*

Apaſtiz, patiz, *the agreement to a contribution.*

Apauvry, *impoveriſhed.*

Apeaus, *appeals.*

Apee, *on foot.*

Apens, *thought.*

Apent, *belongs.*

Aperchenoir, *perceive.*

Apercus de ceo, *informed of it.*

Aperluy, *by itſelf.*

Aperment, *openly.*

Apeſchez, *impeached.*

Apeſer, *to appeaſe.*

Apetiſez, apeticher, appetichie, appetie, *diminiſhed, leſſened.*

Apeu, *a few.*

Apeyne, *ſcarce.*

Apiergent, *they appear.*

Apieroit, *it appears.*

Apoi cheſcun, *every one almoſt.*

Apoincter, *to appoint, direct.*

Apoint, *pointed, ſharp at the end.*

Apoſtiler, *to write notes on.*

Apoſtilles, *additions, obſervations.*

Apoſtle, apoſtal, apoſtoile, apoſtoire, *the pope.*

Apoy ylia demure (qe), *that there ſcarce remains.*

Appaiers, *to be paid.*

Appaiez, *ſatisfied.*

Appairallez, *repaired.*

Apparailementz, *fitting out.*

Apparelez (pur l'), *for repairing of.*

L'endemain de l'apparition, *the morrow of the Epiphany.*

Apparoir, apparoer, apparoier, *to appear, make known.*

Appaſſer, *to paſs.*

Appatiſſiez lieux, *places which agreed to pay a ſum of money to the enemy in compenſation of their towns being ſpared from the ravages of war.*

Appaye (en un), *in one payment.*

Appaye (nent), *not contented, diſſatisfied.*

Appeaux, *appeals.*

Appeirez, *impaired.*

Appele, *called.*

Appellations, *appeals.*

Appellantz (Seignurs), *lords appellants, viz. the duke of Glouceſter, Henry earl of Derby, Richard earl of Arundel, Thomas earl of Warwick, and Thomas earl of Nottingham, earl Marſhal, who were ſo called in* 11 *Rich.* II. *becauſe they were the accuſers in parliament of the then late miniſters.*

Appelliers, *called.*

Append, *pending.*

Appener, *to portion out.*

Appenſer, *to think or conſider.*

Appenſementz, *thoughts.*

Appenſes, *hung, affixed.*

Appente, appient, *belongeth, belonging.*

Apperceivance, *preparations, diſcovery.*

Apperient q̄, *who import.*

Apperil, apparaillez, *ready, apparelled, prepared.*

Appert,

Appert, *openly, in public.*
Appeſer, *to agree.*
Appeſement, *agreement.*
Appiaux, *appeals.*
Appiert evidence, *apparent evidence, juriſdiction.*
Appiſant, *evident.*
Applater, *to make plain.*
Appliantz, *arriving, drove into.*
Applicuer, *to employ.*
Applier, *to ſubmit.*
Applois, *employment.*
Apport, *tax, tallage, impoſition, payment, tribute, charge, expences.*
Apportz(come), *as it ought.*
Appoſer, appoſe, *adjuſt, agree.*
Appoſee, *queſtioned, adjuſted, ſettled.*
Apprailles, *ready.*
Appreciation, *appraiſement.*
Appreignent, *learn, be informed of.*
Appreiſours, *appraiſers.*
Apprentiſe, *a ſtudent of the law, a pleader, a ſerjeant at law.*
Un apprentiz de la court le roy et attourne, *an apprentice of the court of the king and an attorney.*
Appreſter, *ſhould endeavor, ought to be prepared.*
Appreſta (ſe), *ſhould be ready.*
Appreſtes, *payments, loans.*
Appreſte (argent), *money borrowed on loan.*
Appreſtes (per luí), *by him lent.*
Apprimes, *firſt.*
Appriſe, appris, *learned.*
Appriſez de ley, *learned in the law.*
l'Appriſement, *the ſeiſing.*
Approcher lour droit, *to come at their right.*
Appromptes (per), *by borrowing.*
Approper, *to appropriate.*
Approperment, *properly.*
Approperment (per), *by appropriating.*
Approve, *vouched.*
Approvez, *appropriated.*
Approvemenz, *improvements.*
Apprower, *to improve.*
Approwours, *approvers.*
Appruer, *to approve.*
Appruement, *profit.*
Appus, *appear.*
Apree, *afterwards.*
Apres, *next, neareſt to.*
Apres les IIII jours, *within 4 days.*
Apres, *learned, ſkilled in.*
Apreſtay, *I lent.*
Apreſt (d'argent d'), *ready money.*

Apreſt (dettes d'), *debts which ought to be paid down.*
Aprimes (tout), *in the firſt inſtance, immediate.*
Apris le jour, *after the day.*
Apris, *underſtood, valued, appraiſed.*
Apris de da leie, *learned or verſed in the laws.*
Apriſes (des), *from informations.*
Apriſe, *learning.*
Aprivoiſes, *improved, purchaſed.*
Aprocha, *petitioned.*
Aprocher a notre, *come at our own.*
Aprouchier, *proceed.*
Aprove, *improves.*
Aprua ſon waſt, *approved his waſt.*
Apruchement, *approach, arrival.*
Apuril, *April.*
Aquar (Serg.), *ſerjeant of the ewry.*
Aquitantz, *acquittance.*
Aqules, *to which.*
Ara ete, *ſhall have been.*
Arace, *to eraſe.*
Araceez, *tore out.*
Aracher, *to grub up.*
Aracine, *taken root.*
Araer, arair, *to prepare, array, ſettle.*
Arages, *madmen.*
Araies, *array, apparel.*
Araine, *braſs.*
Arant, *plowing, earing.*
Arat, *ſhall have.*
Arbalaſtres, arbaleſtes, *croſs bows.*
Juges arbitrers, arbitrarys, *a private judge choſen by conſent of the parties to determine the matter in difference.*
Arc, *a bow, an archer.*
Arcamentz, *ſecrets.*
Arces, arctz, *burnt.*
Arcewesche, *archbiſhop.*
Arche, *a cheſt.*
Archer, *to ſhoot.*
Arct, *compelled.*
Arctable, *forcible.*
Arcter, *to force, bind.*
Arctors, *the plaintiffs.*
Aſſiſes arannez, *aſſiſes arraigned.*
Ardeit, ardes, *burnt.*
Arden, *a wood.*
Arduys negoces, *arduous buſineſs.*
Que pur l'arduite de lour charge, *as well on account of the arduouſneſs of their charge.*
Are, aret, *a ram.*
Arecountre, *according to.*
Areigne, *happen.*
Areitez, *arrented.*

Aremeuaunt,

Aremenaunt, arenaunt, *for ever after.*

Arenes, aresnes, aresenez, *put to answer, arraigned, called in question.*

Arent, *a certain sum assessed by way of fine for beaupleader.*

Arentes, *let, rented at.*

Arere, *back again.*

Arere (en), *aforetime.*

Arere (joint), *diminution, joined again.*

Areriffment, *hindrance, delay, prejudice.*

Aresme, dareim, *of brass.*

Arest, *stay.*

Arester, areiter, *stop, resist, opposed.*

Arestieu, *seized, detained.*

Arestus, arestutz, *arrested.*

Aret, *an account.*

Arete, areste, *taken or charged with some crime.*

Argouces, *argued, debated.*

Arieres en temps (en), *in times past.*

Arire (rendra), *shall pay back again.*

Arierisee, *injured, hindered.*

Arivail, *arrival.*

Arkes, *bows.*

Arm (de l') de Tamyse, *an arm of the Thames.*

Arme, *weapon.*

Armez, *arms, coat armour.*

Armor, *the sea.*

Armure, *arms, armour, harness.*

Armures (milles), *a thousand armed men.*

Aront, *shall have.*

Arorez, *fodder, soil, compost.*

Arouere, *to answer.*

Arpen, *an acre.*

Arr, *in arrear, arrained.*

Arrablez, *overpowered, oppressed.*

Arracer, *to root up.*

Arrages (gens), *madmen.*

Arraisoner, *put to answer.*

Arramez, *commenced.*

Arramir, *to assemble.*

Arranez, ou arranerz, *arraigned, or to be arraigned.*

Arras (en), *in earnest.*

Arraynement, aresnement, *the arraignment.*

Arre (demaunde), *demand back again.*

Arrect, arrette, *let him impute it.*

Arren, arreyn, arrent, *arraigned.*

Arrer, *to plow up.*

Arrer et semyr, *to plow and sow.*

Arrere (en), *lately.*

Arrerie, *perverted, delayed, frustrated.*

Arreremeyn, *backwards, gradually.*

Arreriſſement, arerifment (en), *in delay, hindrance, annoyance.*

Arreſtre, *to accrew.*

Arreſt, accreſt, *accrews.*

Arreſtent, *take.*

Arrient, *happens.*

Arrier, arrer, *to give earneſt.*

Arriers, *again.*

Arrivails (petitz), *ſmall landing places.*

Arroie (que je), *that I ſhall have.*

Arroit, arroet, *ſhould have, would be.*

Arroul, *inrolled.*

Arrure, *plowing.*

Ars, *burnt.*

Arſines, arſeuns, arſures, *burning.*

Arte, *narrowed.*

Artic, artique, *North.*

Arte (eſt), *is obliged.*

Artex, *compelled.*

Articlarie, *artillery.*

Artus, *Arthur.*

As, *to, into, amongſt.*

As ſiens, *and his.*

As utaves, *on the octaves.*

Aſalt, aſaut, *aſſault.*

Aſaumple, *an example or precedent.*

Aſaudre, *to abſolve.*

Aſcaventer, *to certify or make known.*

Aſchoiſounez, *called in queſtion.*

Aſcavoire, *to be underſtood.*

Aſcenſement, *agreement.*

Aſcent, *aſſent, knowledge.*

Aſcerchez, *ſearched.*

Aſcerte, *certified.*

Aſceverer, *to affirm.*

Aſcient (qui a), *who knowingly.*

Aſcunement, *in any wiſe; ſome of.*

Aſcurrons, *we aſſure.*

Aſierent, *belong.*

Aſoles, *wounded.*

Aſols, *ſatisfied.*

Aſoudre, *to abſolve.*

Aſout, *abſolved.*

Aſoyne, aſone, *eſſoyn.*

Aſperſe, *diſperſed.*

Aſpertee, aſprete, *by rough meaſures, by force.*

Aſprement, *roughly.*

Aſeet, aſſiete, *aſſignment.*

Aſeir, *to ſit.*

Aſelees, *ſealed.*

Aſes, *aſſeſſed.*

Aſquus, *ſome.*

Aſs (l'), *the aſſiſe.*

Aſſa, *Aſaph.*

Aſſach, *a compurgation by 300 men.*

Aſſaeroms, *will attempt.*

Aſſaiants, *aſſiſting.*

Aſſaiant de harneis, *trying, or fitting on of armour.*

Aſſaie (en), *on trial.*

Aſſait, aſſeit, *aſſert.*

Aſſaileront, *aſſault, or ſet upon.*

Assaver 3 mois, *3 months notice.*

Assavoir, *certify.*

Assay, assaye, *endeavoured.*

Assees, *a woodcock.*

Assege, *besieges.*

Assemble, *a collection.*

Assembler, *to meet.*

Assemblee, *an union.*

Assembleement, *meeting.*

Assemle, *together.*

Assener, *to assign.*

Assenoms, *assign, appoint.*

Assenne, *assignment, support, portion.*

Assent, *something to sit upon.*

Assentement, *consent.*

Assentui en judgement, *joined in issue, in judgements.*

Asseours, asseont, *assessors, assess.*

Asseourez, *made safe.*

Assequrer, *to assure, make certain.*

Asser, asseer, asseoir, *to settle, fix, ascertain, assess, keep.*

Assert (d'), *to certify.*

Asserte, *surety.*

Asser (d'), *with steel.*

Asses, *set up, put up.*

Asses (l'), *conjunction, concurrence.*

Assesaunce (a la), *at the assessing.*

Assessors, *abettors.*

Asserera, *will assure, make sure.*

Assere, *drained.*

Asseyly, *assaulted.*

Assez, aseez, assetz, assietz, assau, *enough.*

Assez asser, *enough to do.*

Assiette, assoir, *assessment, tax.*

Assigniers, assinez, *assigned.*

Assis, *situated.*

Assise en ore, *set in gold.*

Assis (jour), *day appointed or fixed.*

Assises, assisserent, *set, appointed.*

Assiduelment, *constantly.*

Assieore, *to prosecute.*

Assiz, *sit.*

Assys, *appointed, affeered, assessed.*

Assoager, *to comfort.*

Assoigne, *essoyn, excuse.*

Assoil, *absolve.*

Assoyl (qe Dieu), *on whom God have mercy, pardon.*

Assoilent, se assoilent, *punish.*

Assoir, *to besiege.*

Assolloms, *we absolve.*

Assommes, *adjusted.*

Assondre (pour), de assouldre, *to absolve, to acquit.*

Assoub, assouth, assous, *acquitted, discharged, resolved.*

Affurrer (d'), *to essay.*
Affure (l'), *the certain.*
Affurrera, *and will assure, covenant.*
Aftallation (l'), *the installation.*
Aftate, *estate, condition.*
Afterlabs d'or, *an astrolabe of gold, an instrument to make astronomic observations.*
Aftonbz, *tin.*
Aftraint, aftructz, aftrictz, *constrained, bound.*
Aftraignons, *to bind.*
Aftre, *a hall.*
Aftre, aiftre, *a hearth.*
Aftrer (home), aftrier, *a man resident, a villein born in a house of the lord's.*
Aftres (treftouz le), *all the houses, fire hearths.*
Aftrus, *hidden, difficult.*
Aftuche (j'), *I conjecture.*
At, *hath.*
At, *and.*
Atachiee, *affixed, annexed.*
Atanys, *attainted, convicted.*
Atat, *estate, purchase.*
Atauntz, atantz, *so many.*
Ateigne pas, *does not come to.*
Ateignent, *which belong to.*
Ateindre jekes a oens, *get at them.*
Ateint, *amount.*
Ateinz, *attainted.*
Ateivament, *effectually.*
Atendre (e fit), *and let it be understood.*
Atent, *attends.*
Atente, atendre, *waiting.*
Atient, *extinct.*
Atornez (a co), *appointed for that purpose.*
Atrait a notre obeiffance, *drawn to our obedience.*
Atret, *drawn aside.*
Atreys, *other.*
Atreent (ne), *do not draw.*
Attacher, *to attack, take place.*
Attacher fon appeal, *to commence, to prosecute his appeal.*
Attach (fe), *attached, come upon.*
Attachent, *buying.*
Attaindre, *understand.*
Attaine, *brought, commenced, seized on.*
Attainables, *to be commenced.*
Attainables (nient), *are not to be brought.*
Attaine (caufe), *cause attached.*
Attainer fa action, *to commence his action.*
Attainre (fil ne puiffe) de prover fa pleine, *if he cannot proceed to prove his plaint.*

Attaintes pur ſerfs, *found by verdict to be villains.*

Attame, attamened, *commenced, attached.*

Attanners, *untanned.*

Attant (pour) de temp, *for ſo long a time.*

Attauntz de noetz, *as many nights.*

Attayner, *treat of, ſhew.*

Atteindre, *to attaint, convict, conviction.*

Atteinſiſt (il), *he had accuſed, impeached.*

Atteint, attaint, *convicted, found guilty, adjudged.*

Atteintable (n'eſt), *is not to be attainted.*

Atteint, atteyntz, *proved.*

Atteinz, *attaints.*

Atteindre (eux), *to convict them.*

Atteindre (pur), *to attain, obtain.*

Atteindre (ſi le tenant le voille, *if the tenant will abide thereby.*

Atteinoit (luy) a grant aleur, *met him with a great train.*

Atteignalment, ateiſament, atteynement, atteynaument, *effectually, ſtrenuouſly, remain for ever.*

Atteignent (ſe), *are committed.*

Atteynours, *perſons who are to attaint the jurors.*

Atteynt, atteinte, *an attaint.*

Atteynt de fauſe pleyne, *convicted of having made a falſe plaint.*

Attemprement, *interpretation.*

Attemptates (pur), *for attempts.*

Attendront a nos, *they ſhall be ſubject to us.*

Attentiſſent (s'), *ſhould be tried.*

Attent (come), *as they ought to have done.*

Atterminement, *reſpite, adjournment, attermination.*

Atterminez, *determinable, reſpited.*

Atterminez (dettez), *debts, for the payment of which certain times were aſſigned; and thoſe were called,* debita atterminata.

Attiegnent, attient, *belong.*

Attier, *appointed.*

Attiles (les), *the ſtores.*

Attilmentz (l'), *the fitting out.*

Attirable, *radicated, waſted.*

Attirent (les), *turn them.*

Attires (ſi). *ſo treated.*

Attitles, *aſſigned.*

Attyrer, *to provide.*

Attyres (mal), *ill repaired.*

Attorte, *raiſed, contributed.*
Attournances, *attornments.*
Attournera, *ſhall aſſign.*
Attournons, *attorneys.*
Attraie a lui, *claims it to himſelf, pretends title thereto.*
Attraire, *to draw.*
Attrapper, *to catch.*
Attrenche, *reſpited, reverſed.*
Attrench (tout), *entirely.*
Attrer, *draws.*
Attret, *treaty.*
Attreztrent, *draw, drew.*
Attrot, *conſent.*
Attroiſtre, *to revoke, withdraw.*
An, *to, or, have, had.*
Avabler, *to deceive.*
Ava fait, *had made.*
Avage le Seigneur, *let the Lord go.*
Avail, *lower*; *as* tenant paravail *is the loweſt tenant, or he who is ſuppoſed to make avail, or profit of the lord.*
Availe, *advantage, benefit, profit.*
Aval, *below.*
Aval (va) la rue, *goes down the ſtreet.*
Avant (que vint), avale del pount de Flete, *which runs down by Fleet-bridge.*
Avalaunt, *deſcending.*
Avale, *lowered, proſtrated.*
Avale (price), *price lowered.*
Avallée, *abaſed, humbled.*
Avaller leur trefs, *to lower their flags.*
Avanchant (eux), *protecting themſelves.*
Avant (de), *before.*
Avant (auxi), *as well.*
Avant (iſſint), *ſo on.*
Avant (en), *hence forwards.*
Avant (ſuiſt), *be ſued forth.*
Avans, *having.*
Avaunt (quil ſoint), *that they are proceeding on the buſineſs.*
Avant (ne ſoit pluis) fait, *be no more done.*
Avanſoier, *to advance.*
Avanthier, *the day before, or yeſterday.*
Avantures, *happening, miſchances.*
Avanture (d'), par aventera, *perchance, perhaps.*
Avanture (en), *for fear, leſt there ſhould be occaſion for.*
Avanture (faire), *cauſe to be ſeiſed.*
Avantures (pur faire), *to recover.*
Avaunt, *forthcoming.*
Avaunt meyn, *before hand.*
Avaunt (plus), *more fully.*
Avayner, *Avenor.*

Auban (St.) *St. Alban.*

Aubelaftiers, *flingers.*

Aubiene, *an alien, a foreigner.*

Aucon, *fome.*

Auctor, les auctours, *the plaintiffs.*

Audant, *imagining.*

Audemoneant, *putting in mind.*

Audiens, *to be heard.*

Audions (ne) mie, *did not imagine.*

Audremantz, *aldermen.*

Ave, *with.*

Ave, *a goofe.*

Avene nous, *come to us.*

Avecent, *who have.*

Aveer, *to avow, acknowledge.*

Avegler, *to blindfold.*

Aveir, aver, averre, avere, *to have.*

Aveir efcut, *refcued cattle.*

Aveir (mettre), *fet forth.*

Aveir (per), *through avarice; alfo, through fear.*

Aveit (il ni) pas, *there is not.*

Aveigne, avenent, *happens.*

Aveigna pryvy (come il), *how he becometh privy.*

Aveigne (fuffifant), *fufficient, indemnity.*

Aveignerie (ferjeant del), *ferjeant of the avary, the officer who is to provide oats &c. for the king's horfes. Minfhew. Or, according to fome, Avary fignifies a poulterer, from* Aviarius. *See Minfh.* Poulterer.

Aveignaunt (al), *to the value.*

Avell, *plucked from, torn off.*

Avenable, *reafonable, convenient.*

Avenant, *value, price.*

Avenant, *to come from.*

Avenant (plus), *more material.*

Avenantement, avenaument, *anfwerably, properly.*

Avenaunte mefure (de), *of a proportionable fize.*

Avenaunt foun (a), *in his ftead.*

Avenage, *pent oats.*

Aveuc ce, avenques che, *moreover, befides this.*

Avendrez, *fhall aver, fhall be admitted.*

Avene, *the river Avon.*

Avener, *get poffeffion of.*

Avener (devez), *ought to be admitted, allowed.*

Aven (a ceo ne poient ils), *they may not be admitted thereto.*

Avenont, *having.*
Avenor, *the king's officer to provide oats.*
Avens, *penthouses.*
Avensit, avenoit, avenge, *happened.*
Aventera (par), *by chance.*
Aventurous, *casual, contingent.*
Aventerousement, *by mischance.*
Avenues (facont lour), *make their entrance, advance, congees.*
Avenuz (il est), *he is come to, become intitled to, admitted to.*
Avers, aver, avier, *money, effects, goods.*
Aver, avor, ave, *cattle.*
Avere, averust (en), *in doubt.*
Averill, *April.*
Averioms, *shall have, having.*
Averroit, avraiettre, *would have.*
Averreier (veuille), *will aver.*
Avesqe, *bishop.*
Aveigne, aveignes, *oats.*
Avide, *greedy.*
Avient (q il y), *that it came to him.*
Avientisement, *avoiding, annulling.*
Avietz, *you have.*
Avilee, *rendered vile.*
Avint, *it came to pass.*
Avirances, *protestations, adjurations; also ejurations.*
Aviscera, *shall add.*
Aviscement, *addition.*
Aviser, *to advise, determine.*
Avisementz, *determinations, discretion.*
Avisement (en), *to advise about.*
Avissi, avisi, *also.*
Avis (vient), *laid open.*
Avit, *habit.*
Avium, *we had.*
Aviz, advice, *the opinion.*
Auference, *taking away.*
Auge, *a trough.*
Augunes genez, *some people.*
Augurim, *foretelling.*
Auke, *any.*
Aukeward, *backward.*
Aule, *a ball.*
Aulm, aume, *soul.*
Aulment, *elsewhere.*
Aultont (d'), *moreover.*
Aume some (d'), *with some sum.*
Aumentist, *removed.*
Aumeyne, aumoinge, *at least.*
Aumones, *alms.*

Auncesserie,

Auncesserie, *auncestry.*
Aune, *inned.*
Aunes, *ounces.*
Aunes, *yards, ells.*
Auner (dras), *to measure an ell of cloth.*
Aunkrer, *anchorage.*
Aunoi, *an alder.*
Aunz, auntz, *years.*
Avoec, auveqs, avoet, avoeckes, *with.*
Avoer, *to have.*
Avoeson, avoueson (l'), *the patronage, advowson, foundation.*
Avoerie (de l'), *of the advowson.*
Avoe (d' lour), *of their patron, lords.*
Avoir, avoyer, *a sum of money, goods, effects, estate, substance, debt.*
Avoir (d'), *of the means, ability.*
Avoir (l'), *the wealth.*
Avoir de pois, *any bulky commodities.*
Avoir (de corps et d'), *with their bodies and goods.*
Avoir (pur d'), *out of greediness.*
Avoir (gentz de petit), *persons of small substance or property.*
Avoirs, avoint, *had.*
Avoies (lais), *lay patrons.*
Avoiers (des), *of the avowants.*
Avolsont, *pluck off.*
Avomps, *we have.*
Avonus use, *have used.*
Avotours des playntes, *bearers of petitions, complaints.*
Avouchez, *advocates.*
Avovers, *avowers.*
Avouerie (par), *by allowance of, by avowal of.*
Avoueynt (s'il), *whether they avowed.*
Avoues (les), *the founders.*
Avour (d'), *to have.*
Avoutir, *adulterer.*
Avoutrie, *adultery.*
Avowa, *owned.*
Avowable, *justifiable.*
Avowe, advowee, *a patron, founder.*
Avoweson (d'autre), *of another's foundation.*
Avower, *to challenge.*
Avoye fet lui, *had been done to him.*
Avoyer, *patronage.*
Avoytaunt, *adding to.*
Avoytes, *have put forth.*
Auplieies, *employed.*
Auques, *also, now.*
Aurees (d'), *other things, goods.*
Aurel, auril, avril, aurilleux, *April.*
Aurenoef, *the new year.*

Aures, auriels, *ears.*
Auriens, *have.*
Aurun, *will have, observe.*
Aus, *to us.*
Aus, auts, *others.*
Aus (d'), *of them.*
Ausint, ausinc, aussin, ausuit, ausoys, ausieu, *also, in this manner.*
Ausint come, *as well as.*
Ausoms (ni), *we dare not.*
Aust, *autumn.*
Auster, *hearth, chimney.*
Austh, *August.*
Austour, *a goshawk.*
Aut, *let him go.*
Aut come je puis, *as much as I can.*
Auter, *an altar.*
Auter (sur haut *), *on the high altar.*
Autel, *the like.*
Autour, *the author, maker.*
Autrecloth, *an altar cloth.*
Autrefez, *at other times.*
Autrem, l'autrin biens, *the goods of others.*
Autreouse, *otherwise.*
Autreyerem, *grant.*
Autresi bien, *as well as, likewise.*
Autresi come, *as if.*
Autresint, *likewise.*
Autretant, *as much.*
Auvablement, *effectually.*
Auvere, auver, *to have.*
Avultere (l'), *the adulterer.*
Avultu, *for one year.*
Avute, *bad.*
Avyne, *happen.*
Avyce, *advice, cause.*
Avynein, *Avignon.*
Avys, *have.*
Auxienes, *any.*
Auxint, *and, whereas, also.*
Auxi toust, *as soon as.*
Awaite, *ambushments.*
Awant le quart degre, *before the fourth degree is passed.*
Awe, *who had.*
Awe, *a goose.*
Aweit, *crimes committed by await.*
Awen, *the current year.*
Awenours, *owners.*
Awer, Awoure, *suspense, doubt.*
Awereftee, awerouft, *doubt, ambiguity, uncertainty.*
Awes, *waters.*
Awey, *avowed, confessed.*
Awoost, *August.*
Axies, *also.*
Ay, *with.*
Ay, *over.*
Aydonqes, *then.*
Aye (a l' de Dieu), *with God's assistance.*
Ayele, *grandmother.*
Ayer, *heir.*
Ayl, *yes.*

* Sir M. Hale's MS.—Not *l'aut*, as Rot. Parl. vol. ii. p. 205.

Ayle,

Ayle, *grandfather.*

Aylienont, *they put off or defer.*

Aylours, *besides, elsewhere, otherwise.*

Aymez, *esteemed.*

Ayn degre, *own consent.*

Ayne o samne, *an ass with a load.*

Ayr, *choler, wrath, anger.*

Ayre (l'), *them.*

Ayrer, *to plow.*

Ayront, *shall build their nest, or breed.*

Ayteles, *to such.*

Az (l' de soye), *a silk lace.*

BA, baa, *Bath.*

Baailler, *to gape or yawn.*

Babé, *Elizabeth.*

Bacelée, bacelete, bacelote, *a damsel.*

Baceyes, *pearls.*

Bacha, *a calf.*

Bachelereux, *hardy, adventurous.*

Bachilier, bachiler, *a batchelor, a young esquire, a knight.*

Bacins, bascins, *basons.*

Badel, *a beadle.*

Badise, *vanity, boldness.*

Baes prise, *low price.*

Bage, *a bag, a coffer.*

Bagnes, *baggage.*

Bague, *a reward, bribe.*

Bahuz, *chests, cloak bags.*

Bailes, *bailiwicks.*

Baillolf, *Baliol.*

Bail de seisine, *livery of seisin.*

Bailement (le), *the lending.*

Baillast arrere, *delivered back.*

Bailler, *to let forth, to lend, to deliver.*

Bailleu, *delivered.*

Bailliff demeyne, *his own delivery.*

Baillons, *we allow.*

Baillye, *a bailliwick.*

Bailours, *sureties.*

Baisser, *to humble.*

Baisser le tete, *to bow the head.*

Balaunce, *suspence.*

Bale, ball, *a pack, a bale.*

Balene, balen, *a whale.*

Baleseitz, baillaitz petits, *small ruby balais.*

Baley, *a broom, besom.*

Balhier, balhif, *bailiff.*

Balhent, *the bailiffs accompt.*

Balinguee, *advised, careful.*

Ballots, *little packs.*

Ban, *outlawry, banishment.*

Bande, *delivers.*

Bander, *to tye, to bind.*

Banderount suis, *shall deliver up.*

Bandoner, *to leave.*

Bandon,

Bandon, *left to oneſelf.*
Bandour, *boldneſs, courage, audacioufneſs.*
Baneres, *knight bannerets, banners.*
Baner deſpleye, *with banner diſplayed.*
Banky, *bench.*
Bannier, *a public cryer.*
Banny, *ſent.*
Bannys, *thoſe that are baniſhed, outlaws.*
Banoors, baneours, *banner bearers.*
Barat, *deceit, ſubtilty, wrangling.*
Barbandier, *a brewer.*
Barbicans, *bulwarks, outworks*
Barbits, barbyts, *ſheep.*
Barder leins, *to beard wool.*
Barein, *barren.*
Barel d' or, *a little bar of gold.*
Bares, *at barrs, a game ſo called.*
Baret, *ſtrife.*
Bareys, *eaves.*
Barges (les),
Barils, *barrels.*
Barnage, *baronage, the body of the nobility.*
Baron, *huſband.*
Barreaux, barrez, *barrs or grates.*
Barrouych, *Berwick.*
Bars, *bargains.*
Bartheu, *Bartholomew.*
Bas cur, *an out yard.*
Baſe meaſon, *low room.*
Baſilique, *a royal palace.*
Baſlard, *buckler.*
Baſſeur, *lowlineſs, familiarity.*
Baſſinet, baſinet, bacinet, *helmet.*
Baſt, *a pack ſaddle.*
Baſtant, beſtant, beſtent, *diſpute, proceſs, conteſt, litigation.*
Baſtes, *convenient.*
Baſtiment, baſſment, *a building.*
Baſtiſe, *battered.*
Baſton de Fleet, *a tipſtaff of the Fleet.*
Baſyns, baſcins, *baſons.*
Batant, batement, batture, *beating.*
Bater, battre, batter, *to beat.*
Bater bledz, *to threſh corn.*
Bateux, batails, battels, bateeves, batelx, *boats, barges.*
Batraunt, *beating, aſſaulting.*
Batuz, *beaten, hammered to pieces.*
Battaillers, *combatants, warriors.*
Baucant, *yellow.*
Bauceant, baucent, *a pavillion.*

Bauciant,

Bauciant, baucent, *a ſpy, an informer.*
Baudement, *fairly, merrily.*
Baudour, *to the encouragement.*
Baudra, *ſhall deliver up.*
Baudra (li), *ſhall take to himſelf.*
Baudront, *ſhall deliver, give.*
Baudroyeur, *a currier.*
Baudure, *courage, be emboldened.*
Baut, *lets.*
Bayle de Lincoln, *the bail of Lincoln.*
Bayler, *to deliver.*
Beal, *well, better, fair, handſome, lawful, good.*
Beance, *intention, deſire, hope.*
Beance, beiance (en), *in expectation of.*
Beat, *bleſſed.*
Beaudes, *bold, emboldens.*
Beau luy eſt, *tis well for him.*
Beaumers, *the Bohemians.*
Beawme (roy), *king of Bohemia.*
Beddes, *beds, pieces of worſted.*
Bedel, *a calve.*
Beeves, *oxen.*
Beins, *goods.*
Beiſtes, *beaſts, cattle.*
Bejure, *drink.*
Bekenes, *beacons.*
Belance, *balance.*
Bele, *handſome, in health.*
Belement, *fairly.*
Beliſtrer, *to beg.*
Bem, *well.*
Beme, *Bohemia.*
Ben, *welfare.*
Ben pleider, *for* beau pleader, *for amendment of a vicious plea.*
Bene, *well.*
Bene, ben (ſi), *as well.*
Bene en tour, *well near, almoſt.*
Benoit, *benedict.*
Bens, benez, benes, bendes, *goods.*
Beof, *an ox.*
Beogaunt, *begging.*
Beoms, *inſtead.*
Beovier, *a neat herd.*
Beoure, *to drink.*
Berbrees, berbets, *ſheep.*
Berce, *a cradle.*
Bercher, *a ſhepherd.*
Bercherie, *a barkary, or tanhouſe.*
Bercil, *a ſheepfold.*
Bere, *beer.*
Bere, *towards.*
Berkſuir, *Berkſhire.*
Berluffer, *a gaſh.*
Bers, biers, *barons.*

Bers (a nobles), *to the noble barons, lords, personages.*

Bery, *the chief ſeat of a manor.*

Beſche, *inqueſt.*

Beſcher, *to dig.*

Beſele, beſleez, beſiletz, *embezzled.*

Beſer, *to kiſs.*

Beſon, beſom, *buſineſs, occaſion, neceſſity, behoveth.*

Beſoigne (plus ſage), *a wiſer ſtep.*

Beſtall, beſtiairies, *beaſts, or cattle of any ſort.*

Beſtez, beſties, *beaſts.*

Beſtourne, *turned out of its courſe.*

Beti, betie, *Elizabeth.*

Beverer, *a watering place.*

Beu pleider, *fair pleading.*

Beuſe, *a widow.*

Beutre, *butter.*

Beuverie, *drunkenneſs.*

Beyſes, *kiſſed.*

Beyver, *drinking.*

Biaus fiez, *good ſon.*

Biche, *a hind.*

Bien voulu, *tenderly loved.*

Bien (de) et de mal, *whether innocent or guilty.*

Bienke, *very well.*

Biens, bie, *intend.*

Biers nobles, *noble perſons.*

Bigue, *a ſhe goat.*

Bile, *a bill.*

Bille, *a label, or note of the value of a thing.*

Bioms, biens, *intend.*

Bions, *effects.*

Bis, *bread or biſcuit.*

Biſſe, *a female ſnake.*

Blake rode, *the black croſs.*

Blamiſement, *infringement, prejudice.*

Blanches paroles, *fair ſpeeches.*

Blanc gaunt, *a white glove.*

Blanc (5l.) i. e. *the king's fermor was to pay either 5l. 5s. or to ſubmit his money to the teſt of the fire, and thereby make good the 5l. in fine ſilver.*

Blaſme et diffame, *blamed and defamed.*

Blauncheours, *blanchers, whiteners, tawers of ſkins.*

Ble, *corn.*

Bleer, *to ſow, to put the ſeed into the ground.*

Blein, *full.*

Blemiſh, bleſmys, *broken.*

Blemiſhment (en), *to the prejudice, infringement.*

Blemiſſement (ſans nul), *without any infringement, diminution.*

Blemure, *a disfigurement.*

Bleſme, *pale, bleak.*

Bleſſies, *damaged, injured.*

Bleuer,

Blester, *to pare.*
Bloy, bloie, *blue.*
Boces d'argent, *bosses, studs of silver.*
Bochers, *butchers.*
Boeitz, *oxen.*
Boidrai, *I will give, deliver.*
Boiens genz, *good people.*
Boillant eaw, *scalding water.*
Boilles ou brases, *tempered.*
Boillure, *bullary for making salt.*
Boisseau, *a bushel.*
Boiste, boist, *a box.*
Boivre, *to drink.*
Bojeaux, *entrails.*
Bok, *Buckingham.*
Bokuyler, *buckler.*
Bond, *limited.*
Bondages, *bond tenants.*
Bondes, les bondes, *an inferior order of free men.*
Bonement purra, *well may.*
Bonnes, *bounds.*
Bonnoizon, *blessing.*
Boon, *good.*
Boord, *at board.*
Borc, bors, bos, *a village.*
Borc, borth (li), *the boroughs.*
Bordeaus, *stews, brothel-houses.*
Bordell d'femmes lovees, *a brothel house for prostitutes.*
Bord, *on board.*
Bordes, *lies, tales.*
Bordez, *boards.*
Borisalderes, *borough-holders.*
Bos, bose, *a wood.*
Bosel, *a bushel.*
Bosoinera, *it shall be necessary.*
Boson, *a buckler.*
Bot, bod, *the extremity, the end.*
Bote, *aid, help, amends, advantage.*
Bote, *put.*
Bota (se), *put himself.*
Boteaux, *boots.*
Bote et espernonne, *booted and spurred.*
Boter, bouter, *to set fire to.*
Botez devant le Roy, *laid before the king.*
Botier, *to put.*
Botons, *buttons, buds.*
Boucher, *to stop.*
Boucher, *to speak.*
Bouch au cour, *an allowance of diet at the king's or a great lord's table.*
Bouchier, *a butcher.*
Boud (au), *at the end.*
Bouger, *to budge.*
Bougeons, bouges, *arrows.*
Bougre, *futil.*
Bouges, bonges, *budgets.*
Boune, *a boundary.*

Bounifas,

Bounifas, *Boniface.*

Bountee, bountez, *goodneſs.*

Bountenouſe, *bounteous, bountiful.*

Bourchemeſter, *burgomaſter.*

Bourdick, boures, *the firſt Sunday in Lent.*

Bourg, *a baſtard.*

Bourgeſſors, *burglars.*

Bouſe, *purſe.*

Bouſquelier, *a woodman.*

Bouſſeaux, *buſhels.*

Bout feu, *an incendiary.*

Boute de la table, *end of the table.*

Bouter avaunt, *produce, put forth.*

Bouter hors, *to put out.*

Boutent (ſe), *put themſelves.*

Bouticari, *an apothecary.*

Boverie de terre, *an ox-gang of land.*

Boviller, *to boil.*

Boyance, *expectation.*

Boyeſte, boyette, *a box.*

Boyure, *drink.*

Brace, *a lance.*

Brace de la meer, *an arm of the ſea.*

Brace et vendu, *brewed and ſold.*

Brachel, *breeches.*

Brachile, *a bracelet.*

Braces, brachies, braches, les bras, *arms.*

Bracer, *to brew.*

Bracereſſes, braceraſſes, *brewers.*

Braceurs des querells, *bracers, or embraceors of quarrels.*

Braconer, *a hunter.*

Bracyne, *a brewing.*

Braez deſtr', *right arm.*

Bragard, bragueur, *a flanting, bragging, ſwaggering perſon.*

Brair, *to cry, to brag.*

Branchies, *branches.*

Brant, *burned.*

Bravement, *fine.*

Brau, *a bull.*

Braudeſters, brouderers, *embroiderers.*

Braul, *a brawl.*

Brauſle (en), *in confuſion.*

Brayard, *a cryer.*

Brayes, breiz, brees, *malt, bread, corn.*

Bre, *pitch.*

Brecatages, *breaches.*

Breche, *an arm.*

Brede, *embroidered.*

Breer, *brewing.*

Bref jor, *a ſhort day.*

Bref (deinz), *ſhortly.*

Brefte, *ſhortneſs.*

Bregheynok, *Brecknock.*

Brek, breche, *a breach or gap.*

Bren,

Bren, *bran.*

Breffine, *a mill to grind malt.*

Bretages, *battlements.*

Bretemeuil, *Bartholomew.*

Brevi, *in brief.*

Brider, *to bridle.*

Bries, brieves, *writs.*

Brieve (deinz), *in a ſhort time.*

Brigain, *contention.*

Brige, *quarrel, diſpute, faction.*

Briqueterie, *brickwork.*

Briſie, *broken.*

Briſtuit, *Briſtol.*

Briſure, *a ſlight ſcar.*

Britaſk, *a fortreſs with battlements.*

Bro, *a diſtrict, a field.*

Broche, *a lance, a needle, a packing needle.*

Broches, *ſpits, gallons.*

Brocha permy le corps, *run through the body.*

Brode, *brood.*

Broggours, broggage, *brokers, brokage.*

Broſe, *canceled.*

Bru, *a noiſe.*

Brudez, *edged, bordered.*

Bruer, *brewing.*

Bruere, *heath.*

Brug, bruge, *a bridge.*

Bruſe, *a purſe or pocket.*

Bruſe, *broken into.*

Bruſey, *heath ground.*

Bruſq, *green.*

Bruſure de pountz, *breaking down of bridges.*

Buant, *a bull, bulling; alſo drinking.*

Buche, *underwood, bruſhwood.*

Buche, *utters, ſpeaks.*

Buche (de), *by word of mouth.*

Buer, *to waſh.*

Bues, buez, bouez, *oxen.*

Buffe, *a blow.*

Bugge, *badger.*

Buiſſons, *thickets, woody places.*

Buizart, *a kite, buzzard.*

Bultel, *a boulting ſieve.*

Bulter, *a bolter or ſieve.*

Bundes, *bounds, limits.*

Bure, *butter.*

Burge, *a purſe.*

Burgerie, *burglary.*

Burgeſſours, *burglarers, houſebreakers, burglars, alſo incendiaries.*

Burghald, *boroughold.*

Burgous, *ſhrubs.*

Burlyng, *burling of cloth.*

Burre, *a veſſel.*

Burt, *borough.*

Buſle, *a pope's bull.*

Buſſel, *a buſhel, a meaſure.*

Buſoignes, *buſineſs.*

Buſoignables, *neceſſary, convenient.*

Buſoignouſes, *the neceſſitous.*

Buſoin, buſun, beſonche, *occaſion, need.*

Buſſuns, *buſhes.*

Buteront feuz, *ſhall ſet fire to.*

Butiner, *to divide the plunder.*

Buzac, *a kite.*

Byan, *to dwell.*

Bye, *thinks, intends.*

Byli, *bill.*

Bynd des anguilles, *a bind of eels.*

Byron (courts de), *courts baron.*

Byſſe, biſſie, *a kind of ſilk.*

Cãe, *cauſe, caſe. giſt.*

c̃a et la, *here and there, hither and thither.*

C̃her, *to be ſearched.*

C̃hres, *charters.*

C̃hun, *every.*

Con̄is, counzance, *confeſſion.*

c̃ teinte, *the ſeiſin.*

Cũ, *as.*

Cabeletz, caables, *trees blown down, branches of trees rent down.*

Cabeſtre, *a headſtall.*

Cablicia, *browſe or bruſhwood.*

Cabre, *a goat.*

Cachereau, *a bailiff.*

Cachereau, *chartulary.*

Cachet, *a ſignet or ſeal.*

Cadeloyne, *Catalonia.*

Cadene, *a chain.*

Cadiere, *a chair.*

Cadonqes, *that, then.*

Cagne, *a dog.*

Calabre (de), *furr of Calaber, a little beaſt about the ſize of a ſquirrel.*

Calamay, Candolaire, *Candlemaſs day.*

Calenge, *an accuſation.*

Calenou, *Chriſtmas.*

Caler, *to hold one's tongue.*

Calſay, *a cauſey.*

Camaen blank, *a white camea.*

Cambe, cambage, *brewhouſe.*

Camber, *a brewer.*

Cambre, *a chamber.*

Cambre, *cieled, vaulted.*

Cãpaine, *bell.*

Campaigne del roy, *the queen conſort.*

Campeſtres, *paſtures.*

Canal, *a kennel, a channel.*

Canape, *hemp.*

Candalle, *Kendal.*

Candeliere, *Candlemaſs-day.*

Canes et foreſtez, *woods and foreſts.*

Canez, canes, keynes, *oaks.*

Cangier, *to change.*

Canibe, *hemp.*

Canonizele

Canonizele escrite, *canon law.*
Cans, *dogs.*
Cap, *the head.*
Capage, *a pole tax.*
Capes, *Capua.*
Capiele, *chapel.*
Captal, *a captain, a chief, a seigneur.*
Caquet, *prattling, scolding.*
Carca, *loaded.*
Carcas, carkoys, *a quiver.*
Cardoil, *Carlisle.*
Cardonel, *a Cardinal.*
Cardours, cardoresses, *carders.*
Carerl, *carriages.*
Cargie, *loaded, charged,*
Cargues, *charges.*
Carkerent, *inquired of.*
Carkes, *compelled.*
Carkoys, *a mast, a carcass.*
Carme ou garme, *the verses and songs which the bards sung before an engagement, to animate the troops.*
Carnels amis, *bosom friends.*
Carpos de l'alliance, *the articles of the alliance.*
Carruweez, *carves.*
Carse ꝑ, *perhaps.*
Caruer, *plowman.*
Carwe de terre, *one plow land.*
Cas d'argent, *a case of silver,*
Cas de frument, *a heap or load of wheat.*
Cas (en lur), *in their persons.*
Cascun, *any one, each.*
Case, *a cottage, a house.*
Case eins (per), *but, and in case.*
Case (en), *in some, in such cases.*
Cassable, *voidable.*
Casse de blee, *stack of corn,*
Casses, *cases.*
Catal, *moveables of any kind.*
Cateau, *a castle.*
Catoour, *one who belongs to the acatry.*
Caver, *a knight,*
Caverre, *plough.*
Cauceage, *toll paid towards repairing causeways.*
Cauces, causies, *causeys or causeways.*
Caunt, *when.*
Causa (a), *by reason of.*
Causeours, *causers, the occasion of.*
Causer, *to cause.*
Cautels, *warnings.*
Cautelle, *craft, guilt.*
Caux, ceux, *those.*
Cauxion, *caution, surety.*
Cayer, *affixed.*
Cayers (les saincts), *the sacred page, text.*
Cavon, *a grandfather.*

Ce, ceo, cetty, cecy, cel, celuy, *this, that, these, he, him, here.*
Ceans, *here, within.*
Cea, *it.*
Cea (jesques en), *to this time.*
Cea enarere, *for the time past, heretofore.*
Ceals, ceax, ceaux, *those.*
Ceau, *heaven.*
Cedules, *seats or pews.*
Ceel, *a saddle.*
Ceerte, *certain.*
Ceincture, ceincte, *a girdle.*
Ceindre, *to girt, or gird.*
Ceinz (de), *of this court, here.*
Ceissents, *ceasing.*
Ceint, ceinture, *a bell, a girdle.*
Ceinturers, *girdlers.*
Celastes, *sealed.*
Celaont, *they divulge.*
Celeement, *secretly, in private, slowly, imperceptibly.*
Celi, *he.*
Celure, cele, *a coverlet.*
Cementers, *bricklayers, masons.*
Cen, *that.*
Cendal, *a sendal.*
Cengle, *a girt.*
Cenrs (a), *to the hearts, intentions, souls.*
Censables (en choses), *in things to be taxed.*
Cense, *rent.*
Censeze, *deemed.*
Censour, *a farmer.*
Centiesme partie, *hundredth part.*
Centurer, *a centeyner.*
Cenz, *hundred.*
Ceo (a), *for this purpose, at this time.*
Ceol, *that.*
Ceol, *heaven.*
Ceoles (en y), *into the same.*
Ceo (in q̃), *in as much as.*
Ceo que, *where.*
Ceoque (que de), *that whereas.*
Ceoset, *seised.*
Ceosq, *for, during, until.*
Ceou (tout), *whatsoever.*
Cep, *stock.*
Ceper (al), *to the gaoler.*
Ceppes (en), *in the stocks.*
Ceps des arbres, *the stocks or roots of trees.*
Cepurqaunt, *notwithstanding.*
Cerchiez, *searched, should search.*
Cere, *a lock.*
Cerifiers, *cherry-trees.*
Cer ke, *what.*
Certefyeassent, *certify.*
Certes, *verily, truly.*
Certes (mais), *nevertheless.*

Cervi, *paid.*
Cervoiſe, *ale.*
Ces, *thoſe.*
Ces freres, *his brethren.*
Ceſourdhuy, *this day.*
Ceſſaunt, *ſixty.*
Ceſſe (le), *the forbearance.*
Ceſſion, *ſeſſion.*
Ceſſou, *ſitting.*
Ceſte (miſe a), *aſcertained.*
Ceſtes, *this.*
Ceſtres de vin, *quarts of wine.*
Ceſtr, *Cheſter.*
Ceſſure (un), *a receiver, a bailiff.*
Ceu, *that, this.*
Ceu (ſaunz le), *without the knowledge.*
Ceue (en la), *on the back, on the cover.*
Ceuls, *thoſe.*
Ceunrey (del), *of the corrody.*
Ceyns, *here.*
Ceynt, ceyntus, *girded.*
Ch' Seig. *dear Lord.*
Chs en Dieu, *dear in God, beloved in Chriſt.*
Chace, chaſe, *obliged, compelled, have recourſe to.*
Chacer deſcharowe, *driver of a plow.*
Chaceez, *driven.*
Chaches, char, charet, charette, *a cart.*
Chaier (leſſer), *let fall.*
Chainant, *exchanging.*
Chair envenomee, *veniſon.*
Chal, *a knight.*
Chalejurs (les), *the challengers.*
Chalkyng (pur), *for chalking.*
Chalment, *clearly.*
Challenger, *to claim.*
Challis (prince), *prince Charles.*
Chalunge, *claim.*
Chambre depinct, *anciently St. Edward's chamber, now the painted chamber.*
Chamber bas, *a jakes.*
Champartors, *thoſe who are guilty of champarty.*
Champart (a), *ſeparate.*
Champeſtre (en), *in country towns.*
Champs (quant des), *how much meadow ground.*
Chancelez, *canceled.*
Chanceaunt, *happening, falling out.*
Chandelor, chaundelure, *Candlemaſs.*
Channte (une bone), *a piece of good fortune.*
Chanoms, *canon.*
Chapel, chappell, *crown, coronet, breaſt plate, helmet.*

Chapellet (environ le), *round the circle.*

Chapell de ferre, de feutre, *a breast plate of iron.*

Chapouns (ne a ouster), *not to take the hats off.*

Chaperon, *a hood, hat, a kind of head dress.*

Chaperon (sans), *bareheaded.*

Chapon, *the crown of the head.*

Charchez, *chartered.*

Charer, *to fall.*

Charetter, *waggoner, carter.*

Charettes (les) de feyn, *cart loads of hay.*

Chargeez, *loaden.*

Charges, *charters.*

Chargeant, *heavy, penal, expensive.*

Chargeance (en) manere, *very earnestly.*

Chargaunte (si), *so weighty, so forcible.*

Charier, *to draw, or drive.*

Charoigne, *carcase.*

Charonies, charounes, *bodies.*

Charnels amys, *bosom friends, allies by blood.*

Chars (jours de), *flesh days.*

Chars, charres, charets, *carts, waggons, ploughs.*

Charrennes, charewes des terres, *carves of land.*

Chartre, *a prison.*

Charners (bestes), *beasts of the plough.*

Chasables, *obliged, compellable.*

Chase, *drift, chase.*

Chaser (et) adresses, *to drive strait along.*

Chaser (de), *from driving.*

Chaste (en toute), *with all expedition.*

Chastel (le), *the chattels, goods.*

Chastelle (Roy de), *king of Castile.*

Chastel neof, *Newcastle.*

Chastirians, *should chastise.*

Chastres, chastris, *gelt.*

Chate, *brought.*

Chate (la), *buys it.*

Chate, *bought.*

Chaton (un), *a cat.*

Chatters, chattres, *commodities.*

Chauces, *causeways.*

Chaucez, *driven.*

Chau (de) ke, *in as much as.*

Chaud melle, *a hot or sudden debate, corruptly called chance-medley.*

Chauncelrie (en la), *in chancery.*

Chaunterent, *declared, pronounced.*

Chaussez,

Chauſſez, *put upon his boots.*

Chauſez, chauſure, *breeches, ſtockings.*

Chaufer, *to warn.*

Chavoynes, *canons.*

Chaulx (de), *of them.*

Chautes (en volles) et gargans de oiſeaux, *in the flight, ſinging, and chattering of birds.*

Chaux, *thoſe.*

Chaxtel, *caſtle.*

Chaye, *fallen down.*

Cheaunce, *an accident.*

Checer in debat, *to come in queſtion or debate.*

Cheet (mout) en age, *is very much in years.*

Cheez (vus), *you fall.*

Chefs (a), *to his head.*

Chefe (a) del an, *by the end of the year.*

Cheitiſment (vivont), *live hardly.*

Cheitivetee (grant), *great hardſhip.*

Cheivalerie du temple (meſtre de la), *maſter of the order of the knights templars.*

Cheines, *chains.*

Cheir, cheyr, checer, cheſer, *to fall, to abate.*

Cheie, cheiez, *fell, happened.*

Cheiſſont ſur, *are made upon, fall upon.*

Cheivſauns, Cheviſſance, *an agreement between debtor and creditor, in relation to the loan of money.*

Chekere, *excheqeer.*

Cheke (ſauf), *ſave that.*

Chele (par la meiſme) grace, *by this ſame grace.*

Chelui (pur), *for him.*

Chemimynaunt, *purſuing his journey on the highway.*

Chentz wyt (trois), *three hundred and eight.*

Chen, chens, *dog-days.*

Cheneau, *a young oak.*

Cheny, *finiſhed.*

Cheount, cheent (ne), *do not fall.*

Chepier, *a gaoler.*

Cher, *dear.*

Cherementes, cheremont, *dearly.*

Cheriſancez, *cheriſhing.*

Cherte, *charity.*

Cheſte, ches (lettres), *theſe letters.*

Chereil, *may happen.*

Cheſer (a), *to fall, or come to, fall out, happen.*

Cheſt, chet a ſavoir, *that is to ſay.*

Cheſcuny, checon (a), *to every one.*

Cheſon, *carried on, defended, occaſioned.*

 Chet,

Chet, *fell out, happened.*
Chetifs, cheytifs, *caitifs.*
Chevage, *poll-money paid by a villain to his lord.*
Chevance, *goods, money, riches, bargains.*
Chevances (a faire), *to borrow, to make bargains for.*
Chevaſſent, *may go over, may perform them.*
Chevauche en hoſte, *heads the army on horſeback.*
Chevalines (beſtes), *beaſts for the draught.*
Chevalines traians, *drawing-carriages.*
Cheventeins, *chieftains, captains.*
Chevetaigne dettor, *principal debtor.*
Chevance (ſa), *his ſubſtance.*
Cheveſtres, *head-ſtalls.*
Cheve, cheveres, chewers, *goats.*
Chevin (donner), *prepare the way.*
Chevin (en), *on his journey.*
Chevir de denier, *to take up money on loan.*
Cheviz, *borrowed.*
Cheviz, *to come to an agreement touching property.*
Cheuz, *happened, fallen.*
Cheryrent (luy ne), *owed no ſervice to him.*
Cheye, *fallen down.*
Cheynes, *chains.*
Cheys, *choice.*
Chi apres, *herein after.*
Chiaus (a touz), *to all thoſe.*
Chi (entre), *between this.*
Chief (ſon), *his head.*
Chief du lyt, *bed's head.*
Chiefs (en foreignes), *in foreign places.*
Chief de mois, *at the end of the month.*
Chief qun, *every.*
Chienquante, *fifty.*
Chier (de), *by a fall.*
Chier, chire, chiertees, *dear, dearneſs, reverence, love.*
Chierions, *will cheriſh.*
Chiery, *favoured, encouraged.*
Chieſt, *failed.*
Chiet (ſon), *his client.*
Chiet a tre, *falls to the ground.*
Chiez d' oſtiez, *the head of a family.*
Chipoteis (des), *in proviſions, rents.*
Chir, *knight.*
Chirk (de), *of this.*
Chiſtel, *caſtle.*

Chite,

Chité, *a city.*

Chivauche (facent la), *cause a perambulation to be made.*

Chivalx, *horses.*

Chivachez, *perambulated, ridden.*

Chivaunch, *were riding.*

Chivanche (in la), *in the expedition, campaign.*

Chivache encontre le roy, *rides against the king.*

Chivaucher, *to ride.*

Chivaus covertz (a), *with horses covered.*

Chivalchier le pais, *over-run the country.*

Chivers, *goats.*

Chivisaunce, *an unlawful bargain.*

Choa (pour) qu, *because that.*

Choces (les), *things, goods.*

Choeur, *choire.*

Choucee (a bout de la), *at the end of the cause-way.*

Choient, *fail.*

Chole, *choler.*

Chose (ne ent mande autre), *does not command to the contrary.*

Chou, chon, chu (a), *to this, that.*

Chou (et tout) que, *and all which.*

Chou (pour qu), *because that.*

Chre, *charter.*

Chuient, *fall off.*

Chun, *every.*

Chun (an), *each year.*

Chun (come ben) servant, *how much every servant.*

Chuny (a), *to every one.*

Chyen (entre) et lieu: *inter canem et lupum, twilight.*

Chynes, *oaks.*

Ci pris, cy mis, *as soon said as done.*

Ciceltr', *Chichester.*

Ciege, *siege.*

Cier, *to mow*

Cierges, *wax tapers.*

Cierve, *a hind.*

Cieus, *here, hither, those, such.*

Cigne (liveree del), *livery of the swan; a swan was one of the badges of Henry the fourth, and was embroidered on the caparisons of his horse when duke of Hereford, at the intended combat between him and the duke of Norfolk. Prince Henry his son bore his achievement, supported by two swans, each holding in his beak an ostrich feather and a scroll.*

Cignettez, *cignets.*

Cil,

Cil, cili, *he.*
Cincaunt, *fifty.*
Cink, *five.*
Ciphe, *a cup.*
Cips, *ſtocks.*
Cis, ces, *they, thoſe.*
Ciſere, *ale.*
Ciſme (la), *the ſchiſm.*
Ciſne, *a ſwan.*
Ciſours, *ciſars.*
Ciſt, *this.*
Citoſt, *as ſoon as.*
Citues, *placed in.*
Cla, *claims.*
Clamant, *claiming, maintaining, commanding.*
Clamur (al), *for proclaiming.*
Clamous pleints, *clamorous complaints.*
Clarifie, *cleared up, made appear.*
Clarre, *claret.*
Clave, *a horſeſhoe.*
Claud, *a ditch.*
Claye, *a hurdle.*
Claymors de franchiſes (les), *thoſe who claim franchiſes.*
Claree (vin de), *claret.*
Clachent lains (qui), *who clack wool.*
Clamour, *impeachment.*
Clefs, *hurdles.*
Cleif, *a key.*
Cleifs, cliefs, *keys.*
Clerkus, clerex, *clergy, clerks.*
Cler jour, *clear day.*
Clere memoire, *of famous memory.*
Cler, *clerk.*
Clerement, *clearly.*
Clergie, *ſcience, literature.*
Clergereſſe, *a learned woman.*
Cliefs, *keys.*
Clier droit, *clear right.*
Clime, *kindred.*
Climacha *, *potius* chivacha †, *rode with.*
Cloiſtres, *incloſed places.*
Cloier, *to prick.*
Clore, *to incloſe.*
Clos (brefe), *a writ cloſe.*
Cloſe (pur), *for fencing, incloſing.*
Cloſture de hayes, *incloſing with hedges.*
Clos (le), *the cloſe.*
Clouſtre (fiſt), *cauſed to be incloſed.*
Clough, *a valley.*
Clowes de gilifer (3), *three cloves.*
Cloy, *pricks.*
Clurs, *clerks.*
Cluſe de paſche (la), *the cloſe of Eaſter, i. e. the firſt Sunday after Eaſter.* Dominica octava paſchæ,

* See Parl. Rolls, vol. II. p. 193. pet. 73.

† Hale's MS.

chæ, dominica post albas, dominica in albis; le dimanche de la quasimodo, *from the service beginning with those words in the Roman Missal.*
Clyens, *clyents.*
Co (estre), *moreover.*
Co (d'), *of this.*
Coaction, coartacion, *compulsion, coercion.*
Coche (fuit), *was laid down in bed.*
Cochin (d'), *from the kitchen.*
Cochoures, *couchers.*
Coe ottroire, *grant this.*
Coe (ou) est, *whether this is.*
Coes les; Coe (la), *the commons.*
Coe (le) boist, *the common box.*
Coelers, *collars.*
Coems, coens de Nichole, *earl of Lincoln.*
Coers, *hearts.*
Coer, *commoner.*
Coers, coerts, *forced.*
Coert (qore), *which is now current.*
Coes (les povs) del roialme, *the poor commons of the realm.*
Coeurs, *course.*
Cofin (un), *a basket.*
Cofre (un), *a trunk or chest.*
Cognizance, *suggestion.*
Coherter, *to force.*
Cohiber, *to restrain.*
Cohues, *assemblies, courts of justice.*
Cojantz, *being compelled.*
Coieres, coirs, coers, *hearts.*
Coictz, *boiled.*
Coievient, *convenient.*
Coignsu, *known.*
Coigne, *coin, money.*
Coigner, *to coin.*
Coiles, *testicles.*
Coil doust, *as he ought.*
Coillage, *collection.*
Coiller, *to assemble, to collect, gather in.*
Coillers d'argent, *silver spoons.*
Coillet, *collected from.*
Coillet, *a lock of wool.*
Coillet (de), *for gathering.*
Coilliant, *gathering.*
Coillours, *collectors.*
Coinistre, *confess.*
Coinonte, *connected.*
Coint, *affable.*
Coinnus, coinus, *rabbits.*
Coitiffe (chastell de), *castle of Cardiff.*
Coitacons, *meetings.*
Coket (payn de), *coket bread.*
Coler, *collar.*
Colere, *colour.*
Colerent, *pretend.*

Coller,

Collet, *taken away.*
Coli, *took.*
Collation, *comparison, simple, coler.*
Collacion (une bone), *a good oration.*
Collision, *collusion.*
Colorers (pluis), *the better to colour over.*
Colourent (se), *pretend.*
Colp, *cut off.*
Colps, *the neck.*
Collusion, *comparison.*
Colx, *a blow.*
Com, *as.*
Coma droit, *common right.*
Comande, *send.*
Comant, *farewell.*
Comaundable, *to be committed.*
Commant, *command, order, bearer, attorney.*
Combatuesse, *beat down.*
Comb, *a valley.*
Combatour, *one who is hired by another to fight for him.*
Combur, *burn.*
Coment, *how, howmany.*
Coment cy que, *although that.*
Come, *when, as soon as.*
Comen some, *common summons.*
Comensables et provables, *commenced and carried on.*
Comesatz, *beginning.*

Cometut, *committed.*
Cominasser, *to have common.*
Comissair du roy, *the king's commissioner.*
Comistre (a), *to speak of.*
Commauvacs, *commotes.*
Comme plance, *common discourse.*
Commettement, *falshood.*
Comminer, *to keep company, to converse with, to have.*
Commineront, *they assembled together.*
Communalment, *generally.*
Communalment, communement, communelment, *in general, commonly, jointly.*
Comūuner, *to meet in common.*
Communal, *common.*
Commune de reaum, *the commons of the cities and boroughs.*
Communaunte, *commonalty.*
Commune (a la), *with the commonalty.*
Commune (sanz) parlement, *without frequent parliaments.*
Comorth, *a subsidy.*
Comognenues, *fellow-monks.*

Comp (a un), *at one payment.*

Compensation, *payment.*

Compaſſer, compaſcer, *to compaſs, imagine, deſign, intend, endeavour, attack.*

Compectant, *competent.*

Comperer, *to ſuffer.*

Compeigney, *company, ſociety.*

Compernant, *compriſing, ſetting forth.*

Compertment, *appearing.*

Compigne, *contain, compriſe.*

Compier, *a godfather.*

Compiere, *as appears.*

Compoir (pur), *to appear.*

Componnent les ſuppliantz, *let the petitioners compound.*

Compliſement (faire) de juſtice, *to do compleat juſtice.*

Compliquer (de), *to fold up.*

Compliſſement, *accompliſhments.*

Comprins, *compriſed.*

Comune (cheſcune), *each of us jointly.*

Comunalte (nule), *nothing that is common.*

Comunalte (aſcunes de), *ſome which concern many perſons; ſome community.*

Comyn (en), *in common.*

Comyns de parlement, *the commons in parliament.*

Comyns, *the common people.*

Con, *as.*

Coña, paſture, *common of paſture.*

Conation, *endeavouring.*

Concauſe * (*potius* l'un cauſe), *one cauſe.*

Conceyvere mon brief, *bring, frame my writ.*

Concey, *framed, adapted.*

Certeignment conceux, *certain information.*

Conceillier, *conſult, adviſe.*

Concubeant, *lying together.*

Condemaundaſſe, *demand.*

Condouner, *to grant.*

Conductz, *lodgers.*

Conduſt (lettres de), *letters of ſafe conduct.*

Conduitz (les), *the attendance.*

Condition (en grant), *in great hazard.*

Coneife, *leave.*

Conefeye bien, *knew very well.*

Coneve, *known, acknowledge.*

Conexes, *connections.*

* See Parl. Rolls, 4 Hen. IV. vol. III. p. 508. pet. 90.

Confer-

Conferromous (si), *if we compare.*

Confesse, *examined.*

Confession, *an answer to interrogatories.*

Confexion (a la), *to the making.*

Confier, *to trust.*

Confourmeront, *informed.*

Confiquez, *confiscated.*

Confors, *comforters, aiding.*

Confrontations, *borders.*

Congye, conge, *leave.*

Congie de soy conseiller, *leave to imparl,* i. e. *talk with the plaintiff.*

Conier, *a place where rabbits and hares were preserved.*

Conigg, *coney ground.*

Conilles, conings, *coneys.*

Coninges, *shillings.*

Conisaunce, *knowledge.*

Conisent (ne les), *do not acknowledge them.*

Conisoit, *he was obliged.*

Conissoms (nous), *we acknowledge.*

Conjouyr (luy), *to congratulate him.*

Conjectement, *conspiracy.*

Connsealx (par les) damperts issue se puisse fair, *by the advice of both parties it may be brought to an issue.*

Connuis, *known, open.*

Connying, *knowledge.*

Conoisse, *acknowledge.*

Conoyssent, *hold cognisance of.*

Conpayne, *companion.*

Conquastere, *to shake, to break to pieces.*

Conquerra, *shall gain, obtain.*

Conquest (de), *by acquisition, purchase.*

Consallatez, *counseled, advised.*

Conseil (tenuz), *kept secret.*

Consent, *acknowledged.*

Consieux (privez), *privy counsellors.*

Consile et plaine, *the church is full and provided for.*

Consommez, *consumed, spent.*

Constitution, *appointments.*

Consul, consealx (du), *one of the council.*

Consute, consu, *annexed, sewed together.*

Cont, *earl.*

Containes, *remote.*

Contal, *of a county.*

Contamus, *we declare, or count.*

Contasse, *countess.*

Conte (a), *at the county day, court.*

Contee,

Contee(le), *the county-court.*
Conte, contes (la), *the accompt.*
Conte (sur la), *upon his account.*
Contean, *contained.*
Conteckours, *brawlers.*
Conteins (soy), *refrain themselves.*
Contek, *a contest, dispute, disturbance, opposition.*
Contemplation, *affection, regard.*
Contenance, *purpose.*
Contenance, countenaunce, *contenement.*
Contenement, *countenance, or freehold land contiguous to his tenement.*
Content (a), *has accounted.*
Contentation, *satisfaction.*
Contentz, conteux, *contentions.*
Contenu, *continued.*
Contenue, *contained.*
Contenunt *, *run.*
Contenz, *contention.*
Conter, *against.*
Conterent (lui), *related to him.*
Conterfait, *resembling.*
Contez (des), *of the shires, counties.*
Contessa, *countess.*
Contessoiz, *contemplation.*
Contetz, *contained.*
Continance, *continuance, observance.*
Continuament, *directly, immediately.*
Continuance †, *his contenement, support, maintenance.*
Continues, *contained.*
Contiraunt, *notwithstanding.*
Contraitz, contraults, *contracts.*
Contrariast, *had contradicted.*
Contrariantz (les), *the offenders.*
Contraster, *to contrast.*
Contresteant (nemye), *notwithstanding.*
Contredie, *refuses.*
Contree (fuit), *was engaged with, opposed.*
Contrefaire, *to imitate.*
Contrelutent, *oppose.*
Contremant, *countermand.*
Contremount, *ascending, uppermost.*
Contremount (en), *in the ascending.*
Contremaunt (degres), *ascending degrees.*
Contreestier, contrester, contrescer, *to prevent, oppose, grieve, oppress.*

* Vid. Rot. Parl. vol. II. p. 190. Pet. 64. Potius *courunt*, Hale's MS.
† Ib. p. 213. Pet. 25. Potius *continaunce*, Hale's MS.

Contremettre,

Contremettre, *to lay against, to impose upon.*
Contrepanel, *a counterpan.*
Contreovez, contrevez, *counterfeited.*
Contreval, *downwards.*
Contreveigner, contravener, *to act contrary to, break, oppose.*
Contreytour, *arch traytor.*
Contrier, *to contradict.*
Contrirerant (nient), *notwithstanding.*
Controue, *controuled.*
Controvee, *contrived.*
Controver, *to contrive.*
Controveures des novelles, *devisers, inventors of tales.*
Contus, *bruised.*
Convainquus, *convicted.*
Conveer, *to convey.*
Conveiez, *conveyed.*
Conevences, *covenants.*
Convensist (il), *it becomes necessary.*
Convent, convenu, *covenanted, obliged.*
Converer, *to cover.*
Converroit, *converse with.*
Conversantz, *abiding, resident.*
Convs, *converse.*
Conussent, *acknowledges.*
Conviront, *shall convey, conduct.*
Convis, *a banquet.*
Convoist (que se), *which consisteth, shews, discovers itself.*
Convyer, *to convince.*
Conyng, *coney, rabbit.*
Cool (le coler du), *the collar from the neck.*
Coonte, *a count, earl.*
Cooperture, *a thicket.*
Cop, cope, coupe, *a blow.*
Copable, *guilty.*
Copie du people, *a great number of people.*
Copier, *to cope.*
Coplice, *an accomplice.*
Coppe (blees en), *corn in cocks.*
Copped, *laid in heaps.*
Copper, *to cut off.*
Copperent, *uncovered.*
Copyl, *a fox.*
Cor, *heart.*
Corage, corouce, *anger.*
Corage, *consent, will, mind, inclination.*
Corage (la), *encouragement.*
Coraunt, *passing, current, limited.*
Cord, *a load.*
Cord (de la), *the agreement, consent.*
Cordeau de soy, *a silk ribband.*
Cordewaners (de), *leather, &c.*
Cordiner, *a shoemaker.*

Core, *heart.*

Coreours de chivalx, *horse-coursers.*

Corer, *to have recourse to.*

Coreute (fust), *was in enmity with.*

Coriage (du) de harang, *of curage, or curing of herrings.*

Cornefer, *maker of horns.*

Cornele de la test, *the crown of the head, the brain.*

Coronoaille, Cornville (duc de), *duke of Cornwall.*

Coronal, *a coronet.*

Coroneis (vins livr' d' esterlins), *twenty pounds sterling.*

Corones (as), *to the coroner.*

Coronse, *enraged.*

Corores laboreres, *runagate laborers.*

Corouce, *a carousal, a great entertainment.*

Corpores, corporez, *corporate.*

Corps presantz, *corse present.*

Correes de battaill, *arrayed for battle.*

Correours, *curriers.*

Correpc', *corrupt, hasty.*

Corrue, *convicted.*

Cors, cort, court, *short.*

Cors (en le), *in the principal.*

Cors (sur peine de) e d' avoir, *on pain of body and goods.*

Cors (sur le) Dieu, *upon the body of God,* i. e. *the consecrated Host.*

Cors, corse, cords, *a body.*

Corse present, *a mortuary.*

Corses, *cloths, kerseys.*

Corsues, *course, corporeal.*

Cort, court, *limited.*

Cortaise, *civil, gentle.*

Cortoise, *courtesy.*

Coruces, *enraged.*

Corue, *course run, ferreted.*

Cor'une, cornus, *horned, tipped with horn.*

Cornwayles (terre), *Cornish land.*

Cosces, *husbandmen.*

Coses, *things.*

Cost, *this is.*

Costages, *cost.*

Costal, coste, *by, present, near.*

Coster, *a rich cloth or vestment, made use of on great festivals.*

Coste, *coat.*

Coste (en) coste, de coste, *collateral.*

Costeins, *neighbouring, near to, on the borders of.*

Cot gare et vileine tuson, *inferior kind of wool.*

Cotellers, *cutlers.*

Cotel, *a knife.*

Coteaux (piene de), *a pair of sciſſars.*

Cotidian, *daily.*

Cotiers, *cottagers.*

Cotte, cote, *a coat.*

Cotu, *cut.*

Cotures, *little houſes, cottages, coverings, incloſures.*

Cotures (quant des), *how much arable land.*

Couche, *double, laid double.*

Coucher, *a couch.*

Couerer (vous voudres), *will ſhelter yourſelf.*

Coues (as) des chival, *at the horſe's tail.*

Couldront, *ſhall coſt.*

Couldront (qu'ils), *which they ſhall think.*

Couler, couller, *colour.*

Coulerou, *anger, paſſion.*

Coulpale, *guilty.*

Coun, Con. *Pudendum muliebre.*

Councelera, *will conceal.*

Counfort, *comfort, aſſiſtance, encouragement.*

Counſaunt (il ſeit), *and he is known.*

Counſeile, *provided.*

Coũſeiler al roy (ſaunz), *without the king being conſulted.*

Counſeyla (il), *he adviſed.*

Countables (en), *in counts.*

Count (en) countant, *in counting.*

Counte, *county-court.*

Counte (de) en counte, *from county court to county court.*

Counte, county, *account, eſtimate, computation, eſteem.*

Countees, *counties.*

Counter, *to count, declare, tell, plead, compute.*

Counte palys, *a count palatine.*

Counter palais, *a county palatine.*

Counter pleadable, *may reply.*

Counterpayne, *a counterpayne.*

Counties, *earls.*

Countinuance (lour), *their contentment.*

Countor, *a count.*

Countors des menſonges, *thoſe who deviſe and relate lies.*

Countradit (ſans), *without oppoſition.*

Countre etre, *to be againſt, oppoſe, reſiſt.*

Countre la pes, *againſt the peace.*

Countre lit, *upon his bed.*

Countre rouler, *controller.*

Countreval, *deſcending.*

Counturs

Counturs le roy, *the king's serjeants.*

Coup de mere (pur), *by force of the sea.*

Coup, *damage.*

Coupable, *guilty.*

Coupe, *in fault, to blame.*

Couperie (de), *of cutting.*

Couper (de), *of blows.*

Couper le tayle, *to cut off or dock the entail.*

Coupiz, *coppices.*

Courade, *the intestines.*

Courage, *encouragement.*

Courajeux, *angry.*

Courece, *provoked.*

Courer (dette), *to recover the debt.*

Courey de battel, *arrayed for battle.*

Courge, course, coure, *to run.*

Courge, court, *runs.*

Courour, *currier.*

Courre, *to course.*

Cours (deux), *two courses.*

Coursables, *current.*

Court, *skreened, constrained, short.*

Court (se), *turns.*

Court (moy) a mort, *which is the cause of my death.*

Court terme (cy), *so short a time.*

Courte (per la), *by the course of.*

Court drap, *cloth, called streits.*

Couseades, *concealed.*

Cousement (de), *of the concealment.*

Couson, *cousin.*

Coustenghes (a nos), *at our own cost.*

Couste (en), *collaterally.*

Courtoist responist, *courteous answer.*

Courtreux, *a garden.*

Coustouses, *costly.*

Coustumers (et a ceo s'est), *and has often practised it.*

Coutes (de deux), *on both sides.*

Coutellours, *cutlers.*

Couvrefeu (l' heure du), *the hour when the coverfeu or curfew-bell was rung, viz. seven in the winter at St. Martin's le Grand.*

Coux, *a cuckold.*

Couz, cous, coust, *cost.*

Covegne, *it behoved.*

Coveigne (gens de), *covetous, greedy people.*

Coveitant, *covetous, desiring.*

Covenable, *proper, apt, sufficient, right.*

Covenablete de tens, *convenient time.*

Covene, *rightful.*
Covent (ai), covenenchiet, *have covenanted, agreed.*
Covent (nous), *behoves us.*
Coventelis, *conventual.*
Covenist (il), *belonged to, it was necessary.*
Coverer (se), *skreen, protect themselves.*
Coverer (pur) eglises, *to cover, or repair churches.*
Covert chival, *a horse arrayed, or harnessed.*
Covetise, coveitese, coveigne, *desire, greediness.*
Coviegne (de sa), *of his own head.*
Covoitoms, *we are desirous.*
Covynes, *their secret places of meeting.*
Cowes (la), *the tail, the end.*
Coylir, *to cock.*
Coyly, *gathered.*
Coyne, *coinage.*
Coyre, *leather, a skin.*
Coyre, coure, *copper, brass.*
Craftus (touz les) du citee de Londres, *all the craftsmen, companies of the city of London.*
Craire, *to confide in, entrust with.*
Crainer, *to refuse.*
Crampus de goute, *laid up with the gout.*
Crastine, *the morrow of any festival.*
Cray (je), *I believe.*
Cray, *betrayed.*
Creable, *to be feared.*
Greablement, creable, *credibly, credible.*
Creacures, creansours, *creditors.*
Creance (la), *the instructions, the articles.*
Creances, et a creanciers, *borrowed, and to be borrowed.*
Creance (a), *upon credit.*
Creantceantz, *borrowed.*
Creaule, *credible.*
Crecefiz, *a crucifix.*
Credibles, *credible.*
Crerez, *created.*
Creez fiablement, *give faithful credit to.*
Creises. *crossed.*
Cremal, *a crimson or purple colour.*
Creme, *burnt.*
Cremeur, *fear, dread.*
Crere, creier, *to believe, give credit to.*
Cresceaunce, croissaunce, *growth.*
Cressom (ke nus), *that we give him credit.*
Cressours (par engendrure de), *by having lawful issue born alive.*
Crest, *rises up, accrues.*

Cret,

Cret, *accrues.*

Cretain de eau, cretange del ewe, *rising of water.*

Cretine, *an inundation.*

Creval oeil, *thrust out the eye.*

Creve, *a wear.*

Creve, *shook, ratled, increased.*

Creues (novelles), *new raised.*

Creum, *we believe.*

Crewe, *grown, incurred.*

Creye, creyer, *believe.*

Cribre, *a sieve.*

Cribre (le payn), *bread of bran.*

Crible, *debated.*

Crichet, *agreement.*

Criegnent (ne), *are not afraid.*

Crie, cry general, *a general proclamation.*

Crier, *to summon.*

Cries la peace, *declare, draw the concord.*

Criesme, *a crime.*

Crieuerie (la), *the office of crier.*

Crikes, *creeks.*

Criler, *to argue, debate.*

Crilz, criz, *cries.*

Crins, *the hair of the head.*

Crire (set), *who knows how to write.*

Crismatorie d'arg dorrez, *a chrism of silver gilt; a vessel in which the ointment with which kings were anointed was kept.*

Crisme, *a crime.*

Crist (Jehu), *Jesus Christ.*

Cristine, *christian.*

Crocq (six harquebuxes de fer a), *six large arquebusses of iron.*

Crochet (dix harquebuzes a) de bronze, *ten arquebusses of brass.*

Croiables gentz, *credible persons.*

Croice (seinte), *holy cross.*

Croire (de) auxi fortement, *should also firmly believe.*

Croise, croisse, crous, cruix, *a cross.*

Croise (et homme), *and there may be reason to believe.*

Croisement, *crusade.*

Croix neitz (sur la), *on the white cross* *.

Croiziex, croyses (des), *persons intending to go to the Holy Land.*

Croke (sanz), *without any iron spike or hook.*

Crome, *crime.*

Croyserie, *crusade.*

Crudes (draps), *raw cloths.*

* Brady in his appendix 32, and in his history 92, translates this; *on the old cross*; but I apprehend the word *neitz* is from *nitidus.*

Crue (char), *raw flesh.*
Crue, *a wear.*
Cruice (icestes), *this cross.*
Crus, cruez, *credited, believed.*
Cry (la), *the proclamation.*
Cũ, *as.*
Cu (un), *a cook.*
Cuchie en son lit, *lying in his bed.*
Cudietz (cum vos), *as you think.*
Cuel, *the neck.*
Cuelly, *collected.*
Cuens Leys (li), *the earl Lewis.*
Cuens de Flanders, *count or earl of Flanders.*
Cueou, *the buttocks.*
Cuer (a), *at heart.*
Cuers, *leather, skins.*
Cuerent, *meet.*
Cueurier, *master of the choir.*
Cui, *whom, to whom.*
Cuide, cuideroit, *thinks.*
Cuille (qui ad la), *which is not castrated.*
Cuil, cuile, cuel, *the neck.*
Cuiller d'or, *a gold spoon.*
Cuiller, *a collection.*
Cuilliz, *gathered, collected.*
Cuir (last de), *a last of leather.*
Cuist, *bakes.*
Cule, *dung, filth.*
Cule nuict, *the night season.*
Culhir, *to collect.*
Culiours, *collectors.*
Culture (un), *a piece of ground.*
Cum, *as.*
Cumbre, *Cumberland.*
Cumpaignie, *company, society.*
Cun, *one alone.*
Cundez, *coined.*
Cunee, cunage, *coined, coinage.*
Cuneuse, *known.*
Cunge, cungie, *leave.*
Cunquestre, *conquest.*
Cunte, *county, earl.*
Cupre (de), *of copper.*
Cur (lunge), *a long purse.*
Cur le roy, *court of the king.*
Cureles, *without cure of souls.*
Curerons, *will take care, will apply for.*
Curge, *short.*
Curge, currye, *runs, to run.*
Curoms, *will take care,*
Curr, *a hide.*
Curreours des quirs, *curriers of leather.*
Curriez, *would run, proceed.*
Curiurs (d'main), *of curriers.*

Currons,

Currons, *will take care.*

Curruz (pur), *through anger.*

Curs (bref de), *a writ of courſe.*

Curſe (la), *the courſe.*

Curt, *court.*

Curteignes pilous, *curtains made of hair.*

Curtiner, *to improve, cultivate, fence in.*

Curtiver, *to plough.*

Curtoiſe, curteiſe, *genteel, civil, courteous.*

Curz, *courts.*

Cuſine, *dyet.*

Cuſins, *kindred.*

Cuſtages (as), cuſtees, *at the coſt.*

Cuſtance, *Conſtance.*

Cuſtefre, *Chriſtopher.*

Cuſtivent, *cultivate.*

Cuſtumer laron, *a common thief.*

Cuſtume (a), *into a precedent.*

Cuſtumiers du courte, *ſuitors of the court.*

Cuſu, *ſewed to, annexed.*

Cuttle, cutle, *a knife, dagger.*

Cuune, *generation.*

Cuyre (eſcu de), *a ſhield of leather.*

Cuyſein, *a cook.*

Cuz, *put.*

Cy, *yes, ſo.*

Cy, *if, ſo, then, alſo, as, here, hereupon.*

Cy apres, *hereafter.*

Cy avant, *as well before.*

Cy bien, *as well.*

Cy court, *ſo ſpeedily.*

Cy (entre), *between this, between this time.*

Cy long, *as long.*

Cy pres, *as near as can be.*

Cy que, *ſo that.*

Cy vivement, *ſo lively.*

Cye per attorney, *here by attorney.*

Cyeinz, cyen, *here, within.*

Cyeit, *let there be.*

Cyel, *heaven.*

Cyens, *his own.*

Cyere, *to-morrow.*

Cymytere, *a church-yard.*

Cynk, *five.*

Cynſours de bourſes, *cutpurſes.*

Cyre (verte); la ver en cite, *green wax.*

Cyſors, *cutters.*

Cytoaen, *a citizen.*

Dam̃s, *damages.*

D anz, *five hundred years.*

Daſſ̃, *of aſſize.*

Dđ, *demand, demandant.*

Dnẽ (y), *demand.*

Dẽe, *to have been,*

Def, Deft, *default, want.*
Dr̃, *right.*
Drence, *difference.*
Deftr̃, *diftrefs, diftrained, obliged.*
Da, dea, *yes.*
Da (ouy), *yes verily.*
Daareim, *the laft day of the month.*
Dabondant, *moreover, befides.*
Dabte, *date.*
Dagge, *a fmall gun.*
Dagnell noire, *black lamb.*
Dagne, dage, *dagger.*
Daie, dait, *ought.*
Daies, *within, concerning.*
Daillours, *others, elfewhere.*
Daine, *a doe.*
Dalphin, *the dauphin, the eldeft fon of the king of France.*
Damager, *to opprefs, injure.*
Dam̃aifgiet, *endamaged, injured.*
Damafches beftes, *tame beafts.*
Dames, *deer.*
Dames de religion, *lady abbeffes, prioreffes.*
Damnable, *to be condemned.*
Damnablement, *grievoufly.*
Damoifells, demicelles, *nobles, the fons of kings, princes, noblemen and knights, fubordinate lords, ladies of quality.*
Damoyfeles, *damfels, female infants.*
Damp, *mafter, fir.*
Dampner, *to be cancelled.*
Danearch, *Denmark.*
Danis, *Dennis.*
Dard, *a dart.*
Dareigner, *to make proof of it, to teftify, to dereign it.*
Darps, draps, *clothing, covering.*
Darrain, darraigne, darren, darner, *laft.*
Darrein, *proof.*
Darreinere paffe, *laft paft.*
Darreignement, *laft.*
Darreirement, *lately.*
Darrener (au) des terms, *on the laft of the terms.*
Darrees, *money, goods, chattels, effects, merchandize.*
Darres (2), *two-pence.*
Daffer, *to affefs.*
Datif, *a thing in gift.*
Dau, daou, *two.*
Daugiers, dangiers, *fifhing-places.*
Daungerous, *dubious.*
Dauqui en avant, *from henceforth.*
Dauft, *Auguft.*
Davant, *before.*
Davenon, *Avignon.*
Dè, *dice.*

Deanie,

Deanie, *deanry.*
Deaufcens, *two hundred.*
Deaux, *two.*
Debas, *under, below.*
Debafe, *below.*
Debafe les ponts, *beneath the bridge.*
Debafe lour eftate, *beneath their eftate.*
Debaffa, *downwards.*
Debat, *oppofition, contention.*
Debatre, *to difpute.*
Debe, *ought, muft.*
Debelle, *overpowered.*
Deberbiz (peaux), *fheep-fkins.*
Debies, *debts.*
Deboter, debouter, *to put out, deforce, deny, hinder.*
Debouche et corn, *hue and cry.*
Debrifant, *refifting.*
Debrifer, *to cancel.*
Debrufure de prifon, *breaking of prifon.*
Debrufez, *broke in pieces.*
Debuferont, *ought.*
Debuient (ne), *ought not.*
Debuoir, debuoiar, *duty, devoir, obeifance.*
Deburg, *in commiffion of a burglary.*
Decea, *from thence.*
Deceder, *to die.*
Decent, *deceit.*
Deceu, *on this fide.*
Decevanche, deceut, *deceit.*
Deceux, decieux, *deceived.*
Deceyvante (en), *in deceivable manner.*
Deceynt, *ungirded.*
Decha, *on this fide, in thefe parts.*
Dechaffer, *to drive away.*
Decheier, *a robbery, to take to robbing.*
Decheues, *decayed.*
Dechyre, *rent, torn.*
De ci en avant, *from hence.*
Deciens, *fince.*
Deciller les yeulx, *to open your eyes.*
Decimeur, *the owner of the tythes of a parifh.*
Declaiera, declarez, delaiera (ne), *fhall not delay, deny.*
Decole, *beheaded.*
Decories, *fkinned, pulled off.*
Deconfort, *difcomfort.*
Decouper, *to cut down.*
Decres, *decreafe.*
Decrefceantz, *arifing, renewing, increafing.*
Decret, decrez, decreis, (doctour en), *doctor in decretals, doctor of law.*
Dectes, *debts.*
Dedeinz, dedinz, dedenz, dedens, dedaynes, dedeynus, *within, in the mean time.*
Dedentre, *within, between.*

Dedie (lu), *consecrated place.*
Dedints, deduits, *duells, trials, amusements.*
Dedisoint, *deny, refuse.*
Dediftz, *denied.*
Dedirz en jugement, *denied in judgment.*
Dedount, *brought, deduced.*
Deduc, deduces, deduft, deduift, deduct, *brought, alledged, determined.*
Deduiz, dedut, deduyt, *recreation, pastime.*
Dedure (a faire), *to bring in question, to bring proof.*
Deduysant, *drawing: also requiring.*
Dedutz, *game.*
Deduz, *during, depending.*
Dēe, *to be.*
Deen, *dean.*
Deenz, *within.*
De entre, *between.*
Deervie (tot nel eussent il), *although they had not deserved it.*
Deface, *defeat.*
Defacum des membres, *loss of limbs, members.*
Defaicts, *defeated, conquered.*
Defaille, *deficiency.*
Defames, *infamous.*
Defauce, *dissolved.*
Defaudroit, *should wait.*
Defauderunt, *shall make default.*
Defaurroit (en cas qu'il), *in case of failure, in case of death*
Defausit, *should die.*
Defaut, *deficiency, default, defect.*
Defawcher, *to mow, reap*
Defayllift, *failed, died.*
Defectz, *destroyed, defeated, undone.*
Defeet, *defeated.*
Defence, defence (en), *in defiance of, in derogation of.*
Defence (en), *fenced off, in several.*
Defencuse (se), *may defend himself.*
Defendaunt (se), *in his own defence.*
Defendeutz, *badly repaired.*
Defender, *to oppose, deny.*
Defend' le droit, *opposes or denies the right.*
Defendre, *to probihit.*
Defens (mises en), *put in defence, prohibited.*
Defense, *prohibition, commandment.*
Defensed plait, *maintain any plea.*
Defenses, *prohibited seasons and places.*
Defent, *defends.*

Defere,

Defere, *ſet aſide, undo, defeat, reverſe.*
Defeſance des templers, *the ſuppreſſion of the order of the knights-templars.*
Defeſant, *undoing, defeating.*
Defez, *done.*
Deffeſance (en), *in prejudice.*
Deffiaille, *breach of faith.*
Deffranchiſſant, *disfranchizing.*
Defie, *miſtruſted.*
Defiete, *loſt, forfeited.*
Definement du terme, *end of the term.*
Defiſtes, *did, gave.*
Deflis, *tired.*
Defola, defoula, defula, defoules, *trodden down, trampled upon, ſpoiled, damaged, ill-treated, abuſed.*
Defont, *defeated.*
Defore, *oppoſe, obſtruct.*
Defover, defower, *to dig or take up again, to uncover.*
Defoulours, *ſpoilers, robbers.*
Defrene vers lui, *recovers againſt him.*
Defretz, *will defeat.*
Defriſher, defriſcher, *to work by tilling the ground.*
Defua ſon baron, *eloped from her huſband.*
Defues, *widows.*
Defuiaunt, *running away, flying from.*
Defula, defola, *took out of the fold.*
Defuont, *run away.*
Degage, *give ſecurity.*
Degages, *replevied.*
Degaſt, degeſt, degata, *ſpoiled, waſted, trod down.*
Degayne, *untilled.*
Degiſe manere, *in an undue manner.*
Degre, *voluntarily.*
Degre voyde, *a void ſpace.*
Degret, *degree.*
Degu, *nobody.*
Deguerre, *in war.*
Deguerpys, *abandoned.*
De guiſſe, *diſguiſed.*
Degun, *any.*
Degutz, *due.*
Deherte de ſa feivre, *ill of her fever.*
Dehors, *in.*
Dehue, *due.*
Dehonneſtation de fammes marriees, *robbing married women of their chaſtity.*
Dei, *finger.*
Deia, *dyed.*
Deignent, *condeſcend.*
Deigner, *grant.*

Deject,

Deject, *thrown down.*
Deins, *teeth.*
Deins aver, *in the hands.*
Deinzseins, *denizens.*
Deinz (de) et jours, *within ten days.*
Deinz, deinz qe, del deins, *within.*
Dejoste, *near.*
Deisiens, *we said.*
Deissiers, *desired.*
Deissoins, *say.*
Deissons, *should say.*
Deit, *owe, owing, owes, ought.*
Deites, *debts.*
Deita, *aforesaid.*
Deiture, *right.*
Deive, ee, *ought to be.*
Deivent, *owe.*
Deiviers, *rights, duties.*
Deivoerent myses, *there ought to be provided.*
De kes en sea, *to this time.*
De kes ore, *hitherto.*
De key, *wherefore, till this time.*
Delair, *release.*
Delair, *the month of December.*
Delairont (se), *shall divest themselves.*
Delaissie (nous avons), *we have given up.*
Delaisser, *to leave, forsake.*
Delaissementz, *releases, acquittances.*
Deleaute, *perfidy, rebellion, infamy, light character.*
Delermer, *to bewail.*
Delers, *besides.*
Deles, *delay.*
Deles, delez, delees, *about, near.*
Delessoms, *we release.*
Delie, *dissolved.*
Delinqetz, *dismiss.*
Delitable, *delectable, dear to him.*
Delitent, *take a pleasure in.*
Deliverant, *the affirmant.*
Deliverance (vers la), *towards the sessions of the gaol-delivery.*
Deliveraunt, *dispatching, performing.*
Deliveraunce (a la), *for the discharge.*
Deliverer (le people), *the people delivered at a gaol-delivery.*
Delleanses, *allegations.*
Delue, *delayed.*
Delyt, *delight.*
Demainer (en son), *in his demesne.*
Demainez, *lords.*
Demaint, *now, presently.*
Demariez, *married.*
Demaunder, *to cry a thing, to send.*
Demaygne (en), *in demesne.*
Deme, *to be.*

Demeanez,

Demeanez, *ordered.*
Demeigne, demenie, demeine, *own.*
Demein, *to-morrow.*
Demeine (en), *in the mean time, again.*
Demeins, *with less.*
Demenez, *agitated, stirred.*
Demenge, *Sunday.*
Dementenant en avant, *from this time forwards.*
Dementers, *while.*
Dementers (en), dementiers, *in the mean time.*
Demesnez, *ruled: demeaned themselves well.*
Demesure (a), *beyond all measure, immoderately.*
Demette (se), *parts with.*
Demettent (sei), *submit themselves, render themselves.*
Demettre, demitter, *to let go, to part with, to put away.*
Demeures, *wait.*
Demierkes, *Wednesday.*
Demittable, *demiseable.*
Demoer, demourier, demoerger, demorier, *to remain, abide, dwell with.*
Demoere (la), *the protest, declaration.*
Demoere (la) le counte de Lanc. *the protestation of the earl of Lancaster.*
Demonstrance, *declaration, count, petition, remonstrance, suggestion.*
Demorant testament, *last will.*
Demorez, *retained.*
Demorer ensemble, *to cohabit together.*
Demustrer, *to shew.*
Demy noet, *midnight.*
Demys (a), *has parted with.*
Demyst (ne se), *did not put himself out.*
Dempt, *taken.*
Den, *dean.*
Dene, denne, *a valley.*
Deneir, *to give.*
Denerie, *deanry.*
Dener, denier, denire, deneres, denerez, denrees, danree, *a penny, money.*
Deners countauntz, *ready money.*
Denier, deniast, *denied, refused.*
Denier parties, *towards the parts.*
Denioms, *afraid.*
Denoicer, *wages.*
Denomination (de lour), *of their own naming.*
Denqui, *beyond.*
Denree de pain, *a penny worth of bread.*
Dent, *give.*
Denueroit en la mercie, *should be amerced.*

Denyer,

Denyer, *dye.*
Denygres, *obliterated.*
Denys (vos), *give you, I lay before you.*
Denz, *within.*
Denzeyn, denzeiſne, *denizen.*
Denzieme, deſein, *decenry.*
Deociſſe, *dioceſe, diſtrict, pariſh.*
Deoſſe, *boned.*
Deotantes, *deodands.*
De par de la, *beyond-ſea.*
Departable, *diviſible.*
Departier (a), *ſeparate.*
Departies, *diſpoſed of.*
Departirent, *divided.*
Departie (la), *the ſeparation.*
Departeement, *ſeverally.*
Departure, *parting.*
Depece, (ſoit denier) des peſce, *let the money be broke to pieces.*
Depeciez, *cancel, tear.*
Depdād, *in the commiſſion of a robbery.*
Depenſements, *ſuggeſtions.*
Deper, *on the behalf.*
Deperdes, *loſſes.*
Depere, *loſt, decayed.*
Depererary, *ſhall repair to.*
Depertier, *to depart with.*
Depertire, *depart from.*
Depeſcer, *to unfold, cut into pieces by retale.*
Depeſcez priſon ont, *have broken the priſon.*
Depeſne (ſon baſton eſt), *his ſtaff is broken.*
Depeſſeront le mur, *ſhall break down the wall.*
Depieca, *lately.*
Depiroient, *taken away, deſtroyed.*
Depiz, *worſe.*
Deplain, *in a ſummary manner.*
Deplayer, *to wound.*
Deprave, *reviled, depreciated.*
Depredative (diſſeiſine), *a diſſeiſin gained by violence, or clandeſtinely.*
Deprovera, *ſhall diſprove.*
Depoos, *a depoſit.*
Deport, *juſt, right, equitable.*
Deport, *reſpect.*
De porte (je me), *I rely upon it.*
Deporter, *to depart.*
Deporter, deſporter, *diverſion, recreation.*
Depoſt d'armes, *laying down of arms.*
De qes en ca, *to this time.*
Deques, *until.*
D' qune, *therefore.*
Deranꝙrs, dereein, *laſt.*
Deraſerent, *broke to pieces, cut to pieces, deſtroyed.*

Derchief,

Derchief, derechief, derichefs, *moreover*, *again*, *repetition*, *from henceforth.*

Dere, *deer.*

Derere eux, *in their abſence.*

Derene, dereinet, *derained*, *deraigned*, *determined.*

Derener, dereigner, dereyner, deraigner, dereiner, derainer, *to prove*, *to clear himſelf*, *to inſtitute*, *to deraign.*

Dereſon, *ſcorn*, *contempt.*

D'reigne, derene, *proof.*

Derire, *behind-hand.*

Deriſe, *mocked*, *laughed at.*

Derognent, *derogate from.*

Deroguer, *to abrogate.*

Deromper, *to break.*

Derrai, *damage.*

Derreiner, *to endeavour.*

Derroin, dereint, *laſt.*

Derroit, *ſhould give.*

Derruide, *in a ruinous condition.*

Des, *from.*

Des accordaunt, *different*, *varying from.*

Deſacort, *diſagreement.*

Deſadunques, *from that time.*

Deſaiſez, *injured*, *troubled*, *hindered.*

Deſapeile, *unfurniſhed*, *unprovided.*

Deſareſtent, *diſcharge*, *releaſe from the arreſt.*

Deſaſſentera, *ſhall refuſe his aſſent.*

Deſaſſurez, *diſheartened*, *diſcomfited.*

Deſaſure *, *unſerved.*

Deſattames, *unfiniſhed.*

Deſautes, defaute (la), *the want.*

Deſavaunce, *unadvanced.*

Deſavowes, *diſclaims*, *diſowns*, *refuſes to ſtand to.*

Deſavowes, diſavowes, *diſavowed.*

Deſavowes, *unwarrantable*, *unjuſtifiable.*

Deſbalmant, *clearing from the accuſation.*

Deſbaz, *diſputes.*

Deſblemies, *unblemiſhed*, *uninvaded.*

Deſboucher, *to unſtop*, *to diſpark.*

Deſceitz, deſcenict, deſoynt, deſceyntz, *ungirded.*

Deſcendue, *determined.*

Deſcendent en enqueſte, *come to an inqueſt.*

Deſcendi (lui), *deſired him.*

* See Rot. Parl. vol. II. p. 76. pet. 18. Potius *deſaſvire*, Hale's MS.

Deſcernez,

Defcernez, *decreed.*
Defceverance, *to the fever-ance.*
Defchauces, *barefoot.*
Defchauncee des foulers, *bare-legged.*
Defchee, *defcribe.*
Defcheiez, *tumbled down, gone to ruin, gone to decay.*
Defchete, *abated, deducted.*
Defcheterie, *efcheator.*
Defchevele, *loofe, difhevelled.*
Defcheu de fa plaint, *lofes the benefit of his plaint.*
Defchevoir, *deceive.*
Defclaire, *declares.*
Defclaree, *explained, declared.*
Defclariffement, *explanation.*
Defclor, defclar, *difclofed, fet forth.*
Defclos, *not inclofed.*
Defcomerfit a nubi, *difclofed to any one.*
Defcortz, *difcords.*
Defcovenable, *unfitting, unlawful, nonjuridical.*
Defcovert (tout a), *openly, fairly.*
Defcoulpe, *excufed, juftified.*
Defcoûte, *uncovered.*
Defcoupant, *exculpating.*
Defcounfeile, defcounfeille, *difcounfeled, not filled up, unprovided.*
Defcres, *decreafe.*
Defcrez, *difcreet.*
Defcrie, *difcovered, perceived.*
Defcripvraj, *I will defcribe.*
Defcroiftre, *to grow lefs.*
Defcrus, decheue, *decayed.*
Defcufer, *to excufe.*
Defcyners, pledges defeines, *pledges in the decenry.*
Defdeigz, *difdain, difdains.*
Defduit, *game.*
Defeefe, defeefi, defeafe, defeux, *uneafinefs, grief, trouble, charge, vexation.*
Defeifez, *difquieted.*
Defemez, *unfown.*
Defempeftre, *to get out of a fnare.*
Defencrefcez, *decreafed.*
Defenhabitez, *uninhabited.*
Deferes (lur), potiùs *defcres, their decreafe.*
Deferit, *deferted, without remedy.*
Deferite, *difinherited.*
Defervie, *not fupplied, unferved.*
Defervy, *intitled to, deferved.*
Defes, *deceafe.*

Defefparur,

Deſeſparer, *to deſpair.*
Deſetereſon, *diſinheriſon.*
Deſevere, *parted, divided.*
Deſeverums, *ſeparate, ſever, cut of from.*
Deſeurer, *to divide, ſeparate.*
Deſeuht eux, *under them.*
Deſeuverte, *uncovered, laid open.*
Desfermez, *unlocked.*
Deſgarnys, deſgarrys, deſgorrie, *unwarned, unprovided, unfurniſhed.*
Deſgaynnes, *untilled.*
Deſgorrie, *unprovided.*
Deſhonte, *without ſhame.*
Deſhors, deſhorſe, *from henceforth.*
Deſia mis en poſſeſſion, *already put us in poſſeſſion.*
Deſimes, *make known.*
Desjoynames, *parted, untied.*
Deſiron, *deſirous.*
Deſke, *ſince.*
Deſkes a ore, *ſo far*
Deſlaez, *delayed.*
Deſleaute, *treachery.*
Deſliez, *looſed from, diſcharged.*
Deſlors, *from that time.*
Deſloyál, deſleal, *unlawful, fraudulent.*
Deſmaintenant, *from henceforth, forthwith.*
Deſmarietz, *unmarried.*
Deſme garb, *the tenth ſheaf.*
Deſmeneront, *ſhall bring, ſhall ſend, remove.*
Deſmes, *deer.*
Deſmeſurable, *unbounded.*
Deſmolicons, *demolition.*
Deſnaturel, deſnatureus, *unnatural.*
Deſnaturee (liè de la), *bound by nature.*
Deſnigrer, *to blacken, to defame.*
Deſnue de amies, *void or deſtitute of friends.*
Deſoient, *ſaid.*
Deſoies, *ſaid; alſo unaccuſtomed.*
Deſolent, *abuſe, ſpoil, trample upon.*
Deſolerent (malement), *evilly treated him.*
Deſooth, *beyond, above.*
Deſordines accomptes, *irregular accompts.*
Deſore, deſhors, deſorenaunt, deſorenavant, deſore en avant, deſorendroit, deſormes, deſoremes, deſormais, *from henceforth, hereafter, from this time forward, for the future.*
Deſovere, *unworked, unwrought.*
Deſouz, deſoz, *under, underneath, hereafter.*

Desouz (mis au), *ruined.*
Desoynte sa cote, *his coat ungirt.*
Desoz, desouz, *hereafter, under.*
Despaiee, *unpaid.*
Despare, *unequal force.*
Desparpler, *to be distributed.*
Despascerent, *eat up, spoiled, wasted.*
Despeca, *on that behalf.*
Despendent (en), *in the expenditure of it.*
Despendre (a), *to lay out.*
Despendues, *dispersed.*
Despenses, *expences.*
Desperager, *to disparage.*
Desperee, *unforeseen.*
Despire, *despise.*
Despiscea, *speedily, before this time.*
Despite (en), despisaunt (en), *in contempt of, in despite of.*
Despitousement, *despitefully.*
Despitz, *contempts, hatred.*
Desplede, *without plea, unanswered.*
Despleyt, *displeased.*
Desplie, *displayed.*
Desplounge, *overflowed, flooded.*
Despointer, *dispute.*
Despores, *spurs.*
Despoit et aes, *their recreation and ease.*
Desportent (il), *they forbear.*
Desportere (lui), *assist, comfort him.*
Desportes, *relieved, excused.*
Desportes de payer, *exempted from paying.*
Desportera (il), *he will dispense with,*
Desport (sans favour ou); sans deport faire a nuli, *without shewing favour to any one.*
Desport (tant), *so long lost, so long been deprived of.*
Despost (mis en), *deposited, laid up in warehouses.*
Despourter, *spare.*
Desprie, *unseised, untaken.*
Despuliez, *despoiled.*
Despurvue, *unprovided.*
Despyt (en) de lour defaut, *by way of punishment for their default.*
Desquarantre, *to discharge.*
Desque, desquel, desqe al jor, *until the day.*
Desreinserement, *lately.*
Desreine, *proved.*
Desrengeront, *shall set out.*
Desreson (la), *the unreasonableness.*
Desrobbez, *robbed, despoiled, wasted.*
Desroy, *to be out of order.*

Desrumputz,

Desrumputz, *squeezed together, burst.*

Dessasseurance, *unsafety, disappointment, discomfit.*

Desseme, *not sown.*

Dessente, *descent.*

Dessevrer, *to put asunder.*

Dessiese, *disseisin.*

Dessouz, desuz, *under, underneath, hereafter.*

Dessoubs (ou), *or thereabouts, or within that number.*

Dessuisy, *seized.*

Dessusditz, deseuredis, *abovesaid.*

Destachez, *untacked.*

Destail (a), *by retale.*

Desteinantz, *will fail, prove bad.*

Destembez, *disturbed.*

Destertre, *desert, leave.*

Destincter, *to distinguish.*

Destopper, *to unstop.*

Destorberoms, *would prevent it.*

Destountz, *unknown.*

Destour, *gone back.*

Destr̃, *distress.*

Destrayiens, *distractions.*

Destre, *held fast.*

Destre, *a large horse, a horse of service for the great saddle in war.*

Destre (au), *on the right hand.*

Destre mayne, *the right hand.*

Destr̃ (a), *over-against.*

Destreint, *straightened, restrained, difficult to come at, expensive.*

Destreit, destroitz, d'estroit, *district, distress*

Destrement, *speedily.*

Destresces, *distresses.*

Destresse, destressce, *compulsion.*

Destresse au roi, *abridge the king.*

Destreynt, *proved a title to.*

Destrier, *to try.*

Destrouses, *destruction.*

Destruer, *to condemn.*

Destrut, *destroyed.*

Destrutz, *put out of, disinherited.*

Desturbance, *impediment, delay.*

Desue, *abused.*

Desuer, *to break through, set aside, undo.*

Desverie, *folly.*

Desuese, *injury, hindrance.*

Desvesties, *naked, uncloathed.*

Desuis, desus, desuys, *above.*

Desuis rendre, *to surrender.*

Desvoier, *to wander out of the way.*

Desurder, *to raise.*

Desunes, *above.*
Desurit, *desires.*
Desvorre, *devoured.*
Desvoye, *deviate.*
Desuis le mot, *under the word.*
Desyra, *tore.*
Det, *said.*
Detrahe, *taken out of the hands of, taken from, withdrawn.*
Detrees (a), *to the decrease.*
Detreie, *withdrawn.*
Detrenchent, *cut.*
Detrie, *tried.*
Detriment (le), *the trial.*
Deu, Deus, Deux, *God.*
Deu, *of.*
Deu, *of the.*
Deu, *a debt.*
Deu, deuz, *due.*
Deuantz, *devotions.*
Deubter, *was afraid.*
Deu cas, *two cases.*
Deues, *two.*
Deura, deurons, *ought.*
Deurees, dueres, deuries, deures, devers, *money, effects.*
Deuroient, *should shield.*
Deuront, deurent, *ought.*
Deurra, *will give, will present.*
Deutz, deubtz, *due.*
Deuvre, *to be indebted.*
Deux, *dies.*
Deux (en), *on God, in God.*
Deux, deus, *two, both.*
Deuxiesme, *second.*
Devaler, *to go downwards, to bring down.*
Devanciers, *aforetime.*
Devanciers, *ancestors.*
Devan luy, *from him.*
Devantement, *devoutly.*
Devates, *disputes, debates.*
Deveier, *will deny.*
Devenent, *which fall, come into.*
Devensit, *had come.*
Devensist enceinte, *became ensient.*
Devenuz, *arrived at, become.*
Devent, *before.*
Devenk, devent, *become.*
Dever, *to dye.*
Dever, *to owe, to be indebted.*
Dever, *duty.*
Dever, devers, *against.*
Devere eaux, *on their part.*
Devers, *dead.*
Devers, *the money.*
Devers le fyn, *towards the end.*
Devers pere ou mere, *of the father's or mother's side.*
Devers la mere, *on the mother's side.*

Deversee,

Deverſee, *with, in the power of.*
Devereire, *devoir.*
Devereit, *ought to be.*
Devereit dire, *ought to ſay.*
Deverait (ne), *ought not to have.*
Deverount (a ceux qui les), *to the owners.*
Deverie (en), *in a delirium.*
Deveſtua (ne), *ſhall not be put by.*
Devez, *deviſed, ſurmiſed.*
Devi, *owes.*
Deviaſt, *dyed.*
Devicoez, *had fell, had come into.*
Devient, *dye; alſo, they owe.*
Devin, *divine.*
Devinar, *divination.*
Devis, *deviſe.*
Deviſable, *diviſible.*
Deviſee, *deviſed, appointed.*
Deviſes (en), *in the diviſion.*
Deviſeement, *ſeverally.*
Devoer, *ability.*
Devoidable, *may be divided.*
Devoir, *to have.*
Devoir, deſtitut, *deſtitute of wealth.*
Devolupa, devolute, *devolved.*
Devomus rien, *we owe nothing.*
Devote (ne), *ought not.*
Devove, *appointed.*
Devouz, *devoted.*
Devoy, *ſubmit.*
Devoyant (en), *in right of*
Devoyer, *endeavour.*
Devy eſpouſera, *ſhall eſpouſe.*
Dewaunt, *before.*
Dewe, *due.*
Dewe, *two.*
Dex, *God.*
Dexcint, *fifteen.*
Dey, *finger.*
Dey apper, *ought to appear.*
Dey, devy, *dieth, died.*
Deycuns, *we ſaid.*
Deyes, *drivers of geeſe.*
Deyne, *his own.*
Deyme, *the tenth.*
Deyms, deynes, *does.*
Deymus, *ſayd.*
Deynt, *alledge, ſay.*
Deyve, deyvent, deiva, deyne, *owe, ought.*
Deze, dez, *ten.*
Dezeyners, *deçiners.*
Dĩ, *half.*
Dian, *dean.*
Diaules, *devils.*
Diaulx, *two.*
Dibendre, *Friday.*
Dibilie, *diſabled, reduced, infirm.*

Dicel, *of this ſame.*
Dicelle (a), *from hence-forth.*
Dici, *of this.*
Dict, *a word.*
Diemane, *Sunday.*
Dieme, *the tenth.*
Diemenches (li rois des), rex dierum dominicorum, *Trinity-Sunday.*
Dien, *they ſay.*
Dienee, *deanry.*
Dient, *ought.*
Dieu, *due.*
Dieux, *two.*
Diez, Dies, Dieux, *God.*
Difalmement, *defamation.*
Diffenſe, *defence.*
Diffet, *defeated.*
Diffinite, *of affinity.*
Diffie (ſoy), *puts himſelf out.*
Diffuantez, *fled.*
Diffuantz le lei, *in defiance of the law.*
Dignier, *a penny.*
Dijau, Dijou, *Thurſday.*
Di jeo, *I ſay.*
Dilai, *delay.*
Dilapidez, *dilapidated, waſted, ſquandered away.*
D'ilent, *of the entire.*
Dillation, *delay.*
Dilleoques, dillouques, *afterwards.*
Dilliours, *of electors.*
Dilueques, *from thence.*
Dimaigne, dimeine, dimeins, dimeignt, dimenche, dimegne, *Sunday.*
Dimar, *Tueſday.*
Dimecre, *Wedneſday.*
Dimiſes, *diſmiſſed.*
Diner, *a penny.*
Dinquios, *as far as, hitherto.*
Dins, *in, within.*
Diole, *a dial.*
Diont, *may ſay.*
Diotre, due, *daily.*
Dious, Dius, *God.*
Direchef, *again.*
Dirept, *took, accept.*
Dirrain, *laſt.*
Dirs enkes, *different inks.*
Dirupt, *broken down.*
Diruite, *thrown down.*
Dis, *ten.*
Diſaſſentz, *diſſent.*
Diſavaile, *diſadvantage.*
Diſavances, *unadvaneed, unprovided for.*
Diſaviſes, *unwary.*
Diſavowable de droit, *againſt law.*
Diſcēte, *he deſcends.*
Diſch, *diſh.*
Diſchapper, *to eſcape out of.*
Diſcheiſit (ren), *any thing ſhould be abated.*
Diſci, dis ſicum, *ſince, for as much as.*

Diſcoiture,

Difcoiture, *difcolouring.*

Difcombrance, *difturbance.*

Difcontinue, *difcontinuance.*

Difconveniable perfons, *improper, unfit perfons.*

Difcorage, *difcouragement.*

Difcourer, *to cleanfe.*

Difcoverirent, *uncovered, difcovered.*

Difcovert, *a woman unmarried.*

Difcrepancie, *a difagreement, difference.*

Difcries enemies, *proclaimed, notorious enemies.*

Difcriver, difcever, *to difcover.*

Difcurrer, *to run up and down, through.*

Difcuter, *to difcufs.*

Difdeinance, *defpifing.*

Difdict, *a yielding or confeffion of guilt.*

Dife, *the tenth part.*

Difeame, *unfowed.*

Difeafe, *trouble, inconvenience, diftrefs.*

Difeafez, *injured, troubled, hindered, difquieted.*

Difenef, *nineteen.*

Difes, *dice.*

Difefet, *feventeen.*

Difette (de), *for want.*

Disfoith ataunt, *ten times as much.*

Difgrade, *degraded.*

Difheritefon, *difinherifon.*

Difinfovie, *unburied, taken up again.*

Difliee, *under no obligation.*

Difliver, *to difplace.*

Difmables, *tytheable.*

Difmarie, *unmarried.*

Difme quinquinall, *a tenth of all goods for five years together.*

Difmenges, *on Sundays.*

Difoitifme, *the* 18*th part.*

Difpaire (en), *in danger.*

Difparagation, *difparagement; the matching an heir, &c. in marriage, under his or her degree or condition, or againft the rules of decency.*

Difpencer, *to difcharge.*

Difpend, *depend.*

Difpendre, *put off, hindered, avoided.*

Difpendus, *difpenfed with.*

Difper, *defpair, danger.*

Difpergez, *difipated, fevered.*

Difport, *diverfion, entertainment.*

Difpit, difpitz, *contempt.*

Difpitoufe, *contemptuous.*

Difplet, *difpleafes.*

Difpos (mis en), *laid up.*

Difporter (eux), *eafe them, excufe them.*

Diſpuceler, *to deflower.*
Diſrobbe, *robbed, ſpoiled.*
Diſſate, *Saturday.*
Diſſeites, *deceits.*
Diſſentez, *diſſenſions.*
Diſſi la qui, *untill that.*
Diſſiny, *performed.*
Diſſiſme, *tenth.*
Diſvyt, dyſwiit, *eighteen.*
Diſſu, *deceived.*
Diſt commun, *common report, fame.*
Diſtaunce, *difference, diſpute.*
Diſtincter, *to diſtinguiſh.*
Diſtintiaunt, *diſtinguiſhing.*
Diſutime, *eighteenth.*
Diſtraction (ſans), *without damage.*
Diſtz articles, *aforeſaid articles.*
Diſtraire, *to withdraw.*
Diſtreaſable, *which may be diſtrained.*
Diſtrictuels, *diſtricts.*
Diſtreindre (ſans rien) en dure mān, *holding him by the hand without ſqueezing it too hard.*
Diſtrent (que), *who alledged.*
Diſtrent (ils), *they ſaid.*
Diſtrover, *to deſtroy.*
Diſtrue, diſtroue, *deſtroyed, diſparaged.*
Diſturbance, *hindrance, prevention.*
Diſturberent (ne les), *did not prevent them.*
Dit, *decree.*
Dit (en), *in word.*
Ditant, *during the time.*
Ditas parties, *the ſaid parties.*
Ditez, *called.*
Dition (en la), *in the power, juriſdiction.*
Divers, *differing, different.*
Diverſement, *diverſely, ſeverally.*
Dividende, *ſchedule, liſt, indenture.*
Divinal, *of divination.*
Diviſe, *given.*
Diviſion, *eſtabliſhment.*
Divont (ne), *ought not.*
Dix, *God.*
Diz, *ſaid, aforeſaid.*
Dm̄, domina, *dame, lady.*
Doayre, doans, *dower.*
Dobbours des draps, *ſellers of cloth.*
Doctrinez (en), *inſtructed in.*
Doel, *grief.*
Doen, *gift.*
Doen eſtat, *due eſtate.*
Doẽs, *given.*
Doi cent (li), *the* 200.
Doiauntz, *who ought.*
Doibt, doi, deux, *finger.*
Doibuent, *ought to be.*
Doient (que il), *what they owe, that they are in debt.*

Doigne,

Doigne, *granted.*
Doigner, *tenders, yields, grants, gives.*
Doine, *ought.*
Doioers, *dowers.*
Doire, *to bear.*
Doirees, *wares, goods, effects.*
Doit, doner, *ought to give, is to give.*
Dol, *ſorrow, grief.*
Dolauz, *aggrieved.*
Doleances, *grievances.*
Dolent, *grieving, troubled.*
Doles (les) de foreſt, *the bounds of the foreſt.*
Dolet, *an ax.*
Dolions, *we complain of.*
Doloir, *to aggrieve.*
Doloroufement, *wofully, grievouſly.*
Domage, *dammage.*
Dome final, *final ſentence.*
Domeſche, *domeſtic.*
Doms eſtre certeins, *ought to be certain.*
Domt, *give.*
Don, *of the.*
Donables, *aſſignable.*
Donance, *giving.*
Donaunt, *procurement.*
Donc, *given.*
Done, doniſſions, *taken.*
Donei, *granted.*
Donerunt, *gave, granted.*
Donewyz, *Dunwich.*
Don lui, *of the place.*
Donnant *reſervation.*
Donne, *a lady.*
Donor (de), *by gift.*
Donqes, *then.*
Donu, doneſein, doneiſon, donyſon, donacioun, *gift, grant.*
Doraunt, *during.*
Dorce, *back.*
Dore, *a door.*
Dorem, Doream, *Durham.*
Dorer (à), *to be given.*
Doreſenavant, *from henceforth.*
Dorra, *ſhall give it, or diſpoſe of it.*
Dorront, *agree, conſent.*
Dorrount, *remain there.*
Dortour novell, *new dormitory.*
Dos (par le), *by the creſt.*
Doſce, *twelve.*
Doſer, doſel, *a hanging or canopy of ſilk, ſilver, or gold-work, under which kings or great perſonages ſit; alſo the back of a chair of ſtate.*
Dotaunces, *diſputes, doubts.*
Dote, *doubtful.*
Dote (nount pas) de treſpaſſer, *are not at all afraid of offending.*
Dotier (il fait a), *there is reaſon to ſuſpect.*
Dotif, *doubtful.*
Dotoient, *feared.*
Dotous, *doubtful, in doubt.*
Douer, *gift.*
Donjours, *of the day.*

Doulce,

Doulce, *gracious, gentle.*
Douloit, *complained of.*
Dounfres, *Dumfreis.*
Dount, *wherefore, from whence.*
Dovorre, *Dover.*
Dour, *given.*
Douree, *Dover.*
Dous, *two.*
Douſt, *ought, muſt.*
Douſtres, duſtres, *leaders, commanders.*
Doutance, doubtantes, *doubts.*
Doutantz (meyns), *leſs fearing.*
Doute, *fear, fears.*
Doute ceo, *apprehends, ſupports it.*
Doute, en doute, *doubtful.*
Douterent, *feared.*
Doutez, *feared.*
Douvent, *give.*
Doux, *two.*
Douyme, *the ſecond.*
Dowarie, *dower.*
Dowe, *endowed.*
Doy, *finger.*
Doy (ne), *I ought not.*
Doy bien avoir (le), *it is right I ſhould have it.*
Doygna, *condeſcended.*
Doygner, doigner, *to give.*
Doynt, *gives.*
Doz (au), *on our backs.*
Doz peres, *the twelve peers of France.*
Dozze, doze, dozime, dozine, *twelve; the 12th.*
Dr̃, drait, *right.*
Dragges, draggus, *little boats or veſſels formerly uſed on the river Severn.*
Dragguent oiſtres, *drag oyſters.*
Drappeaux quarrez, *banners.*
Drechier, *to redreſs.*
Dreċt (par), *by right.*
Dreille, *a ditch.*
Dreine, *produced.*
Drekes, *until.*
Dr̃ence, *difference.*
Drene (il eſt), *he is proved.*
Drenere, *laſt.*
Drengage (en), *the tenures by which the drenches or drengers held their lands.*
Dres, Drez, *right.*
Dreſcent (la), *redreſs it.*
Dreſſer, *to compile.*
Dret, a dret, *overagainſt, oppoſite.*
Drettes, *right, juſt.*
Dretture, *right.*
Dreyn, drein, preſent, *laſt preſentation.*
Dreyn (au), *at laſt.*
Dreyt (tot), *directly.*

Droit

Droit (de), *of law.*
Droit (en), *concerning, in right of.*
Droite mauveſte (p), *out of mere wickedneſs.*
Droiturs et devots, *juſt and devout.*
Dromandes, *dromandes*; *veſſels called by that name.*
Drouſda, *Drogheda.*
Drout, diont, *ſay.*
Druthin Dieu, *the houſe of God.*
Du, *God.*
D'uāt, *before.*
Dublee, *duplicate of, repeated.*
Dublein (treis), *threefold.*
Dubles (treis), *three times twelve.*
Ducatz fetz, *dutchy fees.*
Duce, *kind, tender.*
Duce, *leads.*
Duce (eawe), *freſh water.*
Duchemen, *Dutchmen.*
Dudzime, *twelve.*
Due, *of the.*
Due, *to diſpoſe of.*
Duerent avoir (ne), *might not have.*
Duer, *laſts, endures.*
Dues, *two.*
Dues, *ought.*
Duete (de), *as a duty.*
Duetees, *duties.*
Duez (lui), *due to him.*
Du faire, *to do.*
Dui, *to-day.*
Dui fil, *two ſons.*
Duiſſoy (que jeo), *that I am ſuppoſed.*
Duiſt, *let him give.*
Duiſt aver ēē ouis, *ſuppoſed to have been killed.*
Duit, duiſte, duiſſent, aver eſte, *ought to have been.*
Duitez, duytz, *duties, rights.*
Dulce le roy (tres), *moſt gracious king.*
Dun, *gift.*
Dunes, *downs.*
Dunge, dune, *give, given.*
Dunk, dunc, dunky, *then, therefore.*
Duodes, *twelve.*
Duoirs, *duties.*
Duppur, *duplicate.*
Durement dormy, *ſlept faſt.*
Durer, *continue, remain.*
Dures, *hardened.*
Dureſſe, durette, *hardſhip, difficulty.*
Durete (tanz de), *ſo many hardſhips.*
Durite, durete, durte, *compulſion, dureſs.*
Durmene, *overcome.*
Durra, *will give.*
Durums, *live.*
Dus, *duke.*
Duſcenz, *two hundred.*
Duſeſme, *twelfth.*

Duſkes

Duſkes a chon qe, *until that.*
Duſſe, *two.*
Duſſent, duſont (que), *who ſhould, ought, are ſuppoſed.*
Duſtres, *ring-leaders.*
Duw (en lu), *in due place.*
Duz, *due.*
Duz, dus, dug, *a leader.*
Duſze, duze, *twelve.*
Duzim, *twelfth.*
Dy, *due, juſt.*
Dyent, *ſay, are of opinion.*
Dyent eſtre, *they ſay moreover.*
Dymain (le), *the morrow.*
Dymenges, *Sundays.*
Dymes, *tythes.*
Dymeyne, dymain, *Sunday.*
Dymis, *tythes.*
Dyners, *dinners.*
D'yntruſion, *of intruſion.*
Dys, dyz, *ten.*
Dyſeot livres et neof, *eighteen pounds nine ſhillings.*
Dyſpais (touz), *ever ſince.*
Dyvelyz, *Dublin.*
Dyvent point (ne), *ought not.*
Dyvintz, *divines.*

E, *and.* Ea, *and, alſo, further.*
Eage, *age.*
Eage, *life.*
Eantz, *having.*
Eare, *to plow.*
Eaſe (ſera), *may eaſe himſelf.*
Eaſez, *moderate, eaſy.*
Eaue, eave, eawe, *water.*
Eaux, *ewes.*
Eaux, *they.*
Eaux meiſmes, *themſelves.*
Eauz, eaux, eaus, *them.*
Ebahir, *to be ſurpriſed.*
Eble, *Eubolo.*
Ebrieux, *Hebrew.*
Echeiſt, *falls.*
Echerount, *ſhall fall out, ſhall fall, ſhall eſcheat.*
Echever, *to eſcape.*
Ecil enſens la terre (fore k), *only thoſe within that land.*
Ecumieur, *a pirate.*
Ede, *Eudo.*
Edel, *noble, illuſtrious.*
Edovart, Edvalt, Edwars, *Edward.*
Eẽ (aver), *to have been.*
Een, *be.*
Een fait deins l'an (ne yert), *has not been made within the year.*
Eent, *have.*
Ees, *bees.*
Eeſe, *pleaſure.*
Eeſt, eſt, *Eaſt.*
Eez, *hear, had, have.*

Effertull,

Efferant l', *the proportion.*
Effectull, *effectual.*
Efforablement (tant), *in as a strong manner.*
Efforcer, *to aid, assist.*
Efforcement, *force.*
Efforcez, *strengthened, secured.*
Efforcier peis, *to break a treaty of peace.*
Effouage, *hearth money.*
Effours, *efforts, endeavours.*
Effunder, *to shed, spill.*
Egarri, *healed.*
Egas, *decision, judgement, award.*
Egeceſtre, *Exeter.*
Eggliſe, *church.*
Egiſe, *lyes.*
Egiſtement, *agiſtment.*
Egle, *eagle.*
Egle (de l'honur de l'), *of the honour of the eagle.*
Eguiſer, *to happen.*
Egun, *any.*
Eguunt glia eſte, *they have been.*
Ehonte, *infamous.*
Ei (j'), *I have.*
Eians, *men.*
Eiants, *having.*
Eide, *aid.*
Eiens, *ever.*
Eier veue (l'), *have ſeen it.*
Eies, *forwards.*
Ejets a cuer, *have at heart.*
Eil (s'), *if they.*
Eimient Dieu, *love God.*
Ein, ceo, *rather.*
Eincz ſes hours, *before theſe times.*
Eindegre, *own accord.*
Eine temps (d'), *before, of a prior date.*
Eines, *in, that.*
Eingliſe, *church.*
Ein quy, *within whoſe.*
Einſnes, *eldeſt.*
Eins ceo, *when, unleſs, the ſame, rather, until.*
Eins ceux q le actor, *before the plaintiff.*
Eins (ſi), *before.*
Eins tenus (l'), *in the mean time.*
Einſperker, *impound.*
Einz, *but, in.*
Einz ceo qil, *before that he.*
Einz qe, *before that.*
Eioms, *have.*
Eions (de), *of having.*
Eions (de), *of his.*
Eir (l'), *the eyre.*
Eir, eirs, *heir, heirs.*
Eirent, *wander, ſtray.*
Eires, *ayries.*
Eirie, *to hatch.*
Eirie de eſpernons, *a young brood of hawks.*

Eiſkes,

Eiſkes, *until.*

Eiſſi, *as.*

Eiſſi co eſt a ſaver, *inſomuch.*

Eiſſi ne por quant que, *provided, nevertheleſs, that.*

Eiſſilliez, *exiled.*

Eiſſir, *to go out of.*

Eiſſit, *departure, exit.*

Eiſſo, *this.*

Eiſt (de l'), *on the eaſtern part.*

Eit n', *have not.*

Eivers (de), *of goods found, of cattle.*

Eivos, *behold.*

El, *in*; *nothing.*

Elbit, *eight.*

Elef, elefe, *flux and reflux.*

Eles, *eyes.*

Elevi, *choſen.*

Eleyer (poet), *may chuſe.*

Elez, *on a ſudden.*

Elin, *a gentleman.*

Eliſer, *to chuſe.*

Ellus, *choſen.*

Elegger, *to alledge.*

Eloviaunce, *allowance, connivance.*

Elm, *helmet.*

Elves, *choſen.*

Elus, *uſuages.*

Embandiz, *emboldened, encouraged.*

Embas, *below.*

Embatent (s'), *intermeddle.*

Embeaſiler, *to filch.*

Embellies, *ſet forth, ſhewed.*

Embeſche, *impeached.*

Emblea diſmes, *carries off his tythes.*

Emblear (l'), *the emblements.*

Embleent, *carry out of, remove.*

Embleer, *a ſeedſman, to ſow.*

Emblemy, *unimpeached, unhurt.*

Embler, *to ſteal.*

Emblez, embles, emblees (par), *by ſtratagem, by ſurprize.*

Embloioure (de), *of ſtealing.*

Emboſoigne, *needeth, requireth.*

Emboſoignera (ſil), *if need be.*

Embrace, *undertaken, embraced, purchaſed.*

Embracez (ont), *have ingroſſed.*

Embreaſer, *to burn.*

Embrevure, *a regiſter.*

Embu, *drunk up.*

Embuchement, *ambuſcade.*

Eme, *with.*

Eme, emie, *eſtimation, price.*

Emercient,

Emercient, *amerced.*
Emergentz, *arising.*
Emfle, *puffed up.*
Emfauntz, *children.*
Emi, emmi, *in half, in the middle.*
Emieez, *issued, sent out.*
Eminentz, *impending.*
Emmi, *between.*
Emmorti, *become dead.*
Emmurrer, *to wall about.*
Emoi, *emotion.*
Emoines, *witnesses.*
Emologation de la court de parlament, *the confirmation of the court of parliament.*
Emon, *Edmond.*
Emonit, *admonished.*
Empakkur (l'), *the packing.*
Emparke, emparkez, *impounded.*
Emparkement, *a park, an emparkment.*
Emparnours, *undertakers of suits.*
Empashment (en son), *in his infirmity, impediment.*
Empeche, *impeached.*
Empeirez, empirez, *impaired.*
Empell (q̃ l'), *which is called.*
Empendent, *pendant.*
Empensions, *pensions.*
Emperement, *in ornamenting, repairing.*
Emperez (se soient), *have possessed themselves of.*
Emperler, *to imparle.*
Empernant, *assuming, pretending to.*
Empernent a champart, *take for maintenance.*
Empernour, *the taker.*
Empes chenienz (por divers), *an account of divers impediments.*
Empeschable, *impeachable.*
Empeschement, *impeachment, impediment.*
Empetrer, *to require, to insist.*
Empiel (ley), *imperial or civil law.*
Empiete, *impiety.*
Empire tant nequant, *neither better or worse than before.*
Empla, *stole.*
Emplee (terre), *land sown.*
Emplere, *to fill.*
Empleroms, *we will fulfil.*
Emplevist (se), *got possession again.*
Emplir, *to fulfil.*
Emply, *implyed.*
Emportablez charges, *intolerable, heavy charges.*
Emportunement, *importunately.*

Empotentz,

Empotentz, *impotent, infirm.*

Emprainct, *impressed.*

Empraine, *in band.*

Emprant, *borrowing.*

Emprêiant, *praying.*

Empreigne, emprint, *taken upon themselves.*

Emprent, *borrow; also, taught.*

Emprent, *who undertakes.*

Emprent, *impression.*

Empres, *pledged.*

Empresserent, *engaged, hindered.*

Emprez, empres, *after, afterwards.*

Empriantz, *beseeching.*

Emprimechief, *first of all.*

Empris, *undertaken, taken up.*

Emprisse, *undertaking.*

Empriums, *beg, pray.*

Emprompt z, empraunt, emprant, *borrowing.*

Empuis (d'), *afterwards.*

Empuisse, *may.*

Empuissonement, *imprisonment.*

En, *in, by, within.*

Enaager, *to declare one to be of age.*

Enabyter, *to inhabit.*

En apres, *hereafter.*

Enarer, *in time past.*

Enarer cea, *to this time, heretofore.*

Enavant, *for the time to come.*

En oultre, *furthermore.*

Enbataillez, *in battle array, engaged in battle.*

Enbeverer, *to water, also a watering place.*

Enbeverer (droit de), *right of watering, or taking in water for cattle.*

Enblauncher, *to blanch, to make white.*

Enblee, enblaye de ble yvernail, *sown with winter corn.*

Enbleir, *to steal.*

Enboisinera, *will want.*

Enbosid, *embossed.*

Enbosognez, *engaged in business.*

Enbouellecz, *embowelled.*

Enbrace, *encroached.*

Enbraudez, *embroidered.*

Enbrever, *to minute down, to reduce into writing.*

Enca, *heretofore, some time past.*

Encariez, *carried away.*

Encaver, *to beware.*

Encea, enci, *so, also, afterwards.*

Encepper, *to confine him.*

Encere, *yet.*

Enceynte, *quick with child.*

Encha (depuis huit jours), *within these eight days.*

En chaln, *appease.*

Enchancer,

Enchancer, *to alter, to raiſe.*

Enchappellè, *crowned with a crown, or coronet.*

Encharger, encharchees, *to give in charge.*

Enchaſe, *drove away.*

Enchaſer, *to compel.*

Enchaſconez, *chaſed.*

Enchaſon, encheſon, encheſſon, encheſcun, enchiſon, *cauſe, occaſion, reaſon.*

Enchaunterie, *witchcraft.*

Enchaz et rechaz, *inchace and outchace; the right of driving cattle to and from a common.*

Encheires, *enhanced, made dear.*

Encheiez, *decayed.*

Encherer, *to enhance the price of.*

Encheriſſe (ne), *do not raiſe the price of.*

Encheſcune, encheiſonez, encheſones, encheſon, *puniſhed, called in queſtion, croſs-examined.*

Enchiez, *at, to.*

Enchi la, *there.*

Enchres, *anchors.*

Enci, *ſo, alſo, afterwards.*

Enclaimant, *claiming.*

Enclairſi, *brought to light.*

Enclarre, d'enclore, *to incloſe.*

Encliner del oyl (par), *by a wink of the eye.*

Enclos (le jour), *the day included.*

Encloſe, *to incloſe.*

Encloſtrure, *incloſure.*

Enclouez, *ſtudded.*

Enclowe, *pricked by a nail.*

Encoires, *beſides.*

Encois, *before.*

Encolourerent, *involved.*

Encombremen, *incroachment, incumbrance.*

Encomiter, *to be committed.*

Encon, *on high.*

Encontre, *meets, encountered, oppoſed.*

Encontrer (d'), *to meet.*

Encontre mount, *in the aſcending.*

Encontre val, *downwards.*

Encontrevenent, *undo.*

Enconvent, enconvenancies, *covenanted.*

Encoranement (l'), *the coronation.*

Encorovetz, *encourage.*

Encoru, *accrewing.*

Encorue, encoruz, *barred.*

Encoruz, encoure, encoru, *incurs.*

Encoſte, *collateral.*

Encoſteantes, *on the banks, ſides.*

Encountables, *to the counts.*

Encoupe, *indicted, charged, accused, guilty.*
Encouterable, *counter-pleadable.*
Encoutment com (aincois), *but as soon as ever.*
Encrece du mond (de lour), *of their worldly income.*
Encrecer, *to accrew, to increase.*
Encres, *increase, accession.*
Encrest, *accrews, increases.*
Encroe, *fixed to a cross.*
Encrustrent, *increased.*
Encurru, *come, arrived.*
Encuser, *to accuse.*
Encuserez (n'), *will not accuse.*
Encusement, *indictment, accusation, impeachment.*
Ency, *therein.*
Encz, *but.*
Endeges, *superannuated.*
Endeiront, *will endeavour*
Endentier (d'), *to indent, to be made party to an indenture.*
Endette la maison (il), *he had run the house in debt.*
Endevera, faire (ceo quil), *what he ought to do therein.*
Endeux, *both.*
Endeyvent estre quites (quil), *that they ought to be discharged.*
Endicion, *indiction.*
Endirez, *in like manner may be said.*
Endirra, *will declare.*
Enditement, *interpretation.*
Endivrons, *will assist.*
Endormer, *to charm.*
Endormy (fuit), *was dormant.*
Endosse, *back, encourage.*
Endosser, endocer, *to indorse.*
Endou, *to be endowed.*
Endreit (a feit nous), *hath made us amends, satisfaction.*
Endreyt, *relating to.*
Endroit (l'), *without, outwards.*
Endroit, d'endrett, *in right of, with respect to.*
Endront (en quel), *in what place.*
Enducent, *occasion, bring on.*
Enduceront, *will persuade, induce.*
Enducez (a ce), *brought to that.*
Enduirons (ne), *will not entice, persuade.*
Endurze, *hardened.*
Eneez, *have, received.*
Enemiablement, *in a hostile manner.*
Enente, *ruined.*

Enewance

Enewance de draps, *watering of cloth.*

Enfamant (actions en), *actions of ſcandal.*

Enfamie, *infamy, infamous.*

Enfauncea, enfaunt engendra, *brought forth, or was delivered of a child.*

Enferges, *put in irons.*

Enferment, *confine.*

Enfiace, *mercy.*

Enfile, *twined, twiſted.*

Enfo, enfovie, *buried.*

Enfondre, *broke.*

Enforce, *ſtrengthens.*

Enforfet, *offending.*

Enformer, *to inſtruct, inform.*

Enformeſons, *ſpeeches.*

Enfortune (par), *by miſfortune, accident.*

Enfouncez, *poured out.*

Enfoundrees, *ſunk, overflowed, under water.*

Enfourny, *performed.*

Enfraignance, *infringement.*

Enfralndrant, *ſhall infringe.*

Enfranchiſe (nient), *not of record.*

Enfraunchee (a poi), *almoſt overrun with franchiſes.*

Enfreindre (l'), *the breach.*

Enfrenge, enfreimte, *broken.*

Enfreoms, *we will do therein.*

Enfuiſt, *deſerts.*

Enfytuez (meliùs enſi tuez), *ſo killed* *.

Engage, *mortgaged.*

Engage, *betrothed.*

Engager le batail, *to offer battle.*

Engaigement, *pledge.*

Engaines, *guarded.*

Engarnies, *withheld, ſurrounded, fenced-in.*

Engaux, *equal.*

Engendre (a), *to be begotten.*

Engendrure, *iſſue.*

Engetter, engeiter, *to eject.*

Engin, enghein, enginement (mal), *ill deſign, decit, fraud.*

Enginer (pur), *to cheat, defraud, ſeduce, intice.*

Engineuſement, *groaning, lamenting.*

Englaterra (roy d'), *king of England.*

Englefeld, *England.*

Engleſche, Engles, *Engliſh.*

Englecherie, *proof that a perſon found killed was of Engliſh extraction, and not a foreigner.*

* See Cowel's Dict. Affath.

Engluerount (se), *will fix on themselves the guilt of the crime.*
Engnes, *Agnes.*
Engracious, *ungracious, untoward.*
Engravance, *grievance, molestation.*
Engriever, *to aggravate.*
Engyn par, *by deceit.*
Enhabler, *to enable.*
Enhauce, enhaunce, *raised, exalted.*
Enheritants (les), *the inhabitants.*
Enheriteez (est), *is intitled.*
Enheritementez, *hereditaments.*
Enheritez, *having an inheritance in.*
Enhuiller, *to administer extreme unction.*
Enientez, *rendered null, avoided.*
Enjevin, *of Anjou.*
Enimiste, *enmity.*
Enjojalee, *furnished, provided with jewels.*
Enjont, *enjoining.*
Enjoynte, *joined.*
Enke, *ink.*
Enki, *thus, so.*
Enlaylla, *sent thither.*
Enleist, *delivers up.*
Enli, *instead of.*
Enlost, *in the army.*
Enmediate, *immediate.*
Ennaugerunt, *proceeded on their voyage.*
Ennenti, *defeated.*
Enneur, *honour.*
Ennoliement, *extreme unction.*
Ennoy, *annoy.*
Ennoyastes, *sent.*
Ennoyer, *to send him away, remove him.*
Ennoyez, *troubled, grieved.*
Ennoys, *necessities.*
Ennoyter, enoyter, *to annul.*
Ennuerent, *whom they sent.*
Ennuict, *to day.*
Enombraser, *to shade, cover.*
Enor (l'), *the honour.*
Enordeniant, *in an irregular, undue manner.*
Enordinant, *inordinate.*
Enorez, *honoured.*
Enoultre, *moreover.*
Enoundez, *overflowed.*
Enournez, *adorned.*
Enoyter, *to annul.*
Enpant, *composed.*
Enparkeler, *to fence in.*
Enpaynes, *put to pain.*
Enpechez, *impeached.*
Enpeirant, *impairing.*
Enpeirement, *detriment.*
Enpeirez, *impaired.*
Enpensione, *a pension.*
Enpensones (ne), *don't intend.*

Enperi, *worſe.*
Enpire, *embaſed.*
Enpleynnaunt, *by way of complaint.*
Enploient mye (n'), *do not lay out.*
Enplyes, *employed.*
En poin, *in hand.*
Enpori, *impoveriſhed.*
Enporri (ſi), *ſo ſtale.*
Enportera le realme, *ſhall be king.*
Enporter heritage, *to run away with the inherit-ance.*
Enportez, *carried away.*
Enpres, *after.*
Enp̃igne, *took, received.*
Enpriſant, *deſiring.*
Enpris unt, enpnez, *have undertaken.*
Enpriſt le chymin, *entered upon his journey.*
Enpromptz, *things bor-rowed.*
Enproneroun, *impriſoned.*
Enprovour, *proveditor.*
Enprower (d'), *to improve.*
Enprueez, *improved.*
Enprumptu, *borrowed.*
Enpus, *produce.*
Enque (par), *by the in-queſt.*
Enq̃rg̃ (ſi), *let him in-quire.*
E̲qrere, *to get, take.*
Enquerrez, *inquiries.*
Enquerelant (nul), *no plaintiff, no ſuit.*
Enquerelez, *impleaded.*
Enqueſter, *find out.*
Enquieter, *diſturb.*
Enquore, *yet, ſtill.*
Enracier, enracer, *to pull up by the roots.*
Enrollement de ſes lains, *at the rolling up of his wool.*
Enrollez, *folded up.*
Enroyer (m'), *to grant me.*
Ens, *in, within, between.*
Ens ne ſeit (ſi), *unleſs it be.*
Enſanle, *in blood.*
Enſarchement, *an exami-nation, a reſearch.*
Enſauſie, *exalted.*
Enſayer, enſuer, *to purſue.*
Enſealer, *ſhut up, impound.*
Enſeares, enſeires, *locked up.*
Enſecchi, *dried up, wi-thered.*
Enſegie, *beſieged.*
Enſeigne (loial), *lawful buſineſs.*
Enſeignementz, *qualifica-tions.*
Enſeigner, *to ſhew, ap-pear.*
Enſeignurant ſur l'eſtat le roy, *lording it over the ſtate of the king.*
Enſeintez, *with child.*
Enſeiver, *to ſerve.*

Enſelle, *ſaddled.*

Enſemble, *it ſeems meet.*

Enſement, *likewiſe, in like manner, in the ſame manner.*

Enſencers, *cenſers.*

Enſenie, *inſtructed.*

Enſenſer, *to inform.*

Enſenſes, *incenſed.*

Enſerres, *will be.*

Enſervager, *to enſlave.*

Enſerver, *to ſubject, charge.*

Enſerve, *kept, reſerved.*

Enſervee, *ſervile.*

Enſervir (ne poit l'en), *is not compellable.*

Enſeverit (meuz), *much better know.*

Enſeyner, *to ſhew, point out.*

Enſi enſy, *ſo, thus, alſo, in like manner.*

Enſi pres, *ſo near.*

Enſi totes voies, *provided always.*

Enſier, *to mow or reap.*

Enſigne, *blooded.*

Enſignement, *aſſignment.*

Enſigner, *to ſhew.*

Enſignere (en), *in teaching, inſtructing.*

Enſignes, *occaſioned.*

Enſignition, *enſignment.*

Enſimys, *being.*

Enſivient (qe s'), *which follow.*

Enſiwames, *we followed.*

Enſiwyt il pas, *it does not follow.*

Enſorquetot, *above all.*

Enſſievant (en), *in purſuance of.*

Enſtres, *entries.*

Enſu, enſuyt, s'enſient, *follows.*

Enſuer, *to follow.*

Enſuit, *hereafter.*

Enſuivant, *againſt.*

Enſuivroit (il s'), *it would follow.*

Enſundis, *in that caſe, alſo.*

Enſure, *obey.*

Enſurmettaunt, *ſuggeſting.*

Enſurrer, *to riſe.*

Enſus, *big with child.*

Ent, *in, in the mean time.*

Ent, *thereupon, of them, thereof.*

Ent (d'), *thereof.*

Ent, *intire, whole.*

Entacher, *to infect.*

Entagle, *importuned.*

Entaineez, *entered upon, debated.*

Entamees, *ſtirred, moved.*

Entant come, *ſignifies as much as.*

Entartz, *burned.*

Entaunt, *ſo much.*

Entaunt graunt, *be thereby as good as grants.*

Entechele, *tainted, infected.*

Enteins, *underſtood.*

Entendable,

Entendable, *to be under-ſtood.*

Entendances, *attendances.*

Entendaunt, *thinking, imagining, underſtood.*

Entendement (l'), *the form.*

Entendementz, *meanings, conſtructions.*

Entendiblement, *fully, plainly.*

Entendre (fiſt lui), *made him believe.*

Entendre, *to attend.*

Entenk (jeo) y-entanks, *I think.*

Entent, *underſtand them.*

Entente, *intention, claim, aim, plaint, count.*

Ententivement, *carefully.*

Entenue, *underſtood, heard.*

Enterceur, *the party challenging the goods, he who has placed them in the hands of a third perſon.*

Enterimes, enterinee, enterrine, enterin, enteriene, *entire, perfect.*

Enteriner, *to perfect.*

Enter mains, entre meins, *in our hands, in his hands.*

Enternient, *entirely.*

Enteynont, *hold, keep.*

Enteyſant, *tacitly, by ſaying nothing.*

Entexes, *interwoven.*

Entient, *holds.*

Entier (al), *upon his entering.*

Entiercir, *to depoſit a thing with a third perſon, till the property is proved.*

Entiers (et les), *and entries.*

Entiers, entierent, *intirely.*

Entierte, *the whole.*

Entitle, *qualified.*

Entraihantz, *dragging, drawing.*

Entorſe, entoir, entour, en tour, entur, *about, round, concerning.*

Entoucher, *to give a poiſonous quality to any thing.*

Entover, *to walk about.*

Ent mettra (ne ſe), *will not interpoſe, aſſiſt.*

Entraiter (dereſonable), *unreaſonable, unjuſt treatment.*

Entralliez, *confederated together, bind themſelves together.*

Entraſſemes, *entered.*

Entre, *above, beyond.*

Entre (a l'), *as far as the limits.*

Entre, encre (de), *ink.*

Entreaidions lui uns l'autre, *will mutually aid each other.*

Entrebat, *an interloper.*

Entrebat (par), *by interlopement.*

Entrecoñent point (ne s'), *do not intercommon.*

Entredit (en temp d'), *in prohibited ſeaſons.*

Entreferrent, *engage, fight.*

Entreiſſets (ne), *ſhould not enter into.*

Entrelaſſer, *to put between, interline.*

Entreleſſant, *omitting, leaving out, relinquiſhing, laying aſide.*

Entreleſſe (ne), *would not proceed in.*

Entreliere, *to obſerve.*

Entrelies (ſe fuſſent), *bound themſelves together.*

Entrelignure, *intelineation.*

Entreluterent, *engaged together, fought.*

Entremeiſſent (ſe), *ſhould occupy, be put into, intermeddle with, took upon himſelf.*

Entremelles (accions), *mixed actions.*

Entremellies, *mixed, blended together.*

Entre mellure, *an intermixture.*

Entremiſted inquirer, *authoriſed to inquire, cauſed inquiry to be made.*

Entrendre (fait), *to be underſtood.*

Entreparler, *to conſult together.*

Entrepennent, *conſult among themſelves, enterpriſing.*

Entreres, *to be entered.*

Entrerupt, *interrupted.*

Entreſte (malement), *evilly treated him.*

Entretant, *in the mean while, to fulfil.*

Entretz, *interred.*

Entreval, *interval.*

Entreuls (d'), *among them.*

Entrevyſent (ſe), *have an interview.*

Entricate, *interwoven.*

Entrignier, *accompliſh.*

Entromys (nous) in l'homage, *we did homage.*

Entrovez, *narrow paſſes.*

Entrour, *about.*

Entruſtee, *increaſed.*

Ent tant regard (ni), *neither paying regard.*

Entyvement, *entirely.*

Entz, enz, *but.*

Envaiſemen, *an invaſion.*

Envee, envint, *ſent.*

Enveer avant, *to proceed.*

Enveer (facez), *cauſe to be ſent for.*

Enveierons (lui n'), *we will not condemn him.*

Enveillez, *grown old.*

Envenant, *enſuing.*

Envenoms,

Envenoms, *have ſent.*
Enveogler, *to inveigle, blind.*
Enveoms, enveons, enveuns, *we ſend.*
Enverce, *againſt, towards.*
Enverrez, *inquired into.*
Envers (l'), *within.*
Enveyees, *envoys.*
Enveyer, envoyer, envier, *to ſend.*
Envie (ne), *nor damage, injure.*
Enviroune (mal), *traduced.*
Envis, *with regret.*
Envoderoms, *we would have.*
Envoeglez, *blind.*
Envoez, *become.*
Envore (il), *he ſends.*
Envorrez, *ſhall ſend.*
Envoyable, *ſhall be ſent.*
Envoyellera (poriùs enjojulera), *will provide with jewels.*
Envoyglifment (en), *in avoydance, in deceit of.*
Envyurez, *intoxicated.*
Enuer, *to enure.*
Enwer (en), *in arrear.*
Enyage, *the right of eldership.*
Enz, *in, within, but.*
Eoque, *becauſe that.*
Eofs, eoues, *eggs.*
Eofues, potiùs jeofnes (genz), *young people.*
Eoins (que nous), *that we ſhould have.*
Eoms, *have.*
Eos (al), *to the uſe.*
Eou, *he, him.*
Eours de pite, *works of piety.*
Ephebe, *one who is major.*
Epouvantement, *excuſe.*
Eppoſant, *the petitioner.*
Epprendre (d'), *to take.*
Eps, *a bee.*
Equiture, *to ride.*
Equus (d') le hile dox, *until he hears.*
Erainent, *leaving off, avoiding.*
Eran, *will be.*
Erantz, arantz, *ploughing.*
Erberage, *proviſion for cattle.*
Erberger, *to lodge or harbour.*
Ercedekene, herſedecome, *archdeacon, archdeaconry.*
Ercevefques, *archbiſhops.*
Ercewec, *the archbiſhop.*
Erderont, *ſhall aid, adhere to.*
Ẽre, *be.*
Ere, *ſhall be.*
Ere, erer, *to ſowe.*
Erer, erier, *to wander up and down.*

Eri,

Eri, *I was.*
Erinez, *wasted, ruined.*
Erite (l'), *the inheritance.*
Erite, *an heretic.*
Ermyn, *an ermine.*
Eroer, erver, *to journey, to travel.*
Erra, *shall go.*
Erraunt traitour, *an arrant traitor.*
Erreront, *went the eyre.*
Errisement, *hindrance.*
Erroign, *erroneous.*
Errois, *Irish.*
Erront, *shall hear.*
Errount, *go their heir.*
Ers, *heirs.*
Ersoir, *yesterday.*
Ert, *he was, it was.*
Ert (ne), *shall not be.*
Es, ez, *in, behold.*
Esãple, *sample.*
Esbaiez, esbaiz, esbahi, *abashed, surprised, terrified.*
Esbaire nous (pour), *to recreate ourselves.*
Esbaudes, *imboldened, encouraged.*
Escales, *scales.*
Escar, *estate, condition.*
Escarcetee, *scarcity.*
Escarlate (d'), *of scarlet.*
Escarsement, *scarcely.*
Escarta de ble, *scarcity of corn.*
Escaud, *damage, offence.*
Esceppe, *shipped.*
Eschair, *happen.*
Eschaist, *should intreat; also should escheat.*
Eschant (q'il ne le) de quaunt q'il fait, *that he did not regard or fear whatever he did.*
Eschancier, *to increase, promote.*
Eschaude, *smothered.*
Escheent, *happen.*
Escheere en maladie, *fall sick.*
Escheere (plus), *more dear.*
Eschelement (par), *by escalade.*
Escheler, *to scale.*
Eschement, *shunning, bending from.*
Escheqir, Esquaquer, *exchequer.*
Escher (si), *if it happens.*
Escheterie (d'), *office of escheator*
Escheve, *eschewed, shunned, bent or bowed from.*
Eschever, *to perform.*
Eschever, eschiver, *to shun, avoid, bend from.*
Escheu (plus), *more afraid.*
Escheu, *befallen, happened.*
Eschier (d'), *to fall down.*
Eschier (l'), *the falling.*
Éschire, eshire, eshuer, eshure, eschure, eschete- ter,

ter, eſchever, *to fall or happen unto, to eſcheat, to deſcend, to fall to.*

Eſchiviſſment, *negligence, want of care.*

Eſchiure, eſchiver, eſchure, eſchever, eſchew, *to avoid.*

Eſchua, *pulled down.*

Eſchuable, *avoidable.*

Eſchuit, *avoided, made default.*

Eſcience (leur), *their conſcience, knowledge.*

Eſcient (a), *knowledge, affection, knowingly.*

Eſclairces, eſclaref, eſclarcie, *cleared up, expreſſed, ſettled.*

Eſclariſer (meus) le fet, *to explain the fact better.*

Eſclaunder, *diſcredit, calumny, ſlander, prejudice.*

Eſclore, *to ſhut out.*

Eſcluſe, *a ſluice.*

Eſcluſe de Paſques, cluſe de Paſche, *the firſt Sunday after Eaſter.*

Eſcluz, *packs, bundles.*

Eſcocher (d'), *to ſhoot.*

Eſcomenge, eſcumeng, *excommunication.*

Eſconduit, eſcundit, *denied, rejected.*

Eſconſe, *a ſconce, a dark lanthorn.*

Eſcotchours, eſchorcheours, *thoſe who ſlay cattle for their ſkins.*

Eſcoter, *to pay.*

Eſcoudirad (s'en), *clear himſelf.*

Eſcoult (doner), *give him a hearing.*

Eſcoundre, eſcondire, *to deny, reject.*

Eſcourcer, *to run, be in force.*

Eſcourcer (lui), *excuſe himſelf.*

Eſcourcher (pour) le parlement, *to ſhorten the duration of parliament.*

Eſcoutement, *clearly, intelligibly.*

Eſcraier countre lui, *oppoſe him.*

Eſcreuz, *increaſed.*

Eſcries, *treated of, deſcribed.*

Eſcriez (felons), *notorious, proclaimed felons.*

Eſcrin, *a coffer.*

Eſcrine (j'), *I hope.*

Eſcripre (a fait), *has cauſed to be written.*

Eſcriptura (les), *ſhall write them.*

Eſcrit, *declared, proſcribed.*

Eſcrits, *directed to.*

Eſcriure, *write, certify, deſcribe.*

Eſcrover, *a ſcroll.*

Eſcrowes,

Efcrowes, *rolls of parchment, fcrolls.*

Efcruire (d'), *to write to.*

Efcryeurs, *writers.*

Efcuminges (cum), *by an excommunicato capiendo.*

Efcumers, *pirates, corfairs.*

Efcune, *each, every.*

Efcuquiteur, *an executor.*

Efcurer, *to fcour out.*

Efcus d'or fol, *a French gold coin of the value of fix fhillings.*

Efcufer, *prevent, excufe.*

Efcufement (en), *in excufe.*

Efcutereit (q'il), *that he would liften to.*

Efcuz, *excufe.*

Efcyncilles de feu, *fparks of fire.*

Efee, *eafy, commodious.*

Efement, *commodioufly, an eafement.*

Efez, *eafed.*

Efgarde, *awarded.*

Efgart, efguart (a l'), *judgement, difcretion, award, with refpect to.*

Efgle, *eagle.*

Es jours de feftes, *on feaftdays.*

Efkep, efkip, *fhipped.*

Efkippefon, *fhipping, or paffage by fea.*

Efkirmye, *fighting, defence.*

Efkole, *fchool.*

Efkuyns, *bailiffs.*

Efle, efleeuz, *chofen.*

Eflevera (tort), *fhall do an injury.*

Eflit, *election.*

Efloigne, *difturbed, delayed.*

Efloignement, *excufe.*

Efloignement (pur) du payement, *for enlarging the time of payment.*

Efloigner, *remove from, alienate.*

Efloignez, *prorogued, adjourned.*

Efmercient, *thank.*

Efmerveilluz, *we wonder, is wonderful.*

Efmon, *Edmond.*

Efmovement, *motion, commotion.*

Efmuz, efmeutz, *moved, ftirred up, difturbed.*

Efne fiz, *eldeft fon.*

Efourketot, *moreover, further.*

Efpaigne (monsr̃ d'), *John of Gaunt, king of Caftile and Leon, duke of Lancafter, &c.*

Efpãle, *efpecial.*

Efpanner le cuft, *to fpare the coft.*

Efparni, *fpared, exempted.*

Efparpilent, *branch out.*

Efpec̃, *fpecialty.*

Efpecefier,

Eſpeceſier, *to ſpecify, to contract.*
Eſpeceries, *ſpices.*
Eſpechement (ſans), *without diſturbance, impediment.*
Eſpeciallte, *affinity.*
Eſpecies, *ſpecies, kinds.*
Eſpee, *thigh, leg, foot.*
Eſpeie, eſpeye, eſpye, *a ſword.*
Eſpeir (ſans) de partir, *without hope of ſeparation.*
Eſpeirer, *to reſerve, ſpare.*
Eſpeires, *impaired.*
Eſpelotte, *expeditated.*
Eſpenſies, *ſpecified.*
Eſpenz, *expence.*
Eſperitaux, eſpeulx, *ſpiritual.*
Eſpermrez (n'), *will not ſpare.*
Eſpernies, *ſpared, exempted.*
Eſperons, *ſpurs.*
Eſperuex (au l'), *to the hopes.*
Eſpve, *ſpare.*
Eſpeuteiſoun (pur), *pro expeditatione canum in foreſta exiſtentium.*
Eſpeyere, *a ſpear.*
Eſpiantz, *having in view.*
Eſpiement, *information.*
Eſpier, *to find out, to look out, obſerve.*
Eſpier (que), *who informs againſt, accuſes.*
Eſpies, *watched.*
Eſpinaces (deux), *two pinaces.*
Eſpingles de boys, *pins of wood.*
Eſpiſes, *eſpouſals.*
Eſpitau, *an hoſpital.*
Eſplee le huiſſes, *bolt or lock the doors.*
Eſples, eſpleits (les), *the profits.*
Eſpleit, *needful.*
Eſpleit (final), *final iſſue.*
Eſpleytez, eſploit, eſplotee, *diſpatched, anſwered, ſerved.*
Eſploir, *to requeſt, to implore earneſtly with tears.*
Eſploit (au), *in diſpatch of, in performance.*
Eſploit (pur l') de parlment, *for the diſpatch of parliamentary buſineſs.*
Eſploit (pur l'), *for carrying on, for the expences of.*
Eſploit (qe Dieu l'), *whom God preſerve, give ſucceſs to.*
Eſploiterent, *diſcourſed; performed ſuch exploits.*
Eſploites (etre), *to be expended.*
Eſploitez de la terre, *delivered the eſplees of the land.*

Esploitier (e), *and to display.*
Esploitz (les), *the services.*
Espoirance, *hope.*
Esporouns, *spurs.*
Espose, esposail, *espousal, marriage.*
Espose, *married.*
Espoveri, *impoverished.*
Espresement, *expressly.*
Esprovaunt (al), *to the assertor.*
Esproves, *proved, marked, stamped.*
Espüel, *spiritual.*
Espurger (soy), *to purge, to clear himself.*
Esquel d' argent, *silver spoons.*
Esquelles, *which.*
Esquers, esquiers, *esquires.*
Esquieles, *ladles.*
Esquunes, *sheriffs, magistrates.*
Essaucier, *to cherish.*
Esseketurs, *executors.*
Essent, *extent.*
Essentu, *assented.*
Essientex, *very learned.*
Essire (potiùs eslire), *to choose.*
Essoierent (que ne), *that it belongeth not.*
Essoirent (come ils), *as if they were.*
Essoyer, *to endeavour.*
Est, *the east.*
Estaa, *stands.*
Estable, *a stable.*
Estable (de lour), *under their department.*
Establissement de dower, *settlement, appointment, or assurance of dower, made by the husband or his friends to the wife, before or at marriage.*
Establissements, *acts of parliament.*
Estably, *settled, appointed.*
Estache, *a pier, pile, bridge, stake.*
Estages, *estates.*
Estaignee, *a pool.*
Estalez, estalee, *money to be paid by instalments.*
Estalls, *stalls.*
Estalls, estales, *tools, scales.*
Estanche, *a reservoir for fish.*
Estantz, *standing.*
Estape, *staple.*
Estr, *being.*
Estat (si a), *it is.*
Estat, *statute, condition, health.*
Estat (n'y), *was not there.*
Estat (en l'), *into the place.*
Estature (l'), estatere, *the beam.*
Estatut, *estate.*
Estaul, *firm, stable.*
Estaulx, *the stalls in a choir.*

Estauncher,

Eſtauncher, *to ſtop, to put an end to.*

Eſtaunkes, *ſtanks, dams, wears, pools.*

Eſtauntez, *being.*

Eſtclok (ſon), *his clock.*

Eſte, eſtee (en), *in ſummer.*

Eſte (la mi), *Midſummer.*

Eſteaunce, *being.*

Eſteiant, *ſtanding.*

Eſteient, eſtient, eſteyent, *were.*

Eſteille, *a ſtar.*

Eſteimes (n') eſteiouns, eſtiemes, pas, *we were not.*

Eſteindre, eſteyndre, *to extend to.*

Eſteint, *becomes extinct.*

Eſteint de (qu), *who were of, who ſided with.*

Eſteint, eſtent, *extinct.*

Eſteintz (mort), *quite dead.*

Eſtemaunt, eſtemans, *eſteeming, accounting.*

Eſtemue, *raiſed.*

Eſtendreit, *would be ſufficient, might be extended on.*

Eſtente, eſtant, eſteinte, *extent, value, eſtimation.*

Eſtent (ſe), *extends itſelf.*

Eſtepne, Eſteve, *Stephen.*

Eſtere oveſqe le roi, en ſuſtenance de ſa corone, *to ſtand by the king, in ſupport of his crown.*

Eſterilitat, *ſcarcity.*

Eſterlynge, *a penny, a farthing.*

Eſterniers (en), *in ſneezings.*

Eſterz (vos), *you are.*

Eſtes, eſtez, *condition, eſtate.*

Eſtey, *ſummer.*

Eſteyme, eſtainte, eſtagne, eſtank, eſtonbz, eſteigne, *tin.*

Eſteynant, (en) eſtenyſement, *in extinguiſhing.*

Eſteyndre, *to extinguiſh.*

Eſteynent paye, *ſtop payment.*

Eſthabelere, *to eſtabliſh.*

Eſtiant, *ſtood.*

Eſtiemes (ke preſent i), *who were preſent there.*

Eſtienes, eſtee, eſtei, *been.*

Eſtiens (nous), *we are.*

Eſtient, *knowledge.*

Eſtiez, *ſtood, been.*

Eſtile, *ſtyle.*

Eſtimures, *robbers.*

Eſtlues (par les), *by the ſluices.*

Eſtuz, eſtleu, *choſen.*

Eſtoffer, *to ſtore, ſtock, furniſh.*

Eſtoier, eſter, eſtere, eſtr, *to ſtand to, abide.*

Eſtoiera,

Eſtoiera (ſi luy) la choſe perder, *if he ſhould happen to loſe the thing.*
Eſtoilettes, *gennets.*
Eſtoiroit (ne), *needed not.*
Eſtoite, *was.*
Eſtole, *a ſchool.*
Eſtoppe, *cloſe, confined, dark.*
Eſtorement (a), *in a large quantity, not by retale.*
Eſtorer (d), *to make amends.*
Eſtores, *ſtored.*
Eſtorie (l'), *the hiſtory.*
Eſtors, *ſtock, ſtores.*
Eſtoũa, *ſhall be compelled.*
Eſtouble, *ſtubble.*
Eſtovereit (lui), *it would be incumbent on him.*
Eſtourtre (pour), *to ſtop.*
Eſtoyer, *happen, be.*
Eſtoyent, *were.*
Eſtoys, *ſtands.*
Eſtr, *being.*
Eſtraites, *derived, drawn.*
Eſtrangent, *ſtrangle.*
Eſtraungiez (a luy), *hath reſtrained himſelf, hath forborn.*
Eſtray (j') hors, *I will go out; will eſtrange myſelf from.*
Eſtrayſſauntes, *ſtraying.*
Eſtre, *been.*
Eſtre (l'), *the exiſtence.*
Eſtre ceo (e), *and beſides this.*
Eſtre (del bien), *of the form.*
Eſtre (voille), *will be, ſtand.*
Eſtrectement, *ſtrictly.*
Eſtrein, eſtrain, *ſtraw.*
Eſtreintier, *to contract, take in.*
Eſtreiont, *they ſtray.*
Eſtreites (par), *by eſtreats.*
Eſtreitz, eſtreats, *ſtreets.*
Eſtremes des molins, *millſtreams.*
Eſtrepes, *ſhipped, pulled.*
Eſtret, *ſtands.*
Eſtrete (haut), *high ſtreet.*
Eſtreutz, *extended.*
Eſtreygnaul (en), *in confining.*
Eſtreynerye, *tin-works.*
Eſtreyt, *derived, deſcended.*
Eſtreytes, *limited, contracted, ſtreightened, taken in.*
Eſtrie (laroun), *a notorious thief.*
Eſtrier, *writing.*
Eſtrifs, *ſtrifes, diſputes.*
Eſtrippe, *waſte.*
Eſtrithing, *Eaſt Riding.*
Eſtrivaſſent, *ſtrove.*
Eſtrivens, *ſtirrups.*
Eſtroicter, *to inſtruct.*
Eſtropier, *to ſpoil, waſte.*

Eſtudes,

Eſtudes (es), *in the muſeums, colleges.*

Eſtues, eſtuves, *the ſtews, or brothel-houſes.*

Eſtuffees (noefz), *ſhips manned.*

Eſtuffement (pur l') de la terre d'Irland, *for the peopling of the kingdom of Ireland.*

Eſtuffement, *ſtocking, peopling.*

Eſtuffeures, *ſtores.*

Eſtumers, *pirates, rovers.*

Eſturens, *ſhall chuſe.*

Eſtuſt, eſtut, eſteuſſent, *ſtood.*

Eſuient (ki), *which follow.*

Eſuoies, *hardſhips.*

Eſvos, *behold.*

Eſtroytement, *narrowly, carefully.*

Eſwer, *doubt.*

Et, *hath, had.*

Et, *into.*

Etſi, *although.*

Eu, *or them.*

Eu tens, *in time.*

Evanceant, *promoting.*

Evaunt dit (l'), *the aforeſaid.*

Evangelies, *goſpels, ſentences out of the ſcriptures.*

Eve, ove, *with.*

Eve, evez, eue, *had.*

Eu (nous e), *we have had.*

Eveniſt, *ſhould happen.*

Eventees, *burſt.*

Evenues, *avenues, paſſes.*

Evoms, *we have.*

Evertuer (s'), *to attend to, to employ himſelf, to prepare.*

Everwyk, *York.*

Eves, *deceived.*

Eveſche, *dioceſe.*

Eveſchee, *biſhoprick.*

Eveſky, eveſtres, *biſhop.*

Euez, eues, *had.*

Euf, eof, *an egg.*

Evitier, *to avoid.*

Euiz (nous) deſunes, *we have above mentioned.*

Eulx, eus, euz, yeux, *eyes.*

Eulx, euls, eulz, *them, themſelves.*

Evoluer, *to unfold, open, turn over.*

Evount, *have.*

Evoytement, *increaſe, advancement.*

Eups, *uſe.*

Eure, eur, *hour, time.*

Euree, *happy.*

Eus, *them, they.*

Eus (a l'), *to the uſe.*

Euſe, *had.*

Euſez, *you had.*

Euſoms (nous) euſſouns, *we have.*

Eutaule, *octave, the ſpace of eight days.*

Eutres, autres (d'), *of others, other things.*

Euvres, *works.*

Euvent, *have.*

Euwes, *bad.*

Euwez, ewez, *watered.*

Eux (de), *of the eyes.*

Euximes (ent), *amongst them.*

Euyz, euys, *them.*

Euz, *but.*

Ew, ewe, ewes, *bad.*

Ewangel, *evangelists.*

Ewe, *bad.*

Ewe, *them.*

Ewe (entre), *between them.*

Ewe (alt il), *he must undergo the water ordeal.*

Ewe douce, *fresh water, a stream.*

Ewelles, *gees.*

Eweret (molin), *a water-mill.*

Ewerwick, *York.*

Ewes, ewoz, *waters.*

Ewez, *watered.*

Ewes (en), *in ponds.*

Ex (d'), *from the river Ex.*

Exaltez, *raised.*

Exaucement, *advancement.*

Excitation (al), *at the intreaty, motion, instigation.*

Exciterent le assise, *encouraged the assise.*

Excusation, *excuse.*

Excuserez (ne), *will not reproach.*

Excussion (potiùs execussion), *execution, production, proof.*

Exec, *exception.*

Execuc̃, *execution.*

Executours (les), *those who are to put in execution.*

Execyte, *excited.*

Exeketour des besoignes, *charged with the affairs.*

Exenger, *exercise.*

Exersant, *exercising.*

Exerwick, *York.*

Exes, *eyes.*

Exi, *any, also.*

Eximons, *exempt.*

Exon, *excuse.*

Expause, expousez, *suggested, represented.*

Expecteroit, *should abide.*

Expleiter (facez), *cause to be dispatched, exercised, employed.*

Expleiterent, *discoursed, acted, performed.*

Exploit, esploit, *dispatch.*

Exploiter, *receive the profits.*

Exprumez, *expressed.*

Extentz, *extinguished.*

Ex̃ter, *to execute.*

Extienter, *to extinguish.*

Extimation, *an estimate.*

Extinsement, extientisement, exteynsement, *extinguishing.*

Extorquer,

Extorquer, *to put out by force.*
Extorter, *to drive off, avoid.*
Extrelins, *people of the north.*
Extremiser, *to administer the extreme unction.*
Ey, *a watery place.*
Eyaunce (en), *in ease.*
Eydance, *evidence.*
Eyde, *help.*
Eyde, *aided.*
Eye (p), *by aid.*
Eyens, *but.*
Eyer (unc), *an ewer.*
Eyette, *ye have.*
Eyme nous, *loves us.*
Eyndegre de meyne (de son), *of his own head.*
Eyne date (d'), *of earlier date.*
Eynesce parcener, *eldest partner.*
Eynest, *eldest.*
Eynt (ne) damage, *shall receive no damage.*
Eyntz, *therein.*
Eynzne feffment, *ancient feoffment.*
Eynz q̄, *when, before that.*
Eyr, *the air.*
Eyres, *heirs.*
Eyse, *easy.*
Eysement, *easement.*
Eyt, *eight.*
Eyt, *shall be, will be.*
Ez, *in, within.*
Ez chouses, *in the things.*
Ezi, *his.*
Ezplaye, *spoiled.*

FAAT (le), *a measure called a fat.*
Fablesse, *weakness.*
Fabloir, *to devise stories, to prevaricate.*
Face (premere), *prima facie.*
Facentz leve, *causing to be levied.*
Faceo (ceo), *has done it.*
Fache de l' eglise (en), *in the face of the church.*
Fachon de home, *human shape or form.*
Facion, *fashion.*
Facion (avaunt le), *before the making.*
Fact, *committed.*
Faez, *make, made.*
Faicez faire, *cause to be issued.*
Faici, *did, sent, dispatched.*
Faict, *did.*
Faicte de memoire (a), *through forgetfulness.*
Faie, *faith.*
Faiere, *to do.*
Faiet, faistes, *made.*
Faile, faillie, faillies, *ended, expired.*
Faillent (y), *be omitted.*
Failler, *to disappoint.*

Failler (fist), *caused to be omitted.*

Faillie (soit), *breach has been made.*

Faillons, *neglect.*

Faily, *omitted.*

Fain, *hay; also beach wood.*

Faint, *committed.*

Fairaginous, *maslin, or mingled corn.*

Faire, *to pay.*

Faire en chose, *to deal in matters.*

Faire son ley, *wage his law.*

Faire le difference (a), *to end the difference.*

Fairie, fairez, *to be made.*

Fairs de Germ. *the marts in Germany.*

Fait en fait, *done in deed.*

Fait en, *already.*

Fait (sur le), *ipso facto.*

Fait gaine, *doth gain.*

Fait (ne) my oublier, *it is not to be forgotten.*

Fait soy (se), *is done, may be done.*

Faiterie (par), *through idleness, laziness.*

Faitours, *factors.*

Faitours, *slothful people.*

Faiture, faitours, *making, doing.*

Faitures, *evil-doers.*

Faitz, fait darmes, *feats of arms.*

Faiz, fais, *deeds, facts, business.*

Faix, *times.*

Faix, *a burthen, load.*

Faix, *false.*

Faixime, *deceit.*

Falaize, *a bank or hill by the sea-side.*

Falast, fally, *failed, done wrong.*

Falent (ki), *which ought to have been.*

Fallent (qui vos), *which concern you.*

Falese, falise, *sands, rocks, cliffs.*

Faleste, *a capital punishment inflicted on a malefactor on the sands or sea shore; perhaps by laying him bound on the sands till the next full tide carried him away, or by throwing him from the cliffs* *.

Fali, *Philip.*

Falx, *false.*

Fam, *hunger.*

Fame, *wife.*

Familier de la chauncery, *a clerk belonging to the chancery.*

* Britton 257. b. Mir. 248. Hengham 87. Cowel.

Famuler,

Famuler, familiar, *one of his household, a familiar, intimate friend, a servant.*

Fanez esmailez, *fanes enamelled.*

Fanons (deus), *two fannels or maniples.*

Fany (en), *in the manner.*

Fany (ove le,) *with the manner.*

Faonier, *to fawn.*

Far, fare, *to go, to bid farewel.*

Fardel de terre, *a fourth part of an acre.*

Fare (fut), *was done.*

Farou, *pigged, farrowed.*

Farroms aver *we will cause to have.*

Farce, *a farce.*

Fas (vous), *do unto you.*

Fasoms (nous nous), *we will make ourselves.*

Fast, *was.*

Fasunt (ne) mes, *do not set.*

Fat, *fate, destiny.*

Fat, *does.*

Fate, fatz, *made.*

Fate (poi), *little done.*

Fatou, *a factotum.*

Fau, *a beech-tree.*

Faucer choses, *false things.*

Fauches, *mowed, lopped.*

Faude, faulde, *a pen or fold for sheep.*

Faverer, *February.*

Favie (a), *to do.*

Favissent *favour.*

Fauisses pleints, *false plaints.*

Faulra, *will fail.*

Fault (a), *want of.*

Fault environ, *comes to, amounts to about.*

Faultant, *making default.*

Faultez, *failed of, falsified.*

Faulton, *want.*

Faultont, *complaining.*

Faunt (en cy), *so born.*

Fause, *damaged, spoiled.*

Fauser, fauxere, faucher, *to falsify, counterfeit, forge.*

Fauseours, fauxiers, *counterfeiters, falsifiers.*

Fausine, *falsity, deceit.*

Fausinerie, faussèrie, *the crime of falsifying or counterfeiting the coin, or great seal.*

Fausissons, *should make default.*

Faust, fait, *was made.*

Faustrer, *to deceive.*

Faut, *fails.*

Faut (la), *the end.*

Faut a veir, *we must, or it is needful to see.*

Fautoures, *slothful, idle people.*

Fautours, *abettors.*

Fauxa mie, *be condemned.*

Faymes, *we caused.*
Fayn, *hay.*
Fayn, *a weazle.*
Faynent, *pretend.*
Fayre, *four.*
Faytours, *vagabonds.*
Faz, *make.*
Fe, *fee.*
Feablement, *bona fide.*
Feals, *faithful.*
Feare, *to make.*
Feasors de draps, *cloth-workers.*
Feat, *done, deed.*
Feat (bien), *good deeds.*
Feat (e), *and it is to be.*
Feaw, *fire.*
Feble (si), *in so poor a condition.*
Febles, *weakness.*
Fec, *fire.*
Fecest, *made.*
Fecioms (com nos), *as we would do.*
Fedz, feetz, *fees.*
Fee (a) seyser, *hath caused to be seised.*
Fee (d'asc), *of any woman.*
Feel et leel, *faithful and loyal.*
Feelement, *faithfully.*
Feer, *fear.*
Feer (a resonable), *at a reasonable price.*
Fees (taunt), *as often.*
Feet, feat, *made, done.*
Feetes, *deeds.*
Feez, feetz, *pensions, fees,*
Feez (autre), *heretofore.*
Feez (plusurs), *several times.*
Feffre, *enfeoff.*
Fei, *faith.*
Feibles (les plus), *the worst.*
Feile, *daughter.*
Feimes, feismes, *caused, made, took.*
Feindront (qe se), *who shall make excuses.*
Feins, fene, *hay.*
Feint, *pretended, feigned, slackened.*
Feires, *fairs.*
Feirte, *fealty.*
Feisiens, *we did.*
Feisimes covenentes, *entered into covenants.*
Feisours, *makers.*
Feissent (jurees se), *should be sworn.*
Feissent (s'ils ne), *if they should not make.*
Feistis (que vous), *which you did.*
Feit (unt) entendaunt au peuple, *have made the people believe.*
Feivre, *fever.*
Feiz (une), *once.*
Felasie per fault (potiùs sault), *by leaping from, by being cast from the rocks or cliffs.*

Felesheppe,

Feleſheppe, *fellowſhip.*

Felon neuſement, *feloniouſly.*

Felypp, *Philip.*

Femes liverer, *we cauſed them to be delivered.*

Fenal, *the ſeaſon for cutting hay.*

Fendue, *ſtruck.*

Fene, *hay.*

Fentua, *fled.*

Feobleſce (la) de lour poiars et ſens, *the weakneſs of their abilities.*

Feor, *to make.*

Feous, *faithful.*

Feoſon, *manner, degree.*

Fer, *but.*

Fer (a), *to make, to repair.*

Fer (a) de guerre, *in a warlike manner.*

Ferdekyngs, *firkins.*

Fere, ferre (a), *to do.*

Fere, *to be mad, diſtracted.*

Ferges (en), *in irons, in fetters.*

Feriage, *a payment for croſſing a ferry.*

Feries, *feaſts, feſtivals.*

Feries de Paſche, *the feſtival of Eaſter.*

Feriours, ferrors, *aſſaulters.*

Ferlinges (de), *of a farthing.*

Ferme, *confirms.*

Ferme pees, *firm peace.*

Fermail crois, *vermillion croſſes.*

Fermaille, *a buckle, claſp, button, alſo a chain, enriched with pearls, precious ſtones or enamel, with which ladies enriched their head-dreſs, to keep it faſt.*

Fermatx, *ſhut up.*

Fermetez, *farms; alſo ſecurities, ſtrong holds.*

Fermentat, fermeme, *confirmation.*

Fermez, *faſtenings.*

Fermiſtier, *wage.*

Fermure, *faſtening.*

Perniſt ſa ley, *performed or made his law.*

Feron, *will act.*

Ferrant (ſelonc la); a la ferant, *according to the proportion.*

Ferrement, *ironwork.*

Ferrent (le), *did it.*

Ferri, *Frederic.*

Ferriemes, *we will cauſe.*

Ferreur (ſouth), *under lock.*

Ferruere, *the ſhoeing of horſes.*

Ferthyng, *a farthing.*

Fertre, *ſhrine.*

Ferve, *great heat.*

Ferue, *ſtroke.*

Ferum, *firm.*

Feſables, *to be made.*

Feſauns, feſantz, *pheaſants.*

Feſes, *done, performed.*

Feſiſtres, *you did.*

Feſomes, feſſuns, *we make, do, perform.*

Feſt, feſte, *feaſt.*

Feſt (poent aver), *might have made.*

Feſte, *do.*

Feſtivables (tenent), *hold as feſtivals.*

Feſure, *make, making.*

Fet, fetes, *was, had been, cauſed, done, made; the fact, deed, buſineſs.*

Fet pas (ne), *does not make.*

Fet a demander, *was to be demanded.*

Fete d'archerie (le), *the exciſe of archery.*

Fetes, *kept, watched.*

Feth, *covenant, faith.*

Feth (ly feynt), *be made to him.*

Feth (tote), *always.*

Fetz, *deeds, grants.*

Feve, *zeal, late.*

Feverez, *February.*

Feves, *pulſe, beans.*

Feville (ſus la), *upon the leaf.*

Fevre (en temps de), *in the time of the fair.*

Feu, *chimney hearth.*

Feu, *was.*

Feuaile, feueile, *fewel.*

Feud, *a fee or reward.*

Feu (argent), *pure ſilver.*

Feur (au), *after the rate, in the faſhion of.*

Feute, feuſt, *ſhould be made, was.*

Feur (ſeu), *had fled.*

Feurent tombes (que), *who frequent tombs.*

Feurs, *manners.*

Feuſſiens, *have been.*

Feuſt, *act.*

Feuſt, *faſt.*

Feuſt, *wood.*

Feuſt (ſur le) de la croys que touchons, *on the croſs itſelf which we touch.*

Feuſt noſtre fitz, *our late ſon.*

Feut, *ſon.*

Feute, *fealty, allegiance.*

Feux, *late.*

Fewere, *to dig.*

Fey, *faith.*

Fey, feyets, *deeds, actions.*

Feym, feyn, *famine, hunger.*

Feymes (qe nus), *as we did.*

Feyn, *a fine.*

Feyn, *hay*

Feyne, *feigned.*

Feyne (ſe), *pretend, ſcruple, delay.*

Feynt

Feynt feff, *a collusive feoffment.*

Feynt (que ent se), *which has been made.*

Feyres, *fairs.*

Fez, *fees.*

Fez, *actions, done, made.*

Fez (sun), *his son.*

Fez (a la), *sometimes.*

Feze (treis), *three times.*

Fezer (a), *to make.*

Fiables (gentz), *persons of credit.*

Fiancer (per), *by pledging his faith. This was allowed a poor man, or a foreigner, who brought an action, because he could not find pledges to prosecute.*

Fianchie, *trusting, confiding in.*

Fianssassent, *should make sure, should pledge.*

Fiasmes tant, *did as much as.*

Ficher, *to fix.*

Fidz de chevalers, *knights fees.*

Fie, *fee, salary.*

Fie (de), *of the fee.*

Fie (en), *in fee.*

Fie par fei, *affirmed by his faith.*

Fiebles, *good, fair, honest.*

Fiee, *time.*

Fief (est), *is possessed.*

Fielle, *daughter.*

Fiene, *hay.*

Fient, *trust.*

Fier (ne poems), *we cannot trust to.*

Fier (armures de), *armed with helmets.*

Fier de guerre (a), *as in time of war, in a warlike manner.*

Fiere en ley, *brother in law.*

Fierent (le), *made, did it, caused the same.*

Fierges, *fetters, irons.*

Fierment ancore, *fast anchored.*

Fieront (que rien n'), *who did nothing thereupon.*

Fiertre (le), feretrum, *a case in which the body of some saint, or reliques, was laid up, a shrine, a bier.*

Fiest (tiel), *such business.*

Fieu de chevalier, *knight's fee.*

Fieuz, fiuz, filh, *son.*

Fiew, *fire.*

Fiew tenants, *free tenants.*

Fiez, *fees.*

Fiez, *time, times.*

Fiblez, *weak, feeble.*

Filace (en), *on the files.*

Fil del ewe, *middle of the water.*

File, *thread.*

File (haut), *high tide.*

Fileresses, *spinners.*

Filg,

Filg, *ſon.*
Filicer, *filizer.*
Filles, *ſnares.*
Fillie, filie, *daughter.*
Finable (pees), *final peace.*
Finablement, *finally, totally.*
Finance, *fine, ſubſidy, ranſom.*
Finant, *ending.*
Finaunce (pur), *for fines.*
Fineez, *ended.*
Fineſſe, *fineneſs.*
Finies, *fine.*
Fins, *differences, determinations.*
Finz, *ſon.*
Fiont, *made.*
Firger, *to put in irons.*
Firmaille, *a link, a chain.*
Firmalx, *locks.*
Firmre, firmur, *a pound, a cloſe place.*
Firmite, *a ſtrong hold.*
Firont (lui) entendere, *make him underſtand.*
Fis, *cauſed.*
Fis (que jeo), *which I did.*
Fiſchez, *fixed.*
Fiſechiens, *phyſicians.*
Fiſſend, *ſhould make.*
Fiſt (te), *was made, was in force.*
Fit, *paid.*
Fit aſcavoir, *it is to be known.*
Fites, *ſons.*
Fitz (les), *the fees.*
Fiuz, fiux, fiz, *ſon.*
Fiuz, *done.*
Flair, flaye, *to blow, blown.*
Flecher, *a bowyer.*
Fleſcher, fleſchier (ſanz), *without ſwerving, without favouring.*
Fleuret (le), *the foil or foin.*
Fleurons, *flowers.*
Fley, *a river.*
Flich, floche, *an arrow.*
Florein d'or, *a florin of gold.*
Florons, flourons, *flowers.*
Flos, flot, *a flood, a river.*
Flot & reflot, *ebbing and flowing.*
Flot (un ebbe et un), *one ebb, and one flood.*
Flote, *fleet.*
Flotter, *to float or ſwim.*
Flotus, *little veſſels.*
Flour Delys (les quatre), *the four princes of the blood, viz. Philip duke of Orleans; John Lewis duke of Anjou; John, earl of Poictiers, afterwards duke of Berry; and the duke of Bourbon: four of the hoſtages left in England, for the performance of the treaty of Bretigny; ſigned the 8th of May,* 1360.

Foder,

Foder, *to feed, to dig.*

Foe ſul Deu, *except God alone.*

Foer, *market-price.*

Foer, *to dig.*

Foer (al), *in like manner as.*

Foercher par eſſoigne, *to fourch by eſſoign.*

Foes, foez, *fees.*

Foethe (deus), *twice.*

Foial (home), *faithful man.*

Foialle entent, *true entent.*

Foials, *ſubjects.*

Foialtee, *fealty.*

Foiance, *digging.*

Foier, *to do, to enjoy.*

Foies, *digged.*

Foiet (toutz), *always.*

Foieth, foitz (a la), *ſometimes.*

Foil del coket, *letter of cocket.*

Foill, *a counterpart of an inſtrument.*

Foilles, foil, *leaves, ſheets.*

Foineſun, founeſtoun (en temp de), *the ſeaſon when the hinds bring forth their young, fawning-time, fence-month.*

Foins (come ore), *as we now do.*

Foir (a la) accqras in, *in manner of, reſemblance of.*

Foite de le record (ad le), *at the foot of the record.*

Foites, *deeds, writings.*

Foith (a tant de), *as often.*

Foith (un), *once.*

Foiſon grant des vitailles, *a great quantity or ſtore of proviſion.*

Foit (bonie), *good faith.*

Foit notoire, *openly done.*

Fole, fol, *fooliſh, bad, foul.*

Folement, *fooliſhly, indiſcreetly.*

Folies, *leaves.*

Foly, *fooliſhneſs, ignorance.*

Fomol appel, *a vexatious appeal.*

Fomollement, *vexatiouſly.*

Fonde de lettres, *in virtue of letters.*

Fonde (ſuffiſant), *ſufficient power, authority.*

Fonge dent, *fore-tooth.*

For, forſe, fore, force, *but.*

For ſulciaunt, *excepting.*

Forbanir, *to baniſh.*

Forbare, *excludes.*

Forboins (es), *in the ſuburbs.*

Forc (un), *a box.*

Forche, *force.*

Force, *force, form, virtue of.*

Force du realm, *the ſtrength of the realm.*

Force

Force (en notre), *in our army.*
Force (a), *of neceſſity.*
Force ley (eſt un), *it is a hard law.*
For ceaus, *but thoſe.*
Forhe, *force.*
Forclorra, *ſhall bar.*
Forclorroit, *ſhould bar.*
Forclos, *forecloſes, excludes, deprives, bars; eſtopped.*
Fore (en la), *in the market-place.*
Forein, foreigns, *foreigners.*
Fores, *foreſts.*
Fores (les), *the cuſtoms, privileges, forms.*
Foreingent, *adjudged.*
Foreyn (en), *out of the loras juriſdiction.*
Forf, *forfeiture.*
Fortace, *forfeit.*
Forfiſt, *forfeited.*
Forfit, fortait, *offence.*
Forger (poient), *may frame, contrive.*
Forgerent, *have contrived.*
Forgoor de faire, *ſet about making.*
Foringes, *ouſted, forejudged.*
Forejuge, *forejudged.*
Forjurer, *to forſwear, abjure, renounce.*
Forjure (a), *to be barred.*
Forjuogeable, *diſabled.*
Forke, *but.*
Forment, *grain.*
Forment, *greatly, forcibly.*
Formenteles, *formal.*
Fornage (a), *for fournage, for the oven.*
Forniſſements, formeiſmes, *framing.*
Forniſſors, *framers.*
Forniſt (ſe), *is performed, executed.*
Foront, *ſhall cauſe.*
Forrein circle, *outward circle.*
Fors (al), *with force.*
Fors de la foreſt, *out of the foreſt.*
Fors deſquelles lettres (par), *by force of which letters.*
Forſablement, *forceably.*
Forſclore, *to forecloſe, to ſeize.*
Fors (faiſons), *bind ourſelves.*
Forſelet, fortelet, fortureſce, *a hold, fortreſs, fortlet.*
Forsjuge pas (ne), *ought not to prejudice.*
Forſprendre, *exception.*
Forſprent, *excepts.*
Forſpris, *except.*
Forſſant, *preſs, compel.*
Forſuire (qil) la courte, *that he be forejudged by the court.*

Fort

Fort a un clyent, *hard upon a client.*

Fort (il se ferroit assez), *he will enter into a sufficient obligation.*

Forte chose, *a hard thing, case.*

Fortunement, *perhaps.*

Forveiast de rienz, *mistake any matter.*

Forveier hors de lyne (sil vorroit), *that he should stray out of, deviate from the line; should degenerate from.*

Forz, *strong.*

Fos, *but.*

Fosse, *a ditch, pond.*

Foster, *a park-keeper.*

Fotiels, *foolish.*

Fouage, *chimney-money; a tax imposed by the black prince on Guienne.*

Fovagle, foveant, *digging.*

Fouayne, *a pit; digging.*

Fouler, fowler aux pees, *to tread down, to tread under foot.*

Fouler, *to dig, to cleanse.*

Foulle, *oppressed.*

Foullons, fullons, *fullers.*

Foundement, *foundation.*

Foundez, *foundered.*

Foundue, *melted down.*

Founs de baptesme (de), *from the font.*

Fount, *belong, do, perform.*

Fount (au), *at the bottom.*

Fount adrere, *are in arrear.*

Founz, *fountain.*

Fovoyle, foueil, *fewel.*

Four, *a baking oven.*

Fourche, *to delay, put off.*

Fourches, *stocks, pillory.*

Fourme, *baked.*

Fourmee, *informed against.*

Fourmr, *form.*

Fourmes (robes), *robes made up.*

Fous nastres, *fools born, idiots.*

Fouts, *it behoveth.*

Fow (quarer), *dug in his quarreys.*

Fowalles, fovoyle, a un astre, *fuel for one chimney.*

Fower, *to cut down, to dig.*

Foy (en bonne), *in bona fide.*

Foyablés, *faithful.*

Foyder, *to dig.*

Foyne, foine, *a pole-cat, a wood-martin.*

Foys (per), *by turns.*

Foys (pur), *the agreement, or covenant.*

Fra (ne), *will not make.*

Frache, *freight.*

Fraile, *a basket.*

Fraine, *a bridle.*

Fraint, *should do.*

Fraiz,

Fraiz, frais, fruez, *charges.*
Frũct, *frank tenement.*
Frankises, *franchises.*
Frans, *free, quit.*
Frap de gents (trop de), *too great a retinue of people.*
Frarie, *fraternity.*
Fraude, *foldage.*
Frauldres, *frauds.*
Fraunche ley, libera lex, *frank or free law; so called to distinguish men who enjoy it, and whose best and freest birthright it is, from them that by their offences have lost it, as men attainted in an attaint, in a conspiracy upon an indictment, or in a premunire, &c.*
Fraunchese, *franchise.*
Fraunchement, frauchment, *freely.*
Fraunchise, *freedom, liberty.*
Fraunk sengler, *a free boar.*
Fraunk tor, *a free bull.*
Fray, *made.*
Frayent (qils), *that they would act.*
Frea, *will perform.*
Frealte, *frailty.*
Freceis, *a Frenchman.*
Freatz (ne), *will not make.*
Frees, *brethren.*
Freez, frees, fres, *expences.*
Freetz, *will do.*
Freines, fresses, *young ash-trees.*
Freintes, *broke open.*
Freit, *freight.*
Frenges, *fringes.*
Frere de bast, *a bastard brother.*
Freris, frerez, *brethren, friory, brotherhood.*
Fresche, *fresh.*
Freskement, friquement, freshment, *directly, lately.*
Fresque, *sudden.*
Frettez, frette, *freighted.*
Freyetes, *broken.*
Frie (le) des salmons, *the fry of salmons.*
Friens, *should do.*
Frier, fryer, *brother.*
Frische, *fresh.*
Froise, *broken in pieces.*
Froit, *frost.*
Froms, *we will make.*
Frospris, *except.*
Frounts, *they make.*
Fruez, *fruits.*
Fruisse la pais, *break the peace.*
Fu, *I was.*
Fu, *fire.*
Fuaunts, *refusing.*
Fuax, *false.*
Fuayl, fouoyle, fowalles, *fuel.*

Fue,

Fue, *fire.*
Fueer, *fleed.*
Fuelle, *a daughter.*
Fuer, *to drive away, chase.*
Fuer, *flight, fled.*
Fuer, *to avoid.*
Fuer (au) du temps, *in proportion for the time.*
Fueront, *were.*
Fueust, *was.*
Fugeree (satain), *figured satin.*
Fui, *were.*
Fuison, foison, *plenty.*
Fuison (grant), *great quantity.*
Fuist, *strong wood.*
Fuit (ne soit), *be not made.*
Fuitz (que se port pur lei), *who pretends to be the son.*
Fullours, fullons, foullons, *fullers.*
Fũnche faire, *a free fair.*
Funder, *to ground, found.*
Fundement, *foundation.*
Fundements, *chief rules, grounds.*
Funt, *do.*
Fur (les), *the gallows.*
Fur̃, furoms, *were.*
Furchesces, *forks.*
Furet, *a ferret.*
Furier, *February.*
Furit, *was.*
Furk, *but.*
Furmage, *cheese.*
Furment, *wheat.*
Furni, *performed, executed, given, framed.*
Furnisez, *execute, dispatch.*
Fuse sang, *blood-shed.*
Fust, *be fled.*
Fust, fuz, *wood.*
Fust, fuz (croys de), *a wooden cross.*
Fust, *should be.*
Fust (avoite), *had been made.*
Fustage (arbres), *old high trees of the forest.*
Fusunt (ne), *were not.*
Futz, fustz (gros), *great trees, timber.*
Fut (mettre a), *set fire to.*
Futyf, *a fugitive.*
Fuums, *were.*
Fuyeur, *a run-away.*
Fuyt, fute, *flight.*
Futz, fuyz, *son.*
Fyere (ne poems de tut), *we cannot at all confide in.*
Fyes, fyez, *times.*
Fym, *dung.*
Fyn, *end.*
Fynable disheritance, *to the utter disinherison.*
Fyne (del osse al), *from the bone to the fin.*
Fynes, *fineness.*
Fynnen, *a fountain.*
Fyrene, *made.*
Fyrent, *confided in.*

Fyw (mys a), *lighted up, ſet on fire.*

G~ẽ, g:ce, *grace, favour.*

G~at, *glove.*

~gnt, ~gund, *great.*

Gr~ee, *grant, agreement.*

Gadount, *that then.*

Gaeres de value, *of any value.*

Gage (en), *in mortgage.*

Gager, *to depoſit, to engage or undertake, to wage.*

Gagerie, gagiere, *pledge.*

Gagez, gages, *ſureties, fees, wages.*

Gagez (eient), *have any wages.*

Gahin, gaing, gaaing, *the autumn.*

Gaigeries, gaigenes, *impignorations.*

Gaies, gaiges (lour), *their ſalaries, wages.*

Gaigier (de), *of gain.*

Gaigiers, *hirelings.*

Gaignage, gaignere, *wainage.*

Gaignarie, gainery, *huſbandry.*

Gaigne (noſtre), *our own advantage.*

Gaigner, *to obtain by huſbandry.*

Gainers (a), *to be gained.*

Gaignes (des), *the gains, profits.*

Gaigneurs, *the captors.*

Gaille, *a jail.*

Gaine, gaignent (que), *who plow or till.*

Gainure, *tillage.*

Gairenner (count de), *earl of Warren.*

Gaiſtement, *waſt.*

Gait, guaite (fiſt), *kept watch.*

Galbelton, *Gallbetten.*

Galee, galeis, *gally, gallies.*

Galeys, *France.*

Galeys, *Calais.*

Galeys (Guill. de), *William de Waleys.*

Galles, Galeys, *Wales, Welch.*

Galoges, *galoches.*

Galoie, galee, *galley.*

Galynes, galines, *cocks, or capons.*

Ganer, *to gain.*

Gantier, *a glover.*

Gants, gaunts, ganz, *gloves.*

Ganudir, *to defend, maintain.*

Gar, *guards.*

Garant, *a warrant, commiſſion.*

Garauntage, *warranty.*

Gar~c de c~hre, *warranty of charter.*

Garbes,

Garbes, *sheaves of corn.*

Garbs, *cloathing, vestures.*

Garceons, *servants, journeymen.*

Garda la, *the award.*

Garde (la), *the wardship, the judgement.*

Garde (la) Farndon, *the ward of Farringdon.*

Gardein, *constable.*

Garden (seignour), *lord-keeper, lord-warden.*

Garder (les), *the judgement.*

Garder, *to watch, preserve, to take care of, to cultivate, to observe.*

Gardes (Cur de), *court of wards.*

Gardes voustre challenges, *look to your challenges.*

Gardiouns, *take care.*

Gardior, *guardian.*

Gardure gardeiny (en le), *in the keeping.*

Garee, *fallow.*

Garee (terre), *old fallow-ground.*

Garesun, *recovery.*

Gareison, *a reward, a support.*

Garenner, *to prohibit.*

Gargaus, *chattering.*

Garignier, *to till.*

Garinthes, *the furr of the legs of hares.*

Garisoun, garneison, garnisons, garny, *the providing for the castle, &c.*

Garisun, garison, *support, maintenance, revenue.*

Gariz, garis, garri, *restored to health.*

Garnementz, *garments.*

Garner, garnisher, *to warn, summons.*

Garnesie, *Guernsey.*

Garnestor garnison (le), *the officer who was to provide victuals, arms, &c. for the support and defence of a castle, &c.*

Garnestour, garnesture (en sa), *in his office of garnestor.*

Garnesture de chatel (en), *towards supplies for the castle.*

Garnesture du chastel (en la), *within the precincts of the castle.*

Garnier (sans), *without first acquainting him.*

Garnis, *paid.*

Garnishement, garnissement, garnishant, garnyseint, *warning, summons, notice.*

Garny, *informed, to have notice of.*

Garny de sa maladie, *cured of his illness.*

Garniz, *provided.*

Garrant, *protect.*

Garrant, quarant, *forty.*

Garrantie, *a justice's warrant.*

Garrantizables, *are to be warranted, proved.*

Garranty, garrenty, *warranted, proved.*

Garren, garene, garreyn, garrayn, *a warren.*

Garreteres, *garters.*

Garrifon (le) imprift, *took upon himfelf the cure.*

Garfettes, *girls.*

Garfonnet, *they draw.*

Gart, *keep, perform.*

Gart (vos), *preferve you.*

Garth, *a yard, garden, or backfide.*

Garzon a pee, *a foot-boy.*

Gafcher, *to row.*

Gafconche, *Gafcony.*

Gaftel (le), *waftel bread.*

Gafter, *to wafte.*

Gaftine, *wafte ground.*

Gaftors, *wafters.*

Gafz, *waftes.*

Gat, *a gate.*

Gaul, *garlick.*

Gaule haut, *gule of Auguft* †.

Gault, gaut, *a foreft.*

Gauterent, gaiterent, *intended, lay in wait.*

Gauntz, *gloves.*

Gaway, *Gallaway.*

Gaweleynes (le corps de), *the perfons of the people of Gallaway.*

Gayguafmes, *gained.*

Gaynage or wainage, *all the plow tackle, or implements of hufbandry, of the villain, countryman, or ploughman, which were to be privileged from diftreffes or feizures for fines or amerciaments; for if they were diftrained or feized on fuch account, he would be difabled from carrying on his employment of agriculture, contrary to the fundamental liberty of fubjects, who were fo to be mulcted, fined, or amerced, as fhould punifh them, but not break or undo them.*

Gayne (hors de), *out of the fheath.*

Gayner, *to till.*

Gaynerie, gaynure, *tillage or tilling, or the profit raifed by tillage.*

Gaynours, *the tillers.*

Gayter la mort, *to wait for the death.*

Ge fuy (que) et ceray, *that I am and fhall be.*

† Dr. Brady fays he could not tell what was meant by *l'andemaigne Gaule haut*; but I apprehend it is the day of the date of the record publifhed by him, and that that day was the 2d of Auguft, being the morrow after the *gule of Auguft*. Brady, vol. II. p. 199.

Geans, *people.*
Geaſt, *a gueſt.*
Geaule, *a jail.*
Gehennet, *to avoid.*
Gehis (eient) de eux meſmes, *have the government of themſelves.*
Gehis (il eſt), *he is forced.*
Geiſt, *lies, reſides.*
Geiſt (lour), *their accommodation.*
Geitant, *waſting.*
Geldables, *liable to be taxed.*
Geleyns, gelyns, *hens.*
Geloſie, *fondneſs.*
Gelure (duc de), *duke of Gueldres.*
Geners, *kinds, ſpecies.*
Genices, *heifers.*
Gente, genx (ma), *my people.*
Gentez (les) du people, *the parliament.*
Gentieux hommes, *gentlemen.*
Gentifeme, *a gentlewoman.*
Gentileſſe, *the nobility.*
Genulera, *ſhall kneel.*
Gentz de meſtire, *maſters of trades.*
Geole, *a cave, a priſon.*
Geolier, *a jailer.*
Gerdin, *a garden.*
Gere, *war.*
Gereſie, Gereſeey, *Jerſey.*
Geril, *diſorder.*
Gernettes, *garnets.*
Gerniſons, *garriſons.*
Gerpit, *avoided, abandoned.*
Gers (qils ne doutent), *that they are not afraid to take.*
Gerſonent (ne), *do not rack.*
Geſkerech, *the month of Auguſt.*
Geſt, *yeſt.*
Geſt, gette (le), *the behaviour.*
Geſta, *carried away.*
Geſte, *a gueſt.*
Geſtez, *waſted.*
Geſtoient ſomons, *who had been ſummoned.*
Get (a), *hath begotten.*
Getteis, gets, *jettys.*
Getter ceo la en hochpot, *to throw into hotchpotch.*
Getter, geter (le), *to ſecure, to indemnify him.*
Gettere, *to caſt.*
Gettez de feyn, *cocks of hay.*
Gettu, *thrown, caſt.*
Geynes, *ſheaths.*
Gharand, *warrant.*
Gide, *guide.*
Gie, *governed.*
Gientz, *people.*
Gieu, Geu, *a Jew.*

Gie, gi, *I, I myſelf.*
Gihall, *Guildhall.*
Giloux, *jealous.*
Gipſerrynges, *harneſs for girdles.*
Girome, *Jerome.*
Girra, *ſhall lye.*
Giſarme, *a military weapon like a lance, or long bayonet.*
Giſer (pur) lui overt, *to lay him open.*
Giſt (qi), *who is buried, who lies.*
Giſtance, *caſting up.*
Giſtes, *caſt up.*
Glebe, *a piece of earth or turf.*
Gleyves, *ſwords, bills.*
Gliſes, *churches.*
Gloſgu, *Glaſcow.*
Glyn, *a valley.*
Godetz d'or, *goblets, mugs of gold.*
Gombre, *rejoice.*
Gomme, *gum.*
Goor, *a watery place.*
Gopiele, gopil, goupil, gupil, *a fox.*
Gores de ſeney, *days of recreation.*
Gorre, *a ſow.*
Gors, gorſe, gorts, *a ſtream or pool, a watery place, a wear, a fiſh-pond, a ditch, a dam, a gorce.*
Got, *a ſluice, drain, or ditch.*
Gouette, *a drop.*
Goule d'Aouſt, *the gule of Auguſt, or the firſt of Auguſt.*
Goune, *gown.*
Gourt, *a watery place.*
Gous, *a dog.*
Goy, *God.*
Goy, *lame.*
Grace de founder, *leave to found.*
Graera, *will agree to.*
Graffer, *a notary, a ſcrivener.*
Gram (en), *in grammar.*
Gramaci, *great mercy.*
Grant, graunt, grauntz, *great.*
Grant, *when.*
Grant ſeal, *great ſeal.*
Grant bank le roy (les juſtices deu), *the juſtices of the king's high bench.*
Grante (le teygne), *take it for granted.*
Grants, grauntez, *granted.*
Grantterries, *nobles of the realm.*
Grantz, graunts, grauntez, graints, *great men.*
Graſe, graſs, *grace, favour.*
Gratentement, *readily.*
Gratiffie (ont), *have approved, confirmed.*
Grava, grave, *a grove.*
Graver, *to grieve, aggrieve.*

Graument, *a great deal.*
Graundour, *extent, ſize.*
Graunta (il), *he promiſed, agreed.*
Grauntez, *grants.*
Grauntiers, grannterz, *to be granted.*
Graynour, granour, *great.*
Gre, gree, *favour, grace, concern.*
Greable, *voluntary.*
Greantz, *we grant.*
Gredirnes, *gridirons.*
Gree, grey, *conſent, ſatisfaction, accord, agreement.*
Gree, gre (de), *voluntarily.*
Gree (par), *by agreement.*
Greei, *agreed to.*
Grees (des), *of the parties aggrieved.*
Gref, *grievance.*
Grefs, *grievous.*
Greignour, greynour, grendres, greindre, *more great, greater.*
Greit, *greeteth.*
Greiver, *to affect.*
Greivure, greverement, *more grievous, heavier.*
Gremercy, *great mercy.*
Greo, gres, *ſatisfaction.*
Gres, *great.*
Greſle, *filled.*
Greſſame, *fine.*
Greve nent (ne), *there is no damage.*
Greve (en), *in trouble, affliction.*
Grevoir, *to aggrieve.*
Greyn (boef peu de), *a corn fed ox.*
Greyne, greigne, *grain.*
Grie, *agreement, ſatisfaction.*
Grief, *grievance.*
Griefs, gries, *grievous.*
Grieues, *on the ſhores, banks.*
Grieux, Grieu, Grigois, *Greek.*
Grigner, *greater.*
Grith, *peace.*
Grithſtole, *a ſanctuary.*
Gro, groſſe, *fat, great.*
Groinure teumain (en), *in greater teſtimony.*
Gromet (un), *a ſea-faring boy.*
Groos (en), *in groſs.*
Gros homes, *men of quality.*
Gros nature, *general nature.*
Gros point, *principal point.*
Groſſement enſient, *great, quick with child.*
Groſſeours, *bickerings, affronts, ill-will.*
Groſſier, *to grow big.*
Groſſment, *generally.*
Groſſome, *a fine at entrance.*

Grotz, *groats.*

Grume, grun, *all ſorts of grain.*

Guannys, *huſbandmen.*

Guariſon, *the cure.*

Guaſcon, *a Gaſcon.*

Guay, guey (au), *to the key of the river.*

Gueƈt apent (omicide de), *wilful murder.*

Gueir, *to take care, to ſee.*

Guel ceux (au), *to the care of thoſe.*

Guelle, *throat.*

Guerdon, *a bargain, a reward.*

Guerdonnez, *rewarded.*

Guerniers, garniers, *garners, ſtorehouſes.*

Guerperent p̄ mort, *left him for dead.*

Guerpi, guerpyes, gueppe, *abandoned, left.*

Guerra, *ſhall plead.*

Guertres, *hinders.*

Guerritt (ſil en), *if he be cured of it.*

Guerroier, guerryer, *wage war, go to war with.*

Guertent, *think.*

Guertoient, *forſake.*

Gueyement, *government.*

Gueyet, *governed.*

Guf, *a pit.*

Guiayne, Guiaigne, *Acquitain.*

Guideront, *thought, intended.*

Guier, guyer, *to guide.*

Güier, *guided.*

Guierent (ſe), *conducted themſelves.*

Guildable, *gildable, not within any franchiſe.*

Guindors, *governors.*

Guiſarme, *a military weapon made like a lance.*

Guiſe, guyſe, *method.*

Guiſe (a) de marchant, *as a merchant.*

Guiters, *holes, gutters.*

Gule, *the beginning or firſt day of a month.*

Gurge, *a pond or pool.*

Gurneroit, *warned.*

Gus, *a beggar.*

Guſtera, *ſhall taſte of.*

Gurre, gwer, *war.*

Guyement, *guidance, government.*

Guyen (Monſr. de), *John of Gaunt, duke of Acquitain.*

Guyet, guyer, *governed.*

Guyſe, *faſhion, manner.*

Guytemens de voyes et de chemins, *deſtruction of roads and highways.*

Guyſe (la d'armes), *the cuſtom; law of arms.*

Gwer, *war.*

Gwyene, Guienne, *Acquitain.*

Gylour, *one who deceives the court.*

Gypwyz, *Ipſwich.*

Gyrues, *Jews.*

Gyler, *to lie down.*

HA, *hath, have.*

Haber, *to have.*

Habergiez, *haubergers, a coarſe ſort of cloth.*

Habidõ, *Abingdon.*

Hable, *able.*

Habler, *to enable, to render a perſon capable of inheriting, to reſtore.*

Hables, *havens, ports.*

Habundent, *abound.*

H'cer (a), *to harrow.*

Hacher, *to plunder.*

Haches, hãce, *hatchets.*

Hada, *a haven, port.*

Hagu, *a houſe.*

Haies, *hedges.*

Haies, *heys.*

Haineux, *inimical.*

Haiour, *hatred.*

Hairaſſera, *will harraſs.*

Haiter, haitier, *to rejoice.*

Haits, haitie, heitiez, *lively, active, hearty, in health.*

Hakett, *agate.*

Halberge, *an inn.*

Halt ſaine, *high birth.*

Halx princes, *high, noble princes.*

Halz haz, fet, *has made.*

Ham, *a village.*

Hamele, hamelle, *a hamlet.*

Hamelx, haniells, *hamlets.*

Hames, *haime.*

Hanap, *hamper, cup.*

Hanap d'argent, *a ſilver cup.*

Hanapes (burſels pur), *covers for cups.*

Hane, *hated.*

Hange, *hatred.*

Hanguvelle, *a New-year's-gift.*

Hanſe, *a ſociety.*

Hanſer, *to accuſe.*

Hanſer (le), *the handle.*

Hanſhomes, *the high men, the prelates and great barons.*

Hantaſt (ne) Engleterre, *ſhould not repair into England.*

Hantin, *an uncle.*

Haour, *hatred.*

Happa, *got, took, received.*

Happa (a) ſeiſin, *hath gotten, ſeiſin.*

Happa (que prines), *who firſt happens to have.*

Happe (ne) mie, *does not gain, obtain, get.*

Happee, *taken.*

Harald, harauld, *a herald.*

Harang ſore, ſoer, *herrings.*

Haraus (reys des), *heralds, kings at arms.*

Haras de juments, *a breed of mares.*

Harchiers, *archers.*

Hard (de la), *implements, goods, furniture.*

Hardoyer, *to attack, insult.*

Hardy, *daring, presumptuous.*

Harenguiser, *herring season.*

Harer, harier, *to stir up, provoke, importune.*

Hareusement, *seditiously.*

Harfort, *Hertford.*

Harmoniqueur, *a musician.*

Harneys in, *arrayed.*

Harriez molt, *very sorry.*

Haspe (le), *the hasp, handle.*

Haster (pour droit), *for dispatch of justice.*

Hastier *a minister; to dispatch.*

Hastif, hastyfe, *immature, inconsiderate.*

Hastif (que soit), *which may require dispatch.*

Hastiulement, *in haste, too soon.*

Hativete, *diligence.*

Hattes, *hats.*

Hauberiom, *a coat of mail.*

Hauberk, haubergons, *a halbert.*

Haugh, *a valley.*

Haulement, hauliement, *highly.*

Haulz, *high, great.*

Haume, *helmet.*

Hauncer, haulster, *to raise, erect.*

Hauncer (un), *a weight called the auncel weight.*

Haunge, *contrivance.*

Haunieck, *one born in Flanders.*

Haunt ne repeir, *haunt nor repair.*

Haur, haut, *hatred.*

Hauront, *shall have.*

Haus, *house.*

Haust eschetour, *chief eschetour.*

Hausters, *towers of vessels.*

Haute, hautece, *highness, excellence.*

Hautisme, *most high.*

Hautness, *greatness, heinousness.*

Hauz, haus, haults homes, *men of high degree, the great barons.*

Havement, *greedily.*

Havene, havle, *haven.*

Havcir, *to have.*

Haye, hay, *a hedge.*

Hayer, *to hate.*

Hayes (en), *in ranks or rows.*

Haynge

Haynge (par), *through malice.*

Hayson, *the fencing or hedging-time.*

Haw, *a small piece of land near a house.*

Hawberg (fee de), *a tenure by which the tenant is obliged to defend the land by full arms, that is, by horse, haubert, target, sword, or helmet; a tenure by knight's service.*

Hawyse, *Avice.*

Hear, her, *heir.*

Heaume, *an helmet.*

Hebbyngwerez, *ebbing-wears.*

Hede-penyez, *head-pence.*

Heint, *hatred.*

Heir, *inheritance.*

Heirs (devant ceux), *heretofore, in times past.*

Heis, heies, *hedges.*

Helmot, *sentence, judgement.*

Hely, *Ely.*

Hen, *had.*

Herbage et herberge (sil), *if he lodges or harbours.*

Herbergages (des), *of the apartments.*

Herberger, *to lodge, to dwell in.*

Herberges (a), *at the castle.*

Herberjours, *lodgers.*

Herbette, *dull.*

Herbirent (queux), *who were quartered.*

Herces, *hearses.*

Here, *heir.*

Hereges, *heretics.*

Herit, *an heretic.*

Heritanz, *inhabitants.*

Hernois, herneys, *harness.*

Heroiés, *heroes.*

Heroldes, *heralds.*

Herpe, *a harp.*

Hersedecome, *archdeaconry.*

Hersoin, *yesterday.*

Hertescombe, *the action in the civil law, called actio familiæ erciscundæ; in our law, coparcenery.*

Het, heate, *the heart.*

Hettez, *hearty.*

Heu (jai), *I have had.*

Heudernesse, *Holderness.*

Heuke, huke, *a hood.*

Heurs, *heirs.*

Heurusite, *happiness.*

Heust este, *had been.*

Heybe, *haybote.*

Heynoste (le), *the heinousness.*

Hi, *there, thither.*

Hide, *fright, dread.*

Hidel, *a place of sanctuary.*

Hidous, *frightful, terrifying.*

Hier, *heir.*

Hiytan jour, *eighth day.*

Hille

Hille (le), *the isle.*
Hiluc, *there.*
Hireté, *inheritance.*
Hirland, *Ireland.*
Ho, *stop, cease; the word made use of for the combatants to leave off fighting.*
Hò (k) devereit entendre, *to make one believe.*
Hobeissent, *obey.*
Hobelours, *hoblers, lighthorsemen, halberters.*
Hobyns, *hobbies.*
Hogetz, *young weather-sheep.*
Hoict, *eight.*
Hoirie, *inheritance.*
Hoirs, *heirs.*
Hokes, *hooks.*
Hoketons, aketon, acton, *cloaks or cassocks.*
Homa, *man.*
Home, homa, *homage.*
Homeaus, *the Elms near Smithfield; the place of execution before Tyburn.*
Honayllurs, *at the same time, nevertheless.*
Honeests, *lawful.*
Hones, *honour.*
Honiz, *injured, ruined.*
Honourment, *ornament.*
Honrage, *a seigniory, a great fee.*
Hons, *a man.*
Hont, *have.*
Hontage, *affront, approach.*
Honurement, *honourably.*
Hony, *disgrace, evil.*
Hooland, *Holland.*
Hopulandes, houpelands, furres, 2, *two long coats or cloaks furred.*
Hor est (par le chambirlayne quy), *by the present chamberlain.*
Hore, *hour.*
Hore (a), *at present.*
Hore (que del), *since that, inasmuch as.*
Hore ditte, *given, tendered.*
Hores (toutes les), *whenever.*
Hors d'or (un rubi), *a ruby not set in gold.*
Hors de ceinz, *out of this place.*
Hors dun fine, *upon a fine.*
Hors de possession, *out of possession.*
Hors port, *bringeth forth.*
Hors q̃ houre, *from the time that, as soon as.*
Hors pris, *omitted, excepted.*
Horstreit hors, *drawn out.*
Horstrez, *dragged out.*
Hort, *a garden.*
Hosa, *dared.*
Hostagez, *hostages.*
Hoste, *an host, a guest.*
Hoste, *put out.*
Hoste (luy) de l'eglise, *those who hold of the church.*

Hostel,

Hoſtel, *houſehold, family.*

Hoſtel, hoſt, houſt, *an army.*

Hoſtelage, *entertainment at an inn; the hire of ſtalls in a market.*

Hoſteler, *to put up at an inn.*

Hoſtelier, hoſtillers, oſtillurs, hoſtler, *an innkeeper.*

Hoſtell le roy, hoſteulx, *the king's houſehold.*

Hoſter, *to remove.*

Hoſtery, hoſtry, *an inn.*

Hoſtes (les), *the doors.*

Hoſtes (tut), *entirely removed.*

Hoſtez, *repulſed.*

Hoſtiel, hoſteulz, *houſe, lodging, home, quarters.*

Hoſtielx tenauntz, *houſeholders.*

Hoſtier, *to take out, diminiſh from.*

Houces, *houſings.*

Houches, *cheſts.*

Houghtez, *taken out, eraſed.*

Hountouſement, *ſhamefully.*

Houpells, *tufts, taſſels.*

Houre qes (del), *ſince that, ſo long as.*

Houre ſerra (quant), *when the time comes.*

Hous en hous (de), *from door to door.*

Houſt, *army.*

Houſt, *war, a military expedition.*

Houſtel, *houſe.*

Houſtiel, *houſehold.*

Hovement, *digging.*

Howes, *geeſe.*

Hoz, hoze, *an army.*

Hu, *hue and cry.*

Huches (en lour), *in their cheſts.*

Huches de mariners, *the mariners cheſts.*

Huchet, *a huntſman's horn, from whence comes the word, hue.*

Huchier, *to proclaim.*

Hue, *cry, clamour.*

Huech, *eight.*

Hueil, *an eye.*

Hues, *had.*

Huem, hucm, *a man.*

Huers (paſſet), *paſſed through, out.*

Huevre, *work.*

Huguetto, *Agatha.*

Hui, huy, *to-day.*

Huimes, *now, preſently.*

Huitienes (les), *the octaves.*

Hujus (quatre), *four boundaries, hedges.*

Huiz, *a gate, a door.*

Hum, *a man, any one.*

Hum, *have.*

Humble (al), *to the navel.*

Humbleſſe, *humility.*

Humes,

Humes, *had.*

Hunt, hount, *shame.*

Huntage, *reproach, discredit.*

Hure (al), *at the same time.*

Hurer, *hat maker.*

Hures, hurez, *hats.*

Hurs (sa haie), *thrown down, pulled down his hedge.*

Hus (al), *at the door.*

Husbote, *housebote.*

Huse (de la), *of the house.*

Huseons, husens, *buscans.*

Hussherie de l'eschekere, *the office of usher of the court of exchequer.*

Hust, *has.*

Hustin, hutin, *noise, clamour.*

Huwe, *Hugh.*

Huy, *beard.*

Huy, *to-day.*

Huy (et ceo est), *and this is now.*

Huy ces jour, *at this day.*

Huyctaves, huykes, *octaves, eight.*

Huyer, *to cry out or proclaim.*

Huys, *door.*

Huyse (inner), *inner parlour.*

Hydouses, *hideous.*

Hÿet, *a heriot.*

Hyl, *he, there.*

Hyl (lie), *here.*

Hyne (le maystre), *the head servant.*

Hys, *he, has.*

J, *they, there.*

J, Ja (en), *there is.*

Ja, iaz, *now, already, henceforth, yet, nevertheless, never, whereas.*

Jademains, jadumeis, *furthermore.*

Ja le plus tart, *nevertheless, at the last.*

Ja soit ceo qe, *so long as.*

Ja soit que, *although, that.*

Ja si grant tort (ne fust ceo), *was the mischief never so great.*

Ja seit ce quil eent este, *although they have been.*

Ja seyt isce ke vos seez lye a nos, *although you are bound to us.*

Ja si able person (soit il), *let him be never so fit a person.*

Jace, *lain.*

Jackes, *jackets, coats of mail; also a kind of military coat put over the coat of mail.*

Jacoit, *although, yet. still.*

Jaczoit ce que, *although that.*

Jadumeins, *notwithstanding, also, moreover.*

Jademeyns, *yet.*

Jagan, *a giant.*

Jaiant, *a giant.*

Jaidit, *lately.*

Jaime, Jaume, *James.*
Jake, Jak, Jaky, *James.*
Jalemens, jalemems, ja le meyns, jalemeyns, *always, alſo, neverthelefs, ſtill, yet, ſometimes, as well as, moreover, further.*
Jalun, jalon, *a gallon.*
Jamais (a) et a jamais, *for ever and ever, perpetual.*
Jamme, *a gem, jewel.*
Jammes devant, *never before.*
Jan, *John.*
Janevoir, Janner, *January.*
Jangleour, *a minſtrel.*
Jannz, *furze.*
Janti fame, *a noblewoman, a gentlewoman.*
Janue, *Genoa.*
Japieca, *within a little time.*
Jarcer, *to cleave.*
Jarges, *charged, oppreſſed.*
Jaſoit, *although.*
Jaſoit ce que, *inaſmuch as.*
Jatant, jatardeis, *now of late, neverthelefs.*
Jatarde, *lately.*
Jaulne, *yellow.*
Jaulx, *them.*
Jaunz, *heath, furze.*
Jaur, *a day.*
Jauſé, *Joſeph.*
Jave, *water.*
Jaynuer, *January.*
Ic, *there.*
Iceeplaiz, *theſe pleas.*
Iceleui meimes, *this ſame.*
Icels, iceans, *ſuch.*
Iceo, icen, *this, that.*
Iceſt (d'), *of the ſame.*
Icevoix, *they, them.*
Ichet, *falls.*
Ict, *thrown.*
Idles, *iſles, iſlands.*
Idunk, *then, there.*
Jeane, *Genoa.*
Jeaundie, Jeady, *Thurſday.*
Jecter, *to throw, caſt.*
Jehan de Peſchan, *John de Peckham.*
Jehana, *John.*
Jehane, *Joan.*
Jehu Chriſt, *Jeſus Chriſt.*
Jekes (qe), *than until.*
Jekes a oens, *up with them.*
Jene, *young.*
Jenuer, Jenevoir, Jeonever, *January.*
Jent ne, *have not.*
Jeodi, *Thurſday.*
Jeofneſſe, jeoffneſs, *youth.*
Jeovene (le), *the younger.*
Jer, *firſt.*
Jer, *yeſterday.*
Jerint, *they have gone.*
Jerjour, *firſt day.*
Jerlm, *Jeruſalem.*
Jern, *Yarmouth.*
Iert, *ſhall be.*
Jert, *will be.*
Jeſkes, jeſqueſencea, *till now, hitherto.*

Jeſlamer,

Jeſlamer, *on this ſide the ſeas.*

Jeſq a, *contrary to.*

Jeſques en cea deſoies, de ſoie, *hitherto unheard of, unaccuſtomed.*

Jeſtieſmes (ſe p̃ſent), *if we were preſent.*

Jette fors, *excepted.*

Jeu, *a Jew.*

Jeuſday, *Tueſday.*

Jeuſdye, Juriſdie, *Tueſday.*

Jewiſe (a ſa), *ſee Juiſe.*

Jex, *eyes.*

Iffinite, *affinity.*

Igale, *equal.*

Igliſe, *church.*

Ignier, igny, *to burn, fired.*

Jia (il), *they are.*

J'iere, j'ere, *I was.*

Ilez, *they.*

Illect, *of the ſame place.*

Illee (d'), *moreover.*

Illes, *iſlands.*

Illickes, illeques, illoc, ilokes, illec, alec, *there.*

Illieyt (taunt come), *as long as there are.*

Illiont (ſi), *if they have.*

Illoeqes, *there.*

Illoeſqes, illueſqes, illuſqes (de), *from thence, from that time.*

Illoigner, *eloined.*

Iluccke, *there.*

Imbuent, *they drank.*

Immunite, *freedom, immunity.*

Impareil, *not to be compared with.*

Impayrera (ne), *ſhall not vitiate.*

Impediera, *ſhall hinder.*

Impere, *empire, juriſdiction.*

Impetraceion, *requeſt, ſuit, proſecutions.*

Impierment, *prejudicing.*

Implier, *to fill up, fulfil.*

Importables, *greater than can be born, inſupportable.*

Importunes (jeues), *vain, inconvenient, improper games and ſports.*

Impreſſeur, *a printer.*

Imprimt en le jour, *twilight.*

Improwment, *improving.*

In apres, *thenafter.*

Inanere, *to make void.*

Incarnacum, *incarnation.*

Incedent, *ſet forth, publiſhed.*

Inchoatz, *commenced.*

Incleaſed, *enſnared, entangled.*

Inconnera, *obſtruct.*

Incuter, *to ſtrike.*

Indeu, *indebted.*

Indicte, *pronounced.*

Indire, *to declare.*

Indomit, *untameable.*

Inducaſt, *induced, introduced.*

Induement, *unduly.*

Indueront, *perſuade, bring into temper.*

Induiſant, *perſuading.*

Indult, *young, not of age.*

Induyent, *induct, put into.*

Infamateurs, *infamous.*

Infamiſe (nul), *no infamous perſon.*

Infect, *undone.*

Infer, *hell.*

Inferme propos (eſt il), *hath a firm purpoſe.*

Informacions, *inſtructions.*

Ingen, *wrong, deceit.*

Ingene (mal), *ill will.*

Ingenyès (les), *their wits.*

Ingyſt, *thrown out.*

Inhabilitations, *diſabilities.*

Inhable, *enabled.*

Inhonuteſſe, *ſhameleſs.*

Inhumeynement, *outrageouſly, cruelly.*

Injecture le maines, *laying hands on one.*

Inique, *wicked.*

Iniſe. *See Juis.*

Injuratours (lour), *thoſe who injured them.*

Inlagerie, *inlawry.*

Inneument, *renewal.*

Innig, *June.*

Inomée, *without a name.*

Inorer, *to be ignorant.*

Inquietaunce, *diſquiet.*

Inquietours, *perſons who moleſted incumbents in their benefices, by virtue of proviſions from the pope.*

Inquiſe, *found, inquired.*

Inraſer, *to pull up by the roots.*

Inſciement, *ignorantly.*

Inſeller, *to occupy a ſtall in a church.*

Inſenſes, *informed.*

Inſient, *pregnant.*

Inſtructes, *prepared.*

Inſtrum, *inſtrument.*

Intant a dire, *as much as to ſay.*

Interes, intereſſe, *injuries.*

Inteleſſe, *omitted, interlined.*

Internement, (a l'), *to the determination.*

Inthime, *an enthymeme; intimation.*

Inthimer la election (luy), *to intimate to him the election.*

Intime amie, *my dear friend inwardly.*

Intromittent, *intermeddle.*

Intruſours, *intruders.*

INV, *Jeſus.*

Invaire, *to invade.*

Invaſibles, *any artillery made of in an invaſion.*

Inveigner, *to find.*

Innynde

Inwynde deins la tesone des lains, *in winding within the fleeces of wool.*
Jo, joe, *I.*
Joalx, joiaus, *jewels.*
Joesnes, joesene, *young.*
Joel, joer, *day.*
Joerge, *swear.*
Joesdie, Joefdy, Joeudie, Joedy, Juesdy, *Thursday.*
Joial, *a jewel.*
Joiaus, *jewels.*
Joieront, *shall enjoy.*
Joiex, *joyful, happy.*
Joignet, Joign, Joil, *July.*
Joir, *obtain, enjoy.*
Joitement, *wording.*
Joiz, *enjoyed.*
Jone home, *young man.*
Jones, *John.*
Jonglours, *minstrels.*
Jont, *joint.*
Jor, *to them.*
Jor promis (no unt teu), *have not kept their promise.*
Jor, joure (al), *at the day.*
Jorci (d'), *of York.*
Jorgi, *George.*
Jorer, *to swear.*
Jornaunte (a la), *at day-break.*
Jorne, *day service.*
Jornee, *place, day.*
Jornee (la), *the taking the assize.*
Jorrours, jorres, *jurors, juries.*
Jorney, jorneie (a la), *in court.*
Jose, *thing.*
Jothed, *cast out.*
Jou, *I myself.*
Jou, *a cock.*
Jova, *played.*
Jouene chapon, *a young capon.*
Jouers, *stage-players.*
Jouette, *youth.*
Jougleur, *a minstrel.*
Jour en autre de journement, *daily.*
Jour (desques au) de huy, *to this day.*
Jour de huy en un moys (dedenz du), *within this day month.*
Jouree, *sworn.*
Journante, *before sun-rise, day-break.*
Journe, *a yoke.*
Journe, journee (a une), *at one day.*
Journe (a la), *at the court.*
Journee, *day, time.*
Journee (a la), *at the meeting.*
Jours (apres les), *after the decease.*
Joursmais (a tous), *for ever.*
Jous (tombe), *fell down.*
Joust, *just.*
Jouste, *near.*
Jouste, *according to.*

Joyer,

Joyer, *to enjoy.*
Joynant (del droit), *of the right joining to it.*
Joynture, *junction.*
Joyons, *rejoice.*
Joyssent a tenet, *have a right to hold.*
Joz a (tous), *for ever.*
Ire, *to go, to journey; also angry.*
Iretage, *heritage, inheritance.*
Irreis, Irrys, Irrois, *Irish.*
Irreit a terre, *would fall to the ground.*
Irreit pas (ne), *should not proceed.*
Irrer, *to journey, to perform their iters.*
Irrez avaunt, *shall proceed.*
Irrite, *unjust, void, of no effect.*
Irrours, *indignation.*
Irruer, *to subvert, to rush in upon.*
Is fors (il), *they go out.*
Iscint (de qi), *from whom issued.*
Isse (ne), *shall not issue.*
Isses (bailiffs des), *bailiffs thereof; or bailiffs of the isles, viz. of Sark, Alderney, &c.*
Issiersa, *shall chuse.*
Isoient, *are there.*
Isoit, *should be.*
Isp, *so near.*
Iss (ke), *which they.*
Issent, *they issue.*
Isser (ne pusse), *cannot go out.*
Isserene, *went out.*
Issint, *thus, so.*
Issir, *going out.*
Issist, *he went out.*
Issit, *it issues.*
Issue (lour), *their brood, their young.*
Issue, *an end.*
Issuit, *in such manner.*
Ist, *he shall be.*
Ist, *lies, issues.*
Istal, *such.*
Istra, ister, *shall issue out.*
Itel (d'ascun), *of any such person.*
Itel manere (en), *in such manner.*
Iter, *a ram.*
Juagus, *jewels.*
Jucques au nombre, *to the number.*
Iveer (en), *in winter.*
Juelyn, Yvelyn, Evelyn, *Dublin.*
Juen, *June.*
Juer (eardes a), *playing cards.*
Juerie (justices de la), *justices of the Jews.*
Juers, *George.*
Jues. *punishment, judgement.*
Jues, *Jews.*

Jueſdy, Juoſdy, *Thurſday.*
Juaus, juaux, jueles, *jewels.*
Juez, jues, *games.*
Jug (le), *the judge.*
Juge, *a yoke.*
Jugeable (ne ſoit), *cannot form any judgement.*
Jugeos (ſeront), *ſhall be ſworn.*
Juggrietz, *ſhall judge.*
Jugied, *adjudged.*
Juig, Juignel, *June.*
Juiſe, juiſſe, juyſe, *judgement, ſentence, vulgar purgation, fire-ordeal, water ordeal, ſingle combat.*
Juiſe ſans autre, *without other, judgement being paſſed* *.
Juiſe aut a la, *let him clear himſelf; let him go to his ordeal.*
Juiſe ſicome il appent (face faire), *that they may have ſuch juſtice as they deſerve.*
Jument, *an ox.*
Jumentz, *mares.*
Jundre (a), *to add to.*
Jung, Jun, *June.*
Junz, innz, *inner part.*
Jupardee, *jeopardy.*
Jur, jura, *day.*
Jure, jurere, *to ſwear.*
Juree, *a jury.*
Juree, jures, *an oath, oaths.*
Juretz, jurats, *ſworn.*
Juretz (entre), *took an oath to each other.*
Jurez, *one who is within the law.*
Jurges, *oaths.*
Jurgent, *ſwear.*
Jurifdie, *Tueſday.*
Jurpris, *adjourned.*
Jurre, *a liege-man.*
Jurromy (nous ne), *we do not ſwear.*
Juſte la coſtere, *near the coaſt.*
Juſtice, juſticer, juſticiee, *amenable to juſtice.*
Juſticement fort et dure, *penance fort and dure.*
Juſticer a lui (ne ſe voet), *refuſes to ſubmit to juſtice before him; to appear before him.*
Juſticer (ſe) ꝑ ley, *to juſtify or acquit himſelf by law.*
Juſticerie (de la), *of the juſticiary, to the judges.*
Juſtices, *brought to juſtice, made to do juſtice.*

* The trial by ordeal was aboliſhed in our courts of juſtice in 3 Hen. III. by an order of the king in council.

Juſticiables,

Juſticiables, juſtiſable, juſtifiable, *juſticiable, anſwerable to, ameſnable, liable to be ſummoned.*

Juſtifie per ſon ordinaire (ne voyle eſte), *will not be juſtified by his ordinary, will not offer to obey and perform the ſentence.*

Juſtifiere (a), *that juſtice may be executed.*

Juſtifiers (a), *to have judgement given.*

Juſtifiez, *regulated.*

Juſtizements, juſticements (les), *judgements.*

Juvent (de ſa), *from his youth.*

Juvaſſen, *rejoice.*

Juveſneſſe, *youth.*

Juy, *judgement; that is, of God; the vulgar purgation by fire or water.*

Juygnet, Juig, Juyn, Juyng, *June.*

Juyl, *July.*

Juzzer, *ſwear.*

Iz prion, *they pray.*

KA, *who.*

Kabal, *a horſe.*

Kage, *a cage, a place for confinement.*

Kalendrel (moys), *a calendar month.*

Kallez, *Charles.*

Kan, kes je puis, *as much as is in my power.*

Kardoil, *Carliſle.*

Kare, *for.*

Karreſme, Kariſme, *Lent.*

Kas (en), *in caſe.*

Kaſkun, *every.*

Kaſte, *chaſte.*

Kaunt, kanke, ke, *whatſoever.*

Ke ſe li, *that if the.*

Kee, ke, *that.*

Kelm et Newur (entre), *between Kelham and Newark.*

Kem alaſt, *that we muſt go.*

Kenes, *oaks.*

Kenteys (en), *by the Kentiſh law.*

Ker, *a city.*

Kere (a), *to procure.*

Keries, *carried.*

Kernes, *idle perſons, vagabonds.*

Kerver, *a carver.*

Keu, ko, *a tail.*

Keus, *thoſe.*

Keynes, keins, *aſh-trees.*

Keynes (en couper de), *in cutting down timber.*

Keyns, kiens, keynz, *oaks.*

Kideux, *kiddles.*

Knol, kne, *a hill.*

Knowr, knoppe d'or, *a knob of gold.*

Knout (roy), *king Canute.*
Koke, *a cook.*
Koungres, coungres, *congers.*
Ky, *which, whose.*
Kydes, *young kids.*
Kynebanton (le manoir de), *the manor of Kimbolton.*

L'rer, *to deliver.*
Lr̃es, *lettered, learned.*
La, lac, lat, *milk.*
La ou, la u, *whereas.*
La que (si), *until that.*
La (si), *so long.*
La v, la hu, *where.*
Labeur, *labour, work.*
Labor merted. *the other moiety.*
Labourer (a), *to work.*
Lacaye, *a lacquey.*
Laccat (sur), *when the bargain was made.*
Laces, *snares.*
Laces (per), *by door-falls.*
Lacharad (il), *he bought them.*
Laches, lasche (le plus), *the most lazy, cowardly, base, or pitiful person.*
Lachesse, *idleness, negligence.*
Lacs de seie, *laces of silk.*
Lacy, *there.*
Ladees, *dishes.*
Ladell d'argent, *a silver ladle.*
Laet drap. *broad-cloth.*
Lafferent, *they belong.*
Laganes, lageons, lagons, *gallons.*
Lagette, *a chest, box.*
Lai, laie, *law.*
Lai, laie, laye, *a plaint, complaint.*
Laid, *grievous.*
Laie (en), *for the relief, ease.*
Laie (de) a affeeir, *for assessing aids.*
Laiel, *lawful.*
Laieur, laiture, leur, *breadth.*
Laillent, *leave.*
Laine (que de la), *than of his own.*
Lain waidez, *woaded wool.*
Laingaige, *language.*
Laisant, *idle, slothful.*
Laiseantz arriere, *laying aside.*
Laisnes, *wool.*
Laisser (de), *to transfer.*
Laissier, *to prevent, omit, neglect.*
Laissiees, *neglected.*
Laissresies, *leave.*
Lait, *permit.*
Laituer, *science, erudition.*
Laiz, leez, *a legate.*
Lalt, *the high.*

L'an

L'an apres l'ansiwit, *after the year sued out.*
Lannde, *land, ground.*
Landroit, *again.*
Laners, lavers, *idle, sluggish.*
Lanes (dez), *of the laity.*
Langagiers, *abusive, scurrilous.*
Lange d'Engleterre (la), *the English nation.*
Lange de la balance (la), *the beam of the balance.*
Langue de Norm̃ (en la), *within the allegiance of Normandy, in the Norman language.*
Languyr, *to delay.*
Languy (de), *to wait for.*
Lanns mannus, *the lord of the manor.*
Lanques, langes, *tongues.*
Lanuz, *woollen.*
Lanyers (pointz), *leather points.*
Laoeure, *breath.*
Laps de temps, *loss of time.*
Laq, *lake.*
Larder (bone), *good booty.*
Larder (pur), *for ploughing.*
Lardyner, *the officer in the king's household who presided over the larder.*
Lareim, *larceny.*
Large ouster, *over measure.*
Large (mettre), *to let go at large.*
Largement (plus), *more easily.*
Largesse, *largeness.*
Larouns, *thieves.*
Larroneux, *thievish.*
Laschesse, *negligence.*
Laser, *a leprous person.*
Lasier, *to omit.*
Lasser (a), *to leave.*
Lastels, *hindrances, stops.*
Lasuz, *left.*
Laton, laten, *brass.*
Lature, *breadth.*
Lattiz, *lattice-work.*
Lattre, *the side.*
Lavours, *lavers.*
Lavours de la moneie, *washers of the coin.*
Laues devauntditz (des), *of the aforesaid places.*
Laust, *lawful.*
Laute, *praise.*
Lay (a), *to the law.*
Lay (en), *in allay.*
Lay est (q'a), *which belongs to him.*
Lay foy (en), *on the faith.*
Layde, *law, custom.*
Layes (les), *the laity, laymen.*
Layes (les), *the lackes.*
Layette, *in the box intitled.*
Laynes, *wool.*
Laynz, leans, *therein.*

Lays, *near.*
Laz de soie, *a lace of silk.*
Le, lee, *large, broad.*
Lea ou, *whereas.*
Lea, *pleased, willed.*
Lea, ley, *pasture ground.*
Leans, *within, in this place.*
Lease, *a leash.*
Leaser (p), *by falsifying, leasing.*
Leaure, leur, *breath.*
Leaus, leaux, *lawful, liege people, also loyal.*
Leaument, lealment, *lawfully, justly, loyally.*
Leaues (bailiffs de), *water-bailiffs.*
Leaute, *authenticknefs.*
Leaute (de), *of his legality, of being* rectus in curia.
Leawe, *water.*
Lebardz, *leopards, lions.*
Lebre, lep, *a hare*
Leccon (entendent la), *attend the election.*
Lectee, *milk.*
Lede, *grievous.*
Lede ou bele, *sick or healthy, handsome or ugly.*
Ledenge, ledenges, *damaged.*
Ledera, *shall hurt.*
Ledez, *hurt.*
Lee, *law.*
Lee, *large.*
Lee dever (serra), *shall be contented, glad to have.*
Lee, leeuz, *lead.*
Lees (justices,) *the justices.*
Lees (pur), *by lease.*
Lees, leez, *a lease, release.*
Lees, *them.*
Lees, lieez, lee, *pleased.*
Lees, *advice, award.*
Leesce, leeche, *joy.*
Leez (molt), *very glad.*
Leez, *obliged.*
Leger (de), *shortly.*
Leger (ne le creriez mie de), *would not give him the least credit.*
Legerement, *slightly, easily, shortly.*
Legerement subversion, *speedy subversion.*
Legerment (rewle), *a standing rule.*
Legerte de jaungle (de), *from a levity of discourse.*
Leges snrs (al), *to the liege lords.*
Legier, *brisk, light.*
Legier (de), *easily.*
Legs, *miles.*
Legurement, *slightly.*
Lei, *to him.*
Leias, *lawful.*
Leicher, licher, *to lick.*
Leid, *aid.*

Leie (la), *the law.*
Leigne, *line.*
Leignes, *wool.*
Leinynes, *linen.*
Leins, leing, *afar off.*
Leinz (de), *himself.*
L'eir, *the heir.*
Leir (fil foit), *if he can read.*
Leis, *them.*
Leife, *read, reads.*
Leife de dras, *lift of cloth, breadth of cloth.*
Leife, leiffie, leifible, *it shall be lawful.*
Leifir, leifer, *patience, leisure.*
Leiffe (lei), *omitted it.*
Leift, *deliver.*
Leifure, *reading.*
Leiuz, *therein.*
Leiz, *near.*
Leiz, *Lewis.*
Lem doit (coment), *how one ought.*
Lem foleit faire (fi come), *as used to be done.*
Lendemain de la clufe de Pafque, *the morrow after the close of Easter.*
Lendemeyn, *the morrow.*
Lenge, *linen.*
Lenn, *Lynn.*
Lenne, *Lincoln.*
Lenor, *the honor.*
Lenquaftre, *Lancaster.*
Lentz monet, *the month of March.*
Lenz, *there.*
Leoms Dieux, *we praise God.*
Leoneys, Loeneis (en), *in Lothian.*
Leour, *their.*
Leopertz, *leopards, lions.*
L'quelle (ou come), *as any other.*
Lequelleque, *whether.*
Le quen, *which.*
Ler, *their.*
Lerbe, *the grass.*
Lerce-hound, *a lurcher.*
Lernuement, *the commendation.*
Leiont, *they lie.*
Lerra, *may leave.*
Lerra morir (fe), *shall die.*
Lerre, liare, *a thief, a robber.*
Lerront (ne), *will not fail doing.*
Les, *last.*
Lefchancement (pur), *for the aggrandifing.*
Lefchewes, *trees fallen by chance, wind-falls.*
Lefcuverad, *he must, he ought.*
Lefe, *leave.*
Lefer, *to hurt.*
Les gentz, *lay people.*

Lesion, *hurting, wounding, damage, injury, detriment.*
Lessa, lesse, lessee, *omitted, left.*
Lessacent (qil les), *that they permit them.*
Lesse au baille, *let to bail.*
Lesseiz (ne), *do not omit.*
Lessent (les), *lease; let them.*
Lesser, *to omit, leave.*
Lessez, *disappointed.*
Lessez, lesset, *let go, omit.*
Lessisiems, *would have left.*
Lessoet (ne luy), *will not permit him.*
Lesteigne, *tin.*
Lesue, lesuz, *hurt, injured.*
Leswes, lesues, *pasture-ground.*
Let, *milk.*
Letanies, *littanies.*
Letergersle, *Luggershall.*
Lettereure, lettur (d'apprendre), *to levrn to read.*
Letra (la), *the letter.*
Lettre, *bill.*
Lettrure, *literature.*
Letture, *letter.*
Letuse, letise, *a little beast resembling the ermine, of a whitish grey colour.*
Levannt dit, *the aforesaid.*
Leve, *leave, consent.*
Leve, *risen up, built, erected, cast up.*
Levee (la), *the rising, the insurrection*
Lever, *to display, erect.*
Lever, *to stir up, bring up again.*
Lever (a), *to be levied.*
Lever (apres lur), *after their rising.*
Lever countre li, *rise to him.*
Lever (pur), *to relieve.*
Levere, leverers, leurierers, leveriers, levoiers, *greyhounds.*
Leverer, *a lurcher, a tumbler dog.*
Leverer (a un), *at a drinking place.*
Leverez, *liveries.*
Levours, *those who levy any tax.*
Leu, leus, leust, *lawful.*
Leu e), *the place.*
Leu, lect, lict, *a bed.*
L'eucres, *the increase.*
Leuement, *lawfully.*
Leues, leuis, *ditches.*
Leucz, *placed.*
Leukes (trois), *three leagues.*
Leukes, lewkes, lewes, lenks, *miles.*
Leur, leure, *breadth.*

Leure,

Leure (a meiſmes), *at the ſame time.*
Leures, *hares.*
Leus (de), *of thoſe.*
Leus, leulx (toz), *all places.*
Leute, *loyalty.*
Leuthien, *Lothian.*
Leuve, leuvad, *a foreſt.*
Leux, *their.*
Leux, *lawful.*
Lew, *place.*
Lew (vers la), *towards the eaſt.*
Lewe, *read.*
Lewe gentz, *lawful men.*
Lewes, lewe, leuz, *read.*
Ley (la), *the river Lee.*
Ley court, *lay court.*
Ley (faire la), *to wage law.*
Ley, lea, *paſture-ground.*
Ley (ſuz), *againſt him.*
Leye (la), *the law.*
Leyed, leyde, *heinous hurt, hurtful.*
Leynes, *wool.*
Leyoins, leyns, *therein, within.*
Leyr de la terre, *from the foundation, from the ground.*
Leyres dez chivalers (de la) *of the wages of the knights of the ſhire.*
Leyſe (en), *in breadth.*
Leyſir, *leiſure.*
Lez, *laws.*
Lez, *the.*
Lez, lieux, *them, thoſe.*
Lez, *nigh, near.*
Lez, *glad.*
Leze majeſt, *treaſon.*
Lezs, *in length.*
Li, *his, they, the, to him.*
Li (de), *from him.*
Li ditz, *the ſaid.*
Li du troie, *pound of troy weight.*
Li uſſunt porveu, *had provided him.*
Lia, lie, lieuz, *read.*
Liat, *lawful.*
Liaux, *lawful men.*
Liaz, liacz, *bundles.*
Lib, libe, *life.*
Lib de terre, *liberata terræ.*
Libard (ovec le touche del teaſt de), *with the touch of the leopard's head.*
Liberat, *free.*
Licette, *lawful.*
Liche, *liege.*
Licitement, *lawfully.*
Licker, *to lick.*
Licours, *liquors.*
Lict, lect, liech, *a bed.*
Lie, liée, lieiſon, *bound.*
Lie, *pleaſed.*
Lie (de la), *of the lineage.*
Lief, leof, *rather.*
Liefgent hu et cri, *levy the hue and cry.*

Lieflode,

Lieflode, liflode, *an eſtate for life.*
Lieges, lieux, *leagues, miles.*
Lieges, *leagues, truces.*
Liens, lientz, *therein; places.*
Lieppars, *leopards.*
Lier, *to alledge.*
Lier, *to read.*
Liers, *priſoners.*
Lies (queux ne ſont), *who are not put into the derennary.*
Lievent, *levy.*
Lieves (per), *by miles.*
Lievies (de leur), *of their heirs.*
Lieu, *a wolf.*
Lieu (pur), *by way of exception.*
Lieu en ceo (aver), *take hold of that.*
Lieure, *a pound weight.*
Lieure, leiure (le), *the book.*
Lieures (avant ces), *before theſe times.*
Lieux, *them.*
Lieux (nulle de), *none of the deputies.*
Lieux, *bonds.*
Lieuz, *room.*
Liez, *places.*
Lige, liguie, *bond.*
Liges (ſes), *his liege ſubjects.*
Ligeſſe, *legiance.*
Lighes, *leagues.*
Ligialtie (la), *the allegiance.*
Ligne, *ſex.*
Ligne de pierrereries (un), *a circle of ſtones.*
Lignie, lin, *lineage, race.*
Ligninies, *tribes.*
Liment, *waſh, filt.*
Limiteers, *limited.*
Linage, *blood.*
Linaige de la mer (ſur le), *on the ſea-coaſt.*
Line biline, *the collateral or bye-line.*
Line de Sendale, *linen of Cendal* *.
Linge, *a line.*
Linge teel, *linen cloth.*
Linquer, *to leave.*
Lingues, *tongues.*
Lins, *wool.*
Linure, *lining.*
Lintheux, linthes, *ſheets.*
Lio hyl, *there.*
Liouns, *lions.*
Lire (preſentee en), *preſented in writing.*
Lirr, *their.*
Lirreit mye (il ne), *it would not be lawful.*
Liſre, *to be read.*

* See Du Freſne, *Cendalum.*

Liſt,

Liſt, liſe, liſible, *lawful.*
Litere, littour (de), *litter.*
Lit morant, *death bed.*
Lith (al), *to the bed.*
Littīme, *lawful.*
Live, *livery, or delivery.*
Livelode, *livelihood.*
Livere (a la), *to the delivery, or livery.*
Livere (et vous), *and you deliver it.*
Livere (ſon), *his livery (for a ſervant.)*
Liver e ſoun (potius, limereſoun), *a prebend, a ſervice* *.
Liveree, *pound.*
Liverer ſuys, *to deliver up, ſurrender.*
Liverees, livereſons, *liverys.*
Liveres, *liveries, aſſignments.*
Liveres de terre, *liberata terræ.*
Liveriad, *deliver, offer.*
Liverour, *the perſon who delivered.*
Livers, *hares.*
Liverſe, *deliverance.*
Livrees, *livres.*
Liũ, *book.*
Liu, *place.*
Liu, *bound.*
Liu faire prendre (de), *to cauſe him to be taken.*
Liu eſt grante, *is granted to him.*
Liu (pres de), *near him, about him.*
Liure, *pound.*
Liuree (de foureez), *furred with hair furr.*
Loar, *their.*
Loaumes, *we allow*
Locil (potiùs, loeil) ſur (pour avoir), *to have an eye over.*
Locoice, *bribe* †.
Loctenant, *lieutenant.*
Lodis, *blith, jocund.*
Loe (jeo vous), *I recommend it to you.*
Loement, *judgement, opinion, deciſion.*
Loer, *to commend, praiſe.*
Loer, *leeward.*
Loer enſoit (melius, loez en ſoil) notre Seignur, nous ſumes (come), *as praiſed be God, we are.*
Loeys, *Lewis.*
Loftes, *forſter child.*
Loia, *thanked.*
Loial, *lawful, true.*
Loial avyce, *legal cauſe, advice.*

* See Ryley Pl. Parl. 14 Edw. II. p. 415, and Parl. Rolls of that year.

† Vid. Rot. Parl. vol. I. p. 275. Pet. 13. Potius lowire. Hale's MS.

Loians,

Loians, *hired.*
Loiastes, *permitted.*
Loie, *commend, approve.*
Loiens, *bonds.*
Loient (qe), *who wash.*
Loier, loyer, loiuer, *fee, reward; farm.*
Loiez soit Dieu, *God be praised.*
Lointaignes, *remote.*
Loisible, *lawful.*
Lomez (les), *the looms.*
Longament, lonc tens, *a long time.*
Longayne, *a house of office.*
Longein, *long, a long time.*
Longement (tant), *as long as.*
Longteyne, longetisme pays (en), *in a foreign, distant country.*
Longue (plus), *farther.*
Longue (a la), *at length.*
Looms (nous vous), *we commend you.*
Looms, loaumes, *we grant.*
Loos, *advice, reward, reputation.*
Lor, *them.*
Lor, lower, *hire, reward, bribe.*
Lor (envers les), *towards their men.*
Lors, *their, then.*
Los, lois, loz, *praise.*
Lose chart (en con), *in a loose paper.*
Losereynt (ne), *dared not.*
Loture de money (le), *the washing of money.*
Lotux, *suckles.*
Lou, *place.*
Lou, lieu, *wolf.*
Loueez, *hired.*
Louis, *far.*
Lour (a meisme), *at the same time.*
Lour (e la), *and of their own.*
Lour (de), *of their goods.*
Loure, *them, themselves.*
Lourgulary, lourderie, *inhumanity, or any villainous act.*
Lous (doctour en), *doctor in laws.*
Lous, *the, them.*
Lousement (m̄ney), *much to the surprise* *.
Louy (du), *of it.*
Louz, *estimated, valued.*
Lovage, *hiring, loan.*
Love, *rewarded.*
Lovers, *rewards.*
Lowage, *possession.*
Lowance, lowange, *a hiring.*
Lowe (pur), *to retain, to hire.*
Lower (pur), *for gain, for maintenance.*

* Vid. Rot. Parl. Vol. II. p. 77. pet. 23. Potius m̄veyleusement. Hale's MS.

Lower,

Lower, luer, lowir, *a reward, fee, bribe, wages.*
Lowere (pur), *to work.*
Lowis, Loys, *Lewis.*
Loy (de), *of allay.*
Loyer, *to award, advise.*
Loyer, *reward, service.*
Loys, lois, los, *praise, glory.*
Loyse, *lawful.*
Loysomus, *let us rest.*
Loynteins heires, *remote, collateral heirs.*
Loyntenus gentz, *people who live afar off.*
Loyntime degree, *a remote collateral degree.*
Loz, *praise.*
Lu, *the.*
Lu, *theirs.*
Lu, *place.*
Lu, lue, leu, *light.*
Lude, *play.*
Lue, *he, them.*
Luer, *reward.*
Luer raisonable, *reasonable price.*
Lues, *miles.*
Lues, lus, luwe, luez, *read.*
Lui Rois, *the king.*
Lui seaus, *their seals.*
Lui, luis (seon), *his place.*
Lui (en qui), *in whatsoever place.*
Luie, *a league.*
Luire, *to shine.*
Luist, *lawful.*
Luites de point in point, *read article by article.*
Lum, *a man, any one.*
Lumble, *navel.*
Lumere, *light.*
Lunc dei, *long or middle finger.*
Lundr' (a), *at London.*
Luner (jour), *the lunar day.*
Lung, *the one.*
Lungement, lungge, *long.*
Lure, lur, lurr, lu, *them, their, theirs.*
Luri, *an otter.*
Lus, *places.*
Lus, *read.*
Lus, lius, tenanz, *lieutenants.*
Luse, luce est, *the use is.*
Luse, *playing cards.*
Lute (a la), *at a wrestling.*
Luy (le), *the place.*
Luy, *it.*
Luy, *them.*
Luz, *places.*
Ly, li, *him.*
Ly, *law.*
Lyance, *allegiance.*
Ly ann jour done (en), *and have given him a day.*
Lyaz, files, *bundles.*
Lye, *read.*
Lye, *merry, chearful.*
Lye estes, *you are bound.*

Lyege, *liege subjects.*
Lyens, *therein.*
Lyer, *to bind.*
Lyer (de), *to alledge.*
Lyer (autrement), *in any other manner fix.*
Lyereit bien, *would sufficiently bind.*
Lyeur, *a brook.*
Lym, *lime.*
Lymite, *limits.*
Lymitours, limitours, *limits.*
Lynge tayl, *fringed linen.*
Lysa bien, *read well.*
Lyse, lyst, *lawful.*
Lyt, *bed*; *licence, let.*
Lyu, *place.*

M, *same.*
Mc̃es, *wares.*
Y-me, *house.*
Mẽtz, *best.*
Mesch', *mischief.*
Mk̃s, *marcs.*
Mr̃, mr̃a, *shall shew.*
Mr̃e, *shew.*
Mr̃e, *master.*
Ms̃, *same.*
Mac, *son.*
Macegrefs, *fishmongers, who buy and sell stolen flesh, knowing the same to be stolen.*
Macel, *a butcher.*
Macheniaes, *mathematiciens, persons who pretend to discover secrets by the position and motion of the stars. Those who professed this art were commonly called* mathematici, *drawers of schemes and calculations; under which name they are condemned in both the codes *, and they were infamous, not only under the Christian administration, but also under the old Romans.*
Macheronerie, *masonry.*
Maderez (draps), *cloth maddered.*
Madlard (un), *a drake.*
Madle (heir), *heir male.*
Maein le roy, *hands of the king.*
Mael, *an halfpenny.*
Maénéresse, *a mediatrix*; *a judge.*
Maere, *mother.*
Maester, *master.*
Maeur, *a mayor.*
Maffait (null), *no mischief.*
Magnies, maisnies, mesnie, *family, household, retinue.*

* Cod. Theod. l. 9. tit. 16. Cod. Just. l. 9. tit. 18.

Magre,

Magre, maugre, *in despite of, against.*

Mahemes, mahaigne, mahayn, *maimed.*

Mahereme, *timber.*

Mahi, Mahie, *Matthew.*

Mahom, *Mahomet.*

Maide (si Dieu), *so help me, God.*

Maige (judge), *a judge who presides over a subaltern jurisdiction.*

Mageste (la), *the Trinity.*

Maign, *great.*

Maignee devant, *brought before.*

Maignent, *live, dwell.*

Majeure, *major.*

Mail, maylle, *an half-penny.*

Maimement, *especially.*

Main, *in the morning.*

Main-a-main, *immediately.*

Mainables, *amenable, distrainable.*

Mainburnie, *guardianship or government.*

Maincraftes, *handicrafts.*

Maindres, mains, *small, less.*

Maine en gule (d'), *from hand to mouth.*

Maine (come sa), *as part of his household.*

Maine (a soy defẽdre ꝑ sa), *to wage battle.*

Mainor (le), *the tenancy, the occupation.*

Mainorable, meinorable, *manurable, tenable, demiseable, lying in tenure.*

Main oeure, meinoure, meynoure (a), *with the manor.*

Mainour (la), *the work, the repairing.*

Mainoverer, *to manure.*

Mainpes, *mainprised.*

Mains (per que) quecunque il vient, *howsoever it came to pass.*

Mains (a tot le), *with all the hands, viz. chaplains and singing-men.*

Mains (jureront en noz), *shall swear in our presence.*

Mains vraie, *untrue.*

Maint, *much, many.*

Maintenant, *presently.*

Maintes fois, *many times.*

Maintion, *mention.*

Maintz, maints, *less.*

Mainuelx mestiers, *manual occupations.*

Mainy (ma), *my family.*

Mair, *mayor.*

Maire, *mother.*

Maire (a), *to marry.*

Mairiaux, *material.*

Maisne, *younger.*

Maisne (lor), *their family.*

Maisoner, *to build, repair.*

Maist Diex, *please God.*

Maiste, *majesty.*

Maistrez,

Maiſtrez, *maſters.*
Maiſtrie, *management, influence, power, dominion.*
Maite, *moiety.*
Makement, *contrivance.*
Mal, maletts, malies, *bags.*
Mal (a) tort tiendroit lieu, *with much leſs propriety would it lie.*
Mal (de) ou pyz, *worſe and worſe.*
Mal paiez, *diſſatisfied.*
Mal voillance, malveullantz (p), *through ill will.*
Maladif, maledif, *ſickly, ſick, afflicted.*
Mald, *Matilda.*
Maldiſpouſee (molt), *much indiſpoſed.*
Male (la), *the mail, the portmanteau.*
Male toute, *entirely bad, good for nothing.*
Maleſe (mult a), *very uneaſy.*
Malets, *cloakbags.*
Malfez, *wicked, evil.*
Malmenez, malmeſne, *evilly kept.*
Malney, malvey, *guilty of a miſdemeanor, contumacious.*
Malrais, *evil.*
Maltalent, maltalenz, *ſpite, indignation, rancour.*
Malveilles, malveiſnes, *miſaemeanours.*
Malveiſt, malves, malvois, *evil, an offence.*
Malurez, Cões, *evil, ſeditious commoners.*
Malx, mals (iſſue), *iſſue male.*
Man, *a Norman.*
Manablement eiſſille (per), *perpetual baniſhment.*
Manantz, manans, *reſident.*
Manas (brefe de), *writ of mainprize.*
Manaſors, *pledges, mainpernors.*
Manaſſables, *threatening, menacing.*
Manaunts genz (bon), *houſekeepers of credit.*
Manche (que vous n'aurez), *that you will never fail.*
Manconages, *manſion-houſes.*
Mandaſſent (qils), *that they ſend.*
Mande, *commanded.*
Mande (en tien), *in ſuch manner.*
Mandementz, *writs of mandamus.*
Mandez, *ſent.*
Mandiens, *beggars.*
Mandient, *curſe.*
Mandiſſiens, *commanded.*

Mandre (a), *to amend.*

Maneceantz, *threatening.*

Maner, manoyre, *a manor.*

Maneer (vey le) potiùs, vey le maneer, *will bring* *.

Maneires, maners, manies, maners, *manors.*

Manere (la), *the custom.*

Maneys (en la), *in the hands.*

Manger (sans repris de), *without giving any wages.*

Mangerie (tienge), *keeps a table for his retainers.*

Manguay (je ne), *I did not omit.*

Manguement, *fault, slip.*

Mangeries (a), *in the kitchen, at the table.*

Maniere forsque (en), *in manner but.*

Maniple, *handful.*

Manique, *a madman.*

Manning, *a day's work.*

Manors, *manors.*

Manour (ove), *with the mainour, with the goods in their hands.*

Mans (les), *the evils.*

Manse, *a farm.*

Manses, *hides of land.*

Mante, *he commands.*

Mantinge, *maintain.*

Manuester, *to filch, to thieve.*

Manulx, *manual.*

Manure, *occupy.*

Manusser, manassier, *threatened.*

Manyee, *handled, under consideration.*

Manyemens, *management, conduct, administration.*

Mappe, *a cloth, a table-cloth.*

Maras, mares, marche, marreys, maries, marys, *marsh-ground.*

Marastre, *mother-in-law.*

Marces (se sount), *have settled themselves.*

March (de VIII), *at eight marks.*

Marche, marchie (le), *the market-price.*

Marchande (ville), *market-town.*

Marchant, (nul alleve), ne prive, *no merchant, stranger, or domestic.*

Marche, *territory, neighbourhood.*

Marche (a), *to market.*

Marchees de terre (100), *land valued at* 100 *marks a year.*

Marchent, *adjoin to, are bounded by.*

* Vid. Rot. Parl. vol. I. p. 10. pet. 45. Potius *veyle.* Hale's MS.

Marches (par les), *in the market towns.*

Marches, *marches, frontier cities or towns between England and Wales, England and Scotland.*

Marches, *marks.*

Marchesche, *the feast of the Annunciation, celebrated in March.*

Marchis, *marquis.*

Marchissans (sont), *are bordering.*

Marcier, *to pay.*

Marcolfe (en la chambre), *the triers of petitions in parliament for foreign parts used to sit in this chamber.*

xx l. marcz, 20,000 *marks.*

Mare (de toute), *of all manner.*

Mareanz, maronniers, *mariners.*

Marenne, *land bordering on the sea.*

Mareschall, *marshal.*

Mareschaucie, *Marshalsea.*

Mareſches, *grain sown in March, spring-corn.*

Mariages, *marriage portion.*

Mariage (a son), *for her marriage portion.*

Margeries, *marquisetts.*

Mariole, *the image of the virgin Mary.*

Marisne (loy), *marine law.*

Maritassent, *married.*

Maritismes (charbons), *sea-coals.*

Marlers, *marl-pits.*

Marrie (del), *of the husband.*

Marriglier, merriglier, maruglies, marguelier, *a church-warden, a sacristan, or sexton.*

Marris, *surprised, concerned.*

Marroch (Streites de), *Straights of Morocco or Gibraltar.*

Mars (deux), *two marks.*

Martens, *hammers.*

Marteror, *the feast of all saints.*

Marthied in rei (al), *at the king's market.*

Martirizer, *martyred.*

Martrons (furres de), *furr of martern or marten.*

Marveis, *evil.*

Mary et espeux (a loial), *for her lawful husband and spouse.*

Mas, *but.*

Mase (sergent de), *serjeant at the mace.*

Maser, mazer (un), *a cup or goblet.*

Masere, *entries, passages, walks, grounds.*

Masle (le), *the male.*

Massoner, *to sing mass.*

Mastre, *a martyr.*

Mastres, *mistress.*

Mat,

Mat, *a fool, a ſot.*
Mat le, *the chagrin, concern.*
Mate, *Matilda.*
Maten, *morning.*
Mater, *matter, buſineſs.*
Mater (ſont), *are the means, are contrived.*
Materiells peches, *temporal offences.*
Matta, *placed.*
Mattire, matirez, *matter.*
Mavaſtiers, *wicked doers.*
Mauclerk, *ignorant, unlearned.*
Mauclum (roy), *king Malcon.*
Mauduit, *ill conditioned.*
Mauveiſte, mauveſte, mauvaiſte, mauveys, mavoite, *offence.*
Maufeteur, *offender.*
Maufez, *demons.*
Mauls, *miſchief.*
Maumenes, *ill-treated.*
Maumis, *maimed.*
Maunches reverſes (ſes), *his ſleves turned back.*
Maundaſt, *ſend.*
Maundable, *to be directed.*
Maunder, *to command.*
Maupae, *ill-treated.*
Maupiteux, *inexorable.*
Maures, *a lyar.*
Mauriot ja meſtier (il ne), *there would be no occaſion for me.*
Mauſbaretz, *evil contentions, ill-grounded ſuits.*
Mauſeſheure (pur), *for avoiding it.*
Mavys, mavos, *evil.*
Mayaouſt, *the middle of Auguſt, the aſſumption.*
Maydeneſtan, *Maidſton.*
Mayen (par), *by means.*
Maylee de pain, *a halfpenny worth of bread.*
Mayles, *halfpence.*
Mayn de eſtre, *right-hand.*
Mayn (de) en auter, *laying our hands on the altar.*
Maynauntie, *manſion-houſe.*
Mayne (la), *the maſter and mariners of a ſhip.*
Mayneall, *in company with.*
Maynerent, *maimed.*
Maynes, (de) a mayns, *at leaſt.*
Mayneur, mainour, maynoeure, *work.*
Maynpaſt, meynpaſt, *houſehold, family, dependance.*
Mayns valaynt, *of the leaſt value.*
Mayns, *matins.*
Mayntz demonſtrantz, *many remonſtrances.*
Mayor, *greater.*
Maz, *a maſt.*
Mazer (hanap de), *a bowl made of mazer.*
Meane, *middle.*

Meane (en le), *in the manner.*
Mear, *ſea.*
Meas, *but.*
Meaſon, *room.*
Meaſons, *nitches.*
Meaur droit, *meer right.*
Meaux, *mere*; *beſt.*
Mecogneues, *unknown.*
Mecreance, *ſuſpicion.*
Mectez en execution, *put into execution.*
Mectre, *to expend.*
Medfee, *a reward, a bribe.*
Mediate (per le), *by the mediation.*
Mediſſe manere (par), *in the ſame manner.*
Medle, *mixed, compounded.*
Medleſe, medle, *an affray, diſturbance.*
Medlure de peche (par), *by blending offences.*
Medlure (pur la), *on account of the mixing.*
Medoine, *the river Medway.*
Medu temps (en le), *in the mean time.*
Mee (ne a), *has not.*
Meel, *honey.*
Meement, meeſmement, *namely, eſpecially.*
Meement, *merrily.*
Meen amy, *a middle friend.*
Meen (come), *as a mediator.*
Meener, *to produce.*
Meenereſſe, *mediatrix.*
Meenner, *an arbitrator, mediator.*
Meer (hors de), *beyond ſea.*
Mees, *moved*; *mediators.*
Mees, meeſe, *meſs.*
Mees (des), *of meat.*
Meevement, *diſturbance, commotion.*
Mefet, *offence.*
Meffet, *miſdone.*
Meffere, *to do miſchief.*
Megme (la), *the ſame.*
Megnes, *brought.*
Meheynee (leva la), *raiſed the hue and cry.*
Meiere, *mother.*
Meignal, meynal, *menial.*
Meignee, meime, meiny, *family, houſehold, company.*
Meigte breve (ili ad), *there is many a writ.*
Meilles, *beſt, greateſt.*
Meillour, *mulier.*
Meiltz, *the better.*
Mein, *hand.*
Mein, mien, mines, *mine.*
Meinalx, *meſſengers.*
Meindre age (la), *infancy, the minority.*
Meinere action (de nul), *in any inferior action.*

Meines,

Meines, *inferior perſons.*
Meines ſages, *indiſcreet, illiterate perſons.*
Meines, *nor.*
Meinez, *many.*
Meingtenuz, *maintained, aſſiſted.*
Meinoure, meynours, *with the manor.*
Meire, *mayor.*
Meins q̄, *leſs than, under.*
Meins, meindre, *leſs.*
Meins (a tote le), *at the leaſt.*
Meins bone diſcretion, *indiſcretion.*
Meins de bien meignent, *bring fewer goods.*
Meins (al), *into the hands.*
Meins, meien (sauntz), *without meſne.*
Meins miſes ſur ſeintz, *laying our hands on the goſpels.*
Meinſt (le), *the leaſt.*
Meint, meine, *dwells, reſides.*
Meintenant, *then, preſently.*
Meintenems, *maintain.*
Meint manera, *many ways.*
Meintroms, *will maintain.*
Meinure (la), *the work.*
Meinz choſes, *things of ſmall value.*
Meircient, *buy and ſell.*
Meis, *more.*
Meis, *a month.*
Meiſan, *houſe.*
Meiſent, *put.*
Meiſme, *ſame, the ſame, himſelf.*
Meiſement, *in like manner.*
Meiſnee, meine, *houſehold, family.*
Meiſſent en reſpit, *ſhould be reſpited.*
Meiſſom, *ſhould beſtow.*
Meiſſoins avant, *produce.*
Meiſſoins (que nous), *that we ſhould put.*
Meiſt, meite, *put, contained in.*
Meiſt, *need.*
Meiſter (q'il a), *that it is neceſſary.*
Meiſtr̃, meiſters, meſtre, *maſter.*
Meiſtrie, *maſterſhip, magiſtracy.*
Meiſtrie, *neceſſary.*
Meiſtymours de querell, *maintainers of quarrels, diſputes, ſuits.*
Meiter, meictre, *to put, place.*
Meleour, *better.*
Meliealx, melx, *beſt.*
Melle, *honey.*
Melle, *an affray.*
Melle (ſe) de la vente, *meddle with the ſale.*

Meller (a), *to blend, mix, interfere in, to interpose.*

Mellez (ne se devient), *ought not to intermeddle in it.*

Mellieu, *middle.*

Melz, meltz, *better.*

Membres (per prendre), *by caption of goods.*

Men, *my.*

Men temps, *mean time.*

Mēn (en), *in a state of insanity.*

Menable, *amesnable, brought, induced.*

Menageoers, *farmers, husbandmen.*

Menant, *dwelling, residing.*

Menassables (ne), *not to be menaced.*

Menassent, menastez (lui), *lead him.*

Menauntise, *a settled concern, a place of residence.*

Menbra, *remember.*

Mende (la), *amends, satisfaction.*

Mend' provereit, *should make the best proof.*

Mendinantz, mendians, *beggars.*

Mendre, *least.*

Mendres, *less.*

Mene gentz (de les), *of the middling people.*

Mene judgement (sans), *without mesne judgement.*

Mene pris, *at a low price.*

Menee a r̃, *brought to answer.*

Menee, mene (la), *the hue and cry.*

Menenges, *household, dependants, menial servants.*

Mener, *to manage, conduct.*

Menes, menees, *brought, treated.*

Menestralcie (par colour de), *under pretence of being a minstrel.*

Mengier (de), *from eating.*

Meni, menuz dymes, *small tythes.*

Meniez, *made.*

Menir, *to bring.*

Menis (et volons ja le), *and we will also.*

Menistres, *ministers, officers.*

Menne, mene, menes people, *inferior people.*

Mennes, *less, small.*

Mennes peches, *small offences.*

Mennes keynes, *small oaks.*

Menour, *manager.*

Menour (frere), *friars minors.*

Menre,

Menre, *brought in, drove in.*
Menront (les), *will conduct them.*
Menſoynes, *lies.*
Menſure, *meaſure.*
Ment, *much.*
Mente, *mint.*
Mentineez, *maintenance.*
Mentiner, *mention.*
Mentir, *to lie, to ſay what is falſe.*
Mentor, menter, *a lyar.*
Mentre (foy), *breach of faith.*
Menty, mentu, *have lied, ſaid what is falſe.*
Mentz, a mentz, *for the beſt.*
Mentz (lour), *their beſt.*
Menues baillifes, *inferior bailiffs.*
Menure, *remain.*
Menuz choſes, *ſmall things.*
Meour droit, *the better right.*
Meoſiſme (ſoi) de archer, *went a ſhooting.*
Mer, meer bank, *the ſea-ſhore.*
Mer (de la) d'Eſcoce, *the marches of Scotland.*
Merce, meer, *mercy, grace.*
Mercez, *wares.*
Merchal, *marſhall.*
Merche del merche, *marked with the mark or ſtamp.*
Merchez, *markets.*
Merchie des vivres, *the rate or market price of victuals.*
Merchiez, *ſigned.*
Merci (ſur), *upon favour.*
Mercia, merchia, *thanked.*
Mere, *mature.*
Mere, *only, abſolute.*
Meri et miſti (juriſdictions), *juriſdictions mere and mixed.*
Meriſme, maeriſme, mermi, *timber.*
Meritorie, *meritorious.*
Merk, merches lettres, *letters of marque.*
Merkedy, Merdie, Mercuredi, *Wedneſday.*
Merrour, *a looking-glaſs.*
Mers, *marſhes.*
Mers, mercz, *wares.*
Mers (la), *the mercy.*
Merted, *moiety.*
Mertlage, *martyrology.*
Merture (de ce), *of this matter.*
Meruſt, *cauſeth, occaſions.*
Merym, merime, merin, merrien, meriſme, maeriſme, mermi, *timber.*
Merz, *amerciaments; merchandize.*
Mes, *month.*
Mes, *but, from thenceforth, afterwards, ſtill, again,*

again, no longer, no more, also, us, we.

Mes (a toutz jour), *for ever after.*

Mes ja, *but yet, neverthe-less.*

Mes que per, *but only by.*

Mes sicome est conteyne, *than is contained.*

Mes sil voit server, *but whether it will serve.*

Mes que (que), *that as soon as.*

Mes (pur), *out of mischief.*

Mes avegne, *evil, misfortune happens, befalls.*

Misceient, mescent, *intermix.*

Mesch, *mischief, misfortune.*

Mésces ortieux, *the middle toes.*

Mescez, *accuse.*

Meschet (si il), *if he miscarries.*

Mesconnussant, *ignorant.*

Mescreables gentz, *persons not to be believed.*

Mescreauntz, *miscreants, infidels, unbelievers, heretics.*

Mescruz, *suspected, guilty.*

Mescusse, *excuse.*

Mesease, *trouble, misfortune.*

Mesel, meseal, mesiau, *a leper.*

Mes entendetz (vous), *you misunderstand.*

Meseaux deges, *leprous persons.*

Meseise de cuer (a), *uneasy in our mind.*

Mesfere, *misdeed.*

Mesfesours, *criminals.*

Mesiuil, mesuil, *a messuage, a house.*

Mesire, *monsieur.*

Meskerdy, *Wednesday.*

Mesmes, *himself.*

Mesn en repons, *put to answer.*

Mesnage, *of the household.*

Mesnam (le), *took him, led him away.*

Mesnaunce, *bringing in.*

Mesnauntes, *bringing.*

Mesne (a la), *in the middle.*

Mesne (le court sera), *the court shall be adjourned.*

Mesnee, mesnie, meyne, *family.*

Mésnee (ee de sa), *to be within his jurisdiction.*

Mesnees, *managed.*

Mesner seroit (qant), *when it should come in question.*

Mesnes (par diverses), *by diverse means.*

Mesnier, *a public cryer.*

Mesnours, *leaders, conductors.*

Mesnours

Mesnours des querelx, *bearers of quarrels.*

Mesoing, *negligence.*

Meson, *a house.*

Mesonage, *house-room, warehouse-room.*

Mesprendre, *to misbehave, offend, mistake.*

Mespressure, *offence, misconduct.*

Mespriorai (de ceo), *of this I will exculpate myself.*

Mespris, *offended, done amiss.*

Mesprison, *misprision.*

Mess, *mass.*

Message, *a messenger, one retained in the service of another, a dependant.*

Messagerie (par colour de), *under pretence of being a messenger.*

Messages, *an ambassador, a nuncio.*

Messeist, *evil intreat.*

Messeles, *middle; diseased.*

Messeles (dens), *the cheek-teeth.*

Messer, messour, *an officer in a manor, who had the overlooking and care of the fields in the time of harvest, and for which he was intitled to certain profits.*

Messerie, *seignory, dominion.*

Messilerie, *a lazaretto, an hospital for lepers.*

Messire, *my lord.*

Messire vos garde, *the Lord preserve you.*

Messoins, *had a mind.*

Messoinges, *lyes.*

Messoit, *but had he been.*

Messures, *measures, terms.*

Mester (haut), *grand master.*

Mester de counter (le), *the science of pleading.*

Mester soit (si), *if there be occasion.*

Mestier (le), *the business, trade, occupation.*

Mestre, *mystery.*

Mestre, *be committed.*

Mestres, *masters, clients.*

Mestrier, *to get the mastery, dominion.*

Mesuenges (lour), *their household, dependants.*

Mesurable, *reasonable, moderate, proportionate.*

Mesurable manner (en), *in a proportionable manner.*

Mesurage (pur le), *for the measure.*

Mesure terre, *land containing about forty ox gangs.*

Mesure (le), *the terms.*

Mesure (preigne), *be moderate.*

Mesure

Mesure rase, rasen (par), *by a measure stricken.*

Mesurer, *to mow.*

Mẽt, *to put.*

Met, *puts.*

Met a cõnseil, *asked the advice of.*

Metable a mainprize, *to be let to mainprize, mainpernable.*

Metere (de), *to place, assign, to put.*

Metir, *offers.*

Metre, *to pledge.*

Metre (le), *master.*

Mette peyne (ne), *let them spare no pains.*

Mettes, *bounds.*

Mettes (faux), *false measures.*

Mettid, *charges.*

Mettier, *the moiety.*

Mettive, *harvest-time.*

Mettre (a), *to set, fix.*

Mever (e), *to move.*

Meves, *moved.*

Meu, meus, *commenced, moved, induced.*

Meuchz, meuth, meulx, meux, meuẑ, meutz, meultz, *better.*

Meult (semble pur le), *it seems best.*

Meulz vaues, *most substantial.*

Meur, meour droit, *better, best right.*

Meures, *mature, ripe, steady.*

Meurra (les), *shall muster them.*

Meurisson, *maturity.*

Meurte, *maturity, wisdom.*

Meusengs, *those of his family, his dependants.*

Meusmes (nous), *we moved.*

Meussent, *stirred up.*

Meut, *a kennel.*

Meuth (I vient), *it is better; best.*

Meuz, *many.*

Meymes (de), *of the same.*

Meyn (par le), *by the hand.*

Meyn (la pleyne), *the handful.*

Meyn (a sa soule), *on his own single oath.*

Meyn (avaunt), *before hand.*

Meyn (du), *of my own.*

Meyn en meyn (de), *from hand to hand.*

Meyn le temp (en), *in the mean time, at the same time.*

Meyn ove, *work, labour; used.*

Meyn (sans), *without mesne.*

Meynal, *menial.*

Meynce damage (au), *doing as little damage as possible.*

Meyn-

Meyndre, *leſs.*

Meyne, meyney, *a houſe-hold, family.*

Meyne (lur volunte de), *their own will.*

Meynpaſtes, *houſehold, family, dependance.*

Meyn pris, *let to mainprize.*

Meyns avyſement maunde, *ill adviſedly ſent.*

Meyn ſachantz, *the unwary, the illiterate.*

Meyns remembrantz, *not ſufficiently mindful.*

Meyns (outre), *out of her hands.*

Meyns (entre), *in hand.*

Meyns nues (a), *their hands bare.*

Meyns (en), *under the protection.*

Meyns ſoit priſe (au), *be leſs effectually inquired into.*

Meyns, *leſs.*

Meyns (au), *at leaſt.*

Meynt, meint, *dwells.*

Meynt areſteant, *notwithſtanding.*

Meynte foitz, *then, at the ſame time.*

Meyntenant, *immediately, preſently.*

Meyntent, *maintains, harbours.*

Meynt home, *many a man.*

Meyntz jour paſſe, *long ſince.*

Meyre, *mayor.*

Meys, *month.*

Meys (ove ſa dozyme), *the party himſelf and eleven compurgators.*

Meys, *mouth.*

Meyſun, *houſe.*

Mez, *middle.*

Mi, *me, myſelf, my.*

Mi, *half, middle*; *mixed, put.*

Mi eſte (le), *Midſummer.*

Mice, *part, portion.*

Micoulau, *Nicholas.*

Midivint, *midnight.*

Mie, *not*; *ill.*

Mie (a la), *in the middle.*

Miech-aouz, *the middle of Auguſt.*

Miedi, *in the middle of the day.*

Mielz, mieltz, mielz, miens, miez, miex, mex, *beſt, better.*

Miendre, *leſs, the leaſt.*

Miendres peches, *ſmaller offences.*

Miere, mier, mire, *mother*; *mere.*

Miers, mieeres (les IIII), *the four ſeas.*

Mies, *meſſuage or houſe.*

Mieſtre, *occaſion.*

Mieſtre eſt (que), *than is neceſſary.*

Mieudre,

Mieudre, *better.*
Mieux, *less; rather.*
Mieux (face soun), *do his best.*
Miey, *middle.*
Migne de feer, *mines of iron.*
Miere, mier, mire, mere, *mother.*
Mij quaresme, *midlent.*
Mikiel, *Michael.*
Mileime, *thousandth.*
Milie mars, *a thousand marks.*
Millier, *a thousand.*
Milliou, *better.*
Millort Henry, *my lord Henry.*
Milui, *middle.*
Milveyn frere, *middle brother.*
Millyme deusentyme, *twelve hundred.*
Min (le), *mine.*
Minee, la menee, *those who ought to pursue felons on a hue and cry.*
Minister (a), *to put in.*
Ministralx, *minstrels.*
Ministration, *the management.*
Minnict, *a minute.*
Minovery, *trespass done by the hand.*
Minours, *miners, engineers.*
Miou, *mine.*
Miuodre, *better.*
Miqueou, Micquel, *Michael.*
Mire, miere, mier, *mother.*
Mire, *sea.*
Mire (ne nous deit), *ought not to put us into a worse condition.*
Mirmour, *murmur.*
Mirrour, *pattern.*
Mis, *we, us.*
Mis, mys, *left.*
Miscrew, miscrue, *suspected, guilty.*
Mise, *issue, plea.*
Mise, *the joining issue in a writ of right.*
Mise (sans sa), *without issue joined.*
Mise demene (de vestre), *of your own putting.*
Mises, *expences, costs, tasks, taxes.*
Miseres (feaux), *faithful gentlemen.*
Miseymes, *supposing.*
Misire, *monsieur.*
Mislier, mislyer, *to chuse the wrong, to mistake.*
Misprisel, *mistaking.*
Missions, *mises, expences.*
Missives, *epistles, letters.*
Mist, *left.*
Mist (soy), *appears.*
Mister, *need of, occasion for.*
Mister, *a secret.*

Mistermyng,

Mistermyng, *miscalling*.
Mistioner, *to mingle*.
Mistrent (se), *put themselves*.
Mit (ou il lui), *where he was his attorney*.
Mitaundre, *in the night-time*.
Mitter, *to appoint*.
Mittomus, *we admit, we put the case*.
Mittomous, *let us suppose*.
Mittr̃, *will send*.
Mittre et tenus, *put and kept it*.
Mius, *better*.
Moblys, *moveables*.
Mocke, *a bride, spouse*.
Mod (en la), *in the mud*.
Modifier, *to alter, regulate*.
Moedz de vin, *a hogshead of wine*.
Moel, meel, *honey*.
Moeleen, *millstone*.
Moelt grantement, *very greatly*.
Moement, *especially*.
Moer, *moves*.
Moerge, *dies*.
Moeryer, *to die*.
Moes, *better*.
Moeves, *moved*.
Mogne, *a monk*.
Moi, *may*.
Moien temp, *mean time*.
Moien, *mediation, a mediatrix*.
Moienantz, moiennans, *namely, especially, by means of*.
Moienez, *means*.
Moienne, *moderate*.
Moienner, *to mediate, negociate*.
Moienneresses, *mediatrixes*.
Moient, *administring*.
Moigns pour le, *at least*.
Moillere, *a malier*.
Moillers (dents), *the teeth called the grinders*.
Moils draps, *milled cloths*.
Moine, *money*.
Moinere (en la), *in the least*.
Moirent, *die*.
Mold, *model*.
Moldes, *many*.
Moleins pur freins, *bosses, bits for bridles*.
Molener, *a miller*.
Molicons (des), *demolition*.
Molt poi, *much worse*.
Molours, *mills*.
Molt, *much, very*.
Molument (le), *the emoluments*.
Molyn ventresse, *a windmill*.
Moly sigles, *mill sails*.

Mond

Mond des molyns (pur), *to grind at the mills.*

Mondre (de), *to cleanſe out.*

Moneage, *an aid or preſent to the duke of Normandy once in three years, that he ſhould ſuffer the current money of Normandy to be changed. See charter of Henry I.*

Monemu, *Monmouth.*

Moneſter (a), *to admoniſh.*

Monition, munition, *ammunition.*

Monles (deux), *two floods.*

Monnoyer (argent) ou a monnoyer, *ſilver coined or not coined.*

Monnumentz (nos menementz), *our deeds or muniments.*

Monſer Jehu Chriſt, *my lord Jeſus Chriſt.*

Monſt, mout, *the world.*

Monſter, *to ſhew.*

Monſter, monſtre, monſtrer, mouſter, moſtier, muſtre, *a monaſtery, a church.*

Monſtra, *took it.*

Monſtrable, *to be declared.*

Monſtraunce (par mauveyſe), *by unſkilfully declaring.*

Monſtre, *muſtre of forces.*

Monſtreſon, *the ſhew.*

Montance, *the value.*

Mont de fois, *many times.*

Montz, monſtiers, *mountains, high lands.*

Mordreu, *murdered.*

Moreyns, morivaile, *murrain, plague.*

Moreult, maraſt, mora, morent, *dyed, dye.*

Moreys, *ſtarved, ſtinking.*

Moriance, *death.*

Moriant (en ſon lye), *on his death-bed.*

Morine, merine, *timber.*

Morreue, Morreve, *Murray.*

Mors d'argent, *a button, buckle, or claſp of ſilver.*

Mort-Mahoum, *by the death of Mahomet.*

Mort (a la), *ſitting melancholy.*

Morteus, *deadly, mortal.*

Moruſt de enfaunt, *dyed in childbed.*

Moryn, *wall.*

Morz (q), *as well dead.*

Moſnier, *a miller.*

Moſſy, *Moſes.*

Moſtera, *will ſhew.*

Moſtrance, *remonſtrance.*

Mot et moet, *word for word.*

Mote, motez, *put, expreſſed.*

Motenaux (pels), *ſheepſkins.*

Moties, motee, *mentioned, worded.*

Motons,

Motons, motonus, *weathers, sheep.*

Motye, *moiety.*

Moudes maners, *many kinds.*

Mouldre, moudre, *to grind.*

Moultlouse, *very long.*

Moultons, *weathers.*

Moult pres (eyde), *very much contribute.*

Mound, *the world.*

Mounder, *to cleanse.*

Moundre, *to fence, inclose.*

Mouneyne (seur), *middle sister.*

Mount (tout le), *the whole world.*

Mount (vers), *towards, upwards.*

Mountance, *amount, value.*

Mountaunt, *amounting to the value of.*

Mounture, *a riding horse.*

Mourront (ne), *shall not move.*

Mous, *many.*

Mout, *died.*

Mout, *much, greatly.*

Mout de fois, *many times.*

Mouti, *motive, design.*

Mouth serroit (qe), *which would be best.*

Mouton d'or, *an ancient French gold coin, on which was impressed a lamb, with this inscription, Agnus Dei, qui tollit peccata mundi, miserere nobis.*

Mouys, muys de ferment, *a certain measure of wheat.*

Move (se), *begins.*

Moveementz, *commotions, disturbances.*

Movement (al), *on the motion.*

Moves, moyes, *months.*

Moyen, *mean, indifferent; temperate; middle.*

Moyen (sans), *without mesne.*

Moyennant, *paying, making such payments.*

Moyennant (vous), *you being the mediator.*

Moyennant qu', *provided that.*

Moyenner, *to intercede with.*

Moyes, *months.*

Moymennans, *by means of.*

Moyr, *mayor.*

Mt̃, *death.*

Mu, *incited, moved.*

Muable (home), *an inconstant man.*

Muables, *different, vary.*

Muance, *changing.*

Mucettes, *in secret.*

Mucha, *concealed.*

Mue, muele, *mute.*

Muer, *to change, alter.*

Muerge, *dyes.*

Muete, *sedition.*

Mueth, *better.*

Muins, *warned.*
Muire, *to dye.*
Muit de chiens, *kennel of hounds.*
Mulnes ſoer, *the ſecond ſiſter, or the middle between two.*
Mulnes, mulneſſe, *fulneſs; the leaſt.*
Multe, *the fine.*
Mult puy, *much worſe.*
Mulveyn, mulnes frere, *middle brother.*
Muner, *to warn.*
Muni, *warned.*
Muniment, *evidence, proof.*
Munſeur, *monſieur.*
Munte (qui), *which amounts.*
Munture, *a riding horſe.*
Muovee, *moved.*
Muovent (ſe), *vary.*
Murdre, *kept ſecret.*
Murdreſſours, *murderers.*
Murdriſſent, *keep ſecret.*
Mure, nuyre (pur nous), *to injure us.*
Murement, *maturely.*
Murger, murer, *to periſh, to dye.*
Muriaux, *walls.*
Murours, *men employed in building walls and fortifications.*
Murra, *ſhall dye.*
Murrerent, murrurent, *dyed.*
Murruſt homage, *the homage is reſpited.*
Muſce, muſee, muſſe, mucha, *concealed.*
Muſeaux, *leprous.*
Muſettes (en), *ſecretly, privately.*
Muſſeles, muſcettes (par), *by ſtealth.*
Muſtre fruiſſer (de), *of breaking into a church, or monaſtery.*
Muſtrer, muſtrel, *to ſhew, ſet forth.*
Muſtrerunt, *ſhewed.*
Muſurablement, *according to the meaſure.*
Muſures, *meaſures.*
Mutere (de), *to change.*
Mutua, *pledged, lent, changed.*
Mutuve, *mutual.*
Mutz, *moved.*
Muye (ny vint), *did not come.*
Muygne (un), *a monk.*
My tout, *all parts.*
My (entour la), *about the middle.*
My lieu (clauſe en), *middle clauſe.*
My (per) et per tout, *by the half or moiety and by all.*
Myer, *mother.*
Myeus, *rather.*
Mykareſme, *midlent.*

Myle haut fil (en), *in the main ſtream.*
Mynate, *midnight.*
Myneurs, *minors.*
Myre, *to prejudice.*
Mys, miſe, *left.*
Mys (ſon), *his conſent.*
Mys par gage, *put by gages.*
Myſe, *aſſeſſment, puniſhment.*
Myſe (par ſa), *by his pleadings.*
Myſe (pur), *for lodging, placing, appointing, depoſiting.*
Myſne (temps), *mean time.*
Myſſus, *ſurmiſed.*
Myſt mye (ne), *did not uſe.*
Myſtes, *prelates, biſhops, and archbiſhops.*
Myſtre, *to place.*

NA, nade, *born.*
Naal, Nadal, Nadaou, *Chriſtmas.*
Naam, *replevy, diſtreſs, withernam.*
Naamer, *to diſtrain.*
Naams, names, *diſtrained.*
Nacion, *birth.*
Nadgeres puis, *ſometime ſince, lately.*
Naefs, *ſhips.*
Naffrerent, *wounded.*
Nagement, *ſwimming.*
Nagueres, n'agures, *lately.*
Naidgayers, naidgaris, nadgares, *lately, ſometimes.*
Naif, *natural, lively.*
Naifu clemence (ſa), *her natural clemency.*
Nail, *a nail in meaſure.*
Nails jammes, *nevertheleſs.*
Nailours, *not elſewhere.*
Naiſtres (faux), *baſtards.*
Nammil, nam, *diſtreſs.*
Nanyl, *nothing, not, no.*
Napez, *naped.*
Naplus, *Naples.*
Naſhiſt, *ſhould be born.*
N'aſquit, naſqe, *was born.*
Naſtres (fous), *ideots.*
Nat, net, *pure, clean.*
Natables, *notable, conſiderable.*
Natair defaut, *notorious defect.*
Nattraie, *draws to himſelf.*
Natureſſes, *naturalneſs, natural affection, kindneſs, civil uſage.*
Navant, *they had not.*
Navie, *navy, ſhips.*
Navil, *no, not.*
Nau, *a ſhip.*
Naufre, naures, *wounded, beaten, hurt.*
Naye, *drowned.*
Nayement, nagement, *ſwimming.*
Nayer, *to ſwim.*

Naz, *the noſe.*

Ne, *nor.*

Ne, *born.*

Ne pur quant-quint, *notwithſtanding.*

Ne ad geres, ne advers, *lately.*

Neant, *not, nothing.*

Neatir, *to annihilate.*

Nee (ſeint), *St. Neot's.*

Nee, *a native.*

Neef, *a ſhip.*

Neen, neez, nees, *born.*

Neen (al heure de), *till noon.*

Neent, *have not.*

Neerment, *nearly.*

Nees, *the noſe.*

Nees, *endamaged, drowned.*

Nees, nee, neetz, *ariſen.*

Nees fols, *natural fools.*

Nef, noef, neif, *new.*

Nef, *nine.*

Nefe, *a ſhip, a boat.*

Nefe, neif, niefe, *a bondwoman.*

Nefiſme, *ninth.*

Nefokaſtel ſur Line, *Newcaſtle under Line.*

Nefs, *ſhips.*

Negit, *negation, negative.*

Neiantz, *not having.*

Neicence, *birth.*

Neiens, neins, *neverthe-leſs.*

Neirent, *drowned.*

Neif (le), *the ninth.*

Neiſture, neiſure, *nativity.*

Neint, *nothing.*

Neir, *black.*

Neis, *not yet.*

Neis, *ſhips.*

Neis un (a), *to any one of them.*

Nekedent, *nevertheleſs.*

Nellui, *nobody.*

Nel ret, *of any crime.*

Nemy encontreſteant, *notwithſtanding.*

Nemy pur ces, *notwithſtanding this.*

Nenf, *ninth.*

Nennil, *by no means, not at all.*

Nenparnent, *ſhall not take upon themſelves.*

Nent, *or, nor.*

Nent, *not.*

Nent (ne ſoit), *is only.*

Neof, *nine.*

Neoyt, *night.*

Nepurquant, *nevertheleſs, moreover.*

Neven, *nephew.*

Neq̃e dõt, *nevertheleſs.*

Nes, *ſhips.*

Neſance, neſſaunce, *birth, origin.*

Nes pot, *cannot.*

Neſſens, *ignorance.*

Neſſent, *beget, ariſe.*

Neſſi,

Neſſi, *an ideot.*
Neſtre, *not to be.*
Neſtre, *to accrue to, to ariſe.*
Neſtre (le), neſtree (la), *the birth.*
Neſtre, neſter (p), *by the birth.*
Neſtrioir, *notwithſtanding.*
Noſtroit, *not known.*
Neſtry (pur my bre de), *by writ of nuifty.*
Nettement abatu, *wholly pulled down.*
Nettrez, *educated.*
Nettroit, *would accrue, ariſe.*
Neture, *nature.*
Nevant (nemie), *not before.*
Nevement, *cloſely, nearly.*
Neviſme, nevyme, *the ninth.*
Nevoutz, nevor, *nephew.*
Nevrer, *to afflict.*
Neu, *not.*
Neure, *to hurt.*
Neuſſeez vous ale (qi), *why did you not go.*
Neux, *nine.*
Neuz, *nephew.*
Newel, *Chriſtmas.*
Neweu, newe, *nephew.*
Ney, *not.*
Neye, *drowned.*
Neyez, *have not.*
Neyſture, *birth.*
Neytz, netz (croiz), *the white croſs, viz. of St. Andrew; one of the croſſes on which they uſed to ſwear in Scotland.*
Nez, *a naive.*
Neze, *noſe.*
Ni (un), *not, a denying.*
Niant, *not.*
Niant, *danger.*
Nicement, *eſpecially.*
Nichol, Nicol, *Lincoln.*
Niee, *denyed.*
Nieement, *namely, particularly.*
Niel, *Nigellus.*
Nielment plede, *badly pleaded.*
Nient mienz, *moreover, beſides.*
Nient, *not, have not.*
Nient (a), *for nothing.*
Nient numbrables, *innumerable.*
Nient obſtant, nient areſteant, *notwithſtanding.*
Nient lemeins, *neverthe-leſs.*
Nienteſement, *avoidance, deſtruction.*
Niert jammes, *ſhall never be.*
Nies (unques), *ever was known.*
Nies, niez, *a grandſon, alſo a nephew.*

Niet, *brings, draws.*
Niez, *new.*
Nifle, *a thing of no value, a trifle.*
Nil, *no one, nothing.*
Niffer, *ſhall not iſſue.*
Nitivitee, *nativity.*
Nit meins (ne), *neverthe-leſs.*
Niye, *drowned.*
No, *our.*
No, *nor, not.*
Nõ, *note.*
Noblee (la), *the noble ex-traction.*
Nobleiſe (cy hauts), *ſo high and noble a calling.*
Noef, *nine.*
Noefa, *refuſed, would not, durſt not.*
Noefs, *ſhips, veſſels.*
Noeifs (ſes), *his neifs.*
Noel, Noil, *Chriſtmas.*
Noement, *eſpecially.*
Noemme, noemine, *ninth.*
Noer, *to ſwim.*
Noeſantz, *nuiſances.*
Noet, *night.*
Noetandrement, *in the night-time.*
Noeviſme, noefiſme, *ninth.*
Noez, *our people.*
Noiera (ne), *ſhall not deny.*
Noies (totes), *always.*
Noif, nois, *ſnow.*
Noifte, *neifety.*
Noirent (que ne), *who do not ſend.*
Noiſent, *dare not.*
Noiſiſe, *noxious.*
Noiſmes (pot) voiſines, *neighbours.*
Noix, noitz, *night.*
Nom, *no.*
Nomaſſoins, *had named.*
Nomed (per ſerment), *by ſwearing in a ſet form of words.*
Nomement, noement, no-momentez, *to wit, eſ-pecially.*
Nomerz, nometz, *named.*
Nomis, *names.*
Nom merveill, *no wonder.*
Nonaen, nonain, nonne, *a nun.*
Nonchoſant, *knowing no-thing.*
None, *noon.*
None, *ninth.*
Noneims, *nuns, wives.*
Nonmeſnaunce (la), *the not bringing in.*
Nonn, *name.*
Nonn (an), *in name of.*
Nonſachaunce, *ignorance.*
Nonſauz, *nonſuited.*
Nonſemblablement (le pluis), *the more unlikely.*
Noore, *noon.*
N'ooſa, *durſt not.*
Nore, *a daughter-in-law.*
Norgales, *North-Wales.*
Nori, *a foſter-child.*
Norices, *nurſes.*

Noriſſement, *encouragement.*
Noriſt, *breeds; amounts to.*
Norrour (le), *the gilder.*
Nos, *we, our.*
Noſant, *hurtful.*
Noſaſt, *durſt not.*
Noſe, noſi, *a nut.*
Noſement, *namely.*
Noſeſt, *knows not.*
Noſmes, noſmables, *ſurnames.*
Note (il a), *he has declared, given out.*
Note, *expreſſed, ſpecified.*
Note (hors de le), *out of the note of the fine.*
Notiſons, *make known.*
Notoier, *ſcience, of experienced knowledge.*
Notorement, *notoriouſly.*
Notorie, *material, obſervable.*
Novallitez, novellerie, novellers, *innovations, new terms.*
Noveal, *new.*
Novel (ore de), *now of late.*
Noveletes, *injury.*
Novels porcions, *equal portions.*
Novies foits, *nine times.*
Nou, nouve, *nine.*
Nouches, *knots.*
Noueſtre, *our, ours.*
Noun, *nine.*
Noun (de cheſcun), *for every number.*
Nounne, *noon.*
Noun (p), *by name.*
Noun def, *not, or undefended.*
Noun due, *undue, what is not lawful.*
Nour, *us.*
Nowell, novelle (a), *at Chriſtmas,*
Nowelles, *new.*
Noyer (ne), *knew not.*
Noyes, *drowned.*
Noys, *nuts.*
Noyſaunce, *a nuiſance.*
Noz, *our, us.*
Nu mencion, *no notice.*
Nuce, *a nut.*
Nude empeſchement (p), *by a bare impeachment, without any proof to ſupport it.*
Nuef, nueve, *new.*
Nuire, nuyre, *hurt, injure.*
Nuiſement, *nuiſance, annoyance.*
Nul (ſi), *if any.*
Nulenois, *never.*
Nulh, *any.*
Null (a), *to any one.*
Nulla, *no, none.*
Nulluy, *no one.*
Nuly biens (en), *in any one's goods, any one's property.*

Num, nun (en), *in name.*
Nummez, *named.*
Nun (ky Deu), *which God forbid.*
Nuncie (la), *declare it.*
Nuncie (que), *who may declare.*
Nuof, *nine.*
Nurrer, nurer (pur), *to nourish.*
Nurriz le roy (les), *the familiars of the king.*
Nurture (de sa), *of his own bringing up.*
Nus, *no.*
Nus, *we.*
Nusant alia, *to the nuisance of another.*
Nusse, *nobody.*
Nust dust fere, *ought to do to us.*
Nut, *has.*
Nutauntre, *in the night-time.*
Nute (mi), *mignight.*
Nuyst (ne), *does not hurt.*
Nuyter (a la), nuytandre, *in the night-time.*
Nuytz, *night.*
Nuz (san), *without us.*
Nyant, *not.*
Nycke (nosme), *nick-name.*
Nye, *a nest.*
Nyef, neif, *a woman villain.*
Nyefe, neif, *a ship.*
Ny gist, *does not lie.*
Nyent avant, *they having none before.*
Nyuemant (sy), *so vigorously.*
Nyurent, *endeavoured, commanded.*

O, *or, and.*
O, O, ou, *with.*
Obeissaument, *obedience.*
Obsaires, *uttered.*
Objicet, *to object, lay to one's charge.*
Obit, obites, *dead, forgotten.*
Oblicter, *to sport, rejoice.*
Oblier, *to forget.*
Obligation, *tenure.*
Oblige, *liable.*
Oblivion, *forgetfulness.*
Obmittes, *omitted, left out.*
Obscurity (en), *in a dungeon.*
Oc, *yes, so.*
Ocbeir, *to obey.*
Occluder, *to shut.*
Occupation, *encroachment, seizures.*
Ochoison, ocquison, ocoison, *occasion, accident.*
Ocious vie, *an idle life.*
Ocreis (le), *the increase.*
Octroye, *granted.*
Od, *or, with.*

Od ſei (apeler), *call to him.*

Odible, *odious.*

Odonqs, *then.*

Oefs, *bees.*

Oegles, ogles, oels, *eyes.*

Oel, *ſhe.*

Oel, *equal.*

Oels, *them, the ſame, in like manner.*

Oens (a), *to them.*

Oens (les), *the doors.*

Oept, *eight.*

Oeptaz, &c. *octave, &c.*

Oeptiſme, *eighth.*

Oer (de), *to truſt.*

Oes, oeps, *uſe, benefit.*

Oeſſes del chambre (les), *the doors of the chamber.*

Oet, oete, *eight.*

Oeux, *eggs.*

Of, *with.*

Office (de ſon), *of right, by virtue of his office.*

Offre, *a tender.*

Offres (p) et p demandes, *by queſtion and anſwer.*

Ofiſſes, offiz, *offices.*

Oghſta, *ouſted.*

Oi, *I have.*

Oi, oie, oieetz, *heard, hearing.*

Oi (cours de), *his body.*

Oictouvre, *October.*

Oie, *an ear.*

Oiels, *eyes.*

Oient, *had.*

Oier (d'), *to hear.*

Oier del jurie (al), *to the ear of the jury.*

Oil, oil, *yea, yea, ay, ay; the aſſent of the commons in* 28 *Edw.* III.

Oille, *oil.*

Oingt, *anointed.*

Oioit, *heard.*

Oir, *to hear.*

Oir maſle, *heir male.*

Oirs (pur ſes), *for his heirs.*

Oires (juſques), *to this time.*

Oiſel, oiſeal, *a bird.*

Oiſel St. Martin (le), *a crow; ſo called from its generally being ſeen about Martinmas in France.*

Oiſines, *inactive, idle.*

Oiſmes, *we have heard.*

Oiſt, *eaſt.*

Oiſuir, *leiſure, opportunity.*

Oitaves, *octaves.*

Oit d', *eight-pence.*

Oitement, *advancement.*

Oiz, *heard.*

Olifaunt, *an elephant.*

Oly (d'), *olives.*

Om, omme, *a man, perſon.*

Om meſſeſoit (come ſe), *as if one had offended.*

Omes (prud), *magnates, great men.*

Omicidie (d'), *of homicide, manslaughter.*
Omosnes, *alms.*
On, *in.*
On (un), *an ounce.*
On assent (sans), *without their assent.*
Onche d'or, *an ouche of gold, a brooch, a necklace.*
Oncl, *uncle.*
Oncore, *moreover, again.*
Oncques n'eussent ete, *had never been.*
Ond, *one.*
One, *with.*
Oner (l'), *the honour.*
Onerer (ne dust), *ought not to meddle.*
Oneret (sagement), *wisely to work.*
Onestee, *decency.*
Onfiec de Boun, *Humphry de Bohun.*
Onkore, *yet.*
Onnerount, *will send.*
Onneur (cap d'), *cap of honour.*
Onques, *never, ever.*
Onst eu, *have had.*
Onta, *shame.*
Onur, *honour.*
Oons (nous), *we have.*
Oont et terminent, *hear and determine.*
Oor la reigne (le), aurum reginæ, *Queen gold. This is a royal debt, duty, and revenue of every Queen consort of England, during her marriage to the king, from every person, both in England and Ireland, for every gift, or oblation, or voluntary obligation or fine to the king, amounting to ten marks or more, for privileges, franchises, dispensations, licences, pardons or grants of royal grace, or favour conferred by the king, which is a tenth part, besides the fine to the king.*
Oor de Cypre (de drap d'), *cloth of gold of Cyprus.*
Oosent (n'), *dare not.*
Oost, *army.*
Opposer, apposer, *to appose, examine, question.*
Ops, *choice, will.*
Opse, *use.*
Opteinent, *obtain.*
Oquison, *occasion.*
Or endroit (qui), *who at present.*
Orail, oraille, *an ear.*
Oraire, orarium, *a stole to be worn at all times by the priest: it went about the neck of him that officiated, to signify he*

he had taken upon him the Lord's yoke.

Orat (ori), *heard the cry.*

Oratours, *complainants, petitioners.*

Orce, ors, orſe, *a bear.*

Orde (del), *of commanding, ordering.*

Ordenours, *thoſe prelates and barons who in* 1310, 3 *Edward* II. *were appointed, by virtue of the king's commiſſion, to reform and ſettle the ſtate of the king's houſehold, and of the kingdom.*

Ordemments, *ordinances or ſtatutes.*

Ordes parolles (ove), *with foul words.*

Ordeynement, *determination.*

Ordi, *barley.*

Ordinail, *a book of rules and orders, to direct the right manner of ſaying and performing holy ſervice: the moſt famous of this ſort was that of Sarum, made by Oſmond, biſhop of Saliſbury,* 1077.

Ordinares, ordeners, *ordinaries, biſhops.*

Ordine, *order, rule.*

Ordiner, *to diſpoſe of.*

Ordir, *to be filthy.*

Ordrene, *ordained.*

Ore, *any more.*

Ore (d'), *at preſent.*

Ore (et ja ſoit), *and ſuppoſe.*

Ore (pur ſon), *for her queen gold.*

Oreler, *a pillow.*

Orendreyt lui, *on his part.*

Orendroit, *now, at this time.*

Organes portatifs du roy (les), *the king's portable organs.*

Oriel, *an ear.*

Orier, *to riſe up, the riſing.*

Orila ove le roy, *had a private audience of the king.*

Orir, *to ariſe from.*

Orlage, *a clock.*

Orphays, *orphans.*

Orpheour, *goldſmith.*

Orray, orrount, orreyent, orrent, *ſhall hear.*

Orret, *guilt.*

Orribletee, *horribleneſs.*

Orrie (l'), *the inheritance.*

Ort, *a garden.*

Orteils, *claws.*

Ortieux, *toes.*

Oſannes, Ozanne, *Palm-Sunday.*

Oſi, *alſo.*

Oſſe, *bone.*

Oſſi qe, *ſo that.*

Oſt,

Oſt, *he had.*

Oſt, *hoſt.*

Oſt, oſtel (a), *with an army.*

Oſtage, *hoſtage.*

Oſtagiez, *ſet at liberty.*

Oſtaſſent, *ſhould remove from, ouſt, put out.*

Oſteilx, *houſes.*

Oſtel, *houſehold, at home, an inn, lodging, entertainment, diet.*

Oſtenſion (de faire), *to ſhew, to produce.*

Oſter, *taken away.*

Oſter (mal), *bad underſtanding.*

Os teres, *ſuch lands.*

Oſterons, *will put out.*

Oſtier, *a door.*

Oſtoyt, *ſtood, was,*

Oſtre, *ſhewed.*

Oſtre ceo, *moreover.*

Oſyum leſſer (nus de), *we have adjourned.*

Ot, il ot, *he had.*

Ote, ot, *he hearkens.*

Otel, *as much, the like.*

Oterie (e), *and grant.*

Otioſite, *idleneſs, want of employment.*

Otrée, *granted, conſented, appointed.*

Otrei, *the other.*

Otrei, otri, *leave, conſent.*

Otrie de ceo, *further, moreover.*

Otriemenz, *conceſſions.*

Otroiant, *attending to, regarding, granting.*

Otruoyſons, *grants.*

Ottie, *granted.*

Ottis, *taken away, carried off.*

Otto or Otho de Tillie, *the name of ſome Norman, who built Doncaſter croſs.*

Ottreer (le), *the charter.*

Ottreire, *to grant.*

Ottret, *granted.*

Ottrie de ceo a luy (n'), *does not pretend himſelf to have any title thereto.*

Ottroyent (s'ilz luy), *if they grant it to him.*

Ottroyer, *to contract.*

Ottruyz, *granted.*

Ou, *whereas, whereto, within, with, into, in.*

Ou cas, *in caſe,*

Ou nun, *in the name.*

Ou que ils fuiſſent, *although they were.*

Ou q ſoit chargeant, *wherewith he be charged.*

Oũ, *to open.*

Ouan, *in a year.*

Oucunque, *whereſoever, whatſoever, whenſoever.*

Oue, ouie, *a gooſe.*

Ouen (qi), *who have.*

Oues, *bones.*

Ove, *with.*

Ove et de trove; de eve et de treve; *i. e. free for many descents; from grandfather, and great grandfather's great grandfather; also certain seignioral rights exercised over villains.*

Ovek co, *moreover.*

Ovekes, oveuk, *with.*

Ovel, *new.*

Ovelment, *equally, justly, exactly.*

Ouent, *have.*

Ovenuz, *arrived, come.*

Over, *have.*

Over (de), *to work, to labour.*

Overaigne del Eglise (al), *to the fabric of the church.*

Overe, ouere pur luy, *passed in her favour.*

Overe pur vous (qe), *which is in your favour.*

Overe (par), *by endeavouring.*

Overe en avant (de cel), *from that time forward.*

Overecha, *goes beyond.*

Overee sey, *wrought silk.*

Overeigne (al), *towards building.*

Overeignes, *works.*

Overe mye (ne), *there is no occasion for.*

Overent, *passed.*

Overer, *to proceed, to gain.*

Overrer, *to work.*

Overesces de seie, *silkworkers.*

Overete (en lieu), *in an open place.*

Overez, *built, erected.*

Overre (en), *inquiry.*

Overte (en temps), *in open tide.*

Overtement, *plainly, manifestly.*

Overtes, *open, so as the lord can distrain.*

Oves et seues, *done and prosecuted.*

Ovesqe ceo qe, *except that.*

Ovesque, *also*

Ovestoit, *whilst he was, was heretofore; appointed.*

Oughtee, *ousted.*

Ovient, *often.*

Ovir, *to hear.*

Ouk, *ever.*

Oukuns, *any.*

Oult (au), *on the last day.*

Oultrance, attrenche (a tout), *to the utmost.*

Oultroyse, *granted.*

Oumes, *men.*

Ountement, *openly.*

Ount mester, *hold it necessary.*

Ovoqes tut ce, *besides all this.*

Ouq,

Ouq, *and that, where.*
Oura, *ſhall have.*
Oure, *hour.*
Oure, *to kill.*
Oure, oures, *works.*
Oure (al), *at the time.*
Oureroms (nous), *we will proceed.*
Oures (avant tout), *eſpecially.*
Ourir, *to manage.*
Our ke (del), *as ſoon as.*
Ours (j'), *I ſhall have.*
Ous, *bones.*
Ous (a), *to them.*
Ouſt, *Auguſt.*
Ouſt, *out, has, had.*
Ouſtage, *hoſtage.*
Ouſtantz, *ouſting, turning from.*
Ouſtel (al), *to the door, at the door, at the beginning, at firſt.*
Ouſter auxi, *over, alſo.*
Ouſtrez, ouſtes, *put out, removed, taken off.*
Ouſtr, *over.*
Ouſtre, *removed.*
Ouſtre auter droit, *except what belongs to others.*
Ouſtre quel, *beyond which, after which.*
Out, *above.*
Outel (ſacrement del), *ſacrament on the altar.*
Outere, overte (eſchange), *public, open exchange.*
Outlagari, *an outlawry.*
Outrage, *abuſe, exceſs.*
Outragieuſe, *exceſſive.*
Outre, *over, beſides.*
Outre (d'), *of another.*
Outre (la), doutre le meer, *beyond ſea.*
Outreiz, *granted.*
Outrement (tout), ouvertement, *intirely, utterly.*
Outr quen culture, *over, through which piece of ground.*
Outre (ſa demande tout), *the whole ſhe demanded.*
Ouve, *or.*
Ouvertez, *letters patent.*
Ouwel-main (en), *into an indifferent hand.*
Ouye, ouy, ouyes, *heard.*
Ouyez, *publiſhing, proclaiming.*
Ouzeroient (ne), *durſt not.*
Ouziſme, *eighth.*
Ow, *or.*
Owaille (un), *a ſheep.*
Owe, aue craſſe, *a fat gooſe.*
Owe, *hired.*
Owel, ouelx, *equal.*
Owele main (en), *into an indifferent hand.*
Owele condic̃on (de), *of equal condition.*
Owelment, *equally.*

Oweles

Oweles (Dieux ad comys ſes), *God has committed his ſheep.*
Owells, *eyes.*
Owels, *goods.*
Ower, *oar.*
Oweſter celle awerouſte (pur), *to remove this doubt.*
Owyt, *eight.*
Oy, *hear, heard, audited.*
Oy (demanda), *demanded oyer.*
Oy dire (par), *by hearſay.*
Oye, *an ear.*
Oye, *oyer.*
Oye encor (je n'), *I have not yet.*
Oyels, *eyes.*
Oyer, *eyes.*
Oyer (ſo), *his hearing.*
Oyis, *heard.*
Oyl, *yes, hear ye, an eye.*
Oynt, *eight.*
Oyr no acuntes (de), *to audit our accounts.*
Oyſels, *birds.*
Oyſon, *gooſe.*
Oyſt, *heard.*
Oyt, *eight.*
Oytaves, *octaves.*
Oytieſme, *the eighth.*
Oyzes (kil), *that he hear.*
Ozanne (la fete d'), *Palm-Sunday.*

ꝑ amont eſcrit, *above written.*
Pl, *plaintiff.*
p̃ my, *throughout.*
P noms, *have brought.*
p̃nt, *takes.*
Põnt, *can, may.*
ꝓoirez, *procured.*
p̃pris, *purpriſed, encroached upon.*
Prõu, *profit.*
p̃r tẽẽ, *for their land.*
p̃s, *taken, more.*
p̃s dil ce q̃s, *near unto, almoſt to.*
p̃ſe, *taken.*
p̃ſel, *taking.*
p̃tie, *brought.*
ꝑ uſe, *by turns.*
Paage, *payment.*
Paas, *country.*
Pace, paſſe, *paſſes, exceeds.*
Paces del Eſchekir (en voiez a les), *ſent to the places; i. e. to the courts of the Exchequer, &c.*
Pache, *a convention.*
Pacs, *peace.*
Pae, paemenz, paes, *payment.*
Pae pas (ne ſe), *is not ſatisfied.*
Paee, *payed.*
Paer (l' apoſtoill), *father the pope.*

Paes, *agreement, peace.*
Paes, *countries.*
Paes (nexcede), *do not exceed.*
Paetz, *paid.*
Pagner (per), *by payment.*
Paiages et Rovages; pedagia et roagia, *tributes and rotages. See Roynages.*
Paie (de), *of payment.*
Paie (mau), *displeased.*
Paiere (p la), *by the father.*
Paies, payez (les), *the payments.*
Paigners, *panniers.*
Paile, *omitted.*
Pailement faire, *to do the like.*
Paillettes, *hangings.*
Painer, *to torment.*
Pain-grosse, *brown bread.*
Pains, *loaves; the first Sunday in lent in the Romish church.*
Paintz, *paying.*
Painz (VII), *seven loaves.*
Paiour, *fear.*
Pair, *to pay.*
Paira, *may.*
Pais, paise, *peace.*
Paisement (sur le), *in the appeasing.*
Paisne, *the youngest.*
Paisvile, *peaceable.*
Paisumne (en), *into a Paganish country.*
Paiz, *agreement.*
Pale, pal, pel, *paling, wood.*
Paler, *to speak.*
Palettes, *a military habit.*
Palle, pallees, *spoken of, treated of.*
Paller (sanz ent), *without mentioning the same.*
Panbretat, *mandate.*
Pandecouste, *Penticost.*
Pane, *cloth, a robe.*
Pane, *bread.*
Panes, *skins.*
Panes, *loaves.*
Panetre le roy (serjante de estree), *by serjeantry, to be the king's pantler.*
Pani, *penalty.*
Pans, *he thinks.*
Panse, *the belly.*
Panses, *hung, pendant, affixed.*
Panures, *poor.*
Paor, paoir, *power.*
Paour, *fear.*
Paours, *payers.*
Papa, *the pope.*
Papate (la), *the papacy.*
Papirs, *papers, books of acccunts.*
Papisicke (eglise), *the Romish church.*
Papistine, *a papist.*

Par, *equal.*

Par, *paces.*

Par (de), *of Paris.*

Parachue, paracheve, *finiſhed.*

Parage, *kindred.*

Paraimer, *to love affectionately.*

Parains, padrines, *theſe are perſons who, in the time of combat, performed the ſame office which advocates and pleaders uſe in diſputation of civil cauſes.*

Paramount (eſpecefie), *above ſpecified.*

Paraval les pountz, *below the bridges.*

Paravant, *before.*

Paraventure, *by, between.*

Parautee (eſtat de), *eſtate of peerage.*

Parcas, *perhaps.*

Parcenier, *parcenery.*

Parchemin, parchena, *parchment.*

Par chi devant, *heretofore.*

Parchier (les murs), *break through the walls.*

Par choſe qe, *becauſe.*

Parcloſe chartre, *in the cloſe of the charter.*

Parconniers, *parceners.*

Parcoons, *dilatory.*

Parcſt, *delay.*

Pard, *loſs.*

Pardannt, *loſing.*

Parde, pardoin, *pardon, forgive.*

Pardehors, *outwards.*

Pardehors le roialme, *out of the realm.*

Pardela, *beyond ſea.*

Pardr, *ſhall loſe.*

Parduit, *loſt.*

Pardurable, *perpetual.*

Pardurablement, *for ever.*

Pare, *by.*

Parecherount, pariſhoiront, *ſhall be wrecked.*

Pareil, parile, parole, *peril, danger.*

Pareiſſouſes, *idle.*

Parches, *parcels, pieces.*

Parempler, *to fill up.*

Parency, parenſi qe, *whereby, ſo that.*

Parent, parentz, *kindred.*

Parent que, *whereby.*

Parer point, perpoint, purpoint, *doublet.*

Pares, *peers.*

Pareſce, *idleneſs.*

Parferons, *will perform.*

Parfin (a la), *at laſt.*

Parfond, *deep.*

Parfurnis, parfourny, *performed, executed, completed.*

Pargam, *parchment.*

Pargemin, *a MSS. on parchment.*

Pariage

Pariage (de), *on the part of the father.*

Pariens a mont, *appearing with much greater.*

Parier, *perjured.*

Parites, *parties.*

Parlance, parly (la), *treaty.*

p̱ la ou, *where.*

Parles, *pearls.*

Par li, *for him, on his account.*

Parlire, *to read through.*

p̱lour (lour cõe), *their common ſpeaker, one who will anſwer for the whole body, the ſpeaker of the Houſe of Commons.*

Parlure, *language.*

Parme, parmi, *at, by, with.*

Parmi (et), *and according to.*

Par mi ce, *therefore, on that account.*

Parmi chou ke, *provided that.*

Parmi cy, *by this.*

Parmuer, *to truck, to barter.*

Parmy, *upon.*

Parner, *to take.*

p̱och, *pariſh, dioceſe, territory.*

Paroches, *parts, ſides.*

Paroge, *converſe, have communication with.*

Paroier, *to appear.*

Parol, paralee, *perambulation.*

Parole, *plea.*

Paroles pur les communes (qi avoit les), *who was ſpeaker for the commons.*

Parolys (avons en), *had ſome diſcourſe.*

p̱ouls, *words.*

Parout, *wherefore.*

Parpaie, *fully paid.*

Parplede, *pleaded.*

Parpoint, *a doublet.*

Parquai, *whereby.*

Parquaunt, *when.*

Parquer, *to incloſe, impound, impark.*

Parqui, *in as much as, becauſe.*

Parraies, *walls.*

Parrie, *equality.*

Parrie, *a peer, peerage.*

Parſiver, *to perform.*

Parſon, *perſon.*

Parſone (apres coeverfu), *after coverfu has rung.*

Parſoneable, *perſonable, enabled to maintain plea in court.*

Partage et pannage, *portion and appennage.*

Partant, *therefore, whereupon.*

Partant que, *inaſmuch as.*

Parte des teſtes (per), *by beheading.*

Parte

Parte et parte, *party and party.*
Parte des coiles (la), *the loss of the testicles.*
Partement, *departure.*
Partez, *carried.*
Partirent, *departed.*
Partisons, *divisions.*
Partment, *in part.*
Partot, *in the whole.*
Partront (ne), *will not depart.*
Party (pur la), *by reason of the parity.*
Parvoar (le), *the procuror.*
Parvoisiers (vallez), *valets who were learned in their military exercises.*
Pas, *passes.*
Pas, paes, *peace.*
Pascage, *grazing.*
Pascher, passer, *to feed.*
Pascher (puisse), *might go.*
Pask, *Easter.*
Pasques charnielx, *Mid-lent-Sunday; Dominica Refectionis.*
Pasque florie, *Palm-Sunday.*
Pasqueret, *the season of Easter.*
Pasquerages, *pasture-grounds.*
Passant, *in their journey.*
Passant, *feed on.*
Passaunte, *exceeding.*
Passement, *death.*
Passer (doit), *ought to exceed.*
Passes (sunt), *are made up, comprehended.*
Passionaire, *a book which contains the history of the passion of our Saviour.*
Pastour, *shepherd.*
Pasture (quitz de la), *to be quit of poture.* See *Poture.*
Pasuilement, *peaceably.*
Patere, *Patrick.*
Pateys, putoys (le), *the ceremonies, prayers.*
Pati, ou souffrance de guerre, *abstinence, or cessation of war.*
Patience Dieu (par la), *by God's permission.*
Patins, *pattens.*
Patins, *dishes, plates, or chargers, made of gold or silver, used at the distribution of the host; and these were called patins or patens; a patendo.*
Patron, *pattern.*
Paver, pavoire, *fear.*
Pavis, *a large kind of shield.*
Pau, *a stake.*

Pauantz, paynant, *paying*.

Paulement, *a little*.

Paumaunt, paumes, *touching, laying one's hands upon*.

Paus (a), *in pledge*.

Pax (un), *a box where the ſacrament is put*.

Paye, a paye, *ſatisfied; payment*.

Payeé, *recompenced*.

Payne, *penalty*.

Payntier le roy, *ſerjeant of the pantry to the king*.

Paynim, *a Pagan*.

Pays, payes, *country*.

Payſqes, *Eaſter*.

p̃e, *pray*.

Pc̃he, *preach, declare*.

Pe, pee, peas, *foot*.

Peace le roy (a la), *to the law of the land*.

Peae, peaz, peax, *peace*.

Peae, *feet*.

Peages, *to us*.

Peaiges, *tolls, cuſtoms*.

Peaiſez, *countries*.

Pealx lanuz, *woolfels*.

Peaux deberbiz, *ſheepſkins*.

Peautre, peantre, *pewter*.

Pec (pris le), *price, each*.

Peccherouſement, *wickedly*.

Pecchi (a), *to ſin*.

Peccune, pecunie, *money*.

Pece (grand), *a great while*.

Pecee (abſentent un), *be abſent a little while*.

Pecheries, *offenoes*.

Pechereuſe cite d'Avenon (en la), *in the wicked city of Avignon*.

Pechir, pecher, *to offend*.

Peck (haute), *High Peak*.

Pecker (de), *to break open*.

Peċt, *the breaſt*.

Pecunielle (peine), *pecuniary puniſhment*.

Pedereſte, *a ſodomite*.

Pee, *foot*.

Pee de la fyn, *foot of the fine*.

Pee, *country*.

Peele (entrez en la), *entered in the pell*.

Peer, *a ſtone, fourteen pounds*.

Peer (franche), *free-ſtone*.

Peeres (nous auncients), *our anceſtors*.

Peereſins (pleignanze), *pilgrims complainants*.

Peert, *appears*.

Pees, *peace*.

Pees (un), *a concord*.

Pees (en), *in the country*.

Pees (mettent les), *ſet their feet*.

Peeſe̊, *appeared*.

Peeſe (ove la), *peaceably*.

Pege, *pitch*.

Peiblement, *peaceably*.

Peier

Peier (plus), *worst.*
Pejer, *worse.*
Peies en main, *paid down in hand.*
Peigneresses, *combers.*
Peinbles, *diligent.*
Peinblement (si), *so diligently, carefully.*
Peine, *punishment.*
Peine benite (pur), *for holy bread.*
Peipe (son), *his father.*
Peir, *peer, equal.*
Peir de justices, *two justices.*
Peire, *father.*
Peire (un), *a pair.*
Peir̃ (il puit), *he may pray.*
Peirs, *stones.*
Peirt, *appears.*
Peis, *weights.*
Peis, *peace.*
Peis, peise, *peas.*
Peise (nus), *pressed us, lay upon our hands.*
Peise (e molt nous), *and it gives us great concern.*
Peiser, *to weigh.*
Peisible, *peaceable.*
Peisiblete, *the peaceable state.*
Peison, *mast.*
Peithe, *fails.*
Peitou, *Poictou.*
Peitreux, peitrelx, *that part of the trappings of a horse, which goes across his breast.*
Peiz, *feet.*
Peles, *issues arising from.*
Pelle (le ditte), *the said appeal.*
Pelure, peleure, *skin, furr, clothing.*
Pelrine, *pilgrim.*
Pelter (citizein et), *citizen and skinner.*
Peltrie, *all kinds of furr.*
Pelwoll, *peltwool.*
Pembrugg, *Pembroke.*
Penacles, *pinnacles.*
Penauntz, *penitents.*
Pence, *intends.*
Pendable, *to be hanged.*
Pendaunt, *in suspence.*
Pendent (en), *belonging.*
Pender, *to consider.*
Pendra, *let him pay.*
Pendure (de), *of hanging.*
Pene, *penalty.*
Pene, *punished.*
Penere (a), *to punish.*
Penes, *obliged.*
Penia (tant lui), *made him undergo such duress.*
Peniblement, *with great pains.*
Penie (sans), *without punishment.*
Penne, *a pen.*
Penner, *a pen-case.*
Penra, ponra, *shall take.*
Penre (faitez), *cause to be taken.*

Penſant, *being grieved at, lamenting.*

Penſement (en), *in thought.*

Penſoier (potiùs, puiſſe oier), *may bear.*

Pent, *depends, depending.*

Penyble, *painful.*

Pepul, *people.*

Peraccompt, *fully accompted.*

Per ainſi, *in the ſame manner.*

Peramont, *above.*

Peranite, *eternity.*

Per a per, *peer for peer.*

Percer le denier (de), *to break the money to pieces.*

Perchemyn (un poy denk et), *a little ink and parchment.*

Perchez, parchez, *breaking down.*

Percloſe, *the concluſion.*

Perdant, *a ſufferer, prejudiced.*

Perdecea (nient plus), *no more in this caſe.*

Per de eus, *amongſt them.*

Perdervers lui, *about him.*

Perdeſiſt, *loſe, loſt.*

Perdez, *loſs.*

Pere, peer (gettre de), *ſlinging; one of the ſports prohibited by* 12 *Ric. II. c.* 6.

Pere nues (a), *bare-legged.*

Peregales, *equals.*

Pereies, peres, *ſtones.*

pent au, *praying to have.*

Perent, *thereby.*

Perer, *to appear.*

Peres, *a peer.*

Peres, *ſtones, pearls.*

Perfere, *to execute, perform.*

Perfez perners, *by pernicious acts.*

Perfit, *perfect.*

Perfond, *deep.*

Perforcera, *ſhall endeavour.*

Perfre le jer jour (que fiſt), *who offers himſelf the firſt day.*

Peri, *loſt life or limb.*

Perie (od), *ſet with ſtones.*

pil de miere (en), *in parts beyond ſea.*

Perils de garranties, *peril, hazard of warranty.*

Perira riens al chief ſeigniour del fee (ne), *the chief lord of the fee ſhall not ſuffer.*

pirent, *were loſt.*

Peris, *damaged, ſpoilt.*

Peris a fure (p ſes), *affeered by his peers.*

Periſſe, *be loſt, depart from.*

Perloygnent, *prolongue.*

Permitter ſon loyal trials, *will not abide his lawful trial.*

Perners,

Perners, *perverse.*

Pernez a mal, *take it amiss.*

Perole (p), *by words.*

Peround, *whereby.*

pount, per unt, *wherefore.*

Per pays, *fully satisfied.*

Perpetre, *made, passed.*

Perplede, *to finish, to decide.*

Perpretes, *committed.*

Per qei oy, *in as much as.*

Per qi, perque, *wherefore.*

Perquillye, *fully collected or paid.*

pquisicõns a mortmayn, *purchases in mortmain.*

Perre, *precious stones.*

Perres (p ces), *by his peers.*

Perrez, Pirers, Pirres, Peres, Pere, *Peter.*

Perry (vine), *bad, adulterated wine.*

Pers, *peers.*

Perseveyront, *perceived.*

Personaument, *in person.*

psuy, *pursue.*

Pert, *part.*

Pert, *appears.*

Pertant, *whereby, thereby.*

Pertant (n'est my), *is not on this account.*

Pertie, *part.*

Perveient, *provide.*

Peruch (la compaignie de), *the Prussian company.*

Perview, *provided.*

Pervis, parvis, *the outer court of a palace or great house; a place where clients, when they wanted to be out of the noise and bustle of Westminster-hall, and to consult with their counsel, used to meet. Such was the place in Palace-yard near Westminster-hall, mentioned by Fortescue de Laud. Leg. Angl. c.* 51. *Dugdale also takes notice of the Pervyse of Pawles. " Formerly," says he, " each lawyer and " serjeant, at his pillar " in St. Paul's church, " heard his client's cause, " and took notes thereof " upon his knee." Dugd. Orig.* 195. *b. See Gloss.* X. *Script.* v. Triforium. *The lowest part of the church next to the north and south doors was also called the parvis; a parvis pueris ibi edoctis: and sometimes courts temporal were held there. Staveley's History of Churches, p.* 157.

Pery, *ruined.*
Perz, *loſs.*
Pes, pez, *peace.*
Pes, *breaſt.*
Pes, *paſture.*
Pes (lour), *their feet.*
Peſantie, peſantee, *animoſity, reſentment.*
Peſaunte, *heavy, ponderous.*
Peſch, *depaſtures.*
Peſche, *is faulty.*
Peſchie, peſkerye, *fiſhery.*
Peſczer, *to feed.*
Peſer debatz (de), *to ſettle differences.*
Peſes (trencher en), *to cut in pieces.*
Peſh (de), *of the paſture.*
Peſiblement, *peaceably.*
Peſme, *very wicked, worſt of all.*
Peſoit (li), *propoſed to him.*
Peſs (de), *in the piece.*
Peſſant, *feeding, depaſturing.*
Peſſe d'etoille de lin (par), *for a piece of linen ſtuff.*
Peſſons, peſshens, peſkons, *fiſh.*
Peſſoners, *fiſhermen.*
Peſſounz (jours de), peſſons, *fiſh days.*
Peſtent, peſtre, *feed.*
Peſtereſces, *bakers.*
Peſtez, *baked.*
Peſtour, peſture, peſcour, *a baker.*
Peſtrine, *bakehouſe.*
Peſtzon, peſſon, *maſt, the fruit of a ſpecies of trees, called glandiferous or maſtbearing, as beech, oak, cheſnut, &c.*
Pet (un), *a crack.*
Petentes (lettres), *letters patent.*
Petie, peti, *pity, mercy.*
Petitement, *little, eaſily.*
Petitz gents, *men of ſmall value.*
Pettavin, *a Pictavian.*
Peu, peuſſauntz, *able.*
Peu de greyn, *fed with grain.*
Peult, peuſt, *may.*
Peulx, peaux lanutz, *woolfels.*
Peure, peuir, *fear.*
Peure, *take.*
Peuſons, *might.*
Peutre, *pewter.*
Pew, *few.*
Pex, *pitch.*
Pey de temps, *a ſhort time.*
Peygne, peynez, *pains, penalties.*
Peynymes, *Pagans.*
Peys, *weights.*
Peyſer, *to weigh.*
Peyſuns, *peaſants.*

Peyte,

Peyte, *a piece.*

Pez, *feet.*

Pheli, *Philip.*

Philas (de), *from off the files.*

Phylatteries; phylatteria, *vessels and boxes made of gold, silver, ivory, or crystal, to keep the relics of saints and martyrs.*

Pi, pie, piz, poux, *a well.*

Pice, *peas.*

Pi cea, *already.*

Pices (sur leur), *upon their pyxes.*

Pie de seal, *foot of the seal.*

Piece (a y demorer un), *to reside there some time.*

Piece ad, piez ca, piecea, ja pieca, ja bone piece, *lately, heretofore, hitherto, some time since.*

Piece (grand), *a great while.*

Piece (sunt alees ja une), *may be uniform.*

Pieche de tans, *space of time.*

Piecza donez, *lately granted.*

Pied de mony, *standard or sterling money.*

Pied puldreaux, *a pedlar, from whence the court of justice, called the piepoudre, is derived, or from the dispatch given in this court.*

Pieg, *deer.*

Piere, pier, *father.*

Pier, *worse.*

Pier (le pluis), *the worst.*

Pier, *a tyler.*

Piere de leine, *a stone of wool.*

Piere de la tiere, *a peer of the land.*

Pieroit, *should pay.*

Piers, *pears.*

Piers, peers, *equals.*

Piers, *pieces.*

Piert, pierge, *appears.*

Piert enemy, *open enemy.*

Piete grand, *great charity.*

Pieur, *worse.*

Piez, *feet.*

Piez (la quelle en est), *which is as bad.*

Piges, *pigs.*

Pigne, *a comb.*

Pigne, preigne, *take.*

Pigne (qe au), *who oppress, lay penalties on.*

Pigneresse, *a carder of wool.*

Pignons, *pen.*

pignotary, *prothonotary.*

Piler, pilere, *a pillar.*

Pilers, *piles.*

Piles, pilets, *bolts.*

Pilez, pillie, pilhe, *pillaged.*

Pille, *pile, that side of the coin*

coin which bears the head; cross or pile, a game.

Pilous, *made of hair.*

Pilot d'argent, *a silver dart.*

Pinct (chambre de), *the painted chamber, the room which was antiently St Edward's chamber.*

Pincteur, *a painter.*

Pinsons, *pincers.*

Pioez (ne), *cannot.*

Pipe (qe court en), *which is in charge in the pipe roll*

Piques d'or, *gilt spurs.*

Pire, *a stone.*

Pis, piste, pise, *the breast.*

Pise de formage, *weight of grain.*

Pises, piz, *peas.*

Pissent, *may.*

Pister ou brasier (a), *to bake or brew.*

Pitaunce, *allowance.*

Pite, piteus, *pity, piety.*

Piteousement, *pitiously.*

Piteux regart, *compassionate regard.*

Pitle (un), *a small inclosed piece of land.*

Piz, *pitch.*

Piz, *worse.*

Pl. *plaintiff.*

pla, qil plast, *that he would talk,*

Place de terre, *piece of land.*

Placquer (fait), *caused to be placed, fixed.*

Plage, *beating, stripes, stroke, wound.*

Plai (en), *in full.*

Plain, plein (a), *intirely.*

Plainement, *fully.*

Plainer poour (ou), *with full power.*

Plaisier (por mietz), *for the better compromising.*

Plait, plaid, *plea, proceedings; also the assembly where they were determined.*

Plait (en), *empleaded.*

Plaiz, *differences.*

Plane (de), *plainly.*

Plane (a), *fully.*

Plante (en grant), *in great number.*

Plasse, *a town, hold, or fortress.*

Plat, *metal, iron.*

Plate (de), *coat of metal.*

Plate (le), *gold or silver uncoined, bullion.*

Plauces, *plausible.*

Plauntes, *planted, placed.*

Playe, *a wound.*

Playes Dieu (v), *the five wounds of our Saviour.*

Playn, plein, plain, *not guilty.*

Play plai (u), *in a plea.*

ple, *speaks or expresses.*

Ple,

Ple, *plea.*
Pleaſt, plerra, *ſhall pleaſe.*
Pleaſaunt, *well liked.*
Pledent, *hold plea of.*
Pledu, *pleaded.*
Plegg (pur), *to take pledges, or ſurety.*
Pleggage, *ſuretyſhip.*
Plein des perſones (encountre tout), *againſt all manner of perſons.*
Pleint (le), *the plaintiff.*
Pleint (le grant), *the greateſt part.*
Pleintie, *complaint.*
Pleintivouſe (ſi), *ſo numerous.*
Pleiſne, pleyne, *complains.*
Pleit, plaint, *complaint.*
Plenere, *full.*
Plente, *plenty.*
Pleſaunce (pur), *for the pleaſure, to pleaſe.*
Pleſir, *will, pleaſure.*
Pleſt, ple, pleiſt, *pleaſe.*
Plet, pleit, *plea.*
Pleu, plieu, *pleaſed.*
Pleve ſa foi, *pledged his faith.*
Plevys (lour), *thoſe whoſe pledges they are.*
Pleyn (plus a), *more fully.*
Pleynant, *plaintiff.*
Pleyndre (ne ſe eſcreyent), *may not be afraid to complain, may not be tired out with complaining.*
Pleytrye, *poultry.*
Pleytz, *pleas, plaints, complaints.*
Plez (ſale de), *hall of pleas.*
Plia, *placed, joined together.*
Plien, pline, *full.*
Plieu, *pleaſed.*
Plieur, *pleaſure.*
Plin (de), *completely, fully.*
Pliſt, *plight.*
Plite, pluit, *plait.*
Ploaſt, ploet, *pleaſes.*
Ploite des beſognes (pour les), *for the diſpatch of the buſineſs.*
Plorantes, *lamentable.*
Plot, *it rains.*
Ploy (ſur le), *on the folding up, the label.*
Pluis, *more, moreover, further.*
Pluiſceſtre, *furthermore.*
Pluis puiſne, *much later.*
Plum, *lead.*
Plumbes, *leaden caldrons, leaden pipes.*
Plume, *feathers.*
Plumer bruere, *to cut heath.*
Plunger, *to intrude.*
Plus, *ſurplus.*
Plus pres qu'il pourra etre fait (de ſamble eſtat, au), *of the ſame quality, or as near as may be.*
Pluſoms (a), *to ſeveral.*

Pluſtoſt

Pluftoft (de), *immediately.*
Plux grant, *much greater.*
pnetz, *take.*
Po, pou, poi, pol, *a little.*
Poaer, power, *poſſe.*
Poant, *could.*
Poart (ne), *cannot.*
Pochier (le), *the thumb.*
Poeimes (nous), *we could, we might.*
Poent, *can.*
Poer, poeir, poair, *power, force, authority, ſtrength; realm, territory, juriſdiction; fear, ability.*
Poer (a renable), *at a reaſonable rent.*
Poer mi (ne), *could not.*
Poes, *can.*
Poeſt, *power.*
Poet, *behaviour.*
Poet mye pyre (no), *cannot be worſe.*
Poeur, *fear.*
Poey (ne), *cannot.*
Poeyt (ſe), *ſhould take effect.*
Poi, *little.*
Poi, *more.*
Poi (a), *at leaſt; well.*
Poi des ans (en), *within a few years.*
Poiart, *may.*
Poiement, *payment.*
Poier, poiar, *power, fear, juriſdiction.*
Poies (per), *for fear.*
Poietz tout (vous), *you put the whole.*
Poigne, poine (en), *in his hand, in hand, paid down.*
Poindre, *to paint.*
Poinons, *pendants.*
Poins, poinne, *pains, penalties, puniſhment.*
Point (ou), *in the condition.*
Pointe (mettront), *endeavour.*
Pointes, pointz, *fingers.*
Pointes tretables, *drawbridges* *.
Points, poins, poinz, *points, articles.*
Points, poinctz (potiùs), ponts, *bridges.*
Poir (quatre), *four pair.*
Poires, *peas.*
Pois (pur), *for the weight.*
Poiſa (nous), *affects us.*
Poiſages (les), *the weighing.*
Poiſant coer (avoir), *to be offended at, to bear reſentment.*
Pois-apres, *ſoon afterwards.*
Poiſcans, puiſſant, *powerful, able.*
Poiſes, *weights.*
Poiſes couchantz, *weights couching.*

* Potiùs, *pountes,* 2 Parl. Rolls 218, pet. 51.

Poiſes,

Poiſes, poiſee, *weighed, conſidered.*

Poiſiz (ſur le), *in the weighing.*

Poiſſance, *power.*

Poiſſantz (eſt), *is poſſeſſed of.*

Poiſſe, *could.*

Poiſures (lour), *their weighing.*

Poix (le), *the fiſt.*

Pol, Poul, Pou, *Paul.*

Polail, *poultry.*

Polentiers (les), *malt-makers.*

Poleyns, poleine, pulleyns, *colts.*

Police (p), *by.*

Polls (a), *to the poll.*

Polrieſme faire, *could do.*

Polrons (que nous), *that we can.*

Poltaire, polter, polentier, *poulterer; the officer in the king's kitchin who has the charge of the poultry.*

Polx, *the thumb.*

Polz, *ſkin.*

Polz (al), *the ſkull.*

Pomadre, *powder.*

Pomelx deſpeies, *pommels for ſwords.*

Poms (nous), *we can.*

Ponce, *hand.*

Pondage, *poundage.*

Pondeur (le), *the weight.*

Pondre, pounder, *a weight, the ſame as the auncel.*

Pont (ne), *cannot.*

Pont freint, *Pontefract.*

Ponz, *bridges.*

Pooi, pooir, poor, por, *power.*

Pooires (le), *the power.*

Pooit, *may.*

Pooms, *we may, might.*

Poons (ne), *we cannot.*

Pooſts, *poſts.*

Poour, *fear.*

Populaires, *common, inferior people.*

Por, *power, juriſdiction.*

Por, *on account of, for.*

Por ce, *therefore.*

Por ce que je a parſſui (e), *and as ſoon as I perceived.*

Por ceu kil, *becauſe that it.*

Por le tot, *for the whole.*

Por quei, *wherefore.*

Porcary, *a hogſty.*

Porceſtre, *Porcheſter.*

Porchers, *ſwineherds.*

Porcionur (a), *to apportion.*

Porcoi, *why.*

Poreerra, *ſhall provide, determine.*

Porgiſer, progiſer, purgiſer, *to lay with, violate, defile.*

Poriroit

Poriroit (ne), *could not.*
Porles, *pearls.*
Porom mie (ne), *could not.*
Porport, *purport.*
Porprises (unt), *have made a purpresture upon.*
Porreymes estre (ne), *cannot be.*
Porseor, *possessor.*
Porsise, *possessed.*
Port (li), *the ports.*
Porte (avec), *with the loss.*
Porte paix, *the pax for the holy kiss. In the primitive times, in the eastern countries, a ceremony was used by the Christians after divine service ended, to kiss one another, as a token of mutual amity and peace: to continue and perform which custom with more convenience and decency, in after-times, this invention was devised, viz. a piece of wood or metal, with the picture of Christ upon it, was solemnly tendered to all the people present to kiss; this was called osculatorium, or the pax, to signify the peace, unity, and amity, of all the faithful, who in that manner, by the medium of the pax, kissed one another. Mat. Paris tells us, that, during the great difference between Henry the Second and his turbulent archbishop Thomas Becket, Rex osculum pacis dare archiepiscopo negavit. Mat. Paris,* 117. *And Holingshed says, that the king refused to kiss the pax with the archbishop at mass. Holingshed in anno* 1170. *Staveley,* 191.
Portesmue, *Portsmouth.*
Portetz, *brought.*
Porton, *share.*
Porverra, *shall provide, determine.*
Porvoiance, *providence.*
Pose, *prevented, settled.*
Poser, *to put questions.*
Posez, *put, set at.*
Posoms, *suppose, or put the case.*
Posses (en), *in pulse.*
Possez (jours), *times passed.*
Postoille (la), *the pope.*
Pot, *can.*
Poture, puture, *a claim made by foresters of provisions from those who lived within the purlieus of the forest.*
Pou (si), *so little.*

Povaire,

Povaire, povare, *power*.
Pouces, *fingers*.
Pouchon, *puncheon*.
Poudre de oiseaus et poissons, *semye of birds and fishes*.
Poūe Descose (la), *the poor people of Scotland*.
Poverail del eynee (la), *the poor people in the neighbourhood*.
Pouers, povre, poverez, *poor*; *poverty*.
Pouerté, *poverty*.
Povira (en quanque il), *in as much as shall be in his power*.
Poulare, *powder*.
Poul, *Paul*.
Poulce, *forefinger*, *hand*.
Pouldreux, *dusty*.
Poules, *wards*.
Poults, poulter, *poultry*; *a poulterer*.
Pounage, *paunage*.
Pounsonez, *powdered*, *spotted*.
Pount, *a bridge*.
Pour de mort, *fear of death*.
Poure, pour, pouwer, *power*, *force*.
Pourar̃ homes, *poor men*.
Pour chivalier, *poor knight*.
Pour cheu ke, *because*.
Poures, *poor people*.
Pourfice, *profited*.
Pourkach, pourkars, pourchack, *procurement*.
Pourlesse, *fearless*.
Pourmener, *to go, or walk about*.
Pourpenser, *to devise*.
Pourpoins (en leur), *in their coat-armour*; *with their arms*.
Pourquoy, *on which account*.
Poursigre, *to prosecute*.
Pouryssement, *impoverishment*.
Pous, *fingers*.
Pous (la), *the poor people*.
Pous (par le), *by the inch*; *the thumb's breadth*.
Pouserent leur sealx, *put their seals*.
Pouste, *power*, *jurisdiction*.
Pout, *may*.
Pout (ne), *could not*.
Poutyns, poucins, *pullets*.
Poutz, pouses (deux), *two fingers*, *inches*.
Power, *poor*.
Powers (a), *to the poor*.
Powere (per noz), *by our father*.
Poy, *a little*.
Poy (tout a), *very nearly the same*, *almost the whole of*, *all but a little*.
Poy fait (a), *little practised*.
Poy et par poy (par), *by little and little*.

Poy denk (un), *a little ink.*

Poy a dire (un), *to ſay a word or two.*

Poy de ly (mult), *very lightly of him.*

Poy de temps (par moult), *a very ſhort time.*

Poy voet vivere par ſoy meſmes (qa), *which can ſupport itſelf.*

Poye vaut, *worth but little.*

Poye (a), *at leaſt.*

Poyer de countee, *the poſſe comitatus.*

Poyer de la mort, *fear of death.*

Poyn, poygne, *a hand.*

Poynes, *penalties, pains.*

Poynne, *pains, trouble.*

Poyntes, *pins.*

Poynt ne, *cannot.*

Poyount, *pay.*

Poys, *weight.*

Poys, *peas.*

Poys (de), *of conſequence.*

Poyſe, *thinks.*

Poyſe (lui), *affects him.*

Poyſent pluis, *are of a deeper die.*

Poze, *placed.*

Pr̃a, *may.*

Praefection, *appointing, making.*

Praigne, prange, *take.*

Praiſe des aſſiſes (la), *the taking aſſiſes.*

Praiſmes, *took.*

Pre (plus), *nearer.*

Prechourez, *preachers.*

Preer (de), *to beſeech.*

Prees, *meadows.*

Preerent (nos), *beſeeched us.*

Preeſt (al), *at the meadow.*

Pref (a), *to prove.*

Prefaire, *to perfect.*

Prei, *meadow.*

Preints (que l'en), *that there is inſerted, put.*

Preier (a la), *at the prayer.*

Preies, preyes, *booty, plunder.*

Preignans affaires, *preſſing affairs.*

Preignaunce, *preſſing, taking.*

Preis, *price.*

Preiſe, *acquainted, informed.*

Preiſer, *to appraiſe.*

Preiſſe (moy), *I plead, inſiſt.*

Preiſee, *prized, commended.*

Preiſſoins, *had taken.*

Preiſt (ſe), *may be taken.*

Preiſtr̃ (les), *took them.*

Premerem (le), *the firſt.*

Premeſſes, *promiſes.*

Premis, *promiſed.*

Premiſtrent, *will promiſe.*

Prendrans en bon gree (un), *a taking in good part.*

Prendre (pur), *to undertake.*

Prengnoffatz, *take.*
Prent (luy), *takes himſelf.*
Prente (le), *the impreſſion.*
Prenye, preigne, preagent, *apprehend, take.*
Prererre, *prayer.*
Pres, *preſented.*
Pres (de), *near.*
Pres (plus), *as near.*
Pres nulles (bien), *ſcarce any.*
Pres (ſi), *as near, as well as.*
Preſchanntz, *perſuading.*
Preſchein, *preceding.*
Preſchein, *next.*
Preſeance, *precedence.*
Preſentaines, *preſented.*
Preſente, *preſentee.*
Preſentez, preſantz, *preſent.*
Preſentment, *preſentation.*
Preſone, *priſon.*
Preſs (ſur un), *on a preſentment.*
Preſs la def (de), *to preſent the defect.*
Preſſieux, *precious.*
Preſt, *took.*
Preſt, *made.*
Preſt, *borrowed, ready, a loan.*
Preſt (de), *borrowed on.*
Preſt (ſon), *what he lent.*
Preſta (luy), *lent to him.*
Preſtaige, *prieſthood.*
Preſte lur aver *, *lent their money.*
Preſter (me), *to accommodate me with.*
Preſtier (a), *to borrow.*
Preſtment ſute, *proof ready at hand.*
Preſz, preſtez, preſe, *ready.*
Pretend, *forethought.*
Pretenſez reignez, *pretended reigns.*
Preud home, preux, *great men; a valiant man.*
Preue, pren, *weal, profit, advantage.*
Prevement, p̃vementes, *privately.*
Prever, *to take a view of beforehand.*
Previpſe, *private ſeal.*
Prevuſmes, *intended.*
Preyer, *to pray.*
Preyez, *ſpoil.*
Preymes, preimes, preiſmes, *took.*
Prez, *prayers.*
Pri (vus), *I pray you.*
Pri, prient (ſi), *ſo prays.*
Prie, *takes.*
Prie (de), *worſe.*
Prier, *to pray, intercede for.*
Pries (la), *the taking.*
Prigner, *to take.*
Priggaute, *parity.*
Prime (a heur de), *at one o'clock.*
Primer apres (tot a), *immediately after, ſoon after.*

* *Aver*, in the Stat. of Acton Burnel, 11 edit. is tranſlated, *goods.*

Primerement,

Primerement, *in the first place, especially.*
Primerime (nonante), *ninety-one.*
Primerme devise (a la), *at the first court.*
Primpt (im), *in the twilight.*
Princee de Capes, *principality of Capua.*
Princhē, *prince.*
Principalement, *especially.*
Principallee de Cestre, *principality of Chester.*
Principaltee, *principalship, head of a hall.*
Prins, prinses, *taken from.*
Print, *he takes.*
Prioritie, *priory.*
Prioure de mort, *fear of death.*
Pris sus, *taken up, undertook.*
Pris (sur le), *upon the price.*
Pris de guerre (les), *the prisoners of war.*
Pris (plus), *the more readily.*
Pris, *may* *.
Prise (nous), *concerns us.*
Prisel, *a taking; also a condition, acceptance.*
Priser, *to value, appraise.*
Priserunt (qui), *who appraised.*
Prises qu, droit, *less value than they ought to be of.*
Prisons, *prisoners.*
Prist, *a loan.*
Prist, *borrowed.*
Prist (de), *by borrowing on loan.*
Prist (se), *was taken.*
Pristerent a mayn (ilz), *they undertook for.*
Pristeront repons, *received answers.*
Pristerount ensemble (sey), *assembled together.*
Pristre (se), *were performed.*
Pristine. (sergeant), *serjeant of the bakehouse.*
Prisun, *prison.*
Priu, purru, *deflowered.*
Prium, *we pray.*
Privables, *liable to deprivation.*
Privez, *people of our own nation.*
Privites (les), *the secrets.*
Probation (pur la), *for the proving.*
Procain, *next.*
Proces, *porks.*
Prochī jour, *next day.*
Prochainement, precheinement, *speedily, last, next.*
Prochement, *immediately.*
Procheynete, prochenite, *proximity, nearness.*
Procier (cela), *that proceeded.*
Procincte, *precinct.*

* Potiùs *puse.* Rot. Parl. vol. I. p. 276. pet. 16. Hale's MS.

Procure,

Procure, *a proctor.*
Prodance, *prudence.*
Prode, *produced.*
Proder, *to go out of.*
Prodes, probes hommes, *honest men.*
Prodes homes, *the Magnates and Grands of the counties, the military tenants, the wise discreet men of the nation; also men well-affected.*
Prodome, *a man of some note.*
Profites (les), *the advantages, benefits.*
Progaine, *progeny.*
Progiser, *to ravish.*
Proiere, *prayer.*
Prois, *prayed.*
Prois, *proved.*
Proismes, *near.*
Prolation (la), *the pronouncing, giving.*
Prologner, *to prolong.*
Promes, *promise.*
Promegons (vous), *we promise you.*
Proñ, *neighbour.*
Pronš, *ready.*
Pronunciation, *sentence, decree.*
Pronunciast le dit parlement, *declared the cause of calling the said parliament.*
Pronunciement (en temps de), *at the time of pronouncing.*
Propier, *like to suffer.*
Propitz, *favourable.*
Propos, *purpose.*
Proprement (sa sals), *his own proper hall.*
Proroignement, *prorogation, prolongation.*
Prosme, *a neighbour.*
Prou, proun, *much, enough, a great deal.*
Proute, *ready, quick.*
Prouz, *proved.*
Provable errour, *a manifest, a just or justifiable error.*
Provablement, *plainly.*
Provablement attaint, *provably attainted, i. e. upon manifest evidence.*
Provables (ceux pleas sunt), *these pleas are to be proceeded in.*
Provant (en), *in proving.*
Prouaire, *a priest.*
Proudhomme, proudomys, prudonne (sur la), *on the probity, prudence.*
Prove (de), *of the probate.*
Provenant, *arising.*
Provenders, *provisers, prebendaries.*

Provendre, *a prebend.*
Prover, *to improve.*
Proverifon, *impoverifhment.*
Provers hommes, *poor men.*
Provifent, *fhould prove.*
Provoft, *the provoft, the lord of the vill; the reeve or bayliff of the king, or of the lord of the manor.*
Prowe, proñ, preve, pren, pru, *profit, advantage.*
P̃royt, *may.*
Prud omes, *great men.*
Prudum, *an honeft man.*
Pruerount, *fhall approve.*
Prumeirement, *in the firft place.*
Prufchanament paffee, *laft paft.*
Pruvance, *proof, evidence, property.*
Pruys, *Pruffia.*
Pry, *proper, advifeable.*
Pry (vous), *I pray, I befeech you.*
Pryemes, *took.*
Pryne, *taking.*
p̃s, pris, *taken.*
pts, *lofs.*
Pu, *more.*
Pucillage, *virginity.*
Pucyns, *chickens.*
Pue et pue (al), *by little and little.*
Pueent (il ne), *they may not.*
Pueent pas (ne), *cannot.*
Pueplier, *to publifh.*
Puer, *pure.*
Pues, *fed.*
Pues, *fpoiled, trodden down.*
Pues, *afterwards.*
Puet eftre, *it might be.*
Puet (ne), *cannot.*
Puet unqore, *is yet depending.*
Pueuble, *people.*
Puft l'en dire, *one might anfwer.*
Pugny, *punifhed.*
Puir (potius pair), paternofters, *a pair of paternofters, ftrings of beads for the priefts,* &c. *to number their prayers by. In one of the canons made at a provincial fynod in* 816, *where Wulfrud, Abp. of Canterbury prefided, we meet with* VII *Beltidum Paternofter, which feems to imply that they had in that age a certain number of ftuds faftened into their belts, or girdles, which were then ufed, as ftrings of beads now are, for the numbering of their prayers, but with this*

this difference, that the studs were all of one size; and that every one of them stood for a paternoster; whereas the modern fashion is, to have lesser beads, which stand for Ave Maries, to one larger, which stands for a paternoster. Johnson's Canons, 816.

Pulfre, *a bruise, swelling, scar, wound.*

Pulles esperners, *young hawks.*

Pulleyns, *colts.*

Pulter, *a poulterer.*

Pulter et catour (sergeant), *serjeant of the poultry and of the catery.*

Pulteri, *poultry.*

Pune, *youngest.*

Punee (une), *a younger daughter.*

Punees, *youngest sons.*

Punier, *to punish.*

Puobles Cristiens, *Christian people.*

Puour, *stench.*

Pupplier, *to publish.*

Pur, *by.*

Puralle, puraille, poral, purlieu, *perambulation.*

Pur arestier, *to arrest.*

Pur ceo qe, *from the time that.*

Pur coe que, *forasmuch as.*

Pur coi, *whereby.*

Pur que, *for which.*

Pur chou ke, *because that.*

Purche, *therefore.*

Purtant cum, *as long as.*

Purtant qe, *to the intent that.*

Purceynte, purseynte, *precinct.*

Purch, *purchaser.*

Purcharrent, *proceeded.*

Purchas de courts, *perquisites of courts.*

Purchas (en le), *in the demand of the writ.*

Purchas demeyn (en son), *of his own demanding.*

Purchas (tout), *all his acquisitions.*

Puree, *ascertained.*

Purfit, *on the sides.*

Purgacon, *cleansing.*

Purge, *purgation.*

Purgyser, *to deflower, to defile, to violate.*

Purjace, *purchased.*

Purjoiner, *to put off.*

Purlheynoste, *prothonotary.*

Purparl, *a conference, a treaty.*

Purparlance (sur), *upon a conference, condition.*

Purparler, purparlance, pur-

purparles, purale, *a perambulation.*
Purparler, *to diſcourſe of.*
Purpenſe, prepenſe, *fore-thought.*
Purpernant, *aſſuming.*
Purportaſt, *purported, dictated.*
Purpoſe, *ſet forth, alledged, declared, propoſed.*
Purpreignes, *makes a purpreſture on.*
Purpreſtour, *he that makes the purpreſture.*
Purpris, *taken, purpriſed.*
Purpull, *purple.*
Purres, *adulterated.*
Purris, *rotten, damaged.*
Purrois lieu (en), *in a place full of putrefaction.*
Purruſt, *deflowered.*
Purſauve, *proſecuted.*
Purſourver, *to ſurvey.*
Purſuant, *proſecutor.*
Purſuer (de), *to proſecute.*
Purſui, *purchaſe, obtain.*
Purſuit (en la), *in the precinct.*
Purſuount, *have ſued, applied for.*
Purtenand, *appertaining.*
Purtrere (la manere de), *the manner of drawing it out.*
Purus, *provided.*
Purveaunce de Dieu, *providence of God.*
Purveier, purvoier, purver, purveer, *to provide.*
Purvey, purview, purvieus, purveu, purw, *provided.*
Purvele, *ball of the eye.*
Purvenauntz, *ariſing.*
Purveyance, purview.
Purvieu, purveu, *proviſion, condition, ordinance, ſtatute.*
Pus, puz, puis, *after.*
Pus, *afterwards, ſince.*
Puſams (quant nus les), *at her eſpouſals.*
Puſance, *power.*
Puſeit, *he may.*
Puſel, *a maid, a virgin, a damſel, a little girl.*
Puſelage, *virginity.*
Pus ke, *ſince that.*
Pus qui, *after that.*
Puſſum, *can, may.*
Puſt, put, puiſt, *fed.*
Puſture, *homage.*
Put, *ugly, homely, diſhoneſt.*
Putage, *adultery, whoredom.*
Putaine, putiene louée, *a hired concubine, an harlot.*
Putel, *a well.*
Puthois, putois, *a Fulmart.*

Pu-

Puture, pufture, poture. *See* Poture.
Puy (mult), *much worfe, very lightly.*
Puys (homage), *pure homage.*
Puyer, *to bear up, to fupport.*
Puyr, *pure.*
Puys, *a well, a watery or oozy place.*
Puys apres, *foon afterwards.*
Puys (de), *fince.*
Puyt affettes byen, *might very well.*
Py, pie, pys, *the breaft.*
Pye, *worfe.*
Pye (de), *on foot.*
Pyghenoute, *pendant.*
Pyndes d'ivory, *ivory combs.*

q̃, *who, when, that.*
Qu, *for.*
Qa, *a farthing.*
Qare lou, *whereas.*
Q. d. non, *certainly not.*
q̃r, *quarter.*
Qant, *when, as.*
Qanpeyne, *that fcarce.*
Qar-qare, quair, *for.*
Qarant földz (deinz), *within forty fhillings.*
Qe, *who.*
Qeconqes, *whatfoever.*
Qele meyfon, *what houfe.*
Qenu enfeuerent, *confequence would be.*
Qeft, *who is.*
Qeftes, *who are.*
Qeu, *that.*
Qi (de), *whofe.*
Qi de ceo, *what's that to the purpofe.*
Qi fi, *fuppofe that.*
Qi (fon), *his cries.*
Q'illoms de fa couftome (et), *and the collecting his cuftoms.*
Qiqe lieu, *in whatfoever place.*
Qiqe foit, *whether it be.*
Qoer (vour efmeroient de), *heartily thank you.*
Qoi, *what with.*
Qore eft, *who now is.*
Qua (fi), *fo that.*
Quacorte, *fourteen.*
Quader, *to relate.*
Quanch il aveit, *all that he had.*
Quanque, *whatfoever, all that.*
Quant et quant, *forthwith.*
Quantieme, *the whole quantity.*
Quantqe (en), *in as much as.*
Quantreft, *whatfoever is.*
Quantz, *how much.*

Quaquil, *all, whoever.*
Quare, quar, *for.*
Quarell de arte, ou de fletche, *a trial of ſkill at fencing or ſhooting.*
Quareſme, quereſme (demy, mii), *midlent.*
Quarkes, *oaks.*
Quarre de le main, *the back of the hand.*
Quarreaux, *cuſhions, couches.*
Quarreur, *a ſquare.*
Quarrier, *a quarry.*
Quart, *takes, carries.*
Quarters (par), *by turns.*
Quartier (par un), *by turns, in rotation.*
Quartrover (decoller et), *beheaded and quartered.*
Quaſſentz, *quaſhed, annulled.*
Quaterable, *quarterable.*
Quatreble (du), *in four times.*
Quatruſze, *fourteen.*
Quattezime joar, *fourth day.*
Quaunt, *when, as much as, as to, how much.*
Quaunt (et ne p̃), *and yet, neverthele∫s.*
Quaus deytas (las), *which ſaid.*
Quay (par), *by which means, wherefore.*
Que, *which, whether.*
Que (pour), *for which.*
Que (de), *of which.*
Quer, quey (de), *whereof.*
Queilletzes, *collected.*
Queiſt, *ſhould ſeek.*
Quelm̃t, *cruelly.*
Quelſz genz, *whatſoever people.*
Queņ, *in what.*
Quen breve, *what writ.*
Quen (outre), *over which.*
Quen-part, *whereſoever.*
Quena, *a woman.*
Quene marchaundie, *but one merchandiſe.*
Quens de Flanders, *count or earl of Flanders.*
Quenz, *earl.*
Queor, queur, quoer, quer, queer, quier, *heart, affection.*
Queque, *although.*
Quer, *leather, ſkin, hide.*
Quer deners, *forty pence.*
Quer, queor (en mye le), *in the middle of the choir.*
Querdoner, *rewarded, provided for.*
Quere, *which.*
Quere (a), *to go for, to get.*
Quere hors, *go out of.*
Querele (de la), *of the quarrel, contention, party.*
Querele (par), *by which means.*
Quereler mieuz (e), *and provide*

provide for themselves better.

Querer, queur, querez, querre, quer, *to get, obtain, to enquire, seek for, beg, fetch, bring over.*

Queresteres, *choiristers.*

Querfage, *wharfage.*

Querge (le), *let him seek him.*

Querle (de), *to seek him.*

Queresme, *Lent.*

Querrer, *a quarry.*

Querrour, *a digger of stones.*

Quer son viver, *to get his living.*

Quest (la), *the inquest.*

Quest (le), *the which.*

Queste, *which is.*

Quetment, *quietly.*

Quets, *watch, guards.*

Queue de vin, *a vessel containing about a hogshead and half of wine.*

Queve, quevi (selles en double), *sealed by affixing the seal to a label.*

Queul (le), *which.*

Queulloient, *collect.*

Queurt, *he searches.*

Queux (de), *of whom.*

Quex, *which, who, what.*

Quey, *what.*

Queys, *keys, wharfs.*

Quidaunce, *believing, thinking.*

Quiders, *thoughts, opinion.*

Quidra, *shall think.*

Quie, *whereas.*

Quier, *the heart.*

Quieur (les), *which.*

Quiex (a), *to whom.*

Quil, *he who.*

Quilage, *collection.*

Quillers d'or, *gilt spoons.*

Quillours, quissours, *collectors.*

Quin, *which, who.*

Quincts et requinctz, *the fifth part of the price of the feudal estate sold, and a fifth of that fifth.*

Quinque al foit li (par), *at any time.*

Quinz, quenz, *earl.*

Quinzen (un), *fifteen days.*

Quinzisme, *every fifteenth day.*

Quirre, quiver, *copper.*

Quirs, quivres, *skins, leather.*

Quis, quise, quiz, *sought, searched for, drawn out, entered up.*

Quisent (que), *who expose to sale.*

Quisses, quious, *buttocks.*

Quist, *he searches.*

Quit, *baked.*

Quiteclamaunce, *a release.*

Quitement, *entirely.*

Quitie, *acquits.*

Quittain (la) quictance, *the acquittance.*

Quive, *end, tail.*

Qullie, *collect.*

Quo, *who.*

Quoer, *heart.*

Quoer (ne ferons mie a eese de), *shall not rest satisfied.*

Quoi, *who has.*

Quont, *when.*

Quotes, *quotas.*

Quoue quo, *the tail of an animal.*

Quount, *which have.*

Quoy, *look ye.*

Quoy (p), *how, by what.*

Qux (le), *which.*

Quyke, *quick, living.*

Qu' nr, *fifth.*

Quyr (le), *the leather.*

Quyvre, quirre, quyur, *copper.*

Qwargh, qwerf, *a wharf.*

Qy, *who.*

r̃ *reason; to answer.*

Rv, *received.*

Rec̃, *recovery, shall recover.*

r̃n, r̃ns (en), *in answering.*

Ro, ronn, *answer.*

Rondre, rẽndre, rour̃re, *to answer.*

Rũ, *given.*

Raancon, *ransom. exemption.*

Raap de Lewes, *the rape of Lewes.*

Rabbailer, rabbatre, *to beat down, pull down.*

Racentz, *roots.*

Races, rases, *pulled down.*

Rachapz, *reliefs.*

Rachater, *to redeem, buy out, repurchase.*

Racinetter, *to take root.*

Racions, *articles.*

Racourcir, *to sink together.*

Rad, *firm, stable, alert, gay.*

Raempler, *to fulfil.*

Raencons, raancons, *ransoms.*

Raenpli, *filled.*

Rajes de la meer, *rage of the sea.*

Raim, *branches.*

Raimbre, *to restore.*

Rain (par) et par baston, per annulum et virgam, *by a ring and rod, wand, or staff.*

Raindre hors de prison (pur luy), *to ransom him out of prison.*

Raine, *queen.*

Raisins, *roots.*

Raisnaable, *reasonable.*

Raison (brief), *speedy justice.*

Raith,

Raith, reth, *a term made use of in Wales, and signifies an oath taken by three hundred men.*

Rakkyng de draps, *racking of cloth.*

Ralongement, *prolongation.*

Rama, *full of boughs.*

Ramage, *wild, untamed.*

Ramens, ramans, ramures, *boughs, branches.*

Ramentens, *remembered, recommended to.*

Ramettre, *to replace.*

Ramilles, *ſmall twigs.*

Rampas, Rampau, *Palm-Sunday.*

Ramys, *replaced, fixed on again.*

Rancumpanne, *cloth not well fulled, dreſſed.*

Rancunes, *rancors.*

Rangeous, *rancorous.*

Raof, Raoul, *Ralph.*

Raoſon (par), *by reaſon, by means of.*

Rapelees, *revived.*

Rapt, *ſnatched, forced.*

Raſe, *ſhaven.*

Raſez, *ſtriked.*

Raſez (dras), *ruſſet cloths.*

Raſoure, *a raſure.*

Raſſe, *eraſed.*

Raſure de os, *fracture of a bone.*

Rate del temps (pur le), *for the proportion of time.*

Raube, *robbed.*

Raveſti, *inveſted.*

Raviſt, *raviſhed, took away with force.*

Rauncener, *ranſomed.*

Ravoms, *have recovered.*

Ravoquement, *revocation.*

Ray, le ray, *the array or panel of the jury.*

Ray (robe de), *robe of ruſſet cloth.*

Raytz, *nets.*

Re, *king.*

Read, realt, *had again.*

Real chemin (en le), *in the king's highway.*

Reale dignite, *regal dignity.*

Reaſon, *reaſon, act, title.*

Reatt, *reattachment.*

Reavera (ne), *ſhall not have again.*

Reau, *reverend.*

Reaume, reaugme, reame, *realm.*

Rebatables, *may be objected to, refuſed.*

Rebataunce (la), *the lowering, the abating.*

Rebauderoit, *ſhould redeliver.*

Rebeaux, rebealx, rebeux, *rebels, diſobedient.*

Rebellite,

Rebellite, *rebellion.*
Rebete, rebote, *rejected, put back, put out.*
Reboter, rebutter, rebouter, *to put back, to bar, repel.*
Rebour, *a robber.*
Rebuquiz, *rebuked, discountenanced.*
Rec̃, *recovered.*
Reccimes, *received.*
Reccourt, *record.*
Receboſſatz, *receive.*
Recehantz, *reſiants.*
Receit, *receives.*
Receiventerre, *to receive.*
Recellement, *withdrawing himſelf.*
Recenſement, *a-muſtering.*
Receraſſent, *ſhould receive.*
Recepueurs des peticions, *receivers of petitions.*
Reces (dernier), *the laſt receſs ; abſtinence.*
Reces (lettre de), *letter of receſs; an abſtinence from war.*
Receſt, *reception.*
Receſtes, *received.*
Receta, recia, *received.*
Recettement, *receipt.*
Recettours, *receivers.*
Rechaceables, *remandable.*
Rechat, *buying.*
Rechate, *ranſom.*
Rechater, *to ranſom, ſave.*
Rechept, *receipt, admittance.*
Rechepte, *ranſomed.*
Recherrions, *we ſhould fall again.*
Recheſs, *extended unto.*
Rechevour, *to receive.*
Rechief, recheſſe (de), *again, moreover.*
Rechoive, *receive.*
Rechurent, receheu, recia, *received.*
Reclamant, *making claim.*
Reclame, *reclaimed, challenged.*
Recoeury, *recovers.*
Recognoiſeans, *well knowing.*
Recoiller, *to aſſemble.*
Recoilliſt, *recohabited with.*
Recoipuent (ne), *do not receive.*
Recollant, *recollecting, remembring.*
Recond, *hid, buried.*
Reconiſaunce, *recognition, verdict of the recognitors in an aſſiſe.*
Reconiſaunce (lour), *their confeſſion, acknowledgement.*
Reconſeile, recounſeillez, *reconciled to, employed by.*
Reconuſez, *recogniſees.*
Recops, *receive.*

Record,

Record, *rehearsed, recited, read over.*

Recordes, *recorders.*

Recors (asseez bien), *sufficiently apprised.*

Recovere, *shall restore.*

Recoupe, *cut off, taken back again.*

Recousse, *rebellion; imposition.*

Recoust, recow, *received.*

Recreanncer, *to renounce.*

Recreant, *cowardly.*

Recreantisse, *cowardice.*

Recreaunt lo pees (en), *on proclaiming or drawing the concord.*

Recreces del sarve (deux), *two ebbs of the water.*

Recreu, *tired.*

Recruoz (li soient), *should be restored to him.*

Rects, a sa folly, *imputes it to his own folly.*

Rectu, *imputed, accounted.*

Recuillez, *entertained.*

Reculier, *to gather, to collect.*

Recussez, *relived.*

Recuvere, *return, be restored.*

Redde, reddement, rediment, *speedy, speedily, readily.*

Reddeur del boucher, *turning of the mouth.*

Reddouz, reddure, *rigor, strictness.*

Reddourde droit, *rendering of right.*

Redour de ley uses, *justices requires.*

Redevanche, *debt, duty.*

Redoute seignour, *dread lord.*

Redoubtemout, *is very much afraid of.*

Redresser, redrecher, *to erect and keep up, amend, redress, cleanse, make satisfaction for.*

Redubbours de dras, *redubbers, patchers, botchers, or menders of apparel. Those who buy stolen cloaths, &c. and, that they may not be known, turn them into some other colour or fashion.*

Reeit, *shall have again.*

Reen, *any thing.*

Reenvoions, *we send back.*

Rees, refs, *nets.*

Rees (de), *with reeds.*

Refection, *repairing.*

Refees, *subfees.*

Reffaire, refere, *to rebuild, repair.*

Reffoul, *the emptying a canal or pond.*

Refoil de la mere, *ebbing of the sea.*

Refor-

Reformement, *restoration*; *performance*.
Refoul, *great inundation.*
Refouler (fouler et), *to flow and reflow.*
Refouler (le fouler et), *to empty it and fill it again.*
Refourme, *reformed*; *drawn up.*
Refreindre, *to repress.*
Refrenee, *refrained.*
Refresement (en), *in refreshing, succouring.*
Refresser, *to refresh.*
Refs, *nets.*
Refu, *shelter, refuge.*
Refurment, *reformation.*
Refust, *may resort to.*
Refuys, *refuse.*
Refuye, *refuge.*
Regalie, *royal.*
Regalie (la), *the regality, royality.*
Regarcier, *to thank.*
Regard, *relation.*
Regard (poy de), *little regard.*
Regard corteisie, *regard or service of courtesy.*
Regardant, regardant, *expectant.*
Regarder, *to allow.*
Regardes, *fees, perquisites, services, rewards, expences, share, allowances.*
Regardez (les), *the salaries; liveries, allowances of the judges, &c.*
Regardez, regarde, *awarded.*
Regardez, *rewarded.*
Regermer, *to sprout again.*
Regetes, *rejected.*
Regnation, *reign.*
Regnauble, *reasonable, equitable.*
Regnez, *reign.*
Regnez (trop), *too much emboldened.*
Regracier Dieu, *to thank God.*
Regreind, *regranted.*
Regrettent, *regard.*
Reherceuill, *writal.*
Rei, *king.*
Reiens (ne soit), *knew nothing of it.*
Reignable, *reasonable.*
Reik (le temps de), *time of harvest, vintage.*
Reimber, *to kill.*
Reimbre, *to ransom.*
Reimbre (a nostre), *for redeeming us, for our ransom.*
Rein, *any thing.*
Rein (par), *by a stream.*
Reinement (la), *the arraignment.*
Reint, *ruined.*
Reinterent, *wounded*; *fined, ransomed.*

Reintz,

Reintz, *punifhed, fined, indicted, ranfomed.*
Reis graens, *great nets.*
Rejoier, *enjoy.*
Rejoife (q'il le), *that he join it again to, unite it to.*
Relais, *releafe, relaxation, remiffion.*
Relaxes, relachiez, *releafed.*
Relene, *relinquifhed.*
Reles, *relief.*
Relevaffent, contre nous (fe), *rofe againft us, rebelled.*
Relevation, *relief.*
Relever (in point de), *in danger of being ruined.*
Relies, *are applied.*
Religion (de mefme la), *of the fame order.*
Relinques, *remains.*
Relinquez, *given up.*
Relinquiz, *abandoned.*
Reliveez, *reliefs.*
Reliverer, *to redeliver.*
Rellatues, *relative.*
Relya, *applied, related to.*
Remaide, *remedy.*
Remainable, *to be accounted.*
Remanant (le), *the reft.*
Remaniables forfeit (font), *are to remain forfeited.*
Remanons, *ftay back, forbear going.*
Remaunderunt, *fent back.*
Remediell, *original.*
Remeinte demounftraunce, *frequent remonftrance,*
Remembraunce, (e metere en), *to be enrolled.*
Remembre, *fet down.*
Remenable, *to be reduced.*
Remenaunt (a), *for ever, for ever after, from thenceforth.*
Remener, *to reftore, to bring back, reduce.*
Remeintiner, rementener, *to remind.*
Remerront, *fhall carry back.*
Remes, *remaining, the refidue.*
Remettre (a), *to be reftored.*
Remeyndra, *fhall not prevent.*
Reminant, *remaining, inhabiting.*
Remis & reconfeile, *remitted and reconciled.*
Remife, remys, *releafed, remifed.*
Remife, *received back.*
Remift, *continued.*
Remiftrent, *remained.*
Remitre, *to ranfom.*
Remmeinant de fiecls (a), *for ever after.*
Remonaera le roy, *lay before*

fore the king, represent to the king.

Remoyer, *to remove.*

Remuale, *removable.*

Remue, *removed, entered into.*

Remuement, remoement, *removal.*

Remument (pur la), *for remedying, removing.*

Remy(seint), *St. Remigius.*

Remys, remiz, *left, remains.*

Remys, remise, remist, remistrent, *remained, continued, released.*

Ren, rens, *any thing; nothing.*

Ren de terre, *any land.*

Ren (a), *to any thing.*

Ren (en nule), *any ways.*

Renable, revable, *reasonable.*

Rendage, *delivering up.*

Rendesist (qil), *that he should deliver up.*

Rendrent, *wounded.*

Rendus, *surrendered.*

Rene, *kingdom.*

Rene, renues, *renowned.*

Renees, reneyee, *apostates, renegado.*

Renent, reneign, *deny, refuse.*

Renestre (a), *to be restored.*

Reng, *rank.*

Rengeons, *resign, submit.*

Renk et rebaylle sus, *surrender and deliver up.*

Renner (nul), *no pyker.*

Renniement, potius remuemens, de la guerre, *commotions, disturbances of war*

Renomens, renun, *renown, fame.*

Renoncher, *to renounce.*

Renoyer, *to abjure, renounce.*

Renson, *ransom.*

Rent, reint, *indicted, accused, fined.*

Renuef, *renewed.*

Renuour(de), *to send back.*

Renure, *fame, renown.*

Repaire (lour), *their post.*

Repairons, repeire, repeirast, *return.*

Repansant, *considering, calling to remembrance.*

Reparlances, *conferences.*

Repeir de merchandises, (le), a Caleys, *the repair, or carrying merchandise to Calais.*

Repeirantz, *repairing to, inhabiting in.*

Repeirez uthalez, *outlaws returned.*

Repel, *calling back.*

Repeller, repeler, *to recover, revoke, restore.*

Rependre (a), *to expend.*

Rependre (de), *to open.*

Reperiller, reparilller, reparelere,

parelere, repeller, *to repair.*

Repere, *receptacle, habitation, houſe.*

Repes (de), *repoſe, reſt.*

Replener, *to fill.*

Replietz, *reply.*

Reploy, reply (ſur le), *on the fold.*

Repoir (ſans), *without returning.*

Repoir, *reſort.*

Repoiſer (de), *to be fixed.*

Reponables, *anſwerable.*

Reponces, *repulſed.*

Repoos (en), *at eaſe.*

Report, *brought back.*

Reportez, *obliged.*

Repoſe, *veſts, lodges.*

Repoſer (ſans), *without reſorting back.*

Repoſt (en), *in ſecret.*

Repperes, *repaired.*

Repreciement, *appraiſement.*

Reprehenſailles, *ſeizures, repriſals.*

Repreigner, reprendre, reprender, *to retake.*

Repreiſmes les traitz, *renew the treaty.*

Repreſt, repriſt, *taken back, compelled, reprehended.*

Repreuches, (les), *the acceſſories, appendages.*

Repriont, reprie, *reprieved deductions.*

Repris, repriſes, *deductions and duties yearly paid out of a manor and lands.*

Reproches, *called in queſtion.*

Reprove autentikement (de), *on authentic proof.*

Reprouvez, *reprobate.*

Repue, *fed.*

Repugnables, *reprovable.*

Repus, *concealed.*

Repus (le Dimanche), Dominica de Paſſione, *in the Romiſh Miſſal, and ſo called from the croſſes and the images of the ſaints being then covered.*

Requerum, *we requeſt.*

Requiller en grace, *to take into favour.*

Requiller (de les faire), *to entertain them.*

Requiſe, *inquired into.*

Re (a de), *in arrear.*

Rere, *to raſe, eraſe.*

Rerecounte (en), *in the rear county.*

Rerefiez, *ſub fees.*

Reremain, *backwards.*

Rerement, *rarely.*

Rerie, *delayed.*

Reſaut, *receives.*

Reſayla le ewe, *the water run back.*

Revivement, *arreſtment.*

Reſcoure, reſcore, *to relieve, aſſiſt.*

Reſcous,

Refcous, refcu, refcufa, *refcued, retaken, relieved.*

Refcous, refcufe, recourfant (foleil, folail), *funfet.*

Refcrivre, *to write to, to return an anfwer.*

Refcure, *to refcue.*

Refcyt (del), *of the receipt,* i. e. *of the crime of receiving felons or ftolen goods.*

Refeauntife, *reriancy.*

Refemble, *feems.*

Refemee, *fown again.*

Refervere, *to receive.*

Refon, *truth, right, juftice, title, reafon, act, argument, charge, expreffion, method, cafe, article, point.*

Refon (p la), *in proportion to.*

Refon (per), *by refummons.*

Refon (funde fa), *grounds his title, counts.*

Refon (noz feare), *make us fatisfaction.*

Refone (de), *in reafon.*

Refons (deux), *two circumftances.*

Refons (fes), *his evidences, muniments, arguments.*

Refort (fon), *a term ufed in a writ of Ayel or Coufinage, in the fame fenfe as a defcent in a writ of right.*

Reforty, *reforted, reverted.*

Refoule, *refolved.*

Refpecteres, refpiretz (ne), *will not delay, refpite.*

Refpi, *delay.*

Refpoignent, *defend.*

Refponez, refpoynez vous (qi), *what anfwer do you make.*

Refpofte, *anfwer.*

Refpundre, *to anfwer.*

Refqueufe, *refcue*

Reffeant, refiant deinez le manoir, *one that continually abides within the manor.*

Reffent, *received acknowledged.*

Reffu, *received.*

Reffumes, *received.*

Reftor, reftors, *reftoration, amends.*

Reftreiñconufans, *take cognifance.*

Reftricte, *made narrower.*

Reftut, *reftored.*

Reftz, *judgment, decree, fentence.*

Refu la mort (a poi), *almoft dead.*

Refurdre, *pay again.*

Refwardent mie (ne), *do not regard.*

Ret, reté, retz, retent, *suspected, accused, indicted.*

Retardation, *delay.*

Reteign vers luy, *keep by him.*

Retenantz, *retainers.*

Retenderount, *shall retain.*

Retenet, *to return, revert.*

Retenget (nuls nel), *let no one retain.*

Retenir, reteiner, *to detain, keep back, retain.*

Retenu, *retained, admitted into.*

Retenues, *reservations.*

Retenutz, *reserved, retained.*

Retenuz, *retinue.*

Reteur, retaur, *return.*

Rethes, *nets.*

Retiner a soy (de), *to take to himself.*

Retoundre, *to clip.*

Retoun, retoundu, *clipped,*

Retournent (que a ces les), *who comply with them.*

Retourner (devoit), *was to be reduced.*

Retrachez, *withdrawn.*

Retraict, retrait, retrayt, retreit, retret, retreit, *withdraw, forebore.*

Retraicter, *to withdraw.*

Rereet, *diminution, draw back, draught.*

Retrehere la corage, *to discourage.*

Retret de la meer, *reflux or ebb of the sea.*

Retreter la reconisance, *to withdraw the recognizance.*

Retreus, retreux, *enlarged, a temporary ransom of a prisoner.*

Retrirer, *to take, withdraw.*

Rette, *crime, offence, guilt, suspicion.*

Rettent, *retain.*

Retter a lui mesme, *impute it to himself.*

Revable, *reasonable.*

Revanche, *revenge.*

Revenans, *mustering.*

Revenant, *comes to, amounts to.*

Revener (a!), *at there turn.*

Revensist, *come back.*

Revenue, *return.*

Revenues, reveues, *review, muster.*

Revenuez, revennaus, revencions, *revenues.*

Revereur, *to reverence.*

Reverons, *reverend.*

Reverses (ses maunches), *his sleeves turned back.*

Reversion (a faire la), *to give up again, to restore.*

Revertise le don, *let the gift revert.*

Revilant, *affecting, making so vile.*

Revinge, *come back.*
Revon (a ſon), duſqes *until his return.*
Rewars, *governors.*
Rewle, *rule, order.*
Rewelez, *regulated, ordained.*
Rewme, *realm.*
Reyans, *royal.*
Reynez, *ruined.*
Reynt, *fined.*
Reys, *kings.*
Rhine, *Queen.*
Ri, *omnipotent.*
Ribaud, *one of the rabble, a ſcoundrel, a raſcal, ruffian.*
Ribauds (fortz), *ſturdy beggars.*
Rie (le), *the heir.*
Rielment (pluis), *more ſeldom, not ſo frequent.*
Riens, *backs.*
Rieſgler * (a en), *to inveigle.*
Rieu, *a ſmall brook.*
Riez, *nets.*
Riflez, *rifled.*
Riflure, *a ſcratch, a rifling.*
Rigle, *a rule.*
Rimer, *to examine, ſearch into.*
Riottis, *riots.*
Ripes del'ewe, *by the water-ſide, banks of the river.*
Ris, rix, *rich.*
Rizard, Richart, *Richard.*
Roaiſons, *Rogations.*
Robbes, *taken from, robbed.*
Robiers, *Robert.*
Roboration, *corroboration.*
Robouchez, *ſtopped, forced.*
Roefs, *oars.*
Roge, *red.*
Roiales (autres), *other the king's officers.*
Roignez, *clipped.*
Roion, *kingdom.*
Rokeboruth, *Roxburgh.*
Rol, *a roll, a regiſter.*
Rolles, colles, *necks.*
Rolys, *rolls.*
Romerie, rommerge, *buggary.*
Romeyns (rey de), *king of the Romans.*
Rondles, *rolls.*
Rone fet (lio hyl), potius unt, *they have made.*
Ronne, *anſwer.*
Rope, *rape.*
Ropele (Robt de), *Robert de Roche.*
Rores (cent), *an hundred faggots.*
Roſſe, *heath.*
Rote (le), *the wheel.*
Roumainement (a), *after the manner of the Romans.*

* Potiùs, *a envieſgler.* Rot. Parl. vol. II p. 79. Pet. 28. Hale's MS.

Roupt,

Roupt, rous, *broken.*
Routez, *routs.*
Roveninkmede, *Running-mead.*
Rovenereray, *without return.*
Rowes, *oars.*
Roy qoreeſt (le), *the present King.*
Royal chemin (le), *the king's highway.*
Roynage, roage, rovage, rotage, *a kind of tribute or payment made for damage done to public ways by carriages.*
Royne, *the Queen.*
Royner, *to clip.*
Ru, *noiſe, murmuring.*
Ruaul, rujaul, *royal.*
Rubaignes, *ribbons.*
Rubbouſes, *rubbiſh, filth.*
Ruby baleis, baleſeit, *an inferior kind of ruby, not ſo deep a red as the true ruby.*
Ruche, *a bee-hive made of ruſhes.*
Ruge, rouges, *red.*
Rule, *a roll, a regiſter; alſo a determination.*
Rumme, *Rome.*
Rumour, *tumult.*
Rumperie, *breaking, failing.*
Rumperours de trieues, *truce-breakers.*
Ruwes, rues, *ſtreets.*
Ruyſdeſſe, *ſeverity.*
Ryen, *nothing, not.*
Rymours, *rimers.*
Ryu, ryz, *a brook.*
Rÿvaille, de la meer, *the ſea-ſhore.*
Ryvires, *rivers.*

s̃, S^r, *his.*
Scen̄, *known.*
Ssm̄, *ſeiſin.*
Sn̄s, *lords, owners.*
S^rs eſpeulx, *lords ſpiritual.*
s̃viz, *ſervice.*
Sa et la, *here and there.*
Saals, *ſeals.*
Sa cote (en pure), *in his coat only.*
Sa volunte (encontre), *againſt their wills.*
Saalez du mun ſel, *ſealed with my ſeal.*
Sabbedi, *Saturday.*
S' ãbleront, *ſhall rendez-vous.*
Sablinouſe (feble terre), *poor ſandy land.*
Saca hors du gaunt, *ſhaked out of the glove.*
Sacc, inſtrumentum litis, *the pleadings in a cauſe.*
Sachaant (ent), *knowing thereof.*
Sachache (ſa noun), *his ignorance.*

Sachaument, sachantement, *willingly, knowingly.*

Sache, *sages.*

Sachet, *withers.*

Sachiez, saches, sachez, sachon, *know.*

Sacrabor (par), sakeber, sackber, sacaburgh, *no freeman was to be seised or imprisoned, except by inquest or by sacrabor, or unless he was taken with the mainour.*

Sacraire, *a chapel, an oratory.*

Saeil, saes, *a seal.*

Saeller (fet), *caused to be sealed.*

Saenti, *holy.*

Saettes, saettels, *arrows.*

Saffers (qatre), *four sapphires.*

Sagane, *a sorceress.*

Sage, *seat.*

Sagement, *cautiously.*

Saget, *seal.*

Sagette, *an arrow.*

Sagitture, *archery.*

Sagrea, *agreed.*

Sagrement, *oath.*

Sai, *I know.*

Saichance, *science, erudition.*

Saiel, *seal.*

Saielleees, *sealed.*

Saient, saies, *are, be.*

Saiges homes, *the sages or wisemen of the law, the judges.*

Saiguw, *lord.*

Sailleires, *keepers of the seals.*

Sain, *sound, strong.*

Sainctures, *sanctuaries.*

Saine, *substantial.*

Sainees, *perfect, uncancelled.*

Sainglement, *entirely.*

Saings manuelz, *signs manual.*

Sains, *saints.*

Sains Esperis (li), *the Holy Spirit.*

Saintemant (sy), *so cordially.*

Saintime, *most holy.*

Sairement, *oath.*

Saisisement, *seising.*

Saize, *six.*

Sak, saak, *a bag.*

Sake, *throw.*

Sakent, *steal.*

Sakekent a terre, *sacked, demolished to the ground.*

Sal, *safe.*

Salair, *a reward.*

Salairier, *to reward.*

Saleber, Salebirs, *Salisbury.*

Sa le meins (promettant), potiùs, ja le meins, *promising also.*

Saler,

Saler, *a ſalt ſeller.*

Salfe pledges, *ſafe pledges.*

Saliɕtaire, *wholeſome.*

Salit, *health.*

Saller, *a ſadler.*

Salmonceux, *young ſalmon.*

Salopebyrs, Salobirs, *Shrewſbury.*

Salſez (chars), *ſalt meat.*

Salvage, *wild, ſavage.*

Sälvaigne (p), *by beaſts,* feræ naturæ.

Salvatione, *pardon.*

Salve, *greets.*

Salvoms (nous vous), *we greet you.*

Salvez, *know.*

Salutz, *known, ſafe.*

Saluz d'or, *ſalutes of gold, a gold coin, called ſo from the words,* Salus populi ſuprema lex eſto.

Salyne (un), *a ſalt-pit.*

Samaday, *Saturday.*

Sambre, *viſage, face.*

Samble temps, *the ſame time.*

Sambleront (ſe), *ſhall aſſemble.*

S'ame, *his ſoul.*

S'amie, *his friend.*

Sammelplatz, *place of meeting, or rendezvous.*

Sanc, *blood.*

Sancere, *ſincere.*

Sánte, *health.*

Sanɕtz, ſanntz, ſant, *without.*

Sandewitz, *Sandwich.*

Sangles (en toutz et), *in all and ſingular.*

Sani, *ſound, healthful.*

Sank fin, *the end of the kindred.*

Sanne ceo, *except that.*

Sanneys, *ſauces.*

Sans (du bien), *the good ſenſe, underſtanding.*

Sant, *are.*

Sanz un qeſtoit, *ſave one who was.*

Sanz, *reaſonable, ſolid.*

Saon, *without.*

Sapriſt, *the author of the Pſalms, David.*

Sarcophes (que feurent), *who frequent ſepulchres, graves.*

Sarcueil, *a bier.*

Sarcus, *a ſepulchre.*

Sarke (frank), *free ſtock.*

Sarre, *ſarah.*

Sarve, *Saved.*

Sarura, *a lock.*

Satain, *ſatin.*

Sathenas, *Satan.*

Savagnie, *beaſts of the foreſt.*

Savarne, *the Severn.*

Savant, *ſaving, knowing, notwithſtanding.*

Saver, ſavoer, *to know.*

Saver (fait a), fet aſſau', fet aſſaver, *be it known, underſtood.*

Saver (ceſt a), *to-wit.*

Saver moun, *to know for certain,*

Saver mon coment e le paſſa, *juſt as it was taken.*

Savement, *with a ſaving.*

Saverai (jeo), *I ſhall know.*

Savere (pur), *to ſave.*

Savi, *wiſe.*

Savit mie lire (ne), *cannot read.*

Savite, *ſafety.*

S'avoins (nous ne), *we don't know.*

Savoure, *ſavours, partakes of.*

Sau, *ſalt.*

Sauant, *reſerving.*

Saubar (per), *for ſaving.*

Saubze, *ſixteen.*

Saucerie del faucie, (ſerviens), *the ſerjeant of the ſalſarie,* viz. *that officer in the king's kitchen, who was to provide the neceſſaries for the king's ſauces; or he who had the care of the proviſions which were to be ſalted.*

Sauces del mer, *creeks of the ſea.*

Saucey, *ground where willows grow.*

Saudre (baton de), *a ſtick of willow.*

Saulx, ſaulices, ſawces, *ſallows, willows.*

Saulve, *ſaved.*

Saume, *Pſalm.*

Saunćte, *health.*

Saune, *ſaving.*

Saunete, ſauite, ſauvette (en), *in ſafety.*

Saunk, ſaunc, ſauns, *blood.*

Saunk fine, *the determination of a deſcent.*

Sauntz, ſaunz, *without.*

Saura, *ſhall know.*

Saus, *thoſe.*

Sauſſes, *torn up.*

Sauſſers, *ſaucers.*

Saut purpenſe (a), *with an aſſault prepenſe.*

Saut (un), *a caper, a dance.*

Saut (a la), *at the ſiege.*

Saute, ſautie, ſauvte, *ſafety, health.*

Sauvaigne, ſauvagine, *unreclaimed animals.*

Sauvere, *Saviour*

Sauyz (bien), *let him be careful.*

Sauuz deſerte (pas), *not without reaſon.*

Sauz, *ſaving.*

Sauzims, *ſixteenth.*

Sawes, *ſauce.*

Say, *I may.*

Saybienke, *I know very well.*

Saye ley, *his law.*

Saye (ceint de), *a girdle of silk.*

Sayn (au), *to the care, regard.*

Sayfze, *six.*

Scalpier de draps, *rowing of cloth.*

Scaves, *known.*

Scaves (que), *that you may know.*

Sceivent, scevent, sceynent, *know.*

Scen, *sense, knowledge, experience.*

Scent, scen, *known.*

Sceppt, *stock.*

Scet, *knows.*

Sceu, sceux, *known, knowledge.*

Sceust, *subject.*

Sceuvent, *they know.*

Scey, *a seal.*

Scheftisbury, *Shaftesbury.*

Schopes, *shops.*

Sciat, scieust, sciet, *knows.*

Sciecle (qant a), *as to secular affairs.*

Scein, scienes, *knowledge, science.*

Scient marie (li eir), *let the heir be married.*

Scienz (notoirmenet), *notoriously known.*

Scier, scyer, seyer, *to mow, to cut.*

Sciet, *it becomes.*

Sciet, *voluntarily.*

Scieues, *known.*

Sciez, *sawed.*

Scire, *sir.*

Scisez, *mown, cut.*

Sclatz (peres et), *stones and slates.*

Scochon, *escutcheon.*

Scolers, *scholars.*

Scomers, *scummers.*

Scotter, *to gall.*

Scripture (pur le), *for the writing.*

Scriver, *to write.*

Scutelar (serviens), *serjeant of the scullery.*

Scutelaire, *the officer in the king's household who was to take care of the dishes, &c.*

Scuverad (dunt li), *then it behoves him.*

Scyer, *to cut.*

Se, *if, whether, his, but, except.*

Se leva, *was levied.*

Seal de notre secre, secre seal, *our privy seal.*

Seailles, *harvest-time.*

Seale (del), *of the pound.*

Seant, seants, sejant, seiance, *sitting.*

Seante, *health.*

Seante, *sitting.*

Sear, *a lock.*

Seas, *ſeals.*
Seaſon (la), *the ſeiſin.*
Seaut, *underſtood, knew.*
Sech (harang), *red-herring.*
Secle, *world, age.*
Secle (en le), *in the world.*
Secole, *ſea coal.*
Secondes royes, *ſecondaries, adjutants, aſſiſtants.*
Sedation, *appeaſing.*
See roial, *royal throne, ſeat.*
See, ſeet (ne), *knows not.*
Seeche, *dried.*
Seel, *ſalt, oil.*
Seen, *knowledge.*
Seen (je), *I am.*
Seen (le), *his.*
Seent (ne), *he not.*
Seept, ſeet, *ſeven.*
Seer, *a governor.*
Ser, ſereir, *to ſet.*
Seere, *to buy.*
Seerſus, *over, acroſs.*
Seert, *ſerves, is made uſe of.*
Sees, *ſet ye.*
Sees, *his.*
Seeſſent (ne), *may not ſit, abide.*
Seet, *done.*
Seetes, ſeetz, *arrows.*
Seez (qe vous), *that you be.*
Segerſtain, ſegretain, *a ſacriſtan, a ſexton.*
Seges, ſegez, *ſieges.*
Segne (en), *in ſign, teſtimony.*
Segon, *according.*
Segrament, *oath.*
Segu, *ſure, certain.*
Segu, *ſure, certain.*
Seguadours, *ſawyers.*
Seguar, *to ſaw.*
Segroi, *ſacred.*
Segurement, *ſecurely.*
Seguyn, *ſuit, to follow.*
Sehur conduit, *ſafe conduct.*
Sei, ſein, *himſelf.*
Sei (heir de), *heir of his body.*
Sei funt, *make themſelves; act as.*
Sei (entre), *between them.*
Seicheries, *the ſervice by which a vaſſal or tenant was obliged to attend his lord to the army; profits belonging to a caſtle.*
Seieant, *ſixty.*
Seientement, *knowingly, wittingly.*
Seietz, *placed.*
Seietz a un (que vous), *that you ſtick to one.*
Seif, *a hedge.*
Seif, ſerfe, *a villain, a ſervant.*
Sergn, *ſign, teſtimony, repreſentation, ſymbol.*
Seigniour, *lord, owner.*

Seignurages (les), *the ſeignurage.*
Seignurie (la), *the prerogative.*
Seignurle (la), *the prerogative.*
Seignel, ſeigle, ſegle, *rye.*
Seijor, *abode, dwelling-place.*
Seil, *a ſail.*
Seil, *ſeals.*
Seimes, *made.*
Sein, *ſound, in health.*
Sein, *known.*
Sein, *ſignal.*
Seine, *ſenſes.*
Seins, *ſaints.*
Seigns, ſeignuus, ſeigne, *ſigned, marked.*
Seings manuel, *ſigns manual.*
Seins (luis), *holy, priviledges places.*
Seins meen, *without meſne.*
Seint, ſeien, *be.*
Seint, *bleſſed.*
Seint entendement, *ſound, good underſtanding.*
Seinta (lui), *girded himſelf.*
Seintiſme pier, *moſt holy father.*
Seintiſme temp, *ſeaſon for devotion, holy ſeaſon.*
Seintuaries, ſeintewarie, *ſanctuary.*
Seinture, *a girdle.*
Seiomes (que nous), *that we ſhould be.*
Seiront, *ſhall ſit.*
Seiſier, *to ſeiſe.*
Seiſonables, *in ſeaſon.*
Seiſſons, *might be, cauſed to be.*
Seiſons del an (tous), *all ſeaſons of the year.*
Seiſt (ſi ceo ne), *unleſs it be.*
Seit fet, *be done.*
Seit, *ſeven.*
Seit, *let him, let him be; has, is.*
Seit (ke), *which was.*
Seit fet (nous), *have made us.*
Seiverent, *proſecuted, purſued.*
Seiz, ſeiſitz, *ſeiſed.*
Sek, *dry.*
Sekes a taunt q̃, *until that.*
Sel, ſely, *that.*
Sel (le), *the great ſeal.*
Selar̃ (ſerviens), *ſerjeant of the cellar.*
Seleables, *to be ſealed.*
Selez e enfrenez (viii chivalz), *eight horſes ſadled and bridled.*
Seli, *of this, this.*
Selles, *if they.*
Selor, *then.*
Selparie, *ſalt-petre.*
Sels, *alone.*

Semadi, *Saturday.*
Semaille (pur), *for ſeed.*
Sembillantz, au voſtre commune, *it ſeeming to your commons.*
Semblablez (qi ſont du ſuier), *which are likely to enſue.*
Semblant d'aucuns (ſelonc), *in the opinion of ſome.*
Semblaunt (bon), *good example.*
Semblaunt (par), *at firſt ſight,* primâ facie.
Seme, *ſixth.*
Sememes (cink), *five weeks.*
Semenſes (les), *what is ſown.*
Semente, *cement, annex.*
Semi, *half.*
Semitz, *ſown.*
Semle (ſe), *it ſeems.*
Semoiſons, *ſeed-time*
Semond, *ſummon.*
Sen, le ſen, *his.*
Sen, ſens, *undrſtanding, judgement, diſcretion.*
Sen, ſens (ſans ſon), *without his knowledge.*
Sen vount, *depart.*
Senes (les), *his own.*
Sendes, *ſhops, ſtalls.*
Senee, *wiſe.*
Senglers, *boars.*
Seneſcaucie, *the office of High Steward.*
Seneſtez, ſenefiez, *ſignified.*
Seneſtrement, *ſiniſtrouſly, left.*
Senne de, *his own.*
Sennes (hors de lour), *out of their mind, inſane.*
Senforcent, *endeavour.*
Senglers perſones, *every perſon.*
Sengles, *ſingle, particular.*
Senhor, ſenhur, *lord.*
Senſuit, ſenſeut, *follows.*
Senſures (ꝑ les), *by the cenſures.*
Sent (al), *with the aſſent.*
Sent (qe furent al), *who were aſſenting.*
Sent (ne), *doth not aſſent.*
Sentainement, *ſecret device.*
Sentez ſur, *on the Holy Evangeliſts, on the ſacred Reliques.*
Sente (ſe), *perceives himſelf.*
Sente mort, *put to death.*
Sente, *right, ſound, good, wholeſome.*
Sente, *a pathway.*
Senteront, *intended.*
Sentiers (les), *the entering into.*
Sentre comment, *intercommon.*

Sentu, *felt.*

Sentu, *thought, were of opiaion.*

Senz, *without.*

Seoffrance, *truce, cessation of arms.*

Seoins oufte (si nous), *if we be ousted.*

Seon (le), *the seal.*

Seons (ou que nous), *wheresoever we are.*

Seons (par les), le seon, *by his own people.*

Seont, *know.*

Seoptisme, *seventh.*

Seor, *sister.*

Seor, *sure.*

Seor (la), *the elder.*

Seose (ne), *durst not.*

Seoul (le), *the soil.*

Seourment, *safely, securely.*

Sep, sept, *race, stock.*

Sepmayn, sepmeme, *a week.*

Seps, ceps, cipps, *a pair of stocks.*

Septain(diz et), *seventeenth.*

Septan et noef, *seventy-nine.*

Septsaunt secund, *seventy-second.*

Septembrale, *September.*

Septre, *the sceptre.*

Sepulture (seynt), *holy sepulchre.*

Sequer (doyt etre), *ought to be followed.*

Sequerent, *following.*

Sequestre, *lock up.*

Sequestres, *locks.*

Seq̃stres, *attendants on officers of justice.*

Sequestrour (le), *the sequestrator.*

Sequeur, *secure.*

Ser̃, *shall be.*

Ser, *serves.*

Ser (ke de mon li et), potiùs, ke de meux li set, *who knows it best.*

Sera, *will serve.*

Sercherie (office de), *office of searcher.*

Serchier, serch, *to search.*

Sercle, *a circle.*

Sercler, *to weed.*

Sere, *shall be.*

Seredes (la), *the screens.*

Sereur, *sister.*

Serfe, *a female slave.*

Serfe, *a female slave.*

Serfs, *stags.*

Serjant, serviens, *one in degree next to a knight.*

Seriche, *search.*

Sergeantie (ꝑ defaute de), *for want of counsel.*

Sergeaunte d'Engleterre (tout la), *all the judges of the coif in England.*

Seriete, *serenity.*

Serions, seriemes, *should be.*

Serjours, *searchers.*

Sermentez, *sworn upon the saints.*

Seroruge,

Seroruge, *a ſurgeon.*
Serpentyne, *a kind of alembeck.*
Serra, *ſhall ſit.*
Serrer, *to block up.*
Serrett (ne), *may not be.*
Serreynt (il), *they would be.*
Serruns tenuz, *ſhall be obliged.*
Sers Dieu, *ſervant of God.*
Serten, *certain.*
Servages, ſerviſſes, *ſervices.*
Serve, *a ſtroke.*
Servens (pur le), *for the payment.*
Serveyſe, ſervoiſe, *ſervice, ale.*
Servi la court, *tendered to the court the uſual form of pleading.*
Servie, *obeyed, complied with.*
Serviens empt, *ſerjeant, purveyor.*
Servietz, *ſervices.*
Servir leſtatut, *anſwer to the ſtatute.*
Serviretz, *will ſerve.*
Servitz, ſervy, *paid.*
Servois, *ponds.*
Servy (ſy il ſeyt), *if it be applied.*
Servy qil ſoient, *that they may be paid.*
Ses, ſeſze, *ſix.*
Ses, *without.*
Ses de la chauncelry (ſi), *if they of the chancery.*
Seſerunt, *ſhall ceaſe.*
Seſſante neuyme, *ſixty-nine.*
Seſſine, *ſeiſin.*
Seſtez, *theſe.*
Seze, *ſixteen.*
Set, *ſeven.*
Set, *knows, known.*
Set, *that, this.*
Set (qe), *which reſteth.*
Sete l'apoſtoille, *apoſtolical ſee.*
Sete, *ſet, fix upon.*
Setes, ſeties, ſeetes, *arrows, ſhafts.*
Setors (ſes), *his ſureties; his ſiſters.*
Setors, *ſailors.*
Sett, *be.*
Setta hors (je), *I ſhoot out.*
Setter, *to ſhoot.*
Settle, *known.*
Setus (de), *of this.*
Setyme (dis), *ſeventeenth.*
Seu, *if.*
Sen, ſeucee, *knowledge, known.*
Seu, *ſalt.*
Seu (de plein), *fully, without reſerve.*
Seu (jeo), *I am.*
Seuant, *following.*
Seue, ſeure, ſeuyr, ſeuure, *to ſue, proſecute.*
Seue, *known.*
Seuf, *ſafe.*
Seuil, *I am wont, I am uſed.*

Seulles, *only, alone.*
Seumes (nous), *we are.*
Seuns (ou ke nous), *wheresoever we shall be.*
Seur, *sister.*
Seur, *sure, certain.*
Seur, *against.*
Seur, *upon.*
Seur se, *moreover.*
Seur ceo, *thereupou.*
Seures (par la), potiùs, pur la seures, *for the safeguard.*
Seurplus (le), *the remainder.*
Seurse, *arisen.*
Seus, *alone.*
Seus, *seals.*
Seus (les), *her people.*
Seus (a), *to his.*
Seus (tuz), *all those.*
Seus (de), *of those.*
Seussioms (nos), *we know.*
Seut, *should be.*
Seute, *suit; payment.*
Seute (pur), *for fear.*
Seust, seuwe, seuwy, *knew, known.*
Seux, (a), *to them.*
Seuz, *shillings.*
Sevant, *skilful, exact.*
Seve, seue, *her own.*
Seve (a la), *to his.*
Seveles, *buryed.*
Sevent, *they know.*
Sevent (qui ne), *who are not capable of.*
Sever, *sue.*
Severa, *will serve.*
Severes, *severed, separated.*
Sevi, *sued.*
Sewes, *known.*
Sewet, *suit.*
Sextemen, *the sixth time.*
Sexter, *a measure of corn.*
Sey, *silk.*
Sey, *himself.*
Sey (e), *by itself.*
Sey (endroit de), *in his place, station.*
Sey (que je ne), *that I may not be.*
Se desovere, *unwrought silk.*
Seyant, *sitting.*
Seyast, *hath seen.*
Seye (sil), *if he sit.*
Seyent, seynt, *be, may be.*
Seyent, *let them apply to, let them sue.*
Seyent (qui meiux), *which better suit.*
Seyer, *to cut, mow.*
Seyer, *to know.*
Seyvent, *they know.*
Seyetes, *arrows.*
Seyetz, en la merci, *be in mercy.*
Seyne, *healthful, wholesome, sound.*
Seyng liege (lur), *their liege lord.*
Seyns, *saints.*
Seyns, *furs.*

Seynt,

Seynt, *girt.*
Seyntetee (ſa), *his holineſs.*
Seyremnuz, *oaths.*
Sez, *his.*
Sezaine, ſezzime, *ſixteen.*
Sezile, *Sicily.*
Shaft, ſcheft, *a weight, the ſame as the auncel.*
Shelps, *ſhelves in a river.*
Shout, *a ſmall boat or veſſel.*
Si, *whether, here.*
Si amy, *his friend.*
Sia (et), *and there is.*
Sibn, *as well.*
Sibor, *as well of.*
Siche, *be it known.*
Sicle, *age, world.*
Si come, *as, as it were.*
Sicome (de), *ſince, ſeeing that.*
Sidre, *cyder.*
Sié, *be it ſo.*
Si eins *another time, before.*
Si eſt, *is, belongs to.*
Sie plain (le), *when the ſee is full.*
Siege faire (de), *to beſiege, to beſet, to lay in wait for.*
Siegea qui, *who ſat in the ſee.*
Siegle, *age.*
Siel, *a ſadle.*
Sien, *ſeat.*
Sience propre chouſe, *his own proper things.*
Siens (de), *of his friends.*
Sient pier, *holy father.*
Sier, *to mow, to ſaw.*
Sier blees (en temps de), *in harveſt-time.*
Sieres, *lord.*
Sieremens, *oath.*
Sierges, *wax-tapers.*
Siert (ni), *does not ſerve, lie.*
Siet, *knows.*
Sietans, *ſixty.*
Siet rien (ne), *knows nothing.*
Sieure, *obſerve, purſue.*
Sieute, *ſuit, requeſt.*
Sieux (des), *of thoſe, of ſuch.*
Siex, ſiey, *ſix.*
Siglaunte (nefe), *a ſhip ſailing.*
Sigles (moly), *mill-ſails.*
Signal, *ſeal.*
Signament, *particulary.*
Signe, *badge.*
Signes de palmes, *ſigns in the palms of the hands.*
Signez, *ſwans.*
Signioris, *ſeignory, lord's ſervice.*
Silleurs, *mowers.*
Silloekes, *there.*
Sillours de burſe, *cutpurſes.*
Simayne, ſimoine, *a week.*
Sime, ſyme, *ſixth.*
Simenel (payn de), *ſimnel bread.*

Simeniaus,

Simeniaus, *ſimnels.*
Simian, *Simeon.*
Simitorie, *church-yard.*
Simonys (ſans), *without a reward, gratis.*
Simpliſt (p te), *on account of the ſmallneſs of it.*
Sine, *his own.*
Sine, *without.*
Sines, *ſwans.*
Singulant, *bloody.*
Singuler, *private.*
Singulere, *ſingle.*
Singulerement, *in the ſingular number.*
Singulerte, (in lour), *into ſeparate parts.*
Sinkaunt, *fifty.*
Sinke, ſink, *five.*
Siours (iii.), *three mowers.*
Siqe, *ſo that.*
Si redde ley, *any ſpeedy law.*
Sir li rois (nodit), noſtre ſire le roi, *our ſaid lord the king.*
Sire, ſires gart, *God preſerve.*
Sire de Roos, *lord of Roos.*
Sirs, *the lords.*
Sirps, *a mat, ruſhes.*
Sis, *ſitten, abode.*
Sis, *his.*
Sis lieux, *ſix miles.*
Siſan, *ſixty.*
Siſme, ſiſime, ſiſine, *ſixth.*
Siſſables arbres, *coppices, trees uſed to be cut.*
Siſt, *it behoveth.*
Siſte, *ſixth.*
Siſtront, *ſtopped, ſeized.*
Siſtrunt (en), *ſhall iſſue from them.*
Site, *ſixteenth,*
Siu, *his.*
Siut, *train, followers.*
Sive, *his.*
Siverne, *the Severn.*
Sivre, *purſue, proſecute.*
Siwant, *following.*
Siwe, *purſue, be a tranſcript of.*
Siwent (qil), *that they follow.*
Siwera, *ſhall ſued for, proſecute.*
Siwit, *ſued out, ſued to.*
Siwte, *ſuit.*
Sleies des worſtedes (les), *the ſleyes of worſted.*
Slethe, ſlede, *a bank of a river.*
So, *thus.*
Soaffre, *permit.*
Sobrain, *ſovereign, ſupreme, prevalent.*
Sobrine, *couſin-german, kinſwoman.*
Soceures, *ſuccours.*
Socures, *ſuccoured.*
Sodeynement, *ſuddenly.*
Sodiacre, *a ſub-deacon.*
Soe, *her own.*
Soef, *ſweet.*

Soeffrance,

Soeffrance, *toleration, delay.*

Soeffre, ſoeffier, *to ſuffer, permit; omit.*

Soeffrir, *forbearance, permiſſion.*

Soel, *alone, only.*

Soel, ſoeil (le), *the ſun.*

Soel mayne (en), *into an indifferent hand.*

Soele ſeveral, *ſeveral ſoil.*

Soen, ſyen, *own, one's own, his own, his.*

Soen (le), *his faithful.*

Soen deſirer (que j'euſſe), *that I had reaſon to expect.*

Soen deſtre (en), *in his diſtrict, in the mean time to be.*

Soen (e li), *and theirs.*

Soens, *thoſe.*

Soens (de), *of ſome of his, to them.*

Soens, ſoiens, ſonz (nul de), *any that belong to him.*

Soens (les), *his agents.*

Soer, ſoor (harang), *red herrings.*

Soer (a), *in the evening.*

Soera, *ſiſter.*

Soer feſt, *upon a deed.*

Soertee, *ſafety, health.*

Soerts, *ſorts.*

Soeverrant, *ſovereignty.*

Soffianz, *ſufficient.*

Soffre, *ſuffice.*

Soffrunes, *ſuſpended, reſpited.*

Soi, *I have.*

Soi, *his.*

Soiant, *ſitting.*

Soias (que vous), *that you may be.*

Soiauls, *ſeals.*

Soie enfile, *ſilk twined.*

Soien, *himſelf, he.*

Soier, *to ſaw, to cut down.*

Soiet, *be.*

Soiets, *arrows.*

Soietz, ſoiets, *ſubjects, men.*

Soieur, *ſiſter.*

Soief, *turf.*

Soigner, *to excuſe.*

Soilent, *they uſed.*

Soillure, *ſoil, filth, dung.*

Soine, *ſounds.*

Soingles, *ſingular.*

Soint, *are.*

Soivent, *ſeveral..*

Soixante onze, *ſeventy-one.*

Solacz, *comfort.*

Soldeours, *ſoldiers.*

Soldrad (pur), *as he deſerves.*

Soldz, *ſalaries.*

Sole, ſoil, *ground, ſoil, land.*

Sole, ſoul, ſoeil, ſoleyne, *ſole, alone.*

Soleient, ſolerent, ſoleront, ſolent, ſolioms, ſoloia, *were wont.*

Solein,

Solein, *solemn.*
Selempnise, *formality, solemnity.*
Solempnite des espoſailles, *solemnization of marririage.*
Soler, *to pay.*
Soler (jour), *the solar day.*
Solers, *shoes.*
Soloile recouch, *sun-set.*
Solom, *according to.*
Solonque cesque, *accordingly.*
Solonque un maner, *after a manner.*
Solt(ne), nel sont, nel sout, *did not know.*
Solyer, *a shoemaker.*
Solz, soldz, *shillings.*
Som̃, somez, *summoned.*
Sombreſſer (Charles de), *Charles Somerset.*
Somdant, *arising.*
Some, *summons.*
Somerement, *in a summary way, briefly.*
Somerier, *in short.*
Someyns, *weeks.*
Somis, *subjects.*
Sommage, *burdens.*
Sommeir les besoignes(de), *to consummate the business.*
Sommer, *to summon.*
Somnelentz, *persons troubled with a lethargy.*
Somous *are.*
Son, *are.*
Sond, *wages, pay.*
Sone, les sones, *his, his affairs.*
Sone tens (en le), *in the mean time.*
Sonee, soune, sonnent, *sounds.*
Sonent, sovent (tant), *so often.*
Sonent, *are.*
Sones (par les), *by his confederates.*
Sonette d'argent (un), *a little silver bell.*
Son nour, *his honour.*
Sons, sous, *shillings.*
Sons, *payment.*
Sons, *without.*
Sont, *know.*
Sontent (se), *think.*
Sooton, *Sutton.*
Sor, sore, sors, *upon, above.*
Sor (ceo), *therefore.*
Sorceler, *to bewitch.*
Sore, sord, *sister.*
Sore (harang), *red herring.*
Sores, *you may be.*
Sort, *be.*
Sort, *lot.*
Sortz, *sorts.*
Sorvent (vos), *you may remember.*
Sos, *a fool.*
Sospent (quy), *which are in suspence, which are depending.*

Q Sopescon

Sofpefcon (qui miens feient en), *who are no ways fufpected.*

Softinges, *fupport, uphold.*

Soft..nt, *fupported.*

Sot, *knew.*

Sot (laron nel), *did not know he was a thief.*

Sotiletees, fotinetes, *fubtleties.*

Sotife, fotye, *ideocy.*

Sot naftre, *a fool natural, a fool from his birth, an ideot.*

Soubdaine, *fudden.*

Soublever, *to lift up.*

Soubminifter, *to ferve under another.*

Soubreffe, *fobriety.*

Soubs, *under.*

Soubfcrire, *to underwrite.*

Soubzaage, *under age, minority.*

Soucheefz, *fhillings.*

Souconduit, *fafe-conduct.*

Soucy (fans), *without fufpicion.*

Soudant, *fupporting, fortifying.*

Soude, foulde; foudees, *wages, pay.*

Sou..z de terre (cent), *an hundred fhillings of land.*

Souder, furder, *to arife.*

Soudeyers, foudiers, fouders, foudjours, foudoyers, foudiours, *foldiers.*

Soudoyer, *maintain, keep in pay.*

Soudoyez, *fupplied.*

Soudure, *foder*

Souealx, *fafe.*

Soveners, *frequen..*

Souentifiez, *frequen...*

Souez, *under.*

Souffeft, *fufficient.*

Souffraunce, foffrance, fufferance, *ceffation of arms, a truce.*

Souffrire, *to fuffice.*

Sougiuz, fougies, *fubjects.*

Soul, *alone.*

Soul jour, *a fingle day.*

Soul, potiùs tout, (de), la terre, *of all the land.*

Soule, *fafe.*

Soulement, *only, alfo.*

Souleu, *the fun.*

Soulevation, *revolt.*

Soulez (femes), *femes fole, fingle women.*

Soulu, *forgiven.*

Soulze, fouz, fouce, foubz, fouids, *a fhilling.*

Soumerement, *arbitration.*

Soun piere, *his father.*

Soun (e), *and.*

Soun (ne), *goes not.*

Soune, *founds.*

Soune ne foit, *fhall not be publifhed, fhall not tend to.*

Sour, *upon, againft.*

Sour chou, *thereupon.*

Sour li, *againſt him.*
Sourdlers, *ſhoes.*
Soure (main), *ſafe hand.*
Sourmet, *ſurmiſes, alledges.*
Sourſiſt, *ariſe.*
Sourviſſant, *attending to.*
Souſprendre, *uſurp.*
Souſtretes, *ſubſtracted.*
Sout, *ſuit, ſuit of court, petition.*
Sout, ſot, *knows.*
Sout, ſoute, (jor de la), *day of payment.*
Southaller, *to undergo.*
South boys, *underwood.*
Southes (ſet), *ſeven ſhillings.*
Southminer, *to undermine.*
Southſewantz, *ſubſequent, following.*
Soutre, ſoultre, *underneath, below.*
Soutz pur ſoutz, *ſhilling for ſhilling.*
Soutz eux, *under them.*
Souve, *ſounds.*
Souvement, *ſafely.*
Souvenere pleint, *frequent complaint.*
Souveneres, *heavy, frequent.*
Sovent (deſtreſſe), *continued diſtreſs, diſtreſs infinite.*
Souventfoth, *oftentimes.*
Souveraignement (deſirant), *greatly, earneſtly, above all things deſiring.*
Souveraunce, *guide.*
Souvereign, *ſuperior, next immediate.*
Sovereigne garnement, *upper garment.*
Sovereigne partie, *greateſt part.*
Sovers, *frequent.*
Souz, ſous, *ſhillings.*
Souzmeiſt, *ſubmitted.*
Souzmis, ſoulzims, *ſubſtitute, ſubjects.*
Sovieront autres remedyes (ne), *ſeeing, knowing of no other remedy.*
Sowdan, *ſultan.*
Sown, *ſound.*
Sowne (iſl), *they are.*
Soy, *his.*
Soy, *of themſelves.*
Soy, ſoyer, *ſiſter.*
Soy (ſi jeo), *if I be.*
Soy (coſte de), *a coat of ſilk.*
Soye, *itſelf.*
Soye, ſoy mene, ſoimene, *himſelf.*
Soy fit, *was made.*
Soyen, *are.*
Soyens (ne nul des), *nor any of thoſe.*
Soyer, *to cut.*
Soyetz, *ſubjects, men.*
Soyiont, *paſſed.*
Soy myſt, *put himſelf.*
Soyne, *a ſynod.*
Spanges, *ſpangles.*

 Spar-

Spargiſſent, *raviſh.*

Spaule (lez), *the ſhoulders.*

Spergiſſer, *to violate, raviſh.*

Spernironis (que nous ne), *that we will not ſpare.*

Splatte, *ſplatted, ſplit.*

Spoliation, diſſeiſin, *deprivation.*

Spours, *ſpurs.*

Sprete, *ſpirit.*

Squerer, *eſquire.*

Sqiller (ſergt), *ſerjeant of the ſcullery; the officer in the king's kitchen, who had the care of the diſhes, knives, &c.*

Squillerye, *the ſcullery.*

Srã, *ſhall be.*

Stagne, *a pool, a pond.*

Stat, *ſtand.*

Stater, *firm, binding.*

Stathes *wharfs.*

Station (la), *the ſtanding.*

Statuit, *ſtatute.*

Staunche, *in good order, dry.*

Stefne, *Stephen.*

Steppes (le), *the way, the path.*

Steres, *ſtirred.*

Sterver, *death.*

Sterveth (ce), *it dieth.*

Steym, *tin.*

Stoure, *ſtocked.*

Straict (home), *a man out of his mind, diſtracted.*

Streat, *the ſtreet, the way.*

Streitures des rivers, *the ſtraitneſs, the obſtructions in rivers.*

Strepe, *the ſtirrip.*

Streyte, *ſtrict.*

Streytement, *ſtrictly, haſtily.*

Strome (le), *the ſtream.*

Stuffe (de leur), *for their keeping.*

Stuffez, *ſtocked.*

Stuffure, *ſtuff, lining.*

Stuffure (pur la), *for the repairing.*

Sturroit, *put, forced.*

Stewes (lez), *the ſtews.*

Style deſcrire (le), *the manner of writing.*

Su, *I am.*

Su (le), *the ſouth.*

Sua, *ſued, impleaded.*

Suaf guiage, *ſafe conduct.*

Suantz, ſuaunte, *ſucceeding.*

Subditz, *aforeſaid.*

Subduitz, *ruined.*

Subit, *forthwith.*

Subornatz, *ſuborned.*

Submyſs, *ſubjects.*

Subridendre, *to laugh behind another's back.*

Subroguer, ſurroguer, *to make a deputy or ſurrogate.*

Subroguez, *ſubſtituted.*

Subtiũs

Subtūs, *under.*
Suburg, *ſuburbs.*
Subz umbre, *under pretence.*
Sud (ne), *was not.*
Sue (je), *I am.*
Sue, *his, his own.*
Sue, *known.*
Sue, *followed.*
Sue cornes, *ſhooing horns.*
Sueffrent, *ſuffer, permt.*
Suelt, *accuſtomed.*
Suens(nul des), *none of his.*
Suer, *ſiſter.*
Suer, ſerve, *to follow, purſue, proſecute, enſue.*
Suers, *ſiſters.*
Suertie, *ſafeguard, ſafety.*
Sues, *ye ought.*
Suete (greynour), *more freſh air, a greater range.*
Suette, ſuete, *ſuit.*
Suez vous tot, *although you are.*
Suffenne, *unwholeſome.*
Sufferable cautele, *a prudent patience.*
Sufferaunce (la), *the truce, ſuſpenſion of arms; pardon.*
Suffert, *allowed, permitted.*
Sufficcantie de terre, *ſufficient land.*
Sufficiat, *ſufficient.*
Suffiſablement, *ſufficiently.*
Suffrable, *reaſonable, lawful.*
Suffrable choſe, *a hardſhip.*
Suffrables (les), *things liable to make good a nuiſance.*
Suffrace (en), *in ſuſpence.*
Suffrancie (ſolent la), *according to the proportion.*
Suffreint, *to be born, endured.*
Suffreit (grant), *great want, ſcarcity.*
Suffretz, *hardſhips.*
Suffrir, *delay, put off.*
Suffroit, *would be ſufficient.*
Sugales, *South Wales.*
Sugets, ſugges, ſuggetz, *ſubjects.*
Sui, *followed.*
Sui, *enſued.*
Suis (a luy prendre), *to take him up.*
Suis (les deliverent), *deliver them up.*
Suis (en), *upwards, above.*
Suiſchargiez, *above charged.*
Suis diſt de, *hereafter ſaid.*
Suis dits, *aboveſaid.*
Suiſargentent, *ſilvered over.*
Suiſorre, *embroidered, gilded over.*
Suiſſoins, *had ſued out.*
Suiſt, *be*
Suit, *aforeſaid.*

Suit, ſuyt, *the retinue, chattels, offspring, and appurtenances of a villain.*

Suit, *the witneſſes or followers of the plaintiff; proof.*

Suit, *a path, or track.*

Suit ſon ſeveral, *has ſued out his ſeveral, partition has been made.*

Suix, *upon.*

Suiz, ſuient, *follow.*

S'ul l'ad, *if he has one.*

Sulary, *ſallary.*

Sullerye, *a plow land.*

Sullings, *alder trees.*

Suluc, ſulun, ſullonc, *according.*

Sum, *his.*

Sum̃eigne, *week.*

Sumes, *we are.*

Sumeter, *the proveditor for the garriſons.*

Sum̃m (a), a ſum' damag', *to ſpecify his damage.*

Summa en la teſte, *ſtruck him on the head.*

Summage (ove), *with horſes laden.*

Sum̃mament, *eſpecially.*

Summes ſur chivalls (les), *the ſumms, or package on horſes.*

Sun conduit, *ſafe, ſure conduct.*

Sun fiuz, *his ſon.*

Sun le chef, *the price of his head, his were.*

Sune, ſuns, *his, his own.*

Sunt, *they are.*

Suours, *ſhoemakers.*

Supetencions, *ſuſpected.*

Suppeditee, *in ſubjection.*

Supplecions, *helps, amendments.*

Supportation, *ſupport.*

Suppoſaill, *allegation.*

Suppoſe (enfaunt), *a ſuppoſititious child.*

Suppoũr, *ſub-prior.*

Suppriz, *ſurpriſed.*

Suppweillez, ſupponailleſs, *ſupported, ſuccoured.*

Sup q̃, *whereupon.*

Sur, *upon, againſt.*

Surs, *lords.*

Sur ſe, *therein, thereupon.*

Surachater, *to overbuy.*

Surchetut, *more eſpecially.*

Surcris, *addition, ſurplus.*

Surdier, *to ariſe.*

Surdit, *ſuſpicion.*

Sure, *to proſecute, to follow.*

Surfet de hoſtes (ſanz), *without too many gueſts.*

Surjetter, *to caſt over.*

Surigiens, *ſurgeons.*

Suriplus, *ſurplus.*

Surmeiſſent, *charged with.*

Surment, *oath.*

Surmettent, *take from.*

Sur-

Surmettent (ils), *they ſurmiſe, ſuggeſt.*

Surmitter, *to ſurmiſe, accuſe.*

Surmys (a luy), *alledged againſt him.*

Surorrer, *to gild.*

Surpluis (le), *the ſurplus.*

Surpluſer (le), *the remainder, deficiency, what is behind, or wanting.*

Surppriſes, *encroachments.*

Surprendre, *ſeize.*

Surpris, *undertaken, ſupported.*

Surpriſion (ſanz), *without moleſtation.*

Surquerge, *moleſts.*

Surquidance, *arrogance, preſumption, diſdain.*

Surrection, *ſubjection.*

Surrounder, *to drown.*

Surſane, *rotten, putrid, unwholeſome, ſurfeited.*

Surſer (yl ne poit), *he cannot pay the penalty of ſurſiſe.*

Surſera la ſurſiſe, *ſhall neglect to purſue the hue and cry.*

Surſes (de), ſurceſſer, *to ſurceaſe.*

Surſiſe, ſurfait, *neglect.*

Surſiſe, *a penalty or forfeiture laid on thoſe who neglected paying the duty or rent of Caſtleward at Dover.*

Surſiſe en ple (de doner), *to give orders for a ſurceaſing of the plea.*

Surſiſes, *neglects, ſurſyſes.*

Surſiſt, ſurſys, *neglected, omitted, ceaſed.*

Surte, *ſurety.*

Surveer, *to overlook, ſurvey.*

Survenantz, *ſojourning.*

Survenet, *ſurvey.*

Survenue p̄ malady, *ſeiſed, overtaken with a ſickneſs.*

Surveſquiſt, *ſurvives.*

Surveux, *ſuperintended, examined, ſurveyed.*

Survieu, *ſurvey.*

Survint, *came.*

Survys, *looked upon, deemed.*

Surundes en le meer, *loſt in the ſea.*

Sus, *upon.*

Sus, *ariſe, be.*

Sus e jus, *up and down.*

Suſanné, ſuranné (terre), *land worn out with too long ploughing.*

Suſdit, ſuſditz, *aforeſaid.*

Suſditz (des), *abovementioned.*

Suſduitz, *put back.*

Suſgroſſes, *engroſſe.*

Suſmet, *ſubmit.*

Sus mette (il), *he alledges, charges.*

Sus mettre a nous, *impute to us.*

Suſpetenus, *ſuſpected.*

Suſpirale, eſpirale, *conduit pipe.*

Suſpris de maladie, *ſeized with ſickneſs.*

Suſquiet, *barraſſed, ſearched about for.*

Suſſemee (chair), *unwholſome meat.*

Suſſent (et ſil), *and if they know.*

Suſt, *be.*

Suſtenance de ſa corone (en), *in ſupport of his crown.*

Suſtendroms (ne), *will not ſupport.*

Suſtretz, ſuſtretes, ſuſtreits, ſuſtrits, ſuſtrain, *withdrawn, withheld.*

Sute, *ſuit, proſecution, proof, evidence, inſtance, requeſt.*

Suter, ſeuter, *a ſhoemaker.*

Suterez, *ſuitors.*

Sutes, *ſuits, ſervices.*

Suth (des parties del), *ſouthern parts.*

Suthdit, *hereunder, hereafter ſaid.*

Suthmyz, *ſubjects.*

Suthtry, *withdrawn.*

Sutilte, ſotivite de ſens, *by parity of reaſon.*

Suwe, ſu, *onions.*

Suy, *proceeded.*

Suy, *followed, purſued, proſecuted.*

Suy hoyr, *his heir.*

Suynnant, *following.*

Suyrement, *ſecurely.*

Suyſt, *ſue out.*

Suys preſt, *I am ready.*

Suys (liverer), *to deliver up, ſurrender.*

Suyt, *ſuit, right of proſecution, livery, ſecurety.*

Suyt (a la), *at the requeſt.*

Sux (pur), *for thoſe.*

Suz, *under.*

Suz ley, *againſt him.*

Suzpris, *ſeiſed.*

Swayl (pur), *for fuel.*

Swefe (q'il tenſit), *that he hold it gently.*

Sy, *if, ſo.*

Sy (que), *that he might.*

Sycome, *ſince.*

Syen, *his.*

Syffet, *a puff with the cheeks, a whiſtle.*

Symayne, ſymeigne, *week.*

Symblement, *ſimply.*

Symerement, *purely, ſimply, ſincerely.*

Synkes fielez, *five daughters.*

Syre, *Sr, father.*

Sys, *ſix.*

Sys, *ſet down.*

t̃, teñ, *tenant.*
Teñ, *to hold.*
Teñ, tent, *held.*
Teñ, *ſuch.*
Tenẽz,teñ,tenz, *tenements.*
Teñz, *tenants.*
Tm̃, *only.*
Tñs, trñs, *treſpaſs.*
Tp̃s, *time.*
Tr̃ pled, *plea of land.*
Tabard, *a cloak.*
Tabulet, *a tablet, a portable altar.*
Tache, *infected; tied, fixed unto, tacked together.*
Tache d'or (un), *a cup of gold.*
Taciſſir, *to cough.*
Taile de boys (un), *a tally of wood.*
Tailla (que ſe), *which was pronounced, given.*
Taille, *barred, taxed.*
Taile, taill, *tally.*
Taille (ſe), *are deſirous.*
Taille, taylle le ditz A (a la), *at the dictation of the ſaid A, when the ſaid A pleaſed.*
Taillee, *pronounced, declared.*
Tailler, *to cut.*
Tailler, *to limit.*
Taillera (jugement ſe), *judgement would be given, pronounced.*
Tailleroient (ſe), *ſhould endeavour.*
Tailles, *acquittances.*
Tailletz (covenantz), *covenants limited, expreſſed, made.*
Taillez, taillie, *entailed.*
Taillez (que vous vous), *that you will prepare yourſelf.*
Taillez (un bois), *a coppice, or wood uſed to be cut.*
Taillont, *they limit, they lay.*
Taillours, *taylors.*
Taillur un villain (de), *to recover a villain departed.*
Taiſiblement, *tacitly.*
Taillurs de amans, *cutters of diamonds.*
Talant, talenz, *talent, love, deſire, inclination.*
Talemains, *neverthleleſs.*
Telent, *encouragement, inclination.*
Talent d'amer matrimoyne, *a love for the ſtate of marriage.*
Talent (mau), *ill will, reſentment.*
Talent (vous dites), *you ſay right, truly.*
Talent (p̃), *by means of.*
Talent preigne, *take effect.*
Tales, talys (novelles), *new declarations, tales.*

Tallion,

Tallion, lex talionis, *like fcr l ke.*

Tal. uns (coupes de), *cut off close by the heels.*

Tamps, *time.*

Tangne, *thine, thy own.*

Tan longament, *so long a time.*

Tank, *extended.*

Tannz, *as well.*

Tanqal, tanne, *until.*

Tanqe, *think.*

Tanqe ceo fuit, *until it was.*

Tanque il soit, *until it be.*

Tans, *time.*

Tant, *as well.*

Tant, (per), *thereby.*

Tant (es), *in the tent.*

Tantcome, *in as much as, while, so long as.*

Tantost, *by and by, almost, so much, presently.*

Tantqeu Eyre, *until the Eyre.*

Taper, *to lurk.*

Tapets, *blankets, coverlets.*

Tapiers, *tapers.*

Tapissant, *lying concealed, lurking about.*

Tard (a plus), *at latest.*

Tardance, *delay.*

Tardist, tardiver (plus), *later.*

Targe, targue, *a target.*

Targe, *the impression of the king's arms in the figure of a target, and sometimes called* pes sigilli, *the privy seal.*

Targer, targyr, *o delay.*

Targera, *shall wait.*

Tariez nounduement, *unduly delayed.*

Tart ou tempre, *later or sooner.*

Tape de blee, *stack of corn.*

Taskes, *taxes.*

Tast (par), *by handling.*

Taste (vient), *have found, experienced.*

Taster, *to touch, to endeavour, to find out.*

Tasters, *little cups.*

Taulpinier, *a mole-catcher.*

Taunt avaunt come, *as fully as.*

Taunt come, *as soon as, for as much as.*

Taunt (cest), *thus much.*

Taunt (pe), *by so doing.*

Taunt ne quant (ne est empire), *will be neither better nor worse.*

Taunt qe (jusques a), *until that.*

Taunt soient, *as soon as.*

Taust apres, *soon after.*

Taux, *such.*

Taux (au), *at the assessment, taxation.*

Taxe, *yew-tree.*

Taxer,

Taxer, *to ſettle.*
Taxes, *appraiſed, aſſeſſed.*
Taxus, *taxes.*
Taye, *grandmother.*
Tayl, *tally.*
Tayl (per), *by payment.*
Tayler haut et bas, *to tax a villain at diſcretion.*
Tayler (lui), *prepare himſelf.*
Tayllable, *taxable.*
Tayon, *grandfather.*
Te, *behold.*
Teaux, *ſuch.*
Teaux (qe), *that ſuch are.*
Tebaud, *Theobald.*
Teguler, *a tyler.*
Tei, teie, *thine.*
Teigles, *tile.*
Teigner, *to hold, to take place.*
Teilz, *ſuch.*
Teinable (le plus), *the moſt favourable.*
Teintrere, *to be dyed.*
Teinz (dras), *dyed cloth.*
Teire, *land.*
Teirs, teirce, *the third.*
Teiſſum, *a badger.*
Teizeler de draps, *a teazeller of cloth.*
Teizels, *teazles.*
Tele, *a web.*
Temoniance, temonie, *teſtimony, evidence.*
Temporaute, *temporalties.*
Tempouros, *the four Ember-weeks.*
Tempre (tart ou), *laer or ſooner.*
Temprer (a), *to mitigate.*
Tempriere (la), *temperament.*
Temps (par), *preſently, ſhortly.*
Temps deſcovenables, *non juridical ſeaſons.*
Temps (quatuor), *the Ember-days, at the four different ſeaſons of the year.*
Tempt (les), *held them.*
Tenable, *to hold place, defenſible.*
Tenables pur attaintes, *to be accounted or deemed as attainted.*
Tenaud, *Stephen.*
Tenaunce, *tenancy.*
Tencon, *a diſpute, quarrel.*
Tendi, *intended.*
Tendreche (par), *by the infirmity.*
Tend, tent, *offers, is ready.*
Tendiont, *may hold.*
Tendrez ſecrees, *will keep ſecret.*
Tendroit, *taking away.*
Tendroit (il), *he thought.*
Tendrons, *will reſtore, deliver up.*

Tendroynt

Tendroynt (ils), *they would think.*

Tendumes de lage le roy veantz le), *seeing the tender age of the king.*

Tendy (il n'a), *he did not look upon.*

Tendy, *tendered, offered.*

Tenell du roy (le), *the palace where the king resides; the king's hall, hell house.*

Tener, *to gain.*

Tenet, *Thanet.*

Tenez, *bound.*

Tenge (vous), *keep, preserve you.*

Teñt, teñ, *held.*

Tengent (qe), *that they keep, observe.*

Tenier, *to hold.*

Tenir, *accept, take.*

Tenirs (a), *to be holden.*

Tenk (je), *I hold.*

Tenoins nous, *we think.*

Tenoms, *look upon, regard.*

Tens (ou), *at the time.*

Tens (en), *in time.*

Tenser, *to preserve.*

Tensit covenant, *performed the covenant.*

Tensit ple (quil ne), *that he should not hold plea.*

Tent ausi come si, *in as full manner, as if.*

Tenure, *tenure.*

Tenure, tenuer (le), *the tenor.*

Tenure (a), *to observe.*

Tenz, *kept, observed.*

Terage, *a duty for breaking up the ground.*

Terce, terse, *third.*

Tere, *land.*

Tere de la Comun, *Commons, Community, of the Land,* viz. *the Bishops, Earls, Barons, and great men of the realm; also military men, such as hold Knight's fees or parts of Knights fees, and such as paid scutage.*

Terme, *time.*

Termine, *detained.*

Termine, *determination.*

Terminer, *to atterminate, or assign a time for payment of a debt.*

Terminez, *held, kept.*

Terra *land.*

Terre (est a), *fails, is aground.*

Terrene, terrien, *earthly.*

Tesir, *to be silent.*

Tessaunt (en), *tacitly, by being silent.*

Testez, *heads.*

Testure, *a testern of a bed.*

Tet, *head.*

Tets, tez, *all.*

Teu, *kept.*

Teule, tewle, *tile.*

Teu

Teu lieu, *ſuch a place.*
Teumoine (en), *en witneſs.*
Teu priſons, *ſuch priſons.*
Teus deus, *both.*
Tex, telx, *ſuch.*
Texes, *wove.*
Teyke (de), *with mail.*
Teynont, teynt, *bold.*
Teynte (la), *the attaint.*
Teyſant (en), *by being ſilent, tacitly.*
Teyſe (ſi en), *if he is ſilent.*
Tezeller de draps, *a teazeller of cloth.*
Theflaine, *the Epiphany.*
Theraï (en mon ſerus), *into my ſerious conſideration.*
Tholomeu, *Bartholomew.*
Tholun, tholon, *toll.*
Thrave des blees, *a thrave of corn.*
Thrommes, *thrums of woollen yarn.*
Ti, *thy.*
Tibaud, *Theobald.*
Tiel, toill, teoil, tuaill (unepriere de), *one piece of cloth.*
Tiel moy, *ſuch a one.*
Tielle (en la), *in tail.*
Tien, *thy.*
Tien counſell, *ſuch counſel, advice.*
Tienge, *keep.*
Tienk (jeo le), *I hold it.*
Tient (luy), *acknowledged, owned him.*
Tient mye in moi (il ne), *it is not my fault.*
Tient my lieu (ne), *does not lie, take place.*
Tiercz (par), *by thirds.*
Tierz (lui), *himſelf, and three others.*
Tieux, tieul, tiex, tious, tilz, *ſuch.*
Til, *ſuch a one.*
Tiltre, *title.*
Timer (a), *to fear.*
Timeur, *fear.*
Tin, *the ſound of a clock.*
Tinctours, *dyers.*
Tinel, *a place where juſtice is adminiſtered.*
Tinel, tynel, le roy, *the king's hall.*
Tingue, tinent, *held.*
Tint, *held, obſerved.*
Tinters, *tinkers.*
Tiou, *thine.*
Teraunties, *tirannies.*
Tiphaynei, *Epiphany.*
Tiſeours de draps, *weavers of cloth.*
Tiſſerans, *weavers, embroiderers.*
Tiſtes, *twiſted, fixed.*
Tiſtours, *twiſters.*
Tixtereſces, *weavers.*
Title (ſoit), *be entitled.*
Tiwe, *killed.*
Toat ale, *gone altogether.*

Tochey (je), *I mentioned, proposed.*

Toddels de lane, *tods of wool.*

Toict, tect, *the roof of a house.*

Toient, *hold, keep.*

Toil (le), *the plea, tolt, contest, dispute, the point.*

Toiller, *to deprive.*

Toillier, *a weaver.*

Toldee, *Theodore.*

Tote, tote (sõme), *sum total.*

Toleress, *the person by whom the entry is tolled.*

Tolet, tollet, tolets, tollerent, *deprived, taken away, barred.*

Tolkeps *yards.*

Toloun, *toll.*

Tols, toluz, tolz, *removed, taken away.*

Tolyr eux (a), *to take from them.*

Tonde (ne), *does not signify, cannot be found fault with.*

Tondour de drap, *one who shears the cloth.*

Tondra (ne), *will not take away, deprive.*

Toneiles, *hogshead, tun.*

Tonel, *a kind of prison for night-walkers, a round-house.*

Toni, *Anthony.*

Tonnel, *a vessel, vat.*

Tonneux voides, *empty vessels.*

Tonnu, *toll.*

Toor savage, *a wild bull.*

Torain, *of Touraine.*

Torale, *a kiln.*

Torbes, *multitudes, routs.*

Torcenouse, *wrongful.*

Torcionnieres, *unjust.*

Tormente, *punished.*

Torne de chescũn pleyntyf (pur le entre de la), *for the entry of the attorney of every plantiff.*

Tornei, *tournament.*

Torre, *land.*

Tors, *a tower.*

Torsjors, *always.*

Torteuous, *tortious, wrongful.*

Tosale (un), *a hogsty.*

Toste (se), *so soon.*

Tot, tos, *all.*

Tot, *although.*

Tot fois, tote voies, totebetz, totedys, *always.*

Tot outre, *entire.*

Tot a primer, *as soon, immediately.*

Tot le meins (a), *full at the least.*

Tot en tot, *wholly, entirely.*

Tottee, *totted.*

Touaille, *a towel.*

Touchiez, *handled.*

Toulle, *toll.*

Toul-

Toulliſſent, *ſhould take away from.*

Toumé, *Thomas.*

Toundeſon (ſeiſone du), *ſeaſons for ſheep-ſheering.*

Toundurs de herbis, *ſheep-ſheerers.*

Tounu, *toll.*

Tourbes, *turfs.*

Tourmentes, *tournaments.*

Tourteres, *Tartars, Saracens.*

Touſt (pluis), *as ſoon.*

Touſt que (ſi), *as ſoon as.*

Tout, *yet, although.*

Tout attrenche, *entirely, from beginning to end.*

Tout diz, tous dis, *always.*

Tout dys, *always had done.*

Tout de nette, *entirely.*

Tout net, *altogether.*

Tout outre, *entire, the whole.*

Toutper, *throughout.*

Tout ſoit, *although.*

Toute ſuoies, *always.*

Tout vois, *however.*

Toutz jours (a), *for ever.*

Toutz jours mes, *for ever, for ever after.*

Touzours, *always.*

Toyſon, *fleece.*

Toz, *all, the whole.*

Tozail, toſail, *a brick-kiln, or chimney.*

Trabeation, *Crucifixion. This was an æra from which charters were ſometimes dated*; Anno Trabeationis Dominicæ 1013. *Dufreſne.*

Tracaſſer *to range up and down.*

Tracement, *ſeeking after.*

Tradictions (des). *Part of the ſervice in the Roman Miſſal, and called ſo from the apoſtles upbraiding the Jews for following the falſe traditions of their anceſtors, and neglecting the weightier matters of the law. Inſtruments are ſometimes dated from this day.* Feria IIII. poſt III. Dominic. Quadrag. *Lemoine.*

Traete, *treated.*

Trahes in juries, *drawn in jurys.*

Trahir, *to draw in, to betray, to commit treaſon againſt.*

Trahir (poit), *may commit treaſon.*

Trahy out, *drawn beyond.*

Traictemets (que ſe ſont), *that this is proper treatment.*

Traiet.

Traiet, *drag.*
Traille, *delivered.*
Trailler, *to ſearch after.*
Traillez, *taxed.*
Traine (per), *by drawing.*
Trait (gens de), *croſs-bowmen.*
Tramettre, *to tranſmit.*
Tranchees, *trenches.*
Trans, *over, acroſs.*
Tranſcrire, *to write over, tranſcribe.*
Tranſeſcrit, *tranſcript.*
Tranſiger, *to tranſact.*
Tranſon, *a fragment.*
Tranſportera, *ſhall tranſfer, aſſign over.*
Trara, *ſhall extract.*
Trat (nient), *not drawn out of, taken out of.*
Travailer en jures, *to go far to be on juries.*
Travaille, travayli, *vexed.*
Travaille, *proſecute.*
Travailler, *to vex, harraſs, diſturb.*
Travailler la court, *to trouble the court.*
Travers (pur), *for ſheaves.*
Traverſant, *traverſing, putting upon trial or iſſue, oppoſing.*
Traverſeles (lines), *croſs lines, collateral lines.*
Traverſer, *to meet, intercept, to deny.*
Trayſun, *treaſon.*
Tre, *earth.*
Treacte le ple hors, *draw the plea out.*
Treaſſoms (ne), *may not draw.*
Treatables, *drawn, withdrawn.*
Trebuchables, *are to be caſt down.*
Trebuche, *fell down.*
Treer, *to draw.*
Trees, *drawn.*
Trees, *handled, diſcuſſed.*
Trefue, *truce.*
Treihes hors, *drawn out.*
Trehiſſent (ſe), *ſhould withdraw; ſhould meet.*
Treies, *three.*
Treiſiem (a), e veſſel, *at the mill-hopper and veſſel.*
Treiſiſſent cele part (ſe), *ſhould move towards thoſe parts.*
Treiſent (qils ſe), *that they would treat together.*
Treiſſent (qils ſe), *that they repair to.*
Treit, trait, trat, *arrow, dart.*
Treit, *treated, uſed.*
Treit (ne feuſt mye), *was not advanced.*
Treit (ſoit), *let him be withdrawn, diſcharged.*
Treite, *carriage, behaviour.*

Treitres,

Treitres, *traitors.*

Treittenient, *treat, entertain.*

Tremetoms, *transmit, send over.*

Tremois, *oats, barley, and such like grain; called so* a tribus mensibus, *because they are but about three months on the ground before they are got in.*

Tremor, tremur (pur), *for fear.*

Trencha durement, *cut with all his force.*

Trenche (il), *it enureth.*

Trenche a tout, *it strikes at all.*

Trenche (a), trenchement, *peremptorily.*

Trenche, *divided.*

Trencheours, *carvers.*

Trencher, *to carve.*

Trencheront devant lor seignur (ke), *who eat at their lord's table.*

Trent lieu ici (ne), *it shall not take place here.*

Trentel, *thirty masses.*

Trentisme tierz, *thirty-third.*

Treos (jeo), *I find.*

Trepassent, *passover.*

Trepir, trepier (un), *a tripod.*

Trep legierment, *too hastily.*

Trerche fois (la), *the third time.*

Trere hors (les), *dragged them out.*

Treroms (ne), *will not draw.*

Tresamble, *the like.*

Tresceint, *most holy.*

Tresisme jour, *third day.*

Tresmarry, *very much concerned, sorry.*

Tresor (on), *in the treasury.*

Trespassa, *left this world.*

Trespassauntz, *those who pass by, go backwards and forwards.*

Trespasse (darreinement), *lately deceased.*

Trespasse, *an offence.*

Trespassement du dit nadgairs roy (par le), *by the death of the said late king.*

Trespassement, *miscarriage.*

Trespassement des terms, *making default at the time appointed.*

Trespassent, *pass over.*

Trespasser, *to trespass, to offend, to transgress.*

Trespasset, *death.*

Tresque, *as soon as, presently.*

Tresredout, *most dread.*

Tresreguise (jey), *now very requisite.*

Tressauntz (potiùs cressauntz), *growing.*

Tresseint, *most holy.*

Trestast, *treated, agreed with.*

Trestisme, *thirtieth.*

Trestournes, tresturnes, *turned from their course.*

Trest'out perde, *let him lose all.*

Trestoutz, trestous, trestore, *all.*

Tresublie, *quite forgot.*

Tresze, *thirteen.*

Tret, trete, *agreement conference.*

Tret, *here.*

Tret saunk, *drawn blood.*

Trete, *treaty, conference.*

Tretez, *drawn, induced to.*

Tretable, *tractable, kind.*

Tretans, *as much, as many.*

Treteours, *those who were appointed to manage the treaty of concord and peace between Edward the second and the discontented barons.*

Tretementz, tretis, *treaties, treaty.*

Treter, treitiz, *to treat of, to entreat.*

Trett, *draught.*

Treterez, *will treat, use, entreat.*

Tretuit, *all.*

Treveure, *finding.*

Treveure (d'altre), *of any other thing found.*

Trewe, *truce.*

Treygne (per), *by delays*

Treyne, *to draw, draught, draws, drawn.*

Treyne et pendu, *drawn and hanged.*

Treys, *three.*

Treyt (payn de) *bread of Trete; wheaten bread; one of the kinds of bread mentioned in the Stat. of* 51 H. III.

Treytour, *a traytor.*

Treyturement, treturement, *traiterously.*

Tri, tries, *three.*

Triboill, *troubles disturbances.*

Trie, *tried, examined into, sifted into.*

Triement, *trial.*

Trienalx, *for three years.*

Trier, *to chuse, select.*

Trier, et arraier (les), *to chuse, pick out, and array them.*

Trierz jour, *third day.*

Tries, *proclaimed.*

Tries excepcions, *excepti-ons may be taken.*
Trieux (en temps des), *in time of truce.*
Triours, *triers.*
Trioussent, *find.*
Triowes, trives, trieues, *truces.*
Tripe (un), *a tripod.*
Triplication, *rejoinder.*
Tris jurs, *always.*
Tristur, *sorrow, grief.*
Troboill, *trouble.*
Troc, *bartered, exchanged.*
Troches, trousses (en), *in clusters, bunches.*
Troes, *found.*
Troesse, troessent, *they find.*
Trosse, *idle.*
Troiter, *to treat.*
Trones, *beams.*
Tronour des laines, *weigh-ers of wool.*
Tronquez, *mutilated.*
Trop hant, *too high.*
Trop (par), *too many.*
Trope (met), *put more.*
Trope tost faict (un), *an over hasty act.*
Trop outrement, *too much.*
Tropoy, *too little.*
Troppe, *a mole.*
Trove (de), et de ove, *see* ove de et de trove.
Trovenes de novelles, *in-ventors of news.*
Trove en un default (serra), *shall be turned into a de-fault.*
Trouez, *boxes with slits to receive charity.*
Troums (nus), *we find.*
Trousieme, *the third.*
Trowe, troye, *a sow.*
Trowe, *found.*
Troye, *found.*
Troyes, *three.*
Trube, *trouble.*
True, *truce.*
Truerant, *touching, con-cerning.*
Trusse, *found.*
Truffle, *found.*
Truir, *to find.*
Truisse, trusse, *find.*
Truite, *takes in the fact, catches.*
Trum, *obscure, black, dark.*
Trussez, *packed up.*
Truve, *finds.*
Trynks, trymkes, *trunks, weirs.*
Tuaill, towaill, *cloth for towels.*
Tuche, *touch; touches, concerns.*
Tuement, *slaying.*
Tuerie, *slaughter.*
Tuest (soit), *should be cut out.*
Tuest chescun langue (soit), *that every tongue should be silent.*
Tuey, *killed.*

Tuicion, *protection, reprieve.*
Tuit, tuite, *whole, all; although.*
Tuit, *hold.*
Tuiz ſeintz, *all ſaints.*
Tumbe hors, *fell out.*
Tundu, *cut, clipped.*
Tuors, *ſlayers.*
Tur, *a Turk.*
Tur, *a town.*
Turbeſover, *to dig turf.*
Turbeurs, *diſturbers.*
Turelle, *a little tower, turret.*
Turgent, *remain.*
Turmentyr, *to torment.*
Turnance, *turning.*
Turnereit, *would turn.*
Turnez, turnes, *tourns.*
Turnois noirs (ſeiſſante mile livres de), *ſixty thouſand livres of black Turnois,* i. e. *fifteen thouſand pounds Sterling.*
Tus jours, *for ever.*
Tut, *although.*
Tut ad e primes, *firſt of all.*
Tut le reaume, *the whole kingdom.*
Tution, *defence.*
Tuwant, *kill.*
Tuz ceuz, *all thoſe.*
Tuz ſeynz, *all ſaints.*
Tuzon (la diſme), *the tenth fleece.*

Twaite, *wood grubbed up, and land made arable.*
Tweſdie, *Tueſday.*
Tyelx, *ſuch.*
Tyene, *keep, detain.*
Tyent, tynt, *they hold.*
Tynell, *the hall.*
Tynt, *held.*
Tyois, *the ancient German, or Teutonic language.*
Typhanie, *the Epiphany.*

V, u, *or, whether.*
ũ, *one.*
Vr̃e (a), *to your.*
V-as̃ fait, *would have done.*
ṽs, *towards.*
Vacations, *voidances.*
Vacherie, vacarie (un), *a cow houſe.*
Vacquer, *to be at leiſure.*
Vadat, *let him go.*
Vadlet, valet. *This word has various acceptations; ſometimes it ſignifies the heir of ſome nobleman or knight, who is in ward; at other times, a young gentleman retained in the king's, or ſome great man's family, and a candidate of honour; often a young gentleman who ſerves in the army; and ſuch an one is frequently called,* ſcutiſer, ſerviens, armiger. *Gloſſ.*

x. Script. v. Valettus. *Also a yeoman.*

Vadlettes del corone, *yeoman of the crown.*

Vadletz, *servants, valets.*

Vaer (de), *to go.*

Vagarant, *wandering.*

Vageront (qui), *which shall be vacant.*

Vahuz, bahuz, *vessels.*

Vaie, *way.*

Vail, *under.*

Vailance (a la), *to the value.*

Vailez, *valets, yeomen.*

Vaillament, *valiently.*

Vaille, *sufficient.*

Vaille, *vigil, watch.*

Vaille cruettz, *old cruets.*

Vaillentz de biens, *persons of property.*

Vaillet regarder (qe vus), *that you will have regard.*

Vailliv, *bailiffs.*

Vaine voicle, *common fame.*

Val (encontre), *downwards.*

Valable, *of force.*

Valait riens (ne), *availed nothing.*

Valallument, *the force of it.*

Valaunt (en), *in the descending line.*

Valer, valoir, *avail.*

Valeures (des), *of the lips.*

Valeyent il (ne), *they would not.*

Valez, *farewell.*

Valiaunts serjeaunts (les meulx), *serjeants of the most substance or property.*

Valissant, *to have been worth.*

Valletz, *the next condition to an esquire.*

Valles, vallez, *valets.*

Valoir (le bien), *the welfare.*

Valoit avant, *goes forwards.*

Valoue, *value.*

Valu (aient), *have prevailed.*

Valuble (estre plus), *to be of more force.*

Values arguments, *arguments of weight and force.*

Vancre, *to vanquish.*

Vanez, potiùs vaux, du pais (mieutz), *most substantial or sufficient of the county.*

Vanque, *vanquished.*

Vanra a age, *shall arrive at the age.*

Vansist melz, *it would be better.*

Vant (le), *the aforesaid.*

Vant parlour (office de), *the office of Speaker of the House of Commons.*

Vaollaunce, *value.*

Vaquans, *vacant.*

Vaquier, vaquer (ne peussent), *cannot be at leisure.*

Varech, *shipwreck.*

Variaunse, *change.*

Varles, *servants.*

Varlet, *a yeoman.*

Varleton, *a groom.*

Varraie, *true.*

Varvick, *Warwick.*

Vassalle, vaissels, vassaux, *vessels.*

Vassaux, *men of courage.*

Vast, *waste.*

Vastant, *wasting.*

Vat, *go, extend to.*

Vau, *a valley.*

Vaudra, *shall give up.*

Vaues, vauez, vauiz, vauetz (des meulz), *of the most substantial, worthy.*

Vavetz des countees (des mieultz), *men of the best reputation in the county.*

Vault, *worth, avails, is of force.*

Vault (ne), *cannot be had, faileth.*

Vaultenant (un), *an unthrift, or one that is worth nothing.*

Vaultre, *a mnngrel hound.*

Vaulx, *vallies.*

Vaunt dit (la), *the aforesaid.*

Vausisent (si il), *if they could.*

Vaussiffee, *vouchsafe.*

Vaussissies eschevour (ke vous), *that you would vouchsafe to receive.*

Vaust (il), *it goeth, it endureth.*

Vaxel, *vessel.*

Vay (lune leue de), *one mile of the way.*

Vaylaunce espernes (ne), *sparing no pains.*

Vaylantz, *worthy, valiant.*

Vaylorent (qils), *as they thought fit.*

Vayn, *the autumn.*

Ubblie, *oblivion.*

Ubliaunce, *forgetfulness.*

Ubois, *where.*

Udifs, udyfs (gens), *idle people.*

Udifte, *misery, idleness.*

Udiness, *idleness.*

Ve, *saw.*

Ve, *worth.*

Ve, vée, *true*

Vea (luy), *refused him.*

Vea, veia, *refused.*

Veage, *voyage.*
Veair, *to see.*
Vealletz, *you will.*
Veance (en), *in view, in expectation of.*
Veaude place, *void, vacant place.*
Veault, *he is willing.*
Vedentz, *seeing.*
Vee, *refusal.*
Vee de name (plees de), pleas de vetito namio. *Holding plea of distresses taken and forbid to be replevied.* Name, nam, naam, namps, *and* nams, *which signifies a distress, come from the Saxon verb* niman, capere, *to take.*
Veẽ, *sent.*
Vee mye (ne), *does not intend.*
Veel, *old.*
Veelez viscountz, *old sheriffs.*
Veent, *forbid, deny.*
Veer, *true.*
Veer, *to act, to view.*
Veer (nous voulons), *we will see.*
Veer avant (en), *to proceed.*
Vees, *think.*
Veet le coroner, *let the coronor go.*
Vefue, *widow.*
Vegle, *blind.*
Vei jeo ne, jeo ne veign, *I do not see.*
Vei, veye, *this day.*
Veia, *refused.*
Veiance (par), *by seeing.*
Veici, *behold.*
Veie, ve, *seen.*
Veie (tote), *quite laid open to the sight.*
Veient, *may see.*
Veiers, *true.*
Veies, veez, la vie, *distresses forbidden to be replevied, the refusing to let the owner have his cattle which were distrained.*
Veif, vefve, vefues, *a widow; widows.*
Veifuage, *widowhood.*
Veigle (la), la veille, *the vigil, the eve, the watch.*
Veigne, *offend.*
Veigner, *to come.*
Veille, *will.*
Veillement, *seeing, watching.*
Veiller, *to watch.*
Veilles, *veils.*
Veillez, veiles, *old.*
Veiltee, *old age.*
Vein (en), *in vain.*
Veine, *comes.*
Veinged (si altre), *if any other shall come.*

Veinquemes, *we conquered.*

Veint diſtinctement nomez, *not expreſsly or particularly named.*

Veioins (nous), *we ſaw.*

Veir (mis en), *produced, ſhewn, proved.*

Veir (ſaunz), *without denying.*

Veirge, le, *the verge or bounds limited to the king's court,* i. e. *twelve miles round the ſame.*

Veiſeetz a lier (que vous), *which you ſaw doing.*

Veiſſetz a lier hors, *ſaw going out.*

Veiſtes (vous ne), *you never ſaw.*

Veiſſon (il), *they ſee.*

Veit, *ſees.*

Vel, *I will.*

Vele, *may.*

Veler (en), *in view.*

Velewet, *velvet.*

Velra, *will.*

Velt, veyl, velloit, velee, *will.*

Ven, *viewed.*

Veñ la, *coming thither.*

Veñaiant, *coming.*

Venancez, *coming, haſtening forwards.*

Venanncez (enaux), *in being revenged on them.*

Vedees, *ſales.*

Vendires (a), *to be ſold.*

Vendra, *ſhall come.*

Vendra (ne), *ſhall not challenge.*

Vendre ſoit, *ſale may be made.*

Vendroins (a peyne), *we ſhould ſcarce have come.*

Vendront (contre), *ſhall offend againſt.*

Venelle du lict, *the ſpace between a bed and the wall.*

Veneours, *hunters.*

Venerdy, Venardy, Venredi, *Friday.*

Vengnent, *they come.*

Venials (ſont), *are to be brought.*

Venjaunce, *revenge.*

Venier (pur le non), *for not coming.*

Veniſmus, *we come.*

Veniſſent (qi), *who offend.*

Venku, *overcome, conquered.*

Venours, *huntſmen.*

Venra, *ſold.*

Venre (le), *the ſcull.*

Venſiſt (que il), *that he ſhould come.*

Vent, *comes.*

Vent (ſen), *comes.*

Vent (p̃), *by ſale.*

Vent (ſe), *is ſold.*

Vent preſtz, *ready ſale.*

Ventee, *diſperſed by the wind.*

Ventes, *woods marked for ſale.*

Ventier, ventiler, *to blow.*

Ventiſme jour, *the 20th day.*

Ventrez (rumpes les), *broken-bellied, burſten.*

Venue, de veñne (mal de) *the eſſoign* de malo veniendi.

Veoer, veoir, *to ſee, to inſpect.*

Veoid, *ſees.*

Veoir, *true.*

Veors, *viewers, ſurveyors.*

Veot, *wills, ſhews.*

Veot (unques ne) *never had ſeen.*

Veouns nous, *we ſee; we will.*

Ver, *cattle.*

Ver, *true, appear.*

Ver (a), *to view.*

Ver (pur), *to ſee.*

Ver, *againſt.*

Ver en cite, potiùs verte cire, *green wax.*

Verament, verreyment, *truly.*

Veray, *very.*

Verbatement, *verbally.*

Verdi-aoré, *Good Friday.*

Vereduiſt, *verdict.*

Verek, *wreck.*

Verement (la), *the evrament.*

Vereys, verreys, vers, verri, *true.*

Vergee (ne acree q ne fuiſt unq') *which was never ſurveyed, meaſured, or laid out into acres.*

Verges, *yards.*

Vergis, *young ſuckers.*

Vergnauntz, *coming.*

Vergoignes, viergoigne, vergoyne, *ſhame, reproach.*

Vergonder, *to abuſe, raviſh, violate.*

Veriſemblables, *very likely.*

Verite, *truth.*

Veritee (peuſſe dire ſa groſſe), *may relate the whole truth of his caſe, may tell his own tale.*

Verreyment, *truly.*

Verroie, *true.*

Verroient, *have a mind.*

Verront, verretz, *ſhall ſee.*

Vers eux (de prendre), *to take with them.*

Verſer, *to turn.*

Verſui, *towards.*

Vertie, *truth.*

Ves (autre), *otherways.*

Veſcu (ſi il uſt), *if he had lived.*

Veſnes,

Vefnes, *widows.*
Vefque, vefke, *a bishop.*
Vefquift, vefquirent, vefquiffent, *lived.*
Vefquift (fi il), *if he was alive.*
Veffelmentz, *things appertaining to veffels and shipping.*
Veft, veftus, *vefted.*
Vefter, veftu, *to veft, to enure, vefted.*
Veftes, *wafte.*
Veftre, vefte, *cloathed, covered.*
Veftue, vefte, *clothed, covered.*
Veftue, potiùs vefcu, (en core), *ftill alive.*
Vefture, *crop, growth.*
Vefture, *robes, veftments.*
Vet (s'en), *go therefrom.*
Vetere, *old.*
Veterlokkes, *fetterlocks.*
Vevant, *living.*
Veve, veia (le), *the fight.*
Veve, *a widow.*
Veveres, *widowers.*
Vevete (en fa), *in her widowhood.*
Veu, *your.*
Veue, *a widow.*
Veuez, *will.*
Veugle, *blind.*
Veuls, *calves.*
Veulliant, *willing.*
Veum (nus), *we fee.*
Veure (par), *by being willing.*
Veus articles, *old articles.*
Veufiffiens, *we would.*
Veut (per), *by a way, method.*
Veute (de), *by fale.*
Veuttez mye, *claim nothing.*
Veutz, veuz, greigne, *old grain.*
Vewe, *view.*
Vey (haut), *highway.*
Veye (fi), *if he perceives, if he will.*
Veyer, *to view, to behold.*
Veyer eft, *is to be feen.*
Veyes, *was.*
Veyet, *fees.*
Veyle (le), *the elder.*
Veylles, *towns.*
Veyn, *vain, void.*
Veyner, *to come.*
Veyr, vier, *truth.*
Veyre, *true.*
Veyfin, *a neighbour.*
Vez (vous), *you will, you wifh.*
Viage, *voyage, expedition.*
Vicary, *a vicarage.*
Vice, *a defect, fault, error.*
Vice, *crime, injuftice.*
Vichel (un), *an heifer.*
Vicie, *corrupted.*
Vicint, *come.*

Uictaine,

Uictaine (l') *the octave.*
Vidimée, *a vidimus.*
Vidront, *will.*
Viduele, *widowhood.*
Vie, *the view.*
Vieant, *coming.*
Viec ſtile, *old ſtile.*
Vief naam, *live diſtreſs.*
Viegles hommes, *blind, old, impotent men.*
Viegnes, *vineyards.*
Viel, *ſenior, elder.*
Vieles, viez dettes, *old debts.*
Viel, *calf.*
Viel beſt, *live beaſt.*
Viels, *vills.*
Viendront, *ſhall come; act, offend.*
Viener, *came.*
Vienes (ffiſſent les), *ſhould make the views.*
Vienqe, *comes.*
Vient (que vie, que), *who is deſirous.*
Vient, *they ſee.*
Vient (le), *the 20th.*
Vier, *to deny.*
Vier, puit, *may ſee.*
Vierge ſon marye, *power, controul of her huſband.*
Viergier, *a verger.*
Viergoigne (en), *to the reproach, ſhame of.*
Vieront (al), *they look to.*
Viers, *towards.*
Vies (par pluſors), *by many ways.*
Vieſtes (ou), *where you ſee or find.*
Vieu, *ſight.*
Vieus, views, *widows.*
Viex, viez, *old.*
Viez (toutz), *all ways.*
Vigued, *neighbourhood.*
Viguereuſe (fame), *a virtuous woman.*
Vikere, *vicar.*
Vikeris, *vicarages.*
Vilaine ſerment, *blaſphemy againſt God, the Virgin, and the Saints.*
Vilaint (li), *a villain, the occupier of land.*
Vileins faitz, *vile, baſe, villainous acts.*
Vilenement deſoler, *baſely uſed them.*
Viles, *old.*
Vill, *a village; a villain.*
Villaine, vilenie, *diſgrace, diſgraceful.*
Ville, citee de la, (communaltie) *the community or commonalty of a town, burgh, or city. This always ſignified the mayor, aldermen, and common council, where they were to be found, or the ſteward or bailiff, and capital burgeſſes, or, in*

in ſhort, the governing part of cities and towns, by what perſons ſoever they were governed, or names and titles they were known; and not the commoners or ordinary ſort of burgeſſes or freemen only. Brady, 132.
Villeez, *townſhips.*
Villenie, *villainous.*
Villude (que vous me), *that you will acquaint me with.*
Vil pris, *a low price.*
Vilte, *vileneſs.*
Vilte tenu, *baſeneſs.*
Vinch point (joe ne), *I dont't come.*
Vincle (St. Pere lad), *the feſtival of St. Peter in bonds; 1ſt of Auguſt.*
Vine, vins, vint, *twenty.*
Vinez, vivez, *ſtacked.*
Vingent, *come.*
Vink, vinſeſt, *came, got to.*
Vins vermeilles, *red wines inned, carried in.*
Vinz, aunes, *inned, carried in.*
Vinz liverez e IIII. (VII.) *ſeven ſcore and four pounds*, i. e. £144.
Vinteront, *they tie, or bind.*
Viollent (ne), *they will not.*
Viot, *envy.*
Vioure, *to live.*
Virent (qui), *who ſaw.*
Virge, *a virgin.*
Virolez, *ferrilled, tipped, capped.*
Viron, *about.*
Virtons, veritons, virettons, *arrows.*
Viſ. viſc. viſconte, *ſheriff.*
Vis, *alive, alſo void.*
Vis, viſe, *face, viſage.*
Vis, *foreſeen. perceived.*
Vis, *advice.*
Vis a fair, *thought fit to be done.*
Viſe ne diſtreſs (p), *by ſecret diſtreſs.*
Viſens, viſnes, *neighbours.*
Viſes, *hinds* *.
Viſeur, *the face.*
Viſitatour, *viſitor.*
Viſne, *neighbourhood, venue.*
Viſnees viles, *neighbouring towns.*
Viſſe, *the vizor of a helmet.*
Viſſent, *bad.*
Uiſſerie, *the office of porter.*
Viſt, virent, *ſaw.*
Viſt le coroner, *let the coroner go.*

* Potiùs *biſes.* See Rot. Parl. Vol. II. p. 94. Pet. 22. Hale's MS.

Viſt enfower (per), *by burying alive.*
Viſteconſail, *ſpeedy council.*
Vit, *privities.*
Vit, *eight.*
Vitel (un), *a calf.*
Viteretz (en), *in truth.*
Vivand (en ſon), *in his life-time.*
Vive vois, *by word of mouth.*
Viver (en), et in veſture, *in victuals and cloaths.*
Viver (pur le), *for the livelihood.*
Vivers, *fiſh-ponds, warrens, parks.*
Vivers, *livelihoods.*
Vivi, *alive.*
Vivies, viver, *victuals, diet.*
Viuperons, *ſhall live.*
Viz, *ſeen.*
Ul, *any one.*
Ulle, *any.*
Ulveſtier, *Ulſter.*
Um (l'), *the man.*
Umbracles, *ſecret places.*
Umbre, *ſhadow, colour.*
Umbrez, *coloured.*
Un meſme, *the ſelf-ſame, one and the ſame.*
Uncore, unquore, unques, *ſtill, yet.*
Unement, uniement, *in general; unanimouſly.*
Ung count, *an earl.*
Ung ou deux, *one or the other.*
Ungle, *nail.*
Ungr, *one.*
Uniement, *unanimouſly.*
Unificence, *making one, uniting.*
Uniment, *equally, in union.*
Uniſone, . unz eſme, *the eleventh.*
Unite (d'), *whatſoever.*
Univerſaire, *anniverſary.*
Unzieme, *eleven.*
Unkes (ne), *never.*
Uns, *ſeveral.*
Unſemely choſe (cõe), *as an unbecoming thing.*
Unſzime, unzieſme, unſime, unzim, uniſme, *eleventh.*
Unt, *have.*
Unt, *therefore.*
Unze (les), *any.*
Vo, *or.*
Vo, *yours.*
Voaie, *voyage.*
Voain, vomheri, *Autumn.*
Voair, *ſee, appear.*
Voaſſiſſent a ceo ſomandre, *might ſend to ſummon them.*
Voce, *voice.*
Vocer, *to call.*
Voderunt, *are willing.*

Voe (par nulle), *by any way.*
Voel (ne), *would not.*
Voelliant, *willing.*
Voels, *vows, wiſhes.*
Voer, *to view.*
Voeſon (la), *the advowſon.*
Voeſt (les), *let him vouch them.*
Voet, *requires.*
Voet (qu'il), *that he go.*
Voet (ſi il), *if he will.*
Voeve, voef, *widow.*
Voguement, *paſſing, returning.*
Voguer, *to call again, return.*
Voi, *I am going.*
Voi droit, *the law requires.*
Voidera, *will.*
Voidez, *departed.*
Voidre (a), *to quit.*
Voie, *true.*
Voie deſch, *by way of eſcheat.*
Voie de utre mer, *voyage beyond ſea.*
Voier, voiar, voir, *the truth.*
Voier (eſt a), *is to be ſeen.*
Voier (per), potiùs noier, *by drowning.*
Voies (nul), *no right to accuſe.*
Voiez, *ye ſee.*
Voil (jeo), *I will.*
Voilde Iriſhmen, *wild Iriſhmen.*
Voile (ne), *cannot.*
Voilauncez ſeigniories, *potent lords.*
Voilent, *violent.*
Voiler (malvey), *ill will.*
Voillantz, *men of worth, ſubſtance.*
Voilleit, *named.*
Voiloir, voillour, *will, teſtament.*
Voir (la), potiùs l'avoir, *the riches.*
Voire, voirement, *truly.*
Voiſe encontre, *act againſt.*
Voiſent (ne), *go not.*
Voiſt avaunt, *proceeds in.*
Volant, vollentifs, en volentie, *willing.*
Volatil royal, *a royal bird.*
Volentrine, *giddy, wilful.*
Voler, *to be willing, to wiſh.*
Voler (bien), *endeavoured.*
Volez, *would take away.*
Volg, volie, volys, *will.*
Volles, chautes, et gargaus de oiſſeaux (en), *in the flight, ſinging, and chattering of birds.*
Voloir (male), *ill wll.*
Volvement des toiſons du lein, *winding up of fleeces of wool.*

Volund, *a will or testament.*

Volunt, *meaning.*

Voluntrivement, *wilfully.*

Voluptuosite, *wantonness.*

Von gre (de lor), *of their own accord.*

Voot, voil, voit, *he will, would.*

Vorra, vorroient, *would.*

Vorrount (ou), *or shall hear.*

Vors, *you.*

Vos, *yours.*

Vosdretz vous, *would you.*

Vouch bien (s'il voet), *save if he would bid him welcome.*

Voucher, *to vouch, to call.*

Voudroit notre bien, *wishes our welfare.*

Vove, *a vow.*

Vovèr, *to vow.*

Voulant (bien), *good will.*

Vount, *they go.*

Vounze, *eleven.*

Vousscierent, *will.*

Vous est, *is true**.

Vousist, *should have a mind.*

Voustrent, *would.*

Vous vies (y), *you would.*

Vout, voul, *visage, countenance.*

Voutent bille, *prefer, put in their bill.*

Voy, voye, *way*; *scape.*

Voyce (jeo ne), *I don't see.*

Voyct, *eight.*

Voyer, *true.*

Voyerment, *truly.*

Voyertie, *truth.*

Voyez voluntaries (jeo), *I would be willing.*

Voyez, *woods* †.

Voy fist, *let him go.*

Voylere (il deyvont), *they ought to wish.*

Voys, *voice.*

Voyse, *is directed*; *issues.*

Voysent, *let them go.*

Voysent jurer (qui), *who are to swear.*

Vowe de frank plegge (aver), *have a view of frank pledge.*

Voz (par les) *by yours.*

Vraes, *true.*

Vre, *your.*

Ure, *ure, practice, use.*

Ure (mis en) *put in practice.*

Ure (al) *at the time.*

Ure apprise, *have understanding.*

Ure, *burned.*

Ureisuns, *prayers.*

* Potiùs *voir est.* See Rot. Parl. Vol. II. p. 181. Pet. 25. Hale's MS.

† Potiùs boyez. Ib. p. 190. Pet. 64.

Urent,

Urent avannt, *were foretimes.*

Urera, *ſhall ſerve, ſhall be uſeful.*

Urera (ne) *ſhall not veſt.*

Urgerouſe, *urgent, eager.*

Vrie (per) *by way of*

Urur de eux (per) *by pulling out the eyes.*

Us, *huts, houſe, doors.*

Us, *uſe, cuſtom.*

Us (de) *of them.*

Uſee, *uſage.*

Uſees (rien) *not at all made uſe of.*

Uſents, *uſing.*

Uſez (les) *the profits.*

Uſier, *make uſe of, uſed.*

Uſſent trove (q̃) *that they ſhould find.*

Uſſers et ports, *uſhers and porters.*

Uſſes (fichiez es) *fixed on the doors.*

Uſſey (ſi jeo) *if I had.*

Uſſoit eſtre, *would be, had been.*

Uſſoyt, uſſont, *had.*

Uſum, *hitherto, ſo far.*

Ut, *and.*

Ut, *eight.*

Ute, *the eighth.*

Utes, utas, utaves, utus, *octaves.*

Utiſme, utim, *eighth.*

Utine (d') *of the eighth.*

Utre ceu terme, *beyond that time.*

Uttard, *lately.*

Utter (que) *who gives out, or publiſhes.*

Uttrees, utteres, *uttered.*

Vuech, *eight.*

Vueille, vuellies, *will.*

Vuidoit (ſe il ſe) *if it was robbed, deprived.*

Vuille, *will.*

Vunt, *have*; *go.*

Vus (pur) *for you.*

Vuſe, *uſed.*

Vut, *had.*

Vut, *ſees.*

Vy (jeo) *I ſaw.*

Vyant, *ſeeing.*

Vye, *life.*

Vye, *refuſed, prohibited.*

Vye de (par) *by way of.*

Vyel parol, *old word.*

Vyeu, *ſeen.*

Vyle, vylys, *vill, city.*

Vyncles, *bonds, fetters.*

Vynee (del) *of the neighbourhood.*

Uys, *door.*

Vytime, *the eighth.*

Vz, *your.*

Uxuoſt, *provoſt.*

Uzzans, *without.*

Wacreours, *vagabonds.*

Wacrus viaundes, *rotten meat, corrupted.*

Wage, *gages, ſureties.*

Wage

Wage (feu) *his challenge.*
Waifnez, *waived.*
Waillez ſanz paſtour, *left without a teacher.*
Wainable, *that may be ploughed or manured.*
Wainent lour querells qui, *who gain their ſuits.*
Wakerantz, *vagrants, people who go begging, and ſtrolling about the country.*
Walais, Walaix, Wallois, *Welſh.*
Waleſeh, *the language of the Walons.*
Wallez, *Wales.*
Wandit (le) *the aforeſaid.*
Warandir, *to guarantee.*
Wardees mius, *better kept, obſerved.*
Warneſture, *the neceſſaries for fortifying a place.*
Warretz, *fallow, unploughed.*
Wart l' um, *let a man take care.*
Weſemeſtre, *Weſtminſter.*
Waſkerantz, *wandering abroad.*
Waſt et beal, *handſomely, civilly.*
Waſteynes (lues) *waſte places.*
Wautham, *Waltham.*
Wayour, *a weare, or were.*
Wedues, *widows.*
Wefs, weifs, *waifs.*
Weigher, *to weigh.*
Welogh, *willow.*
Wener (pur) *to conduct.*
Werpir, *to yield up, give up, forſake.*
Werrons, *ſhall ſee.*
Weruſt, awruſt, *doubt.*
Weſtmuſter, *Weſtminſter.*
Weſtours, *waſſailers.*
Weuce, *a widow.*
Weux, *a beggar.*
Weymoſter, *Weſtminſter.*
Weynez, weyna, weyne, *deſerted, relinquiſhed, in a decline.*
Weyve, *waived.*
Weyver, *to waive.*
Wherwes, *wharfs.*
Wiere, *war.*
Windemonet, *the month of October or November.*
Windowe, *a blank place, or ſpace.*
Wis, *wiſdom, prudence.*
Witembre, *October.*
Witime jor, *the eighteenth day.*
Witive, witave, wictieve, *eight, eighth.*
Wombes, *bellies.*
Worſtetz (lit de) *a bed of worſted.*
Wou (un) *a vow.*

Woyle, *will.*

Wuidier, *to evacuate.*

Wyt myle unces d'our (pour) *for eight thousand ounces of gold.*

Wyt (dixe), *eighteen.*

Xenie, *a new-year's gift.*

Xentelle, *a ſpark.*

Xeurté, *aſſurance, promiſe, ſurety.*

Xeut, *follows.*

Xexantes, *ſixty.*

Yalemaines, *at the leaſt, however.*

Yaue, yave, yaiies chaude, *hot water.*

Yaues (par) *by water.*

Yaus (pour) *for them.*

Yauxi (devant leurs) *before their eyes.*

Ycel (en) *in it.*

Ycement, *thus, in like manner.*

Ycen, *this, that.*

Yceſtes (per) *by theſe preſents.*

Yceux, yceaux, yeile, *thoſe, them.*

Yeit (ſil) *if there is.*

Yeme, hyeme, *winter.*

Yemer (a) *to winter.*

Yeoven, yeven, *given, dated.*

Yerledom, *earldom.*

Yeulx, yex, yes, *eyes.*

Yeuſſe jeo eſte (e tut *and although I had been.*

Yeux ont (nous) *we have ſeen it with our own eyes.*

Ygaument, *equally.*

Ygiſe, *lies.*

Ygo, *therefore.*

Yl, *he.*

Yl ſemble, *it ſeems.*

Yl (ke) *that they.*

Yleke, *from thence.*

Ylemans, *inhabitants of the iſles of Jerſey and Guernſey.*

Ylles, yles, *iſles.*

Yloques, *threw.*

Ymage, *an image.*

Ymaginé, *adorned, embroidered.*

Ympnaire, *a book of hymns, with books of conjurations, and church legends.*

Yo, yio, *an egg.*

Yoe, ive, *water.*

Yra (il) *he ſhall go.*

Yraigne, *a ſpider.*

Yraut, *an herald.*

Yraudement, *in a paſſion.*

Yretge, *an heretic.*

Yris, *ivory.*

Yrois, *an Iriſhman.*

Yrra mys (n') *ſhall not go.*

Yſoit, *therein be.*

Yſlement, *an iſlander.*

Yſſir, *to come, to go out.*

Yſt, *he is.*

Yſtrent (ne) *will not go out.*

Ytal,

Ytal, *thus, so.*
Ytel, *such.*
Yve, *water.*
Yvant, *seeing.*
Yver, yvre, yverne, *winter.*
Yvernayle (ble) *winter corn.*
Yver (froidare) *a frosty winter.*
Yveress (per) *through drunkenness.*
Yveroigner (de) *in a drunken fit.*
Yveroynes (les) *drunkards.*
Yvises, *services.*
Ywell (per) *equally.*

Zabulon, *sand.*
Zern, *yarn.*
Zork (duc de) *duke of York.*
Zusche (Sire Aleyn la) *Sir Alan Zouche.*

FINIS.

PRELIMINARY DISCOURSE,

TO THE LAWS OF

WILLIAM THE CONQUEROR.

THE Laws of William I. having at various Times engaged Men of very great Learning and Abilities in different Countries, in tranſlating them into foreign Languages; I hope I need not apologize for endeavouring to give a more perfect Tranſlation of them into our own Tongue, than has yet been done.

The great Selden, in his Notes on Eadmer, was the firſt who attempted to render theſe Laws into Latin; but he left many Parts of them (on account of the Rudeneſs of the Norman Tongue) untranſlated as he found them. The very learned Ducange, at the Inſtance of Gabriel Gerberon, of the Benedictine Order, who publiſhed the Works of Saint Anſelm, tranſlated the whole of theſe Laws into the ſame Language, which Tranſlation is added at the End of Gerberon's Edition. Dr. Wilkins, in his Code of antient Laws, amongſt which he has inſerted theſe of William, has likewiſe tranſlated them into Latin, neither intirely adopting the Verſion of Selden or Ducange; but frequently varying from both.

Mr. Houard, a learned Advocate of the Parliament of Normandy, has, among his antient Laws of the French, given us, in oppoſite Columns, theſe Laws of William, with Selden's and Ducange's Tranſlations in Latin, and his own in French.

Mr. Tyrrell and Mr. Mortimer have tranſlated ſome of theſe Laws into Engliſh, and given the Subſtance of others of them in their Hiſtories of England

They bear a venerable Aſpect, and are the only Laws extant in the Norman Idiom of that Age.

The Title prefixed to theſe Laws of William, imports that they are the ſame [a] as thoſe which King

[a] They are conjectured by Selden to have been a Copy of thoſe Laws, which by public authority had been reviewed and confirmed in the fourth year of William's reign; and that the time of Ingulphus's taking them down to his Abby was after the 15th year of William's reign, Seld. ad Eadmerum, 172; and which Sir Roger Twyſden, has fixed at the 21ſt, Wilk. 216.

The MSS of Ingulphus's Hiſtory of Crowland, with theſe Laws at the end, were, as Selden informs us, in his time, preſerved at Crowland, but that, notwithſtanding all his endeavours, he could not procure the uſe of it; that he therefore publiſhed theſe Laws from a MS of them in his own cuſtody of about 200 years more recent date. Seld. 172, 173.

Sir Roger Twyſden had another MS of theſe Laws, differing but very little from that of Selden's; as likewiſe had Sir Robert Cotton. Wilkins 211. Notes on Forteſcue de Laudibus Leg, Ang. c. xviii. p. 47. London, 1775.

Selden had his Copy from the Chronicle of Litchfield. Wilk. 215. Nicholſon's Eng. Hiſt. Library fol. edit.

Mr. Somner had alſo a MS of theſe Laws, which Wilkins made great uſe of, and which, when he publiſhed his Saxon Laws, was in the Library at Canterbury. Wilkins's Preface.

But the moſt authentic Copy is that which is in the Red Book of the Exchequer.

The 1ſt, 17th, 18th, 20th, and 36th of theſe Laws (they relating to the Church) are inſerted in Wilkins's Concil. from the MS of Ingulphus. Wilkins's Concil. tom. i. p. 313, 314. Whelock's Lamb. Archaion. p. 159.

Edward,

Edward, his Kinſman, had obſerved before him: but this Fact being called in Queſtion by the above learned Advocate in his Preliminary [b] Diſcourſe prefixed to the antient Laws of the French, it will, in order to maintain the Truth of the Title prefixed to theſe Laws, be neceſſary from our own Lawyers and Hiſtorians to give a ſhort Account of the principal Founders and Reſtorers of the Saxon Laws; and, to ſhew how thoſe Laws ſtood at the Entrance of William I. ſome Explanatory Notes alſo are added to the Laws of William, and References made from each of them to the Anglo-Saxonic Laws. Theſe will mutually illuſtrate each other, and we hope will prove that the Aſſertions laid down by Houard are not well ſupported.

The chief Founders and Reſtorers of the Saxon Laws, were Ina, Alfred, Edgar, and Edward the Confeſſor. When King Alfred ſucceeded to the Monarchy of England, founded by his Grandfather Egbert, he collected the various Cuſtoms he found diſperſed in the Kingdom, and reduced aud digeſted them into one uniform Syſtem or Code of Laws in his *dome book*, or *Liber judicialis*; this he compiled for the Uſe of the Court Baron, Hundred, and County Court, the Court Leet, and the Sheriffs Tourn; Tribunals which he eſtabliſhed for the Trial of all Cauſes civil and criminal, in the very Diſtricts wherein the Complaint aroſe; all of them ſubject however to be inſpected, controlled, and kept within the Bounds of the univerſal or Common Law, by the King's own Courts; which were then itinerant, being kept in the King's Palace, and removing with his Houſehold in thoſe

[b] Anciennes Loix des François conſervées dans les Coutumes Angloiſes recueillies par Littleton, par M. David Houard, Avocat au Parlement de Normandie, en 2 Vols in 4to. à Rouen, 1766.

royal Progreſſes, which he continually made from one End of the Kingdom to the other. And this Book we may probably ſuppoſe to have contained the principal Maxims of the Common Law, the Penalties for Miſdemeſnors, and the Forms of judicial Proceedings; but though it is ſaid to have been extant ſo late as the Reign of King Edward IV, it is now unfortunately loſt. 1 Black. 64.—4 Black. 404.

This Code was called the *Weſt-Saxon Lage*, or Laws of the Weſt-Saxons, and obtained in the Counties to the South and Weſt of the Iſland from Kent to Devonſhire.

The local Conſtitutions of the antient Kingdom of Mercia, which were obſerved in many of the Midland Counties and thoſe bordering on the Principality of Wales, and probably abounded with many Britiſh or Druidical Cuſtoms, were called the *Mercen Lage*, or Mercian Laws.

The Cuſtoms which had been introduced on the Daniſh Invaſion and Conqueſt, and which were principally maintained in the North, in the reſt of the Midland Counties, and alſo on the Eaſtern Coaſt, went under the Name of *Dane Lage* or Daniſh Law.

Theſe three Laws were, about the beginning of the 11th Century, in Uſe in different Counties of the Realm; but King Edgar obſerving the ill Effects of theſe three diſtinct Bodies of Laws prevailing at once in ſeparate Parts of his Dominions, projected and began one uniform Digeſt or Body of Laws, to be obſerved throughout the whole Kingdom.

Edward the Confeſſor, his Grandſon, afterwards completed this Deſign; but probably this was no more than a Revival of King Alfred's Code, with ſome Improvements ſuggeſted by Neceſſity and Experience; particularly the incorporating ſome of the Britiſh, or rather Mercian Cuſtoms, and alſo ſuch of the Daniſh as were reaſonable and approved, into the

West-Saxon-Lage, which was ſtill the Ground-work of the whole: This, Blackſtone tells us, appears to him the beſt ſupported and moſt plauſible Conjecture (for Certainty is not to be expected) of the Riſe and Original of that admirable Syſtem of Maxims and unwritten Cuſtoms, which is now known by the Name of the *Common Law*, as extending its Authority univerſally over all the Realm; and which is doubtleſs of Saxon Parentage. 4 Black. 404.

This Edward the Confeſſor effected without Tumult or Contradiction; all theſe three different Laws holding an Uniformity in Subſtance, and differing rather in the Quantity of Fines and Amerciaments, than in the Courſe and Frame of Juſtice. Spelm. Rem. 49.

Forteſcue, indeed, is of Opinion, that thoſe Laws could not be at that Time conſolidated and thrown into one Body of Laws, becauſe each of thoſe Species of Laws were in Force after, and are to be found, not only in Edward the Confeſſor's, but all over William the Firſt's Laws. And not only Mulcts and Fines ſet, according to the *Dane-Laga*, *Saxon-Laga*, and *Mercen-Laga*; but Cuſtoms and Uſages ſet out to be obſerved according to thoſe different Laws. So that he thinks it muſt be meant only, that Edward the Confeſſor made a Collection out of thoſe Laws then extant, as Alfred did before him; and that, ordering thoſe to be obſerved, which had not been obſerved in the ſhort Reigns of Harold and Hardicanute, he may well enough be called the Reſtorer of the Engliſh Laws.

Thus ſtood the Laws of England at the Entry of William I.; and it ſeems plain that the Laws commonly called the Laws of Edward the Confeſſor were at that Time the ſtanding Laws of the Kingdom, and conſidered as the great Rule of their Rights and Liberties; and that the Engliſh were ſo zealous for them,

them, that they were never ſatisfied till the ſaid Laws were reinforced and mingled for the moſt Part with the Coronation Oath. Hale's Hiſt. p. 85, 86.

Accordingly, we find that this great Conqueror, at his Coronation on the Chriſtmas-day ſucceeding his Victory, took an Oath at the Altar of St. Peter Weſtminſter, in Senſe and Subſtance the very ſame with that which the Saxon Kings uſed to take at their Coronations; adding further, that he would make no Diſtinction between the Engliſh and French. Fort. Pref. 26. Arg. Ant. p. 12.

Of all the ſeveral Species of Laws, the *Dane Lage* pleaſed William beſt; and he declared, that as his Anceſtors and moſt of his Norman Barons came from Norway, and were of Norwegian Extraction, he ought to govern the Realm by theſe Laws. However, he was at laſt, by Tears, and Prayers, and Adjurations by the Soul of Edward, who bequeathed him his Kingdom, diverted from his Purpoſe; and at Berkhamſtead, in the 4th Year of his Reign, in the Preſence of Lanfranc Abp. of Canterbury, for the quieting of the People, he ſwore, that he would inviolably obſerve the good and approved antient Laws which had been made by the devout and pious Kings of England, his Anceſtors, and chiefly by King Edward; and we are told, that the People then departed in good Humour.

William I. having now ſolemnly bound himſelf to govern chiefly by the Laws of Edward the Confeſſor, it became neceſſary, as his Followers were Foreigners, and Strangers to the Engliſh Laws and Cuſtoms, to have them aſcertained, and for this Purpoſe he ſummoned 12 Saxons from every County, to inform him and his Lords upon Oath, what the antient Laws were; and Alured Abp. of York, who had crowned William, and Hugh, Biſhop of London, by the King's

Command, wrote down with their own Hands the Return made by theſe Jurors.

And to bring the Matter ſtill nearer Home, Ingulphus, who was an Engliſhman, who had been Secretary to the Conqueror, and afterwards made by him Abbot of Crowland, has tranſmitted to Poſterity this Account of his Laws. " I brought this Time " with me (ſays he) from London to my Monaſtery " the Laws of the moſt juſt King Edward, which " my Lord William, the renowned King of England, " had proclaimed to be authentic, and to be always " inviolably obſerved through the moſt grievous Pe- " nalties, and commended them to his Juſtices in the " ſame Tongue they were ſet forth, leſt through Ig- " norance we or ours might happen to offend." Ingul. Hiſt. Seld. Ead. p. 172. Whelock's Edit. of Lambard's Archaion, 158, 159. Wilk. Leg. Saxon. 216.

Having given an Account how the Laws ſtood at the Entrance of William I; we will now lay before the Reader what Houard has advanced in Oppoſition thereto, and make ſome Obſervations on thoſe Paſſages.

His Aſſertions, amongſt others to the like Effect, are theſe:

1. *Guillaume le Conquerant défendit ſes nouveaux Sujets de ſuivre d'autres Coutumes que celles de ſon premier domaine.* Diſc. Prelim. p. 23. 31.

William the Conqueror forbad his new Subjects to follow any other Cuſtoms than thoſe of Normandy.

Our Obſervation on this, is, that as William at his Coronation ſwore that he would govern by the Laws of Edward the Confeſſor, confirmed theſe Laws by his Charter to the Citizens of London, and renewed this Oath afterwards at Berkhamſted; it can never be imagined that after ſuch Solemnities all theſe Laws

Laws were cancelled and aboliſhed: and indeed we have on the contrary, many Proofs from our Hiſtorians of the Obſervance of the Laws of Edward in his Reign.

2. *Les Loix de Guillaume n'ont rien emprunté des Loix d'Edward.* Diſcours Prelim. p. 32.

The Laws of William have borrowed nothing from thoſe of Edward the Confeſſor.

Here we muſt remark, that Ducange, who tranſlated theſe very Laws, ſays, that William did not dictate to the Engliſh new Laws, ſo much as confirm the old, eſpecially the Laws of Edward, to which he made ſome Additions. Ducange, Dict. Lex Angl. Vol. ii. p. 265.

Theſe Laws of William compriſe the Ordinances of the Kings Ina and Ethelred, and more eſpecially of Canute. Wilk. Leg. Angl. Saxon. p. 229.

Rapin tells us, that the Cuſtoms now practiſed in England are, for the moſt Part, the ſame as the Anglo-Saxons brought with them from Germany. Diſſertation on Government of Anglo-Saxons, Vol. ii. Oct. Ed. p. 138.

M. Lacombe, in the Preface to his Supplement to the Dictionary du vieux Langage François, ſpeaking of William the Conqueror, ſays, "Ses Ordonnances "ſont les mêmes que celles d'Edouard ſon Prédéceſ-"ſeur." Pref. p. 13. His Laws are the ſame as thoſe of Edward his Predeceſſor.

3. *A l'avenement de Guillaume au Trône, les Loix Saxonnes étoient abrogées depuis long temps en Angleterre. Celles d'Edward, qui ne conſervoient aucunes traces de ces Loix, les avoient remplacées.* Prelim. Diſc. p. 34.

The Saxon Laws had been abrogated a long Time in England before William I. came to the Crown. The Laws of Edward, which preſerved no Traces of thoſe Laws, had ſucceeded in their Room.

Surely

Surely nothing can be further from the Truth than this.

All Hiſtorians agree, that the Laws which William I. ſwore to obſerve, were, "bonæ et approbatæ antiquæ Regni Leges," the good, approved, and antient Laws of the Realm. Pref. 8 Coke.

That theſe Laws were no other than the Laws of Edward the Confeſſor; and that, ſo far from not preſerving any Traces of the Saxon Laws, Coke ſays, they contain the Subſtance of all thoſe; and that what was Law in thoſe Days is ſtill the ſame in ſeveral Inſtances. Pref. to 6 Coke.

This will appear from the Laws themſelves, for many of the Laws of Edward the Confeſſor are the very ſame as in former Saxon Kings; and many Expreſſions and Words, and moſt of the Terms in William I's Laws, are mere Saxon, and derived from that Language, but put into Norman French. Forteſcue's Pref. to Reports.

The Common Law, though ſomewhat altered and impaired by the Violence of the Times, has in a great Meaſure weathered the rude Shock of the Norman Conqueſt. Black. Vol i. p. 17.

The Laws of William I. are in general little other than Tranſcripts of the Saxon Laws or Cuſtoms. Sullivan, Lect. xxviii. p. 288. 292.

4. *Littleton diſtingue en chaque Article de ſon Recueil ce qui eſt de la commune Loi; c'eſt à dire, de la Loi établie par Guillaume le Conquérant d'avec ce qui a été inſtitué par des Chartes, Statuts, ou Edits poſtérieurs.* Diſcours Prelim. p. 42.

Littleton diſtinguiſhes in every Section of his work, what the Common Law is; that is, the Law eſtabliſhed by William the Conqueror, from that which has been ordained by Charters or Statutes ſince his Time. Diſc. Prel. p. 42.

This

This Norman Jurist seems to have a very imperfect and inadequate Idea of what we understand by the *Common Law*, when he tells us, it is the Law established by William the Conqueror. Let us consult our own Lawyers and Historians, and they will inform us, it was called *Folc-Right* in the Saxons Times; that Alfred, Edgar, and Edward the Confessor, were the great Compilers and Restorers of the English Laws; and that these are the Laws which our Ancestors struggled so hardly to maintain under the first Princes of the Norman Line, and which so vigorously withstood the repeated Attacks of the Civil Law; and that these (and not the Law established by William) gave Rise and Original to that Collection of Maxims and Customs which is now known by the Name of the *Common Law*. 1 Black. 66.

To these Laws, William, at the latter End of his Reign added some of his own, which were the Means of establishing the Feudal System in this Nation; and, by his Charter, he commanded that all his Subjects should enjoy the Laws of King Edward in all Things, with those *Additions* which he had appointed for the Good of the English.

Si me errasse deprehenderis, in viam revoca; et Ducem sequar manibus pedibusque. Houard, Title, Vol. ii.

LAWS

THE

ANGLO-SAXON LAWS

REFERRED TO,

As found in WILKINS.

THE Laws of Æthelbirht p. 1
He was King of Kent, and the first Christian King of the Saxons. He began his reign 561 and died in 616.

The Laws of Hlothare and Eadric p. 7
They were Kings of Kent; the first began to reign about 673, and died 685; the other was his nephew, and reigned but about a year and half after him.

The Laws of Wihtræd p. 10
He succeeded his brother Eadric as King of Kent, and died 725.

The Laws of Ina p. 14
He was King of the West Saxons; began his reign 688 and died about 728.

The Laws of Alfred p. 28
He was grandson of Egbert and King of the West Saxons; succeeded to the throne in 872 and died 901.

Foedus Alfredi & Guthruni p. 47
Guthrun the Danish general was invested by Alfred with the title of King of East Anglia about 878.

Senatus

THE

LAWS

OF

WILLIAM THE CONQUEROR.

WITH NOTES AND REFERENCES.

References to the Anglo-Saxon Laws.

*** The principal deſign of making the References, from the Laws of William the Conqueror to the Anglo-Saxon Laws, and thoſe of Hen. I.; is to ſhew, that the Laws of William, notwithſtanding what has been aſſerted by *Monſ. Houard,* ſtand greatly indebted to the Saxon Laws; in the next place it is hoped theſe References will not a little tend towards illuſtrating both Laws; and at the ſame time, preſent the Reader with a ſhort view of what the greateſt part of the Public or Common Law in thoſe ages conſiſted; as well as in ſome degree facilitate, what is greatly to be wiſhed for, a regular digeſt of that moſt antient body of Laws.

LEGES

GULIELMI CONQUESTORIS.

Hæ sunt Leges & Consuetudines quas WILLIELMUS *Rex concessit universo Populo* Angliæ *post subactam Terram. Eædem sunt quas* EDWARDUS *Rex, cognatus ejus, observavit ante eum.*

Ces sont les Les & les Custumes que li Reis WILLIAM [a] *grantut a tut le Peuple de* Engleterre, *apres le* [b] *Conquest de la Terre. Ice* [c] *les meismes que le Reis* EDWARD *sun Cosin* [d] *tint devant lui.*

I. *De* Asylorum [e] *jure & immunitate Ecclesiastica.*

SCilicet; Pax Sanctæ Ecclesiæ cujuscunque Forisfacturæ quis reus sit hoc tempore; & venire potest ad Sanctam

CO est a saveir; [f] Pais a Saint Yglise; de quel forfait que home out fait en cel tens; e il pout [g] venir a Sainte Yglise; out

NOTES.

[a] *Grantut.*—In the fourth year of his reign.

[b] *Conquest de la Terre.*—According to Sir Mathew Hale, Blackstone, and others, the word Conquest signifies no more than Acquisition or Purchase; but according to Dr. Brady and many more, it is taken in the sense Wilkins here understands it, for absolute Conquest. Hale's Hist. Law, p. 86. 2d Black. 48. 242. *Brady.*

[c] *Les meismes.*—They were translated from the Saxon by the command of William, into the Norman Language, and then confirmed by him; and there are not any Laws which are wrote in the Norman Idiom of that Age extant besides these.

But still we must remember, that though these Gallo-Normannic Laws, as well as some others in Latin of Edward the Confessor, have been handed down to us; yet that we must consider them only as a manual of those Laws, and that the greater part of the Laws of Edward are the immemorial Custom of the Realm. Wilk. 219. Seld. 189. Hale's Hist. p. 86. Sulivan's Lect. p. 233.

[See a further account of these Laws in the Preliminary Discourse.]

 Eclesiam;

THE LAWS OF WILLIAM THE CONQUEROR.

These are the Laws and Customs which WILLIAM *the King granted to all the People of* England *after his Conquest of the Realm; being the same as those which King* EDWARD, *his Cousin, observed before him*, viz.

1. *Concerning the Privilege of Asylums, and Immunity of the Church.*

LET Holy Church enjoy her Peace; whatever forfeiture a man hath incurred to this time, if he can come to Holy Church, let him have Peace of life and limb; and if any man lay hands on him who

NOTES.

[d] *Tint devant lui.*—Observed before him; not tulit, enacted; therefore some are of opinion, that these Laws were framed and promulgated by some of the predecessors of Edward the Confessor, and especially by Canute. See Wilkins's Concilia, tom. i. p. 313.

[e] *De Asylorum jure.*—The numbers and titles prefixed to each Law, were added by Selden. Seld. 194. Wilk. 215.

REFERENCES.

Holy Church, Inæ, c. v. p. 15.—Alfr. c. ii. v. p. 34, 35. c. xxxviii. p. 43.

Asylums to the King, Archbishop, Nobleman, Bishop, Lib. Constit. Temp. Athel. p. 110, 111, 112, 113.

Peace, Fœd. Edw. & Guth. p. 51. L. 1.—Edg. p. 76. 1.—Can. p. 127. ii. iii.—Hen. I. p. 243. xi.

Eccleſiam; Pacem habeat vitæ & membri. Et ſi quis injecerit manum in eum qui matrem Eccleſiam quæſierit, ſive ſit Abbatia, ſive Eccleſia Religionis, reddat eum quem abſtulerit, & centum ſolidos nomine Forisfacturæ: et Matri Eccleſiæ Parochiali xx ſolidos: et Capellæ x ſolidos: et qui fregerit pacem Regis in Merchenelega centum ſolidis emendet, ſimiliter de compenſatione homicidii, & de inſidiis præcogitatis.

pais de vie & de membre. E ſe alquons meiſt main en celui qui la mere Ygliſe requireit, ſe ceo fuſt u Abbeie, u [h] Ygliſe e de Religion, rendiſt ce que il javereit pris, e cent ſolz, de forfait, e de Mer Ygliſe de Paroiſſe xx ſolz, e de Chappelle x ſolz, e que enfraiant la pais le Rei en Merchenelae cent ſolz les amendes, altreſi de [i] Heinfare [k] e de aweit purpenſed.

N O T E S.

[f] *Pais a ſaint Ygliſe.*—Pax Eccleſiæ frequently occurs, and ſignifies the immunities and privileges the Church was intitled to, and whoever broke them was ſaid to break the peace of the Church. If any brawls or contentions aroſe in the Church, the peace of the Church was violated, and a double mulct was to be paid according to the dignity of the Church; from 5l. to 30s. Æthelbirht, l. 1. Wihtred, p. 10. S. 3. 4. Inæ, l. 5. Lib. Conſtitut. p. 151. c. ii. Fœdus Edw. & Gut. l. 1. Canut. l. 2, 3. Edw. Conf. l. 2. 7. Edgar l. 1. Concilium Ænhamenſe, p. 121. Sec. 2, 3.

Thoſe who fled to the Church for refuge, were ſaid to have the peace of the Church. See next page, note g.

Our Saxon and Norman anceſtors called thoſe days and parts of the year that were aſſigned to God, Dies Pacis et Eccleſiæ, and the reſidue allotted to the King, Dies or tempus pacis Regis; and in the Laws of Edw. the Conf. Term time is called, Dies Pacis Regis; and Vacations Dies Pacis Dei, et Sanctæ Eccleſiæ Spel. Rem. p. 79. Ed. Con. l. 3.

has ſought the protection of the Mother Church, whether it be an Abby or a Church of Religion, let him deliver him up whom he has taken, and pay 100s. as a forfeiture, and 20s. to the Parochial Mother Church, and 10s. to a Chapel; and whoſoever breaks the King's peace, the ſatisfaction, by the law of the Mercians, is 100s; the ſame for Heinfare and premeditated aſſaults.

NOTES.

g *Venir a ſainte Yglise*—Churches had this privilege from the time of Conſtantine, though there are no Laws about it older than Theodoſius, either in the Juſtinian or Theodoſian Code. By the ninth Law of Alfred, the Criminal had Sanctuary for three days. Æthelſtan extended it to nine days. Æthelred, l. 9. to nine or more. By the 6th Law of Edw. the Conf. he could be taken from Sanctuary by none but the Pope, or one authoriſed by him. The King, Archbiſhops, Noblemen, and Biſhops, had alſo this privilege. Conſtitut. Æthelred, p. 110.

h *Yglise de Religion.*—A Monaſtery or Church dedicated to any religious Order. Wilkins. As to the degrees of Reverence and Privilege, and the puniſhment of violation; Churches were thus differenced, viz. into Eccleſia Capitalis, Eccleſia Mediocris, and Eccleſia Campeſtris. Jo. Brompton 918.

i *Cent ſolz de forfait e de mer Yglise de paroiſe* xx *ſolz.* fani æditais 120 ſolidorum numeratione pacis Eccleſiæ violatæ pænas luito, Leg. Alfr. c. 1.

k *Heinſare*—this is ſometimes wrote Hainfare and Hamfare—Inſultus factus in Domo; and ſeems here to ſignify the ſame as Hamſocen, and not ſervi tranſitum, from Hein ſervus & far tranſitus; or Homicidii compenſationem, as it ſometimes does. Hamſoken & Hamfare are often uſed as ſynonymous in ancient Hiſtorians; and the amends is the ſame.

E de aweit purpenſed—præmeditatus aſſultus, L. Hen. 1. p. 242. l. 10. or it may ſignify any offence committed by await, or malice prepenſed.

2. The

2. *De Hominum Regis privilegio.*

Hæc placita pertinent ad Coronam Regis. Et si aliquis aut aliqua vexaverit, (molestaverit aut) malefecerit hominibus illius Ballivæ & de hoc sit attinctus per Justitiam Regis, Forisfactura sit dupla illius quam alius quispiam forisfecerit.

Icee plaiz asierent a la Coroune le Rei; & se alquens [k] u quens uxuost messeist as homes de sa [l] baillie, e de eo suist atint de la justice du Roi, forfait fust a duble de ce comme altre fust forfait.

3. *De Pacis publicæ violatoribus.*

Et qui in Danelega violaverit pacem Regis, cxliv libris emendet: Et Fortisfacturæ Regis quæ pertinent ad Vicecomitem xl solidi in Merchenelega, & l solidi in West-Sexenelega. Et de libero homine qui habet Sac & Soc &

E que en [m] Danelae fruisse la pais le Roi vii vins livres e iiii les amendes; e les forfaiz le Roi qui asierent al Vescunte xl solz en Merchenelae, e l solz en West-Sexenelae. E al frans home qui aveit [n] Sac e [o] Soc e [p] Tol e [q] Tem e

NOTES.

[k] *U quens uxuost*—"Soit Comte soit Prevôt," Houard; whether Earl or Provost; and indeed Quenz or Quens frequently signifies Earl. See Laws of William, xvii. Quens de Flanders—Treatise on prerog. Queen consort, p. 11.–Seld. Tit. Hon. p. 115.

[l] *Baillie*, i. e Jurisdiction, Province, *Wilkins.*

[m] *Danelae.*—The Danelae, the Merchenlae, and the West-Sexelae are all here taken notice of, as Fortescue has observed; which seems to countenance his opinion, that those Laws were not all consolidated or thrown into one body of Laws; but that Edward the Confessor made a collection out of these Laws then extant, as Alfred did before him. *Fortescue's pref.* 23.

[n] *Sac*, *Soc*, *Tol*, *Tem*, and *Infangthief*, contain privileges enjoyed by Lords of Manors, and Freemen.

Tol

2. *The Privilege of the Men of the King's Bailiwick.*

These pleas belong to the King's crown, namely; if any one whether Earl or Provost, shall evil entreat the men of his Bailiwick and be convicted thereof in the King's court; let him forfeit double what another would have forfeited in the like case.

3. *Of the Violators of the public Peace.*

He who is guilty of a breach of the King's peace, shall, according to the Law of the *Danes*, pay 144 l.; and the King's forfeiture, which belong to the Sheriff, is by the Law of the Mercians xl s. and by the Law of the West Saxons L s. As to a freeman who has sac and soc, tol and tem, and infangentheof, if he is im-

NOTES.

[o] *Sac* from ꞅace, is that priviledge which a Lord of a Manor enjoys of holding pleas and punishing offenders within his Manor.—It also signifies the right of taking the forfeitures or mulcts arising from thence.

[p] *Soc* from ꞅocn, is the territory, precinct, or circuit, wherein the privileges of Sac, Tol, Team, Infangthefe, &c. are exercised; it also imports a liberty, immunity, franchise, priviledge, or jurisdiction. Gloss. Dec. Script.—Somner Gav. 134.—Spel. 51. Ducange. *Houard*, v. ii. p. 118.

[q] *Tol*, the privilege of buying and selling within his own Manor, L. Edw. 24, Brac. 55, b; also of taking Toll of what is bought and sold there. To be exempted from taxes or tolls for what was sold off his own domaines. *Houard.* To be quit from paying toll in any part of the kingdom. *Bract. Flet.* p. 62. S. viii.

REFERENCES.

Alfred, p. 43. xxxvi.—Edward, p. 49. iv.—Athelst. p. 63. iii.—Canute, p. 127. ii.—Edw. Conf. p. 199. xii. p. 203. xxx, xxxi.—Wm. I. p. 228. li.—Hen. I. p. 273. lxxxi.

pleaded

Tol & Tem & Infangentheof & implacitatus fuerit, & ad Forisfacturam pofitus in Comitatu, pertinet Forisfactura ad opus Vicecomitis xl Oræ in Danelega, & de alio homine qui ejufmodi Libertatem non habet oræ xxxii. De his xxxii oris habebit Vicecomes ad ufum Regis oras decem, & is qui eum implacitaverit habebit in remedium verfus eum oras xii, & Dominus in cujus finibus manferit x oras. Hæc eft in Danelega.

[q] Infangenetheof, fe il eft emplaide e feit mis en forfeit en le Counte, afiert il forfait a oes le Vefcunte xl [r] ores in Denelae, e de altre home qui ceft franchife non ad xxxii ores. De ces xxxii ores, arat fi Vefcunte a oes le Roi x ores, e cil qui li plait aurat de remied vers lui xii ores, e le Seigneur, en ki fin il maindra, x ores; co eft en Denelae.

NOTES.

q *Tem*, from Tyman propagare, to teem or bring forth. A privilege granted to a Lord of a manor, of having, reftraining, and judging bondmen, thieves, and villains, with their children, goods and chattels, in his court. *Gloff.* X. *Script. Latro.*

r *Infangthief*, from the Saxon in infra, ꝼanꝫan capere, and ꝺeoꝼ fur. Is that priviledge which the Lord had of trying and hanging a thief on his own gallows, who was taken with the goods ftolen upon him, within his manor. All thefe prerogatives were granted to freemen for the encouragement of hufbandry.

Confiderable farms could not be managed by a fingle family; from thence it became natural for the owners to truft the cultivation of part of thofe farms to poor people and flaves; and that he fhould have the liberty of chaftifing them without obferving the forms of law, and to be anfwerable for wrongs they might do to fuch hufbandmen as lived alfo under his dependence. *Houard*, p. 119.

4. De

pleaded, and a forfeit is laid upon him in the county court, the forfeit ſhall go to the uſe of the Sheriff; 40 ores, according to the laws of the Danes, and as to any other man not having ſuch franchiſe, 32 ores; and of theſe 32 ores the Sheriff ſhall be anſwerable for 10 to the King's uſe; and the proſecutor ſhall have 12 towards his damages, and the Lord within whoſe juriſdiction he reſides ſhall have 10 ores. This is the Law of the Danes.

NOTES.

[a] *Ores.* Spelman and Somner are of opinion, that there was no ſpecific coin called an ore, but that it ſignified the ſame as our ounce. It differed according to the variation of the ſtandard, and was ſometimes valued at 12d. ſometimes at 16d. and at other times at 20d. See Gloſſ. X. Script.

Tale manerium dedit 10, 20, vel 30, libras denariorum de 20 in ora. *Domeſday.*

Solebant dare pro filiis ſuis maritandis duas oras quæ valent 32 denarios. *Pla. Mic.* 37 H. III.

4. *Con-*

4. *De Latrocinii reo, & fidejuſſore qui morum ejus periculum in ſe ſuſceperat.*

Hæc eſt Conſuetudo in Merchenelega; ſi quis appellatus fuerit de Latrocinio, ſeu de Furto, & plegiatus fuerit venire ad Juſtitiam, & fugerit interim, Plegius ejus habebit iv menſes & unum diem ad eum quærendum, & ſi poſſit eum invenire, juret ſe duodecima manu, quod tempore quo eum plegiavit Latro non fuerat, neque per eum eſſet quod fugerit, nec eum prehendere poſſit. Tunc reddat Catallum, & xx ſolidos pro capite, & iv denarios ei qui ceperit ipſum, & unum obolum pro inqui-

Coſt eſt la cuſtume en Merchenelae, ſe alquens eſt apeled de larciu, u de roberie, e ſeit plevi de venir a juſtice, e il ſeit fuie dedenx, ſon plege ſi avera de iv meis e i jour de quer le, [t] e ſi il le pot truver, ſi jurad [u] ſe dudzime main que a l'ure que il le plevi, [w] Laron nel ſot, ne pur lui ne ſent eſt fui, ne aveir nel pot dunc rendrad le chattel [x] e xx ſolz pur la teſt, e iiii den. al ceper, e une maille pur la baſche, e xl ſolz al Rei. En Weſt-Sexenelae cent ſolz al clamur pur la teſt, e iv livres al Rei. E en

NOTES.

[t] *E ſi il le pot truver*—and if he can find him ; but the ſenſe ſeems to require, that it ſhould be ; *and if he cannot find him* ; proviſion being made in the latter part of this Law ; in caſe the thief was taken.

[u] *Se dudzime main.* See note on L. 17.

[w] *Laron nel ſot.*—Latro non fuerat, *Wilk.* One would rather think it ſhould be ; latronem eſſe neſcivit, *did not know he was a thief,* as in Law 48. See alſo L. 41.

[x] *E* xx *ſols pur la teſt, e* iv *den. al ceper, e une maille pur la beſche.* Houard renders it thus, xx s. for proſcribing the fugitive, 4d. to the gaoler, and a maille to the hundred to make up for the loſs of the labour of the abſent perſon.

ſitione,

4. *Concerning him who is guilty of Larceny, and his Surety.*

The cuſtom of the Mercians is this; that if one who was appealed of larceny or robbery, and was pledged that he ſhould be amenable to juſtice, ſhall in the mean time flee; his pledge ſhall have four months and a day to ſeek him up; and if he can find him, he, with 11 compurgators, ſhall ſwear, that at the time he became a pledge for him, he did not know that he was a thief, that he had not any hand in his eſcape, and that he cannot find him; then he ſhall make amends for the the thing ſtolen, and pay 20s. for the head, and 4d. to the gaoler, and a halfpenny for the inqueſt, and 40s. to the King. By the Weſt-Saxon Law, 100s. to the hue and cry for the head, and 4l. to the King; and according to the Law of the Danes,

REFERENCES.

Of Pledges, Alfr. p. 35. iii. p. 41. xxix.—Edg. p. 78, vi.—Edw, Conf. 201. xx.

Theft above 12 *d. and the thief above* 12 *years of age; the puniſhment, and forfeiture,* Jud. Civ. Lond. p. 65. ii.

Theft from the King, how to be compenſated, Athelb. p. 2. iv.

Of theft committed by a freeman, Hloth. and Ead. p. 8. v.—Alfr. p. 29. xv.—Inæ, p. 22. xlvi.—Edw. p. 50. ix.

Of the killing a thief, Whil. p. 12. viii.—Inæ, p. 20. xxxv. p. 17. xvi.

Of thieves when taken, their puniſhment, Inæ, p. 17. xii. p. 18. xviii. p. 19. xxviii.

Of the accuſation of theft, Inæ, p. 22. xlvi.—Edw. p. 49. vi.—

Of intercepting things ſtolen, or being found in the poſſeſſion of another, Hloth. and Ead. p. 8. vii.—Inæ, 22. xlvii. p. 26. lxxv.—Hen. I. p. 262.

the

ſitione, & xl ſolidos Regi. In Weſt-Sexenelega c ſolidos ad clamorem pro Capite, & iv libras Regi. Et in Danelega, Foriſfactura eſt viii libræ. xx ſolidi pro Capite, & vii libræ Regi. Et ſi is poteſt intra annum & iv dies invenire Latronem, & eum perducere ad Juſtitiam, redhibebunt ei viginti ſolidos quos acceperent, & fiat Juſtitia de Latrone.

Denelae, le forfait viii livres; les xx ſolz pur la teſt, e les vii livres al Rei. E ſil pot dedenz un an & iv jurs trover le larun e amener a la juſtice, ſi li rendra les vent ſolz, kis aurad ont, e ſeit faite la juſtice de Larun.

REFERENCES.

Of compenſation of theft, Æthelbirht, p. 4. xxix.—Inæ, p. 24.—Athelſt. p. 56. i.

Of purgation of theft, and of receiving things ſtolen, Inæ, p. 22. xlvi.

Eſcape of a thief, how puniſhed, Inæ, p. 20. xxxvi.—Canute, p. 138. xxvi.—Hen. I. p. 244. xii. p. 263. lxv.

Of the Reward for taking a thief, Whit. p. 12. x.—Inæ, p. 19. xxviii.—Jud. Civ. Lund. p. 67. iv.

5. *De*

the forfeiture is 8l. of which xxs. for the head, and 8l. to the King. And if he can find the thief within a year and four days, and bring him to justice, let the xxs which he paid be returned to him, and let justice be executed on the thief.

REFERENCES.

Of a thief taken with the manour. Wiht. p. 12. ix. Athelst. p. 56. i.—Can. p. 143. lxi.—Edg. p. 78. vii.—Hen. I. p. 259. L. lix. —Wm. Conq. p. 224. xxxi.

Of theft, where wife and children are privy to it, Inæ. p. 16. vii.

Where Master privy. Æthel. p. 57. L. iii.

Theft committed by a servant, who are to be his pledges, Edw. p. 49. vi.

By a freeman and servant together, which to be punished, Hen. I. p. 259. lix.

Where by several servants concerned in one theft, how to be punished, Hen. I. p. 259. lix.

5. *De Latronis prehenſione.*

Is qui prehenderit Latronem abſque ſecta & abſque clamore, quem dimiſerit ei cui damnum fecerit, & venerit poſt ea, *Juſtitiam poſtulaturus*, rationi conveniens eſt, ut det x ſolidos de Hengwite & finem faciat Juſtitiæ ad primam Curiam, & ſi confirmetur in Curia[a], abſque licentia Juſtitiæ, ſit foriſfactura de xc ſolidis.

Cil ky prendra Larun ſanz ſuite e ſanz cri, [y]que cil en leiſt a qui il aurad le damage fait, & vinge [z]pois apres, ſi eſt raiſun, que il dunge x ſolz de [b]*Hengwite*, e ſin face la juſtice a la primere deviſe e ſil paſſe la deviſe ſans le conge a la juſtice, ſi eſt forfait de xl ſolz.

6. *De Animalium Redemptione.*

Is qui Averium replegiaverit, aut Equos, aut Boves, aut Vaccas, aut Porcos, aut Oves, (quod

Cil ky aveir eſcut, u Chivals, u Buefs, u Vaches, u Porcs, u Berbz, que eſt [c]*Forfengen* Eng-

NOTES.

[y] *Que cil en leiſt*—et in ejus poteſtatem tradiderit, deliver up. *Ducange*.

[z] *Pois apres*—ſoon afterwards, the word *pois e poit*, being frequently taken in this ſenſe.

[a] *Si confirmetur in curia*, *Wilkins*—but the words in this Law are, "ſil paſſe la deviſe." The puniſhment inflicted by this Law on the party robbed, is but juſt; as by his neglecting to raiſe the Hue and Cry, the neighbourhood might have harboured a robber without ſuſpecting him to be ſuch. *Houard*.

[b] *Hengwite*, *Hangwith*, or *Hengwith*, from hanᵹian, ſuſpendere, and piꞇhe, mulcta.

A mulct for hanging a man without due judgment, or for having eſcaped out of his cuſtody.

Alſo the liberty granted to a man to be quit from ſuch mulct. *Ducange*.

[c] *Forfengen*, *Forfang*, *Forfeng*, *and Forefeng*, from ꝼoꞃe ante and ꝼanᵹ captio; uſually ſignifies the taking of proviſions in fairs

5. *Of the apprehending a Thief, without Hue and Cry,*

If any one, without purſuit and hue and cry, apprehends a thief, and delivers him up to the party robbed, and applies ſoon afterwards for a reward, it is but reaſonable there ſhould be given him x s. for *Hengwite*, and that a fine be paid to juſtice at the firſt court; but if that court be paſſed over without leave of juſtice, let the forfeiture be 40 s.

6. *Of the reſcuing Cattle.*

Where cattle are reſcued, whether horſes, oxen, cows, hogs, or ſheep (which in Engliſh is called *Forfengen*) he who claims them ſhall give to the provoſt

NOTES.

and markets, before the king's purveyor; but it cannot be here applied in that ſenſe, but muſt rather be taken, as in the Laws of King Ina, for a certain ſum of money given by the owner of things ſtolen, to him who received them out of the hands of a thief; or to one who had found cattle which had eſtrayed, and brought them to the owner.

Selden, *Ducange*, and *Wilkins*, ſeem to conſider this chapter as treating of Replevyns; but with deference to ſuch great authorities, the Reader will judge whether it does not either relate to things taken out of the hands of a thief, or to cattle eſtrayed and brought back to the owners, or to the reſcuing cattle which had been diſtrained. The words "*eſcut*, *leſcuſſum*, *lecus*," come from excutere, eripere de manibus alterius—Nemo namium excutere præſumat—Qui namium excuſſit, reddat, &c. Let no one preſume to reſcue a diſtreſs; let him who reſcued a diſtreſs, reſtore it, &c. L. Hen. I. 51. p. 255. Qui rem furto ablatam de manibus latronum excuſſit. Who ſnatched from the hands of a thief, the thing ſtolen. *Ducange*; *Excutere*, *Forſang*.

REFERENCES.

L. 5.

Inæ, p. 20. xxxvi. p. 25. lxxii.—Canute p. 138. xxvi.—Hen. I. p. 244. xii. p. 203. lxv.

in

Foꞃꝼenᵹen Anglice dicitur) is qui poſtulat, dabit Præpoſito, in toto, pro Averio replegiato viii denarios, nec tamen habeat plus, qui centum habet pro obolo, non dabit pluſquam viii denarios, & pro Porco iv denarios, & pro Ove denarium unum, & pro alio unoquoque quod vivit iv denarios, nihilominus neque habebit, nec dabit pluſquam viii denarios, & dabit vadios, & inveniet plegios, ſe, ſi aliquis venerit ad probationem intra annum & diem ut Averium petat, ad rectum habiturum in Curia, eum de quo is Averium replegiaverit.

leis apeled, cil qil clamed durrad al groſs al [c] provoſt, aveir pur leſcuſſum viii den. [c] jatant ni ait meis quil ont cent al maille, ne durrad que viii den. e pur un Porc iv den. e pur un Berbz i den. e iſitres que vit pur chaſcun iv den. ne jatant ni aurad ne durrad que oit. d. e durra wage, e truverad plege, que ſi altre veinged a pref dedenz lan e un jour pur laveir demander, [d] quil i ai a droit en la Curt, celui de que il aveir eſcus.

NOTES.

[c] *The Provoſt*, or *Præpoſitus*, was that perſon, who in the Pleas of the Foreſt, at the County Court, and Sheriff's Turn, repreſented the Lord of the Manor, whereof he was the *Præpoſitus*; and he was no other than the Lord's Reeve, or as now called, his Bailiff; one that managed his manor and lands for him. Sometimes he is called *Serviens Villæ*; and if more Lords than one in a Town, then *Servientes Villæ*.

The Lord anſwered for the town where he was reſident; where he was not, his Dapifer or Seneſchal, if he were a Baron; but if neither of them could be preſent, then the Reeve, and four of the beſt men of the town. *Brady's Introduction*, vol. i. *Gloſſary*, *Laws of Hen.* I. c. 7. p. 57.

REFERENCE.

Hen. I. p. 255. li.

in the whole 8d. for the cattle refcued; and if all the cattle together are not worth more than 100 halfpence, he fhall ftill give no more than 8d. for a fingle hog 4d. a fheep 1d.; and for every other living animal 4d. each; neverthelefs there fhall be no more given or taken than 8d.; and he fhall give gages, and find pledges, that if any other perfon fhall come with proof within the year and a day, and demand the cattle, the perfon, from whom he refcued the cattle, fhall be amenable to juftice.

NOTES.

Whatever thing was found, was by the next law to be fhewn to the principal perfons of the vicinage; by the Confeffor's laws, it was to be produced before the parifh prieft, the *præpofitus* of the vill, and four of the moft fubftantial men of it. *L. Edw. Conf.* 28. p. 202.

Houard thinks this was the officer who was appointed to take care of the cattle which had eftrayed.

[c] *Jatant ni ait meis quil ont cent al maille, ne durrad que* viii. *deniers* "But if all the cattle together are not worth more than 100 mailles, he fhall ftill pay only 8d." *Houard.*

[d] *Quil i ait a droit en la Curt, celuy de que il aveir efcus*—or whether this may not be rendered, "that he will be amenable to "the court of him from whom he refcued the cattle."

7. Con-

7. *De rebus forte inventis.*

Similiter de Averio vaganti & alia re inventa. Oſtendatur tribus partibus Vicineti, ut teſtimonium habeat de inventione, ſi aliquis veniat ad probationem ad rem poſtulandam, det vadios & inveniat plegios ſe, ſi alius quiſpiam poſtulaverit Averium intra annum & diem ad rectum exhibiturum in Curia, id, invenerit.

Altreſi de aver endirez e de altre troveure; ſeit muſtred [e] de treis pars del veiſined, que il eit teſtemonie de la troveure, ſi alquens vienge a pref pur clamer la choſe duiſt wage e trove pleges que ſe altre clamud laveir dedenz lan e un jour qui il ait a droit en la curt, celui qui lauerat troved.

8. *De Homicidio & Capitis æſtimatione, ſeu* Wera.

Si quis alium occiderit, & ſit reus confidens, & emendare negaverit, det de ſuo Manbote Domino pro libero homine x ſolidos & pro ſervo xx ſoli-

Si home occit altre, [f] e il ſeit counſaunt, e [g] il denie faire les amendes, durrad de ſa [h] Manbote al Seignor pur le franc home x ſolz, e pur le ſerf xx ſolz; la

NOTES.

[e] *De treis pars del veiſined*—ante Eccleſiam ducat, et coram Sacerdote Eccleſiæ, et prepoſito villæ, et melioribus hominibus totum oſtendat inventum quicquid ſit. *L. Ed. Con.* p. 202. l. 28.

[f] *E il ſeit counſaunt*, and confeſſes it; or perhaps it may be rendered, and is known; the word *ſeit* ſeems to anſwer *ſit*, and is in other places taken in that ſenſe. See *L. Hen.* I. 280. l. 91, 92.

[g] *Il dinie*—In Ducange's Gloſſary, under *Manbote*, is read *il deive*—he ought.

[h] *Manbote*, from Man and Boat. Compenſation, is that part of the price of a man killed, which was paid as a compenſation to the Lord of the deceaſed.

dos.

7. *Concerning Things found by Chance.*

What is ſaid of cattle may be applied to any thing elſe which is found; let it be ſhewed in three parts of the vicinage, that there may be evidence of the finding; and if any one brings proof and lays claim to what is found, let him give gages and find pledges, that if any other perſon ſhall claim the cattle within the year and a day, the perſon who found them ſhall be amenable to juſtice.

REFERENCE.

L. 7.

Edw. Conf. p 202. xxviii.

8. *Concerning Homicide, and the Were or Price ſet on each Man's Head.*

If one man kills another, and confeſſes it; yet refuſes to pay the uſual compenſation: there ſhall be given out of his manbote, to the Lord, for a freeman

REFERENCES.

L. 8.

Homicide, kinds of, Hen. I. p. 267. lxxii.
Committed by thoſe in Orders, Edg. p. 90. ix. xi. Hen. I. p. 268. lxxiii. p. 263. lxvi.
Committed on a miniſter of the Altar. Canute, p. 140. xxxviii.—Hen. I. p. 263. lxvi.
On Infants. Alfr. p. 37. viii. Edg. p. 93. xliii. Hen. I. p. 266.
On a woman big with child. Alf. p. 37. ix. Hen. I. p. 266.
In the King's Courts, Palace, &c. Æthelbrit, p. 3. xiii.—Hen. I. p. 272. lxxx.
On his Lord, Hen. I. p. 268. lxxv.
On a Dane, Æthelr. p. 105. v.
On a Welſhman, Sen. Conf. p. 125. v.
On a Frenchman, Wm. I. p. 228. liii.—Hen. I. p. 269. lxxv. p. 280. xci, xcii.
On an Engliſhman, Hen. I. p. 265. lxix.
On a Freeman, Æthelb. p. 2. vi.—Wiht. p. 12. x.
By a Gueſt, Æthelb. p. 3. xxvi. p. 4. xxvii.
Where many are aſſembled, Alf. p. 40.
Caſual Homicide, Hen. I. p. 267. lxxii. p. 278. xc.
Juſtifiable, Alf. p. 30. xxv.
Aſylum, Æthel. p. 113. i.—Alf. p. 29. xiii.—Edm. p. 74. iv.
Purgation, Hen. I. p. 268. lxxiv.

dos. Wera Thani eſt xx libræ in Merchenelega, & in Weſt-Sexenelega. Et Wera Villani c ſolidi in Merchenelega, atque etiam in Weſt-Sexenelega.

[i] Were del Thein xx li. en Merchenlae e en Weſt-Sexenelae, e la wer del Vilain c ſolz en Merchenelae, e euſement en Weſt-Sexenelae.

REFERENCES.

L. 8.

How compenſated or puniſhed, Æthelbirt, p. 3. 20, 21, 22.—Æthelr. p. 111. iv. p. 105. v.—Inæ, p. 25. lxx.—Edm. p. 72. iii. p. 73. i.—Canute, p. 134. vi.

Murder, what, Hen. I. p. 280. xcii.

How puniſhed, Alfr. p. 29. xiii.—Hen. I. p. 267. lxxi. p. 278. lxxxix.

The Mulct on the Vill or Hundred where the Murderer could not be found, Edw. Conf. p. 199. xv.—Hen. I. p. 280. xci. xcii.

9. *Quibus Capitis æſtimatio ſeu* Wera *ſolvenda.*

Quod ad Weram attinet, primo reddat is qui eſt de nobili ſanguine Viduæ & Orphanis x ſolidos, & quod ſupereſt Orphani & Cognati inter ſe dividant.

De la were, primerement rendrat l'um de halt Sainc a la Vidue a as Orphanins x ſolz, e le ſurplus Orphanins e les Parens departent entr'els.

NOTES.

[i] *Were, Weregild, Weregeld.* Æſtimatio capitis—Head money. The price or ſum (when certain crimes were puniſhed by pecuniary mulcts inſtead of death) ſet on every mans head, according to his condition and quality, who had been guilty of ſuch offences as were redeemable.

10. *Ani-*

10s.; and for a villain 20s. The Were of a Thane in the Mercian and West Saxon Law is 20l. and by the same Laws, the Were of a villain is 100s.

9. *To whom the Price of the Head or Were is to be paid.*

As to the Were; for one who was of noble extraction, let there be paid to the widow and orphans x s.; and let the orphans and the kindred divide the remainder between them.

NOTES.

This custom was derived to us, in common with other northern nations, from our ancestors, the ancient Germans.

In the Laws of King Athelstan, we find the several *Weregilds* for homicides established in progressive order from the death of the ceorl or peasant, up to that of the King himself; the Weregild of a ceorl was 266 thrymsas, that of the King 30,000; each thrymsa being equal to about one shilling of our present money; and in the Laws of Hen. I. we have an acount of what offences were then redeemable by *Weregild*, and what were not so.

When the ransom was settled, the offender was to find Were Pledges for the payment of it at stated times, and then he was restored to the King's peace; but if he could not find any pledges, he was doomed to perpetual bondage.

This *Weregild*, when the crime was homicide, was divided into several parts, and paid under different denominations; one proportion of it was paid to the kindred, another to the King, and another to the Lord.

If the party denied the fact, then he was to purge himself by the oaths of several persons, according to his degree and quality.

10. *What*

10. *Animalium aliquot valor, in Capitis æſtimatione cenſenda.*

In Wera reddere poterit quis Equum non caſtratum pro xx ſolidis, & Taurum pro x ſolidis, & Jumentum pro v ſolidis.

En la were purra il rendra Chival qui ad la cuille pur xx ſolz, e tor pur x ſolz, e afer pur v ſolz.

11. *De percuſſore.*

Si quis alium percuſſerit, & negaverit ultra emendare, primo illi reddat caput ſuum *(id eſt, capitis pretium, vulgo Wergildum)* & illi percuſſor juret ſuper Sancta quod aliter non potuerit facere, nec ex malitia quacunque ille fuerit in terram dejectus, id quod *(cauſa)* doloris eſt.

Si home fait plaie a altre, e il denie otrei fair les amendes, primerement li rende ſun le chefe, e li plaiez jurraz ſur ſentez, qui pur mes nel pot fair ne pur haur ſi chjer nel ſiſt deſarbore cho eſt de la dulor.

12. *De vulnere indito.*

Si plaga alicui eveniat viſui aperto, capite toto viſo iv denarios *det per-*

Si la plaie lui vient a vis en deſcuuert al polz tote veie iv den. & de tanz

NOTES.

[k] *Afer*, Dr. Wilkins reads *Afer*, which he renders *Jumentum*; Ducange and Houard tranſlate it *Verrem*; but it is ſubmitted to the Reader, whether *Iter*, as in Lambard, is not the true reading, and whether *Iter* may not, from *Aries*, ſignify a ram.

cuſſor

10. *What Beasts may be taken instead of the Weres.*

Instead of the were of xx s. A stone horse may be rendered; a bull for that of x s.; and a ram for that of v s.

REFERENCES.

L. 10.

Were, xx s. Hen. I. p. 270. latter end of the Law.
Of assaulting another, Alfr. p. 38. xiii. xv.

11. *Of one striking another.*

If one wounds another and refuses to make him amends, in the first place let him pay his Were, and also swear upon the Gospels to the person wounded, that he could not avoid doing it, and that it was not through hatred.

12. *Of the wound given.*

If any one is wounded, so as that the scull is laid open, there shall be paid 4d.; and also the like sum

NOTES.

[1] *E li plaiez jurraz,* &c. Ducange translates the passage thus, "Et plagatus jurabit super sancta, quod pro minori (emenda) non "potest tacere, nec pro odio cariorem (vel majorem) fecerit de sar-"bota, id est de dolore." Houard has followed Ducange, but I have adopted the translation of Wilkins; though this must be confessed to be a very obscure Law.

for

cuſſor, & de omni oſſe, quod quis traxerit ex plaga, oſſe toto viſo iv denarios, poſtea compoſitio ei fiat, ſecudum honores quos ei *(os vel caput)* fecerint; hoc cum fecerit, ſi cor ſuum ei benevolum monſtraverit, & conſilium ſuum ei donaverit, accipiat ab illo quod ei obtulerit.

os cum hom trarad de la plaie al os tote veie iv den. pois acordement ſi li metrad avant honours qui ſi illiont fait, co quil ad fait a lui, ſe ſon queur li purportaſt, e ſon conſeil li donaſt, prendreit de lui ce quil offre a lui.

13. *Membrorum præciſorum æſtimatio.*

Si acciderit ut quis pugnum cujuſpiam abſciderit aut pedem, reddat ei medietatem Weræ, ſecundum id quod *factum* eſt. Sed pro pollice reddat medietatem manus. Pro digito qui pollici proximus xv ſolidos, de ſolido Anglicano, hoc eſt, quatuor denarios. Pro digito longo xvi ſolidos. Pro altero qui portat annulum xvii ſolidos. Pro digito minimo v ſolidos. Si unguem quis præciderit, pro quolibet v ſolidos de ſolido Anglicano, et pro ungue digiti minimi iv denarios.

Si co avent qui alquen colpe le poin a altre, u le pied, ſi li rendra demi were, ſu luc ceo q'il eſt. Mez del pochier rendrad la meite de la mein, del dei apres le polcier xv ſolz de ſolt Engleis, co eſt quer deners; de lunc dei xvi folz, del altre qui ported l'anel xvii ſolz, del petit dei v ſolz, del ungle ſi il colpe de caſcun v ſolz de ſolt Engleis; al ungle de petit dei iv den.

14. *De*

for every bone which appears to be extracted from the wound; but if the wound be afterwards compounded for by his Lords, at his own inſtance, and with his own conſent, then let him accept what is offered.

13. *The Rates to be paid for the loſs of Limbs, &c.*

If any perſon happens to cut off the fiſt or foot of another, let him render to him the half of a Were according to the condition of the perſon; for a thumb he ſhall render the half of the price for a hand; for the forefinger 15s. Engliſh, that is 4d. to every ſhilling; for the middle finger 16s.; for the ring finger 17s.; for the little finger 5s. If a nail is cut off, for every nail 5s. of the Engliſh ſhilling; and for the nail of the little finger, 4d.

REFERENCES.

L. 12, 13.

Wounds, Compenſation for, Æthelbirt, p. 4. Law 33d. and the 38 following Laws.—Alfr. p. 44. xl.—Hen. I. p. 281. xciii.

14. *Of*

14. *De adulterio.*

Qui desponsatam alterius vitiaverit, forisfaciat Weram suam Domino suo.

Ki altrei espouse purgist, si forfait la were vers sun Seignor.

15. *De Judice corrupto.*

Etiam qui falsum tulerit Judicium, Weram suam perdat, nisi super sacrosancta *(Evangelia)* probare poterit, se melius judicare nescivisse.

Altresi qui faus jugement fait, pert sa were, si il ne pot prover sor Saintz qui melz ne pot juger.

16. *De purgatione illius qui Furti reus est.*

Si quis alterum appellet de Latrocinio & is sit liber homo, & habeat exinde verum testimonium de legalitate, purget se per plenum Sacramentum, & alter qui infamis ante fuerat per Sacramentum nominatum videlicet xiv homines legales; attamen si is habere eos poterit purget se

Si home apeled altre de Larcin, & il sot francz home, & il ait ondca verre testemonie [m] de lealte, sen escoudirad per plein serment, & altre qui blasmed ait ested per serment nomed, co est a savoir, quacorte homes leals, per non si il aver les pot, si sen escoudirad sei dudzime

NOTES.

[m] *De lealte*, legality, that is, of his being *rectus in curia*, not outlawed, excommunicated, &c. Hence legality is taken for the condition of such a man. Leg. Edw. Conf. p. 201. xviii. the opposite is *Deleaute*, perfidy, disloyalty, infamy.

Legality sometimes signifies judiciary dignity, power of judging, and jurisdiction or franchise. *Decem Scriptores.*

The *simplex Lada* here corresponds with *Sacramentum planum*, and signifies a purgation or excuse by the simple oath of the party accused. *Ducange*, *Lada.*

duodecima

14. *Of Adultery.*

If one violates the wife of another, let him forfeit his Were to his Lord.

REFERENCES.

L. 14.

Adultery, puniſhment of it, Æthelbirht, p. 4. xxxii. p. 7. lxxxiv.—Wiht. p. 10. v.—Alfred, p. 37. x.—Edmund, p. 73. iv.—Edgar, p. 90. xvii. p. 91. xviii, xix, xx. xxiv. p. 92. xxxiii, xxxiv, xxxv. —Canut. p. 134. vi. p. 141. xlvii. p. 142. l. li.—Wm. Conq. p. 225. xxxvii.

15. *Of a corrupt Judge.*

Alſo he who pronounces a falſe Judgment, ſhall loſe his Were; unleſs he can prove, by ſwearing on the Goſpels, that his ſentence was according to the beſt of his Judgment.

REFERENCES.

L. 15.

Edg. p. 77. iii.—Wm. Conq. p. 226. xli.

16. *How one is to purge himſelf who is guilty of Larceny.*

If one appeals another of Larceny, and he is a Freeman, and has all along had good proof of his Legality, let him clear himſelf *per plein ſerment*; and if the accuſed has heretofore been rendered infamous, *per ſerment nomed*, that is to ſay, by 14 lawful men named; let him, if he can, clear himſelf by 12 com-

REFERENCES.

L. 16.

Plenum Sacramentum. Hen. I. p. 263. lxvi.
Nominatum Sacramentum, Edw. p. 48. i.—Athelſtan, p. 58. ix. —Hen. I. p. 263. lxvi. p. 264. lxvii.

purgators;

duodecima manu, & si habere non possit, se defendat per judicium, & Appellator jurabit (præter eum jurent vii homines nominati) quod propter malitiam non fecerit nec propter aliam causam, quam quia jus suum persequeretur.

main, & si aveir nes pot, si se defende per ivis, e li apeleur jurra sur lui jur set homes nomes, qui pur haur nel fist, ne pur altre chose, si pur son dreit non purchacer.

17. *De eo qui Templum aut Domum fregerit.*

Et si quis appellatus fuerit de fractione Monasterii aut Cubiculi, neque fuerit infamis a retro, se purget per xlii legales homines nominatos duodecima manu, & si alias infamia notatus fuerit, purget se per triplum, videlicet per xlviii homines legales nominatos trigesima sextu manu, & si illos habere nequierit eat ad judicium per triplum si audeat ad triplex plenum Sacramentum, & si is a retro latrocinium emendavit, eat ad aquam

E si alcons est apelez de muster fruisser, u de chambre, e il ne ested blamed enarer, sen escoudit per xlii leals homes nomez sei dudzime main, e sil eit altre siee ested blamed, sen escoudied a treis dubles, ceo a savoir per xlviii homes leals nomes sei trentesiste mein, e sil aveir nes pot, aut a la ivise a treis dubles, si coil doust a treis du plein serment, e sil ad enarer Larcin amended, alt al ewe. Li Arcevesque averad de forfaiture xl solz

REFERENCES.

L. 17.

Church, breaking into; *punishment*, Athelst. p. 30. xxv.—Edmund, p. 74. vi.—Canut. p. 142. lix.

isfactura

purgators; and if he cannot, then let him defend himſelf by ordeal. Let the Appellant alſo himſelf, with ſeven others named, ſwear that what he did was not through hatred, or any other motive, than that of proſecuting his Right.

17. *Concerning him who breaks into a Church or Houſe.*

If any one, who has not in Times paſt been rendered infamous, ſhall be appealed of breaking into a [n]Church, or [o]Monaſtery, or inner part of a Houſe; let him clear himſelf by [p]xlii lawful Men named, he himſelf making the twelfth; and if he has at any other Time been adjudged infamous, let him clear himſelf by [q]three times that Number, that is to ſay, by [r]xlviii lawful Men named, he [s]himſelf making the 36th; and if he cannot procure that Number, let him go to the triple ordeal, as he muſt have three times taken the *plein Serment*. And if he has heretofore made Satisfaction for a Larceny, he muſt undergo the water [t]ordeal. In

NOTES.

[n] *Muſtre*—The Party here being accuſed of a Crime of a deeper dye than that in the former Law, he muſt in the firſt inſtance clear himſelf by twelve Compurgators, though his Character till that time ſtood unimpeached.

[o] *De Muſter fruiſſer, u de chambre*—for breaking of a Monaſtery, or of any private Room in it. Johnſon's Collection of Canons, &c. Vol. I. 1065.

[p] xlii *leals homes*—this ſhould be xii, as appears by the *duodecima manu*, and Ducange has rendered it ſo.

[q] *A treis dubles*—lege *dudzes*; thrice 12. Ducange Juiſium, p. 140.

[r] *xlviii*—This I apprehend ſhould be xxxvi, *i. e.* 3 times 12; the Purgation being *trigeſima ſexta manu*, that is 35 Compurgators and the Party accuſed.

[s] *Sei—ſe* himſelf; the Party being included in the 36th.

[t] *Aut a la Juiſe a treis duble*—It is apprehended, this was to be *Fire Ordeal*, as being more reputable than that of *Water*, and the Party accuſed had been only defamed before, but not convicted. The *triple Fire Ordeal* was by the ſuſpected Perſon carrying in his Hand a Bar of red hot Iron of three Pounds Weight; the *ſimple Fire Ordeal*, of one Pound only. Laws Hen. I. p. 64, 67.

(i. e. judicium aquæ). Archiepiscopus habebit de forisfactura xl solidos in Merchenelega, & Episcopi xx solidos, & Comes xx solidos, & Baro x solidos, & Villanus xl denarios.

en Mercheneale, e lui Evesques xx solz, e lui Quinz xx solz, e le Baron x solz, e li Vilain xl den.

REFERENCES.

L. 17.

Church, breaking into; punishment, Athelst. p. 57. v.
House, Alfred, p. 30. xxv.—Edmund, p. 74. vi.—Canute, p. 142. lix.

18. *De Denariis S.* [n] *Petri, seu Vectigali Romano.*

Liber homo qui habuerit averia campestria xxx denarii æstimanda, dabit denarium S. Petri. Pro iv denariis quos donaverit Dominus, quieti erunt Bordarii ejus & ejus Scabini & ejus Servientes. Burgensis qui de propriis Catallis habet id quod di-

Franc home qui ad [m] aver champester trente deners vailaunt, deit doner le [n] dener Seint Pere. Le Seignur pur iv den. que il dourrard si erent quietes ses [o] Bordiers e ses [p] Bonerz & ses Serjanz. Li Burgeis qvi ad en soud propre chatel demi marc

NOTES.

[m] *Aver champester*—Omnis qui habuerit xxx denaritus vivæ pecuniæ, in domo sua de suo proprio, dabit Denarium Sancti Petri. Leg. Edwardi, p. 198. x.

[n] *Le dener Seint Pere*,—*Peter Pence, Romesoc, Romescot, Rome pennying*. A yearly Pension or Alms of 1d, out of every family; first granted by Ina King of the West Saxons for support of an English College founded by him at Rome; it was called *Peter Pence*, because collected yearly on the feast of St. Peter ad Vincula, i. e. on the 1st of August. This

REFERENCES.

L. 18 and 20.

Peter-Pence—Romscot.
Forfeiture for non-payment. Fœd. Edw. & Guth. p. 52. vi.—Northum. Presbyt. Leges, p. 101. lviii. lix.—Lib. Constit. temp. Æthel. p. 114. iii.—Canute, p. 130. ix. Edw. Conf. p. 198. x.
In what proportion to be paid. Edw. Conf. p. 198. x.
By whom to be collected, North. Presb. Leg. p. 101. lvii.

midia

this Case the Archbishop, by the Mercian Law, shall have for his Share of the Forfeiture xls. the Bishop xxs. the Earl xxs. the Baron xs. and the Villan xld.

18. *Of Peter Pence.*

A Freeman who has Beasts for Agriculture, to the value of 30 d. ought to give 1 d. to St. Peter. The Lord, for 4 d. which he shall give, shall have his Bordmen, the Overlookers of his Cattle and his Servants quit. A Burgess who has Chattels of his own

NOTES.

This was afterwards by succeeding Kings extended throughout all England, and settled at £. 201 6s. a year; and in process of time, the Popes, pretending it was a tribute paid to St. Peter and his successors, collected it to their own use, till it was prohibited by 25 Hen. VIII. and entirely abolished by 1 Eliz.

[o] *Bordiers.* Tenants who held a Bord or Cottage under the service of Bordage from Boꞃꝺ, domus; they are distinguished from servants and villains, and were liable to the most abject services. Ducange.

[p] *Bovers.* Whelock's Edit. *Boners.* Those who held Bonnaria, or Lands set out by certain Bounds. Id.

Tenants who lived in cottages on the Lord's waste. Johnson's Canons.

midia Marca æſtimandum eſt, dare debet denarium S. Petri. Qui in Danelega eſt liber homo, & habet averia campeſtria quæ dimidia marca in argento æſtimantur, debet dare denarium S. Petri. Et per denarium quem donaverit Dominus, erunt quieti ii qui reſident in ſuo Dominio.

vailant, deit doner le dener Seint Pere. Qui en Daneiae francz home eſt e il averad demi marc en argent vailant de aveir champeſtre, ſi devrad doner le dener Seint Pere. E per le dener qui li Seignur durrat ſi erent quietes ceals, qui meinent en ſon demainer.

19. *De muliere vi compreſſa & pudicitia luctamine tentata.*

Qui fœminam vi compreſſerit, forisfacit membra ſua. Qui proſtraverit fœminam ad terram & ei vim inferat, mulcta ejus Domino eſt x ſolidi. Si vero eam compreſſerit, forisfacit membra.

Ki purgiſt femme per forze forfait ad les membres, ki abate femme a terre, pur faire lui force, la multe al Seignur x ſolz, ſil la purgiſte, forfait eſt de [q] membres.

NOTES.

[q] *Forfait eſt de Membres.* Under our Saxon Kings, the puniſhment of Rape was only pecuniary, and the only expreſs Laws on this head are thoſe of Æthelb. p. 7. lxxxi.—Alfr. p. 40. xxv. and Canute p. 142. xlix.

20. *De*

to the value of half a Mark, ought to give 1 d. to St. Peter. By the Danish Law, a Freeman who has Beasts for Agriculture, to the value of half a Mark of Silver, ought to give 1 d. to St. Peter. And for the 1 d. which the Lord shall give, those who dwell in his Domain, shall be quit.

19. *Concerning Rape, and an Attempt on a Woman's Chastity.*

Whoever shall forcibly defile a Woman, shall be punished by loss of his Members; and whoever throws a Woman on the Ground, with an Intent to violate her, the Mulct to the Lord is 10 s. But if he defiled her, he forfeits his Members.

REFERENCES.

L. 19.

Of Rape the Punishment. Æthelbirht, p. 7. lxxxi, lxxxii, lxxxiii.—Alfred, p. 40. xxv.—Canute, p. 142. xlix.

Of Fornication, punishment. Alfr. p. 36. viii.

With a Nun. Edm. p. 73. iv.—Edgar, p. 92. xxxii.—Northum. Presbyt. Leg. p. 102. lxiii.—Concil. Ænham. p. 123. iv.

With others. Æthelbirht, p. 2. x. p. 3. xi, xii. xiv. xvi.—Alfred, p. 31. xxix. p. 40. xxv.—Edgar, p. 91. xxiv, xxv.—Concil. Ænham. p. 123. iv.

Fornication to be avoided. Lib. Constitut. temp. Ethelr. p. 108. iv. Concil. Ænham, p. 120. viii.—Canute, p. 132. xxiv.

Chastity solicitation of, punishment, Alfred, p. 37. xi. p. 38. xviii.—Edgar, p. 92. xxxiii, xxxiv, xxxv, xxxvi.

Adultery, punishment, See L. 14.

20. *De iis qui vectigal Romanum seu D. Petri non pendunt.*

Qui retinet denarium S. Petri, denarium reddat per Justitiam S. Ecclesiæ & xxx denarios forisfacturæ. Et si de ea re est implacitatus per Justitiam Regis, forisfaciat Episcopo xxx denarios, & Regi xl solidos.

Ki retient le dener Seint Pere, le dener rendra par la justice de Seint Eglise e xxx den. forfait. e si il en est plaide de la justice le Rei, le forfait al Evesque xxx den. den. e al Rei xl solz.

21. *De Oculo effosso.*

Si quis alteri oculum effoderit infortunio quocunque, emendet lxx solidis solidorum Anglicanorum. Et si visus ei restituatur, dimidium duntaxat reddatur.

Si al alquns criene[1] l'oil al altre per aventure quel que seit, si amendrad lxx solz del solz Engleis, e si la purvele i est remis, si ne rendra lui que la meite.

NOTES.

[1] *Criene l'oil.* The Law of Alfred is very similar to this—"Si "oculus alicui excutiatur, dentur ei sexaginta sex solidi et sex de-"narii, et tertia pars denarii pro compensatione. Si oculus in ca-"pite sit, et ille tamen videre nequeat, retineatur tertia pars com-"pensationis illius."

20. *Concerning the Refusal to pay Peter Pence.*

He who witholds Peter Pence, ſhall be compelled by Holy Church to pay it; and ſhall forfeit 30 d. And if he ſhall be impleaded for it in the King's Court, he ſhall forfeit to the Biſhop 30 d. and to the King 40 s.

21. *The Puniſhent where an Eye is put out.*

If any one, by what Accident it will, ſhall put out the Eye of another, let the Amends be 70 s. Engliſh. And if the Ball of the Eye remains, only half that ſum ſhall be payed.

REFERENCES.

L. 20. See 18.

L. 21.

Æthelbirht, p. 5. xliv. p. 7. lxxxvi.—Alfred, p. 30. xix, xx. p. 45.—Hen. I. p. 281. cxiii.

L. 22, 23, 24. 29. 40.

Heriot—what to be paid, Canute, p. 144. lxix.—Hen. I. p. 244. xiv. *Where the Tenant died in Battle by the Side of his Lord*, Canute, p. 145. lxxv.—Edw. Conf. p. 205.

22. *De Relevio ſeu εισδεικτικῳ Comitis.*

De Relevio Comitis, quod ad Regem pertinet viii Equi ephippiati & frænis ornati, iv Loricæ, & iv Galeæ, & iv Scuta, & iv Haſtæ, & iv Enſes, alii cæteri iv Neredi & Palfredi cum frænis & capiſtris.

De releif al Cunte, que al Rei afiert viii chivalz ſelez, e enfrenez, les iv Halbers, e iv Hammes, e iv Eſcuz, e iv Launces, e iv Eſpes, [s] les altres iv Chaceurs e [t] Palfreis a frenis e a cheveſtres.

23. *De Relevio Baronis.*

De Relevio Baronis iv Equi cum ſellis & frænis ornati, & Loricæ ii, & ii Galeæ & Scuta ii & ii Haſtæ, & ii Enſes ; & alii cæteri ii unus Veredus & unus Palfredus cum fræno & capiſtro.

De releif a Barun iv Chivalz enſeles e enfrenes, e ii Halbers, e ii hammes, e ii Eſcus, e ii Launces, e ii Eſpes, e les altres ii un Chaceur, e un Palefrei a frenis e a cheveſtres.

24. *De Vavaſoris Relevio.*

De Relevio Vavaſoris ad legitimum ſuum Dominum. Quietus eſſe

De releif a Vavaſour a ſon lige Signeur, deite eſtres quite per le Chival ſon

N O T E S.

[s] *Les altres IV.* This part of the Law ſeems to have been miſunderſtood ; the words *les altres IV.* plainly refer to ſome former part of the Law ; therefore we apprehend that after the words *viii. chivals*, there followed in the original text, *les iv.* that is four of them were to be horſes for war with all their furniture ; and the other four were to be hunters, and palfreys.

The 69th Law of King Canute will, we hope, juſtify this remark.

debet

22. *Of the Relief of an Earl.*

The Relief which an Earl is to pay to the King, is 8 Horſes ſaddled and bridled, 4 Coats of Mail, 4 Helmets, 4 Shields, 4 Spears, and 4 Swords; the other 4 Horſes for hunting and palfreys, with Bridles and Head Stalls.

23. *Of the Relief of a Baron.*

The Relief of a Baron is 4 Horſes ſaddled and bridled, 2 Halberts, 2 Helmets, 2 Shields, 2 Lances, and 2 Swords; of the other 2, one ſhall be for hunting and one a palfrey, with Bridle and Head Stall.

24. *Of the Relief of a Vavaſor.*

Of the Relief of a Vavaſor to his lawful Lord; he ought to be quit, on yielding up the Horſe of his

NOTES.

The Heriot of an Earl by that Law was 8 equi, 4 ſellati, 4 inſellati, &c.

Of the King's Thane, 4 equi, 2 ſellati, 2 non ſellati, &c.

See alſo the Laws of Hen. I. ch. XIV.

The names of *Count*, *Baron*, *Vavaſour*, and *Villain*, were Norman, and were ſubſtituted in the room of the Saxon titles of Earl, Thane, Theoden (or leſſer Thane) and Churl, when the Laws of Edw. the Confeſſor were tranſlated into the Norman tongue.

So likewiſe the Normans conceiving the Saxon Heriot to be the ſame that their Norman Relief was, they tranſlated the word Heriot by the Releviamentum or Relevium, and raiſing the form of their Feudal Law in England, drew the Saxon Cuſtoms to cohere therewith as much as might be; but as Sir Henry Spelman obſerves, there is great difference between Heriots and Reliefs. Spel. Rem. 32. 2 Black. 65. 8 . Suli. Lect. 281.

[t] *Palfreis.* The Palfrey was a horſe of parade; ladies in Romances are always mounted on a Palfrey, as were Princes often, when they made a public entry.

Father,

debet per Equum patris sui talem qualem habuerit tempore mortis suæ, & per Loricam suam, & per galeam suam & per scutum suum, & per hastam suam, & per ensem suum, & si adeo fuerit inermis ut nec equum habuerit nec arma, per centum solidos.

peipe tel quil aveit a jour de sa mort, e per son Halbert, e per sa Launce, e per Sespe, sil fust des apeille, quil ne ont ne Chival ne les armes per ç solz.

25. *De re intestata, aut de rebus ereptis penes alium deprehensis.*

De averio quod *quis* in manibus habet, qui velit postulare furto sublatum, & ille vult dare vadios & invenire plegios ad prosequendum appellum suum, tunc incumbit illi qui *rem* habuerit in manibus, nominare warrantum suum,

De entremeins aveir kil voldrad clamer emblet, e il volge doner wage trouver plege a persuir son appel, dunt li scuverad a celui quil auverad entre meins nomer son guarant sul lad, e si il nel ad dunt nomerad son [u] *Heuvelborh*

NOTES.

L. 25.

[u] *Heuvel borh.* Fidejussor, from healꝼ, dimidius, and boꞃᵹh, debitor, vel etiam fidejussor; unless this should be the same as Headborough. Ducange.

[w] *Sci siste main.* See Leg. Athel. p. 58. l. 9. ei ex vicinis nominantor viri quinque.

[x] *Non posuerat suum Warrantum.* The original is, *ne set*, non scit,—*does not know*.

REFERENCES.

L. 25.

Inæ, p. 22. xlvii. p. 26. lxxv.—Æthelst. p. 58. ix.—Æthelred, p. 103. iv. p. 105. ix. p. 106. x.—Canute, p. 137. xxi. xxii.—Edw. Conf. p. 202. xxv.—Hen. I. p. 248. xxxi. p. 254. xlix.

si

Father, ſuch as he had at his death, and his Halbert, his Helmet, his Shield, his Lance, and his Sword; but if he died ſo unfurniſhed with theſe Things as to have neither Horſe or Arms, then he muſt pay 100s.

25. *Of Goods ſtolen, and challenged by the Ownr.*

With reſpect to Goods found in the Hands of another; if any one will challenge them as ſtolen, and is ready to give Gages, and find Pledges to proſecute his Appeal, then the Poſſeſſor of the Goods muſt name his Voucher, if he has one, and if not, his *Heuvelborth* and his Witneſſes, and produce them,

NOTES.

[y] *Od.* I rather think this ſhould be tranſlated, *with*, inſtead of *Octo.* 8. as in Wilkins. See the ſame word in L. 46.

[z] *Ses teſtimonies.* By the Law of Athelſt. if the goods were under the value of 20 d. then the party, under whoſe cuſtody the things were found, and only one of his witneſſes; and the claimant and two of his were to be ſworn; if above 20d. then the whole number that were choſen were to be ſworn. Leg. Athelſt. p. 58. l. ix.

[a] *Plein ſerment.* See note on L. xvi.

[b] *Son Seignor—i. e.* to his landlord or owner of the farm. Ethelr. 103. iv. Mulctum (cui jure debetur) perſolvito. Canute, p. 137. l. xxii.

[c] *De ſa Nurture.* Ex propria re pecuaria natam pecudem. Leg. Athelſt. p. 58. l. ix.

if

ſi eum habuerit, & ſi non habuerit eum, nominabit ſuum vadem primarium, & teſtes ſuos, & habebit eos ad diem, & ad terminum ſi eos habeat aut eos habere poterit, & intertiator tradet in vadium ſe ſexta manu, & alter mittatur in manum ſui warranti aut ſui vadis primarii, & habeat ille teſtes quod tradet mercatui Regis, & quod ille non [x] poſuerat ſuum warrantum in plegio vivo nec mortuo id jurent octo teſtium ſuorum per plenum Sacramentum; *aſt* perdat catallum ſuum, ſi is teſtimonium perhibeat quod vadem primarium accuſaverit, & ſi non poterit habere warrantum nec teſtem, perdat & pro debito perdat Weram ſuam Domino ſuo. Hoc obtinet in *Merchenelega*, & in *Danelega*, & in *Weſt-Sexenelega*. Non vocabit quis Dominum ſuum ad Warrantum de hoc quod poſitum eſt in vadio, & in *Danelega* confirmet in

e ſes teſtemonies e ait les a jur e à term, ſil les ad, u ſil lès pot aver, e li enterceur liveriad en guage ſei ſiſte [w] main, e li altre le mettrad en la main ſon warrant va ſon *Heuvelborth*, & il ait teſtimonies que il lacharad al marchied du Rei, e quil ne ſeſ ſon warrant en le plege vif ne mort, co jurad [y] od [z] ſes teſtimonies per [a] plein ſerment; ſi perdra ſon Chatel ſi il teſtimonient qui il *Heuvilborh* empuſed, e ſil ne pot aveir guarant ne teſtimonie ſi perdrad, & pur ſoldrad pert ſa werre vers ſon Seignur, coeſt en Merchenelae e en Danelae e en Weſt Sexenelæ. Ne vocherad une [b] ſon Seignor warrant iceo qui ſeit mis en guage, e on Danelae mettred en vele diſſi la, qui il ſeit derained e ſil pot prover qui ceo ſoit de ſa [c] nurture per treis partz ſon [d] vigued ſe il averad derained. kar puis que ſerment li eſt jugied

N O T E S.

[d] *Per treis partz ſon vigued.* Three parts of his neighbourhood: compare this with l. vii.

faciem

if he has them, or can have them, at the Day and Place affigned. And the Party challenging the Cattle fhall offer himfelf and five others as Gages; and as for the other, let his Voucher or his *Heuvelborth* be anfwerable for him; and let him bring Witneffes that he bought them at the King's Market, and that he does not know his Voucher or Pledge dead or alive. This he fhall fwear with his Witneffes *per plein ferment*; but let him lofe his Chattels if his Witneffes declare that it is in his Power to produce his Voucher. And if he can neither produce Voucher or Witnefs, the Matter fhall be determined againft him, and let him, as he deferves, forfeit his Were to his Lord. This is the Law of the Mercians, Danes, and Weft-Saxons. One need not vouch his Lord to warrant that which is put in Pledge, and by the Danifh Law he may put it in, till the Matter is determined; and if he can prove by three parts of his Neighbourhood, that the Cattle were of his own bringing up, Judg-

ment

faciem dictum ibi, quod is sit disrationatus, & si potest probare quod hoc sit de sua nutritione, per tres partes sui victus illi fuerit disrationatum. Nam post quam Lex sacramentalis sibi est adjudicata, inde non potest postea quæstio moveri per judicium Angliæ.

ne len pot pas puis lever per le jugement de Engleterre.

26. *De centuriæ mulcta, ubi reus homicidii judicio non sistitur.*

De Murdo Francigenæ occisi, & homines hundredi non prehendunt & ducunt ad Justitiam infra viii dies ut ostendat ob quam causam fecerit, reddant murdri nomine xlvii Marcas.

De murdre freceis [e] occist, e les homes del hundred nel prengent e amenent a la justice de denz les [f] oit jours per mustrer [g] pur qui il la fait, sin rendrunt le murdre [h] xlvii Marc.

NOTES.

L. 26.

[e] *Freceis occist.* Ducange, and Houard drop the word *freceis.* Selden places it in *Italic*, as difficult to be made out; but comparing this Law with the 53d of Wm. I. and 91st of Hen. I. and others, it seems to relate to the murder of a Frenchman or Norman, as Wilkins has rendered it; and to have been added when these Laws were translated—if not, it signifies a recent murder.

The title of the 53d Law is De Normanni seu Francigenæ cæde. L. Wm. I. p. 228. l. liii.

Si quis Francigena, vel Normannus occidatur. L. Hen. I. p. 280. l. xci.

[f] *Oit jours.*—This is the time assigned by the Law of Edw. Conf. p. 199. l. xv.—By the Laws of Wm. I. in Latin 5 days.—Wm. I. p. 228. l. liii—by the Laws of Hen. I. 7 days. Hen. I. p. 280. l. xci, xcii.

[g] *Pur qui.* Ob quam causam; Selden and Wilkins; but Ducange à quo, which last I have followed.

[h] *xlvii Marc*—By all the above Laws 46 marks.

ment ſhall be in his Favour; for after he has been put to his Oath, the Queſtion, by the Law of England cannot be agitated again.

26. *Of the Mulct on the Hundred, where the Murderer is not amenable to Juſtice.*

Where a Frenchman is killed, and the Men of the Hundred do not apprehend the Murderer and bring him to Juſtice within eight Days ſo as that it may appear who committed the Murder, they ſhall pay, in the Name of Murder, 47 Marks.

REFERENCES.

L. 26.

Edw. Conf. p. 199. xv. p. 200. xvi.—Wm. Conq. p. 228. liii.—Hen. I. p. 280. xci. xcii.

27. *De clientis actione versus Dominum.*

Si quis vult disrationare conventionem de terra sua versus Dominum suum per pares suos eadem tenura quos vocavit in testimonium, debet illud disrationare. Nam per extraneos non potest disrationare.

Si home volt derainer covenant de terre vers [i] son Seignor per ses pers [k] de la tenure meimes que il apelerad a testimoines lescuverad derainer. Kar per estranges nel purra pas dereiner.

28. *De Placito.*

Qui placitat in Curia, cujuscunque Curia sit, excepto ubi persona Regis est, & quis eum sistat super eo quod dixerit, rem quam nolit confiteri, si non potest disrationare per ii intelligentes homines qui interfuerunt placito & videntes, quod non dixerit, recuperet juxta verbum suum.

Home qui plaide en Curt, a qui Curt qui co seit fors la ou le cors le Rei est, e home li mettid sur quil ait dit chose qui il ne voille coinistre, se il ne pot derainer per ii entendable home del pleidant & veant qui il nel aurad dit [l] recovered a sa parola.

29. *De Servorum Relevio.*

De Relevio Villani. Melius animal quod ha-

De relief a [m] Vilain. Le meillur aveir quil avera u

NOTES.

L. 27.

[i] *Vers son Seignor*—By Lord, here, is meant only the Proprietor of an estate, not a Lord of a fee. Houard preuves, Iust. p. 120.

[k] *Per ses Pers de la tenure meimes*—*i. e.* by freeholders within the same Hundred.

[l] *Recovered a sa parola*—Recurretur ad ejus Sacramentum. Ducange; Houard—In misericordia domini Regis remanet. Glanvill, l. x. c. 12.

buerit

27. *Of the Clientary Action of Covenant against the Lord.*

If a Tenant would deraign an Action of Covenant concerning Land againſt his Lord, he muſt deraign it by his Peers of the ſame Tenure as he produced for Witneſſes; for it cannot be deraigned by Strangers.

28. *Concerning Pleaders.*

If a Perſon pleading in a Court, (whoſeſoever the Court is, except the King is preſent) be charged with having ſaid ſomething which he will not own; if he cannot in ſuch Caſe prove by two intelligent Men, who were preſent at the Plea and ſaw him, that he did not ſpeak the Words he is charged with, he muſt have Recourſe to his Oath.

29. *Of the Relief of a Villain.*

As to the Relief of a Villain, he ſhall give to his Lord the beſt Beaſt he has (whether Horſe, Ox or

NOTES.

L. 29.

a *Vilain.* The Villain mentioned in this Law is not to be underſtood a Bondman, but a *Ceorl, Churl, or Huſbandman.* He was of free condition, and was valued as a member of the Commonwealth in the Saxon Laws; whereas a bondman was not valued at all, but was part of his maſter's ſubſtance, therefore could have nothing whereout to pay a Heriot or Relief. Spel. Rem. 14, 15. See note, Law 22. Judicia Civitatis Lundoniæ, p. 71.

REFERENCES.

L. 27, 28.

Hen. I. p. 253. xlviii.

L. 29. See L. 22.

Edw. Conf. p. 199. xii.

Mulct for not repairing them, Canute, p. 143. lxii.

Cow)

buerit id (five Equus fit, five Bos, five Vacca) donabit Domino fuo pro Relevio, & poftea fint omnes Villani in franco plegio.

Chival, u Buf, u Vache, donrad a fon Seignor de releif & puis fi ferait touz les Vilains en franc plege.

30. *De viis publicis.*

De tribus viis, videlicet *Wetlingftreet*, & *Ermingftreet* & [o] *Foffe*. Qui in aliqua harum viarum hominem itinerantem five occiderit five infilierit, is pacem Regis violat.

De iii chemins co eft a faveir *Wetlingftreet* & *Ermingftreet* & *Fos*. Ki en alcun de ces chemins oceit home qui feit errant per le pais u afalt, fi enfreit la pais [p] le Roi.

31. *De Latrone, cum latrocinio feu* ἐπαυ]οφόρῳ, *prehenfo.*

Si latrocinium fit inventum in cujufcunque terra fit & latro fimul, Dominus terræ & Uxor ejus habebunt medietatem bonorum Latronis & vendicatores eorum Catalla fi illa invenerint, & alteram medietatem, fi repertum fit intra *Sache* & *Soche* perdat Uxor, & Dominus habebit.

Si larecin eft troved, en qui terre qui ceo feit & le Laron [q] ovefque, le Seignor de la terre, & la femme averunt la meited del aveir a Laron, e les chalenurs lor chatel fe ille trovent e latre meited fil eft trove dedanz [r] *Sache* & *Soche*, fil perdra la femme & la Seignor laverad.

NOTES,

[o] *Foffe*—there was another public Way called *Ikenildftreet*. Hen. I. p. 199. l. xii. xiii.

[p] *La pais le Roi*—Thefe four royal Ways were faid to have the Peace of the King, becaufe whofoever committed any Offence on them was to be punifhed in the King's Court only. Ducange, *Ermingftreet.*

32. *De*

Cow) for ſuch Relief; and afterwards let all ſuch Villains be admitted into Frank Pledge.

30. *Of the public Ways.*

Of the three public Ways, *viz.* Watling-ſtreet, Erming-ſtreet, and Foſs; whoſoever kills or aſſaults a Man travelling on either of theſe Ways, he is guilty of a breach of the King's Peace.

31. *Of a Thief taken with the Thing ſtolen upon him.*

If a Thief be apprehended with the Goods ſtolen upon him, let it be on whoſe Land ſoever, the Lord of the Land and his Wife ſhall have a Moiety of the Goods of the Thief; and the Challengers their own Goods, if they find them, and the other Moiety; but if found within Sache and Soche, the Wife ſhall loſe her Share, and the Lord have it.

NOTES.

L. 31.

q *Et le Laron oveſque*—Selden underſtands this Law of a Thief taken with the Manour; in the Saxon Laws, called *Handebind, and Backberend*; and by thoſe Laws if the Thief was under 12 Years of Age, or the Thing ſtolen not of the value of 8d. he was to be pardoned for the firſt Offence. Athelſt. p. 56. l. i. Hen. I. p. 257. l. lix.

r *Sache & Soche.* See Law III.

REFERENCES.

L. 31.

Wiht. p. 12. ix.—Athelſt. p. 56. i.—Canute, p. 143. lxi.—Hen. I. p. 259. lix.

32. † *De Senefchallo.*

A Senefchallo de unaquaque Hidarum Hundredi, homo intra feftum S. *Michaelis*, & S. *Martini*, & Ballivus habebit xxx hidas quietas pro labore fuo, & fi averia fuperent limites, aut aqua iis denegetur, & non poffit quis oftendere nec clamorem nec vim quæ eis facta fuerit, reddat averia.

De [q] Strewarde de chefcon des hides del hundred un home dedenz la fefte Seint *Michiell* & le Seint *Martin*, & *Wardireve* fi aurad [r] xxx hides quites per fon travaile, & fi aveir [s] tres paffent [t] per ilot [u] u il denient waiter, e il ne puffent muftrer ne cri ne force, qui lour fuft faite, fi rendifent laveir.

33. *De colonis & glebæ Afcriptitiis.*

Eos qui colunt terram non debet quis moleftare, præterquam de corum debito cenfu. Nec licet

Cil qui cuftinent la terre ne deit l'um travailer, fe de leur diotre cenfe. Non ne leift a [x] feignurage

NOTES.

† This is a very obfcure Law.

[q] *Strewarde*, this feems to be the Officer who was to take care that the Cattle did not eftray, therefore I have not followed Wilkins, but Lambard, where the Text is *Streward*, and not *Stewarde*, Senefchallus.

[r] *Si aurad xxx hides quites*, "Aura, a raifon de chaque charrue "de terre de l'Hundred ou il fera fa garde, l'exemption de la-"bourer 30 hides;" fhall have for every Plow Land of the Hundred where he guards the Cattle, an Exemption from tilling 30 Hides. Houard, Preuves Juft. p. 103.

[s] *Tres paffent*—moriantur, die. Selden, Ducange.

[t] *Per ilot*—periclitentur—expofed to Danger. Ducange.

[u] *U il denient Waiter*—vel labe aliqua infecta fint, or become infected with any Diforder. Ducange. Selden reads, *devient*.

a Domino

32. *Of Stray Wards, and Ward Reeves.*

A Stray Warde and Ward Reeve ſhall be appointed out of every Hide of Land of the Hundred between Michaelmas and St. Martin, and he ſhall have 30 Hides quit for his Labour; and though ſome of the Cattle died, were expoſed to Danger, or caught ſome infectious Diſorder, yet unleſs proof can be given of ſome violence being offered to them, let him be acquitted, on the Cattle being reſtored in the Condition they are in.

33. *Of the Coloni and Naifs.*

No one ought to exact more from thoſe who till the Land than their due Taſk, nor is it lawful for

NOTES

L. 33.

[x] *Seignurage.* Selden paſſes over this Word; Ducange and Wilkins underſtand it as of the Lords of the Fee; but Houard ſays it has no relation to them, and that in order to comprehend the force of this Expreſſion, we ought to recollect that a Hundred was compoſed of 100 Families. That every one of theſe Families made a Roll of the Freemen, Slaves, and Children belonging to them, of above 12 Years old, and preſented this to the Governor of the Hundred; that the Governor, with 12 of the moſt diſcreet, choſen out of all the Families, twice a Year made proviſional and œconomical Regulations for the Diſtribution of the Works neceſſary for the Cultivation of the Lands; and that the Head of every Family was obliged to ſee theſe Regulations executed within his own Diſtrict. Now theſe Heads of Families, ſays Houard, were what they called the Seignurage; and they could not exact of the Coloni, who were ſubordinate to them, greater Taſks than the Hundred had appointed them to do; and that theſe Coloni depended ſo little on the Heads of the Families, that they could not diſmiſs them while

REFERENCES.

L. 33.

Servants—Homicide committed by them on their Lord—puniſhment. Hen. I. p. 268. 75.

On a Nobleman, Hlothar. & Eadr. p. 7. 1.

 Lord

a Domino feodi amovere Cultores de terra ſua quamdiu rectum ſervitium ſuum facere poſſint. Nativi qui diſcedunt a terra ſua non debent cartam falſæ nativitatis quærere, ut non faciant ſuum rectum ſervitium quod ſpectat ad terram ſuam. Nativum, qui diſcedit a terra unde eſt Nativus & venit ad

departir les cultiuurs de lur terre per tant cum il puſſent le dreit ſerviſe faire. Les [y] naifs ki departet de ſa terre, ne devient cartre faut naivirie quere, qui il ne facent lur dreit ſervice, que apend a lor terre. Li naifs ki departet de ſa terre dunt il eſt nez, e vent a autri terre, [z] nuls nel retenget

NOTES.

they were about their Work ; and when any of them died or ran away, they were obliged to find others in their ſtead ; or in caſe of their Neglect, the Hundred Court did it. Houard, Preuves Juſtificat. p. 122. : but with Deference to Houard, the Subject Matter of this Law ſeems to be the Tenures of Villan-Socage and pure Villenage.

The *Villain-Sockman* at that Time, as well as when Bracton wrote, was diſtinguiſhed from the *pure Villein*, in that he could not be removed from his Eſtate at the Will of the Lord, " a gleba " amoveri non debet, quamdiu velit et poſſit facere debitum ſervi- " tium." Bract. l. i. c. ii. S. I.—l. iv. p. 209. Blackſtone's Conſ. on Copyholders, p. 122, &c.

[y] *Les Naifs*, i. e. Nativi or Villeins by Birth held in pure Villenage; they could not quit their Lands without their Lords Permiſſion, and were obliged to do whatſoever their Lords commanded them. Bract. ut ſup.

[z] *Nuls nel retenget.* Si quis abeat a Domino ſuo abſque venia ipſius, vel in aliam provinciam fugiat, et ille deprehendatur, abeat ub prius fuit. Leges Inæ, p. 21. xxxix.

Nemo ſuſcipiat alterius Servum abſque venia ejus quem antea ſequebatur. Leges Athelſtani, p. 60. xxii.

alteram,

Lords to eject them, ſo long as they perform their right Service. Naifs who leave their Land ought not to procure a Charter of falſe Naifty, on purpoſe to avoid the Service appendant to their own Land. If a Naif abandons the Land of which he is a Naif, and goes to another, let no one retain either him or

REFERENCES.

L. 33.

On a Freeman or others, Æthelbirht, p. 7. lxxxv.—Hlothar. & Eadr. p. 8. iii.

By command of his Lord—Penance—what, Hen. I. p. 265. lxviii.—

Theft, by them—puniſhment, Æthelbirht, p. 7. lxxxviii. lxxxix.—Wiht. p. 12. xi.—Ina, p. 18. xxiv.—Athelſtan, p. 57. iii. Jud. Civ. Lond. p. 66. viii. p. 67. i.

Lying in wait for their Lord—puniſhment, Athelſt. p. 57. iv. Edg. p. 78. vii.

Deſerting their Lord in Battle—puniſhment, Can. p. 145. lxxv.—Hen. I. p. 144. xiii.

Working on the Lord's Day, or not obſerving Faſt Days—puniſhment, Wiht. p. 11. iv, v. ix, x.—Fœd. Edr. & Gut. p. 53. viii.—Canut. p. 140. xlii. 141. xliii.

Purgation and Examination, by Ordeal—puniſhment, Leg. Wight. p. 12. v. vi. vii.—Æthelred, p. 103. iii.—Canute, p. 139. xxix.

Not to quit their Service without leave, Ina, p. 21. xxxix.—Edw. p. 50. x.—Hen. I. p. 251. xli.

Killing a Servant, Mulct, Wiht. p. 12. xi.—Alfr. p. 29. xvii.—Hen. I. p. 264. lxviii.

Beating him, or putting him in Chains. Æthelbirht, p. 7. lxxxvi. lxxxvii.

Not to be ſold into a foreign Country. Wm. Conq. p. 226. xli. p. 229. lxv.

Manumiſſion—what would intitle him to it. Wiht. p. 11. iii.—Alfr. p. 39. xii. p. 30. xx.—Canut. p. 141. lxii.—Wm. Conq. p. 229. lxvi.

The Form of it. Wm. Conq. p. 229. lxv.—Hen. I. p. 270. lxxviii.

Dying in Defence of his Lord—the Heriot to be remitted, and his Inheritance deſcendible. Canut. p. 149. lxxv.

Fighting in defence of his Lord, juſtifiable. Alfr. p. 44. xxxviii—Hen. I. p. 274.

 his

alteram, nullus retineat, nec eum, nec catalla ejus, sed redire cogatur ut faciat servitium suum tale quod ad eum spectat: si Domini non faciunt alterius colonum venire ad terram suam, Justitia id faciat.

ne li, ne se chatels, enz le facet venir arere a faire son servise tel cum [a] a li apend, si les seignurages ne facent altri gainnys venir a lor terre, [b] la justise le facet.

N O T E S.

[a] *A li apend.* Ad eum spectat. The Villein by Birth, performed his Services in respect of his own personal Condition. Blackstone's Considerations on Copyholders, p. 119.

[b] *La Justise le facet.* Breve de nativo habendo. Reg. Br. p. 87. De villanis Regis subtractis reducendis, p. 87. vi.

34. *Ne quis Domino suo debitas præstationes subtrahat.*

Nemo Domino suo subtrahat rectum servitium suum, propter ullam remissionem quam ei antea fecerit.

Nullui ne toille a son Senior sun dreit servise, [c] pur nul relais, que il li ait fait en arere.

N O T E S.

[c] *Pur nul relais.* On account of any relaxation of his Services. If the Villein ran away, and the Lord put in his Claim within the Year, so as to shew he did not wave his sovereign Power, the Villein did not by his Absence gain his Freedom. Non currit Tempus contra Dominum, cum Res per clameum appositum efficiatur litigiosa. Brac. l. i. c, x. s. III.

his Goods, but compel him to go back to perform his due Service; if Lords don't make ſuch as till the Lands of others return to their Land, Juſtice muſt do it.

REFERENCES.

L. 33.

Lord anſwerable for their Eſcape, or Flight. Hlothar. & Eadr. p. 8. ii. iv.—Athelſt. p. 57. iii. p. 60. xxii.—Jud. Civit. Lond. p 67. iii.—Æthelred, p. 102. i.—Canut. p. 139. 28.—Edw. Conf. p. 202. xxi.—Wm. Conq. p. 227. xlvii. xlix.—Hen. I. p. 241. viii. p. 258. lix.

Entertaining the Servants of others without Leave. Inæ, p. 19. xxx.—Æthelſtan, p. 60. xxii. p. 62. i.

Servants not under the Protection of any Lord, how conſidered.—Æthelſtan, p. 56. ii. p. 57. viii.—Hen. I. p. 257. lviii.

34. *Of Services witheld from the Lord.*

Let no one withold from his Lord his due Service, on account of any Indulgence his Lord may have before ſhewn him.

35. Of

35. *De Fœmina gravida quæ capitali supplicio damnatur.*

Si morti damnata sit aut membrorum mutilationi fœmina impraegnata, de ea non fiat justitia priusquam parturierit.

Si femme est jugee a mort, u a defacum des membres, ki seit enceintee, ne faced lum justice des quele seit delivere.

36. *De Intestatorum bonis.*

Si quis intestatus obierit, liberi ejus hæreditatem æqualiter dividant.

Si home mort sans devise, si departent les enfans [d] l'erite entre sei per u wel.

NOTES.

[d] *Si departent les enfans l'erite entre sei.* A succinct Account how Lands have descended in England from the Time of the Britons to our Days may not be unpleasing to the Reader.

The Succession of all the Sons was the ancient customary Law among the British in Wales, and was continued to them by the Stat. Walliæ, 12th Edw. I. Hale's Hist. p. 221.

By the Law of England in the Saxons Times, Lands descended equally to all the Males, the Relicks of which remain in the Gavelkind of Kent, Hale 221. Sull. Lect. p. 149.

Our subsequent Danish Predecessors seem to have made no Distinction of Sexes, but to have admitted all the Children at once to the Inheritance. 2 Black. p. 213.

De intestato mortuis.

Sive quis incuria, sive morte repentina fuerit intestatò mortuus, dominus tamen nullam rerum suarum partem (præter eam quæ jure debetur Hereoti nomine) sibi assumito. Verum eas judicio suo uxori, liberis, et cognatione proximis, juste (pro suo cuique jure) distribuito. Canut. p. 144. l. 68.

The above 36th Law of William's is the only one touching Descents; and Lord Chief Justice Hale says, that from this Law, it seems that, until the Conquest, the Descent of Lands was at least to all the Sons alike, and, for aught appears, to all the Daughters also;

35. *Of a Woman enceinte, condemned to Death.*

If a Woman quick with Child is condemned to Death, or Loſs of Limb, let Execution be reſpited till after her Delivery.

36. *Of the Effects of Inteſtates.*

If a Man die inteſtate, let his Children divide the Inheritance equally between them.

NOTES.

and that there was no Difference in the hereditary Tranſmiſſion of Lands and Goods, at leaſt in reference to the Children. Hale's Hiſt. p. 222.

Afterwards, when William, by Conſent of Parliament, eſtabliſhed the Feudal Syſtem, Lands deſcended to the eldeſt Son only.

Henry the firſt moderated this, and directed the eldeſt Son to have only the principal Eſtate, "primum patris feudum;" the reſt of his Eſtate, if he had any others, being equally divided among them all. Hen. I. l. lxx. p. 266. 4 Black. 414.

In the Reign of Henry II. the Right of Primogeniture ſeems to have tacitly revived, being found more convenient for the Public, than the parceling of Eſtates into a Multitude of minute Subdiviſions; but if there was any uncertainty and unſettledneſs in the Buſineſs of Deſcents or Hereditary Succeſſions in his Time, yet in the Reign of Hen. III. the Law ſeems to be unqueſtionably ſettled, that the eldeſt Son was of common Right Heir, not only in Caſes of Knight Service Lands, but alſo of Socage Lands, unleſs there were a ſpecial Cuſtom to the contrary, and has continued ſo down to theſe Days. Hale's Hiſt. p. 232.

REFERENCES.

L. 35.

Woman big with Child, ſtriking,—puniſhment. Alf. p. 30. xviii.

L. 36.

Of Succeſſion. Can. p. 144. lxviii.—Hen. I. p. 266. lxx.

37. *De adultera a patre deprehensa.*

Si pater deprehenderit filiam in adulterio in domo sua, seu in domo generi sui, bene licebit ei, occidere adulterum.

Si le Pere trovet sa file en adulterie en sa maisonn, u en la maisonn son gendre ben li leist occire ladultere.

38. *De jactu velut ad Legem Rhodiam.*

Si quis ex necessitate alterum occiderit aut propter gubernationem faciliorem, ego jecero res tuas de navi ob metum mortis, de hoc non potes me implacitare. Nam licet alteri damnum inferre ob mortis metum quando periculum evadere non potest, & si de hoc me accuses quod ob metum mortis nihil feci de hoc contemptu & ea quæ in navi restant dividantur in communi secundum Catalla, & si quis jecerit Catalla extra navim, absque necessitate ea restituat.

Si [e] home en puissuned altre seit occis, u per manablement eissilled, Jo jettai voz chosez de la nef pur pour de mort, & d'eo ne me poez enplaider, kar leist a faire damage a altre pur pour de mort quant parele ne pot eschaper, e si de co me mescez, qui pur pour de mort nel feisse de co mespriorai, e les choses qui sunt remise en le nef, seient departis en comune sulun les chatels, e si alcun jetted les chatels hors de la nef, senz busun, sil rendet.

NOTES.

[e] *Si home en puissuned altre seit occis, u per manablement eissilled.*— Si quis alterum imposionaverit, interficiatur, vel perpetuo Exilio damnetur. Ducange.

One would imagine this was a distinct Law, it having no Connection with what follows.

Venefici relegentur ex Terra. Edw. & Guthrun. p. 53. l. xi.

See other Laws de Veneficis.

37. *Of a Daughter taken in Adultery by the Father.*

If a Father ſhall take his Daughter in the Act of Adultery in his own Houſe, or in that of his Son in Law, it is lawful for him to kill the Adulterer.

38. *Of caſting Goods Over-board agreeably to the Rhodian Law.*

If one poiſon another, let him ſuffer Death, or perpetual Baniſhment.

If I caſt your Goods Over-board through fear of Death, you cannot implead me of this; for we may juſtify doing an Injury to another, when there is no other Way of avoiding the Danger of Death: and if you accuſe me of having done this, not through Fear of Death; I will exculpate myſelf of it; and the Goods, which remain in the Ship, muſt be divided in common, according to the Quality of them; and if any one caſts Goods Over-board when Neceſſity does not require it, he ſhall render the value of them.

REFERENCES.

L. 37, See L. 14.

L. 38.

Poiſon—the Puniſhment of thoſe, who by Poiſon wrought pernicious Effects on others. Inæ, p. 26. lxxvii.—Fæd. Ed. & Gut. p. 53. xi.—Athelſt. p. 57. vi.—Edgar. p. 92. xxxix. p. 93. xli.—Northum. Preſ. Leg. p. 100. xlviii.

Spoliation of Goods, puniſhment. Æthelred. p. 104. iv.

39. *De judicio in socium absentem.*

Duo sunt participes ejusdem Pacis, & unus eorum implacitatus absque altero, si negligentia sua perdit, non inde debet damnum cedere alteri, qui absens fuit. Nam quod judicatum est inter eos non debet præjudicare iis qui absentes fuerunt.

Dous sunt perceners d'un [f] ᵹnıþe, e est lun enplaide sans laltre & per sa folie si pert, ne dit per co laltre estre perdant, qui present sud, kar chose juge entre eus, ne fors juge pas les altres, qui ne sunt a present.

40. *De Relevio eorum qui clientes censum pendunt.*

Eorum qui fundum suum tenent ad censum, sit rectum Relevium tantum quantum census annuus est.

Cil qui tenent lur terre [g] a cense, soit lur droit releif a tant cum a cense est d'un an.

41. *De Judiciis.*

Caute prospiciant ii quibus cura incumbit judicia facere, ut judicent uti petunt quando dicunt *dimitte nobis debita nostra*, & prohibemus ut homo christianum extra terram

Ententivement se purpensent cil qui les jugementz unt a faire, que si jugent cum desirent quant il dient [h] *dimitte nobis debita nostra*, & nous defendonz qui lum Chri-

NOTES.

[f] Ᵹnıþe. Lambard, Selden, and Houard, read *Cricbet* instead of ᵹnıþe, and Houard renders *Cricbet*, a Horse.

[g] *A Cense.* This was free Socage. Where the Service was by Fealty only, or by Rent and Fealty only, &c. that Tenure was called *liberum Socagium* or *free Socage.* Blackstone's Considerations on Copyholders, p. 114.

39. *Of Judgment against an absent Partner.*

Two Persons are equally interested in the same Contract, and one of them is impleaded without the other; if Judgment through his Negligence is given against him; yet the other, who was not present, shall not lose his Right; for a Judgment between them ought not to affect those who were absent.

40. *Of the Relief of those who hold by a certain Rent.*

Those who hold their Land at a stipulated Rent, let their right Relief be so much as the annual Rent is.

41. *Of giving Judgment.*

Let those, whose office it is to pronounce Judgment, take particular Care they judge, in like Manner as they pray; when they say—" Forgive us our " Trespasses." And we forbid any one to sell a Christian

NOTES.

L. 41.

[h] *Dimitte nobis peccata nostra, & nous defendonz qui lum Christien*, &c. See Leges Canuti, p. 133. ii. and p. 134. iii. from whence this is plainly taken.

REFERENCE.

L. 39.

Hen. I. p. 248. xxxi.

L. 40. See L. 29.

non vendat, nec præſertim in paganiſmum. Caveat homo quod quis animam ejus non perdat quam Deus vita ſua redemit. Qui injuriam elevaverit, aut falſum judicium hinc proferet aut odii aut avaritiæ gratia, ſit in forisfactura Regis de xl ſolidis; ſi non poteſt allegare quod plus recti facere noluerit, perdat libertatem ſuam, niſi juxta beneplacitum Regis illam ab eo redimere queat. Et ſi ſit in *Danelega*, ſit Forisfactura

ſtien fors de la terre ne vende nen ſurchetut en paiſumne. Wart lum qui lum lamne ne perde qui Deu rechatat de ſa vie. Ki tort eſlevera, u faus jugement fra purcurruz, ne per hange [i] u pur aveir, ſeit en forfeiture le Rei d' [k] xl ſolz, ſil ne pot aleier qui plus dreit fair [l] nel ſont, ſi perdre ſa Franchiſe, ſi al Rei nel pot rachater a ſon plaiſir, e ſil eſt en *Danelae* ſeit forfait de [m] Laxlite, ſil alaier ne ſe pot qui il melz faire ne

N O T E S.

[i] *U per aveir.*—Si quis ira, vel odio, vel timore, vel amore, vel cupiditate, &c. injuſtum judicet, L. H. I. c. xxxiv. therefore the word *aveir* may probably be rendered fear; *en awer*, in doubt Britton, 13. a.—*awoure*, Doubt. Reg. 229. b.

[k] *xl s.*—By the Laws of Hen. I. cxx s. Qui injuſti judicabit cxx s. ſolid. reus ſit, et dignitatem judicandi perdat, niſi redimat erga Regem. Hen. I. c. xxxiv. p. 249. c. xiii. l. p. 244.

[l] *Nel ſont.*—See Law 4.

[m] *Laxlite*, *Lahſlite*, *Laſhlite*,—ruptio Legis, tranſgreſſio Legis, pœna violatæ Legis, from laȝh Lex, ꞅlıe, ruptio, violatio. It denoted the Daniſh Common Forfeiture, which was 12 Ores, or one Pound ſterling; but it varied according to the Condition of the Offender. A Thane paid 5 Marks. He that had Bocland 3 Marks, and a Ceorl 12 ores. *Lahſlite*; *and Overſeuneſs*, *Overſameſſa and Overherniſſa* are ſometimes put as ſynonymous; but the laſt more particularly ſignifies a Contumacy or Contempt of the Court, or a neglect of Duty; it alſo ſignifies the Forfeiture for ſuch Offence, from the Saxon oꝼeꞃ ſuper, and hẏꞃan audire, auſcultare. Ducange. Gloſſ. X Script.

de

ſtian out of the Land, but more eſpecially into a Paganiſh Country; let us take care that that Soul which God redeemed with his own Life, be not loſt. Whoſoever promotes Injuſtice, or pronounces falſe Judgment, through Anger, Hatred, or Avarice, ſhall forfeit to the King 40 s.; and if he cannot prove he did not know how to give a more right Judgment, let him alſo loſe his Franchiſe, unleſs he can redeem it at the King's good Pleaſure: And if he lives under the Daniſh Law, he ſhall forfeit *Lahſlite*, if he cannot

REFERENCES.

L. 41. See L. 15.

Dombec, or Liber judicialis, what. Edw. p. 48. i.—Athelſtan, p. 57. v.—Edgar, p. 77. iii.

Judgment to be impartial. Alfr. p. 32. xliii.—Edw. p. 48. i.—Edgar, p. 77. i.—Canut. p. 133. i.—Hen. I. p. 247. xxviii.

Unjuſt Judgment, the Mulct. Edgar, p. 77. iii.—Canut. p. 135. xiv.—Hen. I. p. 249. xxxiv.

Juſtice, the Denial, or Obſtruction of it; Mulct. Edw. p. 49. ii.—Athelſtan, p. 56. iii. Concil. Ænham. p. 123. iii. p. 124. ii. Canut. p. 135. xiv.—Hen. I. p. 249. xxxiv.

Mercy, to be exerciſed with Judgment. Canut. p. 133. ii.

Appeals to the King, in what Caſe allowed. Edg. p. 77. ii.—Canut. p. 136. xvi.

Judges, who ought to be. Hen. I. p. 241. ix. p. 247. xxix.

de *Lahſlite*, ſi allegare non poteſt quod melius facere non voluerit & quod rectam legem & rectum judicium recuſaverit, ſit foriſfactura erga illum ad quem jus hoc pertinuerit; hoc eſt, ſi ſit ergo Regem, vi libræ, ſi ſit erga Comitem xl ſolidi, ſi ſit in Hundredo xxx ſolidi, & erga omnes eos qui Curiam habent in Anglia, hoc eſt, juxta ſolidos Anglicanos. In *Danelega* qui rectum judicium recuſaverit, ſit is in miſericordia de ſuo *Lahſlite*, nec bene faciat querelam Regi de hoc quod quis ei defecerit in Hundredo aut in Comitatu.

ſolt, e qui dreite lei e dreite jugement [n] refuſerad, ſeit forfait envers celi ki dreit, co eſt a aveir, ſi co eſt envers li Rei vi° Livres, ſi co eſt envers Cunte xl ſolz, ſi co eſt en hundred xxx ſolz, e envers touz i cons ki Curt unt en *Engleterre*, co eſt al ſolz *Engleis*. E en *Danelae* qui dreit jugement refuſerad, ſeit en la mercie de ſa Lahſlite, e ne face [p] bon plainte a Rei dici qui lun li ſeit de faili el hundred u el Conte.

N O T E S.

[n] *Refuſerad*—with great deference, I think this ſhould rather be tranſlated, *gainſay, call, in queſtion, or oppoſe*, than *recuſaverit*, as in Wilkins. The Law of Hen. I. will throw ſome Light on this Paſſage. Qui juſtum judicium ordinabiliter habitum, et legitime redditum improbaverit, ſi Regis Actio ſit, *overſeuneſſe* judicetur, I. L ſol. in Weſt-Sexa. L. Hen. I. Chap. xxxiv. p. 249. See alſo Leg. Canut. p. 135. xiv.

prove that he could not judge better; and whosoever shall oppose right Law, and right Judgment, let the Forfeiture go to him who ought to have had that Right; that is, if the King, vi l.; if an Earl, xl s. If it be within a Hundred, xxx s.; and to all those who have a Court in England, this must be according to the English Shilling. By the Danish Law, he who opposes right Judgment, shall be amerced his Lahslite; and he will very improperly appeal to the King's Court under a Pretence that there has been a Failure of Justice in the Hundred or in the County.

NOTES.

• *vi Livres*, Law Hen. I. l. 41.

p *Bon plainte*—Et nemo apud regem proclamationem faciat de aliquo qui ei secundum legem rectum offerat in Hundredo suo. Leg. Hen. I. p. 250. Leg. Edgar, p. 77. ii. Canut. p. 136. xvi.

10. *Con-*

42. *De pignore quod Namium vocant capiendo.*

Non capiat quis Namium aliquod in Comitatu, nec extra usque dum ter rectum petierit in Hundredo, aut in Comitatu, & si ad tertiam vicem rectum non potest habere, eat ad Comitatum & Co-

Ne [q] prenge hum nammil en Conte, ne de fors d'ici quil eit tresfois demand dreit el hundred u el Conte, e sil a la terce fiee ne pot dreit aver, alt a Conte, e le Conte len a sete le quart jurn, e se cili

NOTES.

L. 42.

[q] *Ne prenge hum nammil*—Houard endeavours to prove that this Law is Norman; but we hope to shew that it is of Saxon Origin. The Passage runs thus, Art. 63. "Des Loix recueillies par Selden, le "Conquérant, en recommendant d'observer les Statuts d'Edouard, "avoue qu'il y a ajoute plusieurs dispositions, *Adauctis his quas* "*constituimus*, *&c.* Et on ne peut douter que celle du 42 Article "ne soit de ce nombre. Il est intitulé *De Pignore quod namium* "*vocant.* Le Gage connu sous le nom de *namps* parmi les Nor-"mands, ne l'etoit pas des Anglois, puisqu'en leur imposant "l'usage, le Legislature est obligé de leur donner en l'inter-"prétation." Disc. Prelim. p. 33. Tom. I. Note 39.

"Il ne fut donc pas difficile à ce Soverain de faire insérer dans "les Statuts d'Edouard quelques Maximes relatives aux Coutumes "de Normandie qu'il avoit résolu de leur substituer; et la traduc-"tion qu' il fit faire de ces Statuts en langue Normande, lui four-"nit un Moyen aisé de parvenir à ce but. Car, sous prétexte de "rendre intelligibles certains droits particuliers à l'Angletterre, on "se servit de noms qui étoient consacrés à désigner des droits Nor-"mands qui n'avoient avec les premiers que des rapports fort "éloignés; et insensiblement la conformité des noms fit confondre "cés différens droits auxquels on les avoit indistinctement ap-"pliqués." ibid. p. 33.

The Conqueror, (says Houard) in the 63d of his Laws given us by Selden, avows his having made several Additions to the Laws of Edward; *Adauctis his quas constituimus*, *&c.* and there is no doubt but that the 42d Law is one of that Number. It is intitled "*De Pignore quod Namium vocant.*" The Pledge, known under the Name of *Namps* among the Normans, could not have been in use among the English, since at the Time of instituting this Usage, the Legislature was obliged to give them an Interpretation of it.

42. *Concerning taking a Diſtreſs, which is called Namium.*

Let no one take a Diſtreſs either within the County or out of it, till he has demanded Right to be done him three Times in the Hundred or County Court; and if he cannot have Right the third Time he demands it, then let him apply to the County Court, which ſhall appoint him a fourth Day; and if the

NOTES.

It was not difficult then for this Monarch to cauſe to be inſerted among the Statutes of Edward ſome Maxims which bore Relation to the Cuſtoms of Normandy, which he had reſolved to ſubſtitute in their Place; and the Tranſlation which he cauſed to be made of theſe Statutes into the Norman Language furniſhed him with an eaſy Means of attaining that End. For, under Pretence of rendering intelligible certain Rights peculiar to the Engliſh, he made uſe of Terms which were appropriated to ſignify ſome Norman Rights which had only remote Connections with the others; and the Conformity in Terms inſenſibly occaſioned theſe different Rights, to which they had been indiſcriminately applied, to be confounded.

Our anſwer to theſe Aſſertions is, that it is very true that William added the Laws, by which feudal Tenures were eſtabliſhed, to thoſe of Edward; but then he at the ſame Time expreſsly ordained that the Laws of Edward ſhould "*in omnibus rebus,*" with thoſe additional Laws, be obſerved; theſe laſt are ſuppoſed to have been enacted ſeveral Years after the Publication of Edward's Laws, and they are in Latin, and not in Norman French. The Titles make no Part of the Original, they being added by Selden; but if they were, it is preſumed that the 42d Law cannot be one of thoſe new Laws, as this learned Author conjectures; for the Term *Namps* a Diſtreſs, though made uſe of by the Normans, comes from the Saxon Verb namian, *capere,* to take; and like many other of our Law Terms, which although they ſeem to be French, are only diſguiſed in a Norman Dreſs, and really have a Saxon Original; and as in the Grand Cuſtumiere of Normandy there is a Chapter of *Nampcs,* there is great Reaſon to believe that the Normans borrowed this and many other of their Laws from the Engliſh, inſtead of the Engliſh from them, as Monſ. Houard would perſuade us. Seld. Eadmer. 194. Fort. Pref. p. 46. Arg. Ante Norm. 121. Pref. 6. Rep.

REFERENCES.

L. 42.

Canute, p. 136. xviii.—Wm. Conq. p. 229. lxiv.

mitatus præfigat ei diem quartum & ſi ipſe defecerit de quibus ipſe poſtulat, tunc licentiam accipiat, ut poſſit Namium capere pro ſuo homine & teſtimonio.

defait de ki il ſe claime, dunt prenge conge qui il puſſe nam prendre [r] pur le ſon lum e pref.

NOTES.

[r] *Pur le ſon lum e pref*—I have followed Ducange—Pro ſua utilitate et proficuo.—Canute, p. 136. l. xviii.—Ut proprium ſuum perquirat.

43. *Ne quis rem aliquam emat ſine teſtibus.*

Nemo emat quantum iv denariis æſtimatur, neque de re mortua neque de viva abſque teſtimonio iv. hominum aut de Burgo, aut de Villa. Et ſi quis rem vendicat, & is non habeat teſtimonium; ſi nullum habeat Warrantum reſpondeat alteri Catallum ſuum, & foriſfacturam habeat qui habere debet, & ſi teſtimonium habeat ut jam diximus advocet tribus vicibus & vice quarta diſrationet, aut rem reddat.

Ne nul achat le vailiant de iv den. de mort, vif, ſans teſtimonie ad iv hommes u de Burg, u de Vile; e le lum le chalange e il nen ait teſtimonie, ſi nad nul Warrant rende lun al hum ſon chatel, e le forfait ait, ki aver le deit; e ſi teſtimonie ad, ſi cum nous eviz deſunes [s] voeſt les treis foiz, e a la quart foiz le dereinet, u il le rende.

NOTES.

L. 43.

[s] *Voeſt les treis foiz*—Ducange and Houard, in their Tranſlations, ſeem to have miſtaken this Paſſage. Selden left it unrendered; but when the Words "*voeſt les treis foiz*" are attended to and

44. *De*

Perſon againſt whom he complains, makes Default; then let him have Leave to take a Diſtreſs ſufficient to make himſelf Amends.

43. *That nothing ſhall be bought but in the Preſence of Witneſſes.*

Let no one buy either dead or live Goods of the Value of 4 d. without the Teſtimony of four Men, either of the Borough or Vill; and if the Thing be challenged, and he has no ſuch Teſtimony, he ſhall not be allowed to litigate the Matter, but muſt reſtore the Goods to the Owner, and let the Forfeiture go to him to whom it belongs; and if he has ſuch Witneſſes as above mentioned, let him vouch them three Times, and at the fourth either prove his Right to the Goods, or reſtore them.

NOTES.

L. 43.

compared with the Law of Canute, which ſays, "*tunc Advocatio* "*fiat ter*," the Difficulty ſeems to vaniſh. Canute, l. xxii. p. 317.

REFERENCES.

L. 43.

Lothar. & Eadr. p. 9. xvi.—Edw. p. 48. i.
Athelſtan, p. 58. xii. p. 61. xxiv.—Edgar, p. 80. viii.—Æthelred, p. 103. iv.—Canut. p. 137. xxii.—Wm. Conq. p. 218. ii. p. 229. lx.

44. *De appropriatione rei.*

Nobis rationi consonum non videtur, ut quis propriationem faciat supra testimonium quod cognoverit id quod interest, & quod nihil quis proprium faciat ante terminum vi mensium postquam averium furto sit ablatum.

Nus ne semble pais raison que lum face pruvance sur testimonie ki conussent co que entre est e qui nul nel prust devant le terme de vi meis, apres ico qui laveir su emble.

NOTES.

L. 44.

This Law was totally unintelligible to Selden; and Ducange, Wilkins, and Houard, differ very much in their Interpretation of it; but I think the following Law of Canute explains it best. Nobis etiam non videtur justum, quod quis possideat aliquid, cum adsit testimonium, et cognoscere possint, quod furto sit ablatum; quod nemo possit appropriare sibi aliquid citius quam post sex menses postquam furto fuerat ablatum. Leges Canut. p. 137. xxii.

45. *De vadimonio deserto.*

Et qui retatus est, & testibus convictus de rebellione, & implacitatus tribus vicibus vitavit, & ad

E cil qui est redte, e testimoniet de [t] deleaute, e le plait tres foiz eschuit e al quart mustrent li su-

NOTES.

L. 45.

[t] *De deleauté*—Spelman, Ducange, and Houard, read, *de leaute*; but I apprehend it should be *de deleaute*, as in Wilkins, and that such Reading will be warranted by the Laws of Edgar, Æthelred, and Canute. Si quis (cujus apud omnem populum labefacta est fides) sæpius fuerit incusatus. Leg. Edgar, p. 78. l. vii. Æthelr. p. 103. v. Canute, p. 137. l. xxiii.

See Note on L. xvi.

quartam

44. *Of claiming Things ſtolen.*

It does not ſeem juſt that any one ſhould keep what is ſtolen, when there is Evidence of its being ſo; or that he ſhould gain any Property in the Thing, till ſix Months after it has been ſtolen.

REFERENCES.

L. 44.

Inæ, p. 22. xlvii.—Æthelred, p. 106. x.—Canut. p. 137. xxii.—Hen. I. p. 262. lxiv.

45. *How to proceed againſt contumacious Offenders.*

If any one who has forfeited his Character among his Neighbours ſtands accuſed of any Crime, and has avoid-

REFERENCES.

L. 45. See L. 50.

Edgar, p. 78. vii.—Æthelred, p. 103. v.—Canute, p. 137. xxiii, p. 138. xxvii, p. 139. xxx. p. 136. xx.

quartam vicem ostendat summonitor tria ejus crimina, nihilominus mandetur homini ut plegium inveniat & veniat ad jus, & si nolit, si non viderit hominem vivum aut mortuum, capiat quantum habet & reddat petenti catallum suum & Dominus habeat medietatem residui, & Hundredum medietatem. Et si nullus Parens aut amicus istam Justitiam deforciaverint, forisfaciant erga Regem vi libras. Et quærat latro quicquid poterit invenire, non habeat warrantum de vita sua, nec per prohibitum placitum poterit aliquid recuperare.

menour de se treis defautes, uncore le mande lum que il plege truse, e vienge a dreit, e sil ne volt, si ne vist lum vif u mort, si prenge lum quanque il ad e si rende lum al chalangeur sun chatel, e [u] li Sire ait la meite del remenant, e le Hundred la meite. Et [w] si nul parent nami ceste justice [x] deforcent, seient forfeit envers li Rei de [y] vi lib. e quergent le larun nen en ki poeste, il seit trove neit warrant de sa vie, ne per defensed plait nait mes recourer.

N O T E S.

L. 45.

[u] *Li Sire ait le meité*—alteram bonorum partem fundi dominus, alteram centuriati habento. Leg. Edgar. l. vii. p. 78. Houard is of opinion, that the *Sire* in this Law is not be understood of a Lord of the Fee, but of the Land; and that the Person accused is not to be considered as a Vassal, but as a Member of the Hundred; and that for this Reason the Hundred is intitled to the remaining Half of his Effects. Houard Preuves Justificat. L. xlv. p. 123.

46. *De*

ed appearing at three Courts, and his three Defaults are proved by the Summoners at the fourth Court; then let him be commanded to find Pledges, and ſtand to Juſtice; but if he will not, nor can be found either alive or dead; then let all which he hath be ſeized and the Value of the Thing claimed be paid out of his Effects to the Claimant; and let one half of the Reſidue go to the Lord, and the other half to the Hundred. And if any of his Kindred or Friends obſtruct ſuch Judgment, let the Forfeiture be 6l. to the King, and Search made after the Thief; and in whoſoever Cuſtody he be found, no Pledge ſhall be taken for his Life, nor ſhall he ever after be allowed to plead any thing in his Defence.

N O T E S.

L. 45.

[w] *Et ſi nul parent nami ceſte juſtice deforcent*—the Forfeiture here ſeems to ariſe from reſiſting the Law; therefore I have taken the Liberty of differing from Selden, Ducange, and Houard, by tranſlating "ſi nul parent n'ami,"—*if any of his Kindred or Friends*, inſtead of *if none*; nul being frequently uſed in this Senſe. *A nul*, to any one, Mir. 332. Haw. Stat. i. 26—*ſi nul*, if any one, Prynn 400—Selden choſe to leave this Part of the Law from the word *null*, as he found it.

[x] *Deforcent*—difforciare rectum; dicitur is qui contra rectum agit. Ducange, difforciare. L. Hen. I. p. 260. l. lxi.

[y] *VI.* lib. See Law 41.

46. *Of*

46. *De Hospitibus.*

Nemo alium recipiet ultra iii noctes nisi is eum illi commendaverit, qui ejus fuerit amicus.

Nuls ne receit hom ultre iii [z] nuis, si til ne li command od qui il fust amy.

NOTES.

[z] *Ultre iii nuis*—This Law is plainly taken from Canute's, "Nemo alterum suscipiat diutius quam tres Dies, nisi ille cui "antea servivit, eum commendaverit." Can. l. xxv. p. 138.

47. *De famulis.*

Nemo hominém suum a se discedere patiatur antequam [b] retatus fuerit.

Ne nuls ne lait sun hum de li partir, pus qui il est [a] rete.

NOTES.

[a] *Rete*—with this nearly agrees the Law of Canute, "Nemo "servum suum a se amoveat, antequam se purgaverit ab omni "suspicione, cujus prius accusatus erat." Canute, l. xxv. p. 138. Bract. 124. l. iii. c. x. S. I.

[b] *Antequam*—rather *postquam*, agreeable to the Text, *pus qui.*

48. De

46. *Of Guests.*

Let no one harbour another more than three Nights, unlefs recommended by him who laft entertained him.

REFERENCES.

L. 46.

Stranger, entertaining three Nights, to be anfwerable for him. Hlothar. & Eadr. p. 9. xv.—Canute, p. 138. xxv.—Edw. Conf. p. 202. xxvii.

If only two Nights, not anfwerable. Ed. Conf. p 202. xxvii.

Villain Fugitive harbouring, to be anfwerable for him. Inæ, p. 19. xxx.

Violator of the Peace—what Purgation. Æthelred, p. 118. x.

47. *Concerning thofe of a Man's Houfhold.*

Nor let any one fuffer his Man to quit his Service, after he has been fufpected of any Crime.

REFERENCES.

L. 47. See L. 33.

Athelftan, p. 60. xxii.—Canut. p. 138. xxv.—Hen. I. p. 251. xli.

48. *De eo qui furibus obviam dederit, & abire permiserit.*

Et qui Latroni occurrerit, & fine clamore eum permiserit abire, emendet juxta valorem Latronis, aut se purget plena lege, quod illum Latronem esse nescivit: Et qui clamorem audierit & supersederit, supersessione Regis emendet, aut seipsum purget.

E ki larun encontre, e sanz cri a acient li leit aler, si lamend a la vailaunce de larun, u se nespurge per [c] plener lei, qui il larun nel sout; e ki le cri orat e sursera, la [d] sursise li Rei amend, u sen espurger.

N O T E S.

[c] *Plener lei*—This is the same as *Lex plenaria*, and *Lex apparens*; *viz.* the Trial by Ordeal or Battle, and called so, because from the Event, the Truth of the Matter in Controversy, as was believed in those Days of Ignorance and Superstition, evidently appeared.

This Law is borrowed almost Word for Word from the 26th Law of Canute; and adopted by Hen. I. in his 65th Law.

[d] *Sursise*—in Saxon Oferhennyrre, in the LL. Hen. I. *Overseunessa.* See Note on Law 41.

49. *De hero ut familiæ sistendæ fidejussor sit.*

Quilibet etiam Dominus habeat servientem suum aut plegium suum, quem, si non retatus fuerit, habeat ad rectum in Hundredo.

E chascun Seniour eit son Serjant, u sun plege [e] que si nele rete, que ait a dreit el Hundred.

N O T E S.

[e] *Que si nele rete*—quem, si non retatus fuerit, Wilkins—but I apprehend there must be some Mistake, the Sense being quite the contrary; and the Law of Hen. I. is " Ut omnis Dominus secum " tales habeat, qui justiciabiles sint, et teneat familiam suam in " plegio suo, et si accusetur in aliquo, respondeat in Hundredo suo, " &c." L. Hen. I. p. 251. xli.

48. *The Mulct for letting a Thief go without raiſing the Hue and Cry.*

And whoſoever meets a Thief, and ſuffers him to eſcape without raiſing the Hue and Cry; he ſhall make Amends to the Price of the Thief, or clear himſelf by Plener Lei that he did not know he was a thief: and whoſoever hears the Hue and Cry and neglects to purſue it, he ſhall make Amends to the King for the Neglect, or clear himſelf.

REFERENCES.

L. 48. See L. 33.
Inæ, p. 20. xxxvi.—Canut. p. 138. xxvi.—Hen. I. p. 263. lxv. p. 244. xii.

49. *Every Lord to anſwer for his Servant being amenable to Juſtice.*

Let every Lord be Pledge for his Servant, ſo that if he ſhall be accuſed of any Crime, he ſhall be amenable to Juſtice in the Hundred.

REFERENCE.

L. 49. See L. 33.
Æthelr. p. 103. i.—Canut. p. 139. xxviii.—Edw. Conf. p. 202. xxi.—Hen. I. p. 251. xli.

50. *De incredibili accuſato in Hundredo.*

Si quis intra Hundredum incuſatus fuerit, iv homines eum retineant, ſe duodecima manu purget, & ſi aufugerit pendente accuſatione, Dominus reddat Weram ſuam, & ſi Dominus incuſetur quod per eum abire permittitur, ſe purget ſexta manu, & ſi non poſſet, emendet verſus Regem, & ſit utlagatus.

Si eſt alquon qui blamet ſeit de dinz le Hundred iv humes le retent, ſei xii main s'eſpurget, e ſi il ſen fuiſt dedenz la chalenge, li ſire rende ſun were, e ſi lun chalenge le Seignour qui per le ſen ſeit ale ſi s'eſcundie [f] ſei vi main, e ſil ne pot envers li Rei lament, e [g] cil ſoit utlage.

NOTES.

[f] *Sei vi main*, i. e. He himſelf making the 6th. See L. 17.

[g] *E cil ſoit utlage*—et ſit utlagatus. Lambard, Selden, Ducange, Houard. This laſt Part of the Law does not ſeem to have been thoroughly attended to by any of the above learned Authors; for by comparing the Words "*cil ſoit utlage*;" with the LL. of Æthelred, Canute, and Hen. I.; it is evident, "*cil*," muſt refer to the Party accuſed, and not to the Lord; as the Puniſhment by Outlawry would not only be too ſevere, but abſurd alſo, after making Amends.

Sit Fur exlex. Æthelred, L. i. p. 103 —Sit Homo exlex. Canut. L. xxviii. p. 139—Qui fugit, Utlaga ſit. Hen. I. L. xli. p. 251.

50. *How one of bad Character, if accused in the Hundred, is to purge himself.*

If any one, whose Character has been impeached within the Hundred by four Men, stands accused, let him acquit himself by 12 Compurgators; and if he flees, depending the Prosecution, the Lord shall pay his Were; and if the Lord be charged with being privy to his Escape, he must clear himself by the Oaths of six Persons; and if he cannot do that, he shall make Amends to the King; and let the accused Person be outlawed.

REFERENCES.

L. 50. See L. 45.

Æthelred, p. 102. i.—Canut. p. 138. xxvii.—Hen. I. p. 263. lxv. p. 264. lxvii.

INTRODUCTORY PREFACE

To the 52d, 55th, 58th, 59th, and 63d,

LAWS OF WILLIAM THE CONQUEROR.

MY firſt Intention was only to have tranſlated the Laws of William I. which are in the Norman Tongue; but as the Landed Property of England underwent ſo great an Alteration by his Eſtabliſhment of the Feudal Syſtem, I judged it might afford ſome Entertainment to the Reader to take a View of the above Laws of William in Latin, which effected this great Change; for this purpoſe I have given a Tranſlation of them, and added ſome Notes from various Authors who have conſidered theſe Laws.

William I. ſoon after his Conqueſt transferred almoſt all the Lands of England to his Followers, and made them Inheritances deſcendible according to the Norman Law: but as thoſe which remained in Engliſh Hands would have gone on in the old Courſe, and been free from the Burthen of Feudal Tenure, it was neceſſary to proceed ſomewhat further; for this Purpoſe, in ſome ſubſequent Part of his Reign, the *commune Concilium* of the Nation was convened, and Laws made, which, in the Event, altered the Military Policy of the Kingdom, aboliſhed the *trinoda Neceſſitas*, and made the Lands of the Engliſh and of the Church liable to Knights Service, as he had done the Lands granted to the Normans; and the Syſtem was thereby rendered uniform.

The Æra of formally introducing the Feodal Tenures by Law into this Nation, is not free from Incertainty. Sullivan places this in the 4th Year of King William's Reign; but Blackſtone, from the Saxon Chronicle, is of Opinion it was in the 20th, the latter End of the Year 1086, when William was attended by all his Nobles at Sarum, and all the principal Landholders did him Homage and Fealty; and he thinks it probable that the very Law thus made at that Council, is the 52d Law of this King; and that the Performance of the Military Feodal Services, as ordained by that general Council, are exacted by the 58th Law. Sull. 287.—2d Blackſtone 49.

L. 52.

Statuimus [a] ut omnes liberi [b] homines fœdere [c] et Sacramento affirment, quod intra et [d] extra universum regnum Angliæ Regi Willielmo Domino

We ordain that all Freemen ſhall oblige themſelves by Homage and Fealty, that within and out of the Dominions of England, they will be

NOTES.

[a] *Statuimus*—This implies it was not by the King alone, but by the *commune Concilium*, or Parliament; for the Style of the King of England, when ſpeaking of himſelf, was for Ages after in the ſingular Number. Sull. 288. Wright. 2 Black. p. 49. See Law 58.

[b] *Liberi Homines*—Theſe were Tenants in Military Service, and were the only Men of Honour, Faith, Truſt, and Reputation, in the Kingdom; and from ſuch as theſe, which were not Barons, the Knights did chuſe Jurymen, ſerved on Juries themſelves, bare Offices, and diſpatched all Country Buſineſs. Brady's Anſwer to Petit, p. 39.

[c] *Fœdere et Sacramento affirment.*—*Fœdus* is the Homage, and *Sacramentum* the Oath of Fealty, and they are placed in the Order they are to be done. Sull. 288.

[d] *Intra et extra univerſum regnum Angliæ*—Theſe Words are particularly to be obſerved; for they made a Deviation from the general Principles of the Feudal Law, and one highly advantageous to the Kingly Power. By the Feudal Law, no Vaſſal was obliged to ſerve his Lord in War, unleſs it was a defenſive War, or one he thought a juſt one; nor for any Territories belonging to his Lord that was not a Part of the Seigniory of which he held; but this would not effectually ſerve for the Defence of William. He was Duke of Normandy, which he held from France; and he knew the King of that Country was very jealous of the extraordinary Acceſſion of Power he had gained by his new territorial Acquiſition, and would take every Occaſion, juſt or unjuſt, of attacking him there; in ſhort, that he muſt be always in a State of War. Such an Obligation on his Tenants, of ſerving every where, was of the higheſt Conſequence for him to obtain: nor was it difficult; as moſt of them alſo had Eſtates in Normandy, and were by Self-intereſt engaged in its Defence. Sull. 289.

[e] ſuo fideles [f] eſſe volunt, terras et honores illius omni fidelitate ubique ſervare cum eo, et contra inimicos et alienigenas defendere.

faithful to King William their Lord, his Lands and Honours, with all Fidelity every where with him will preſerve, and againſt all Enemies, foreign and domeſtic, will them defend.

L. 55.

Volumus etiam ac firmiter præcipimus et concedimus ut omnes liberi homines totius Monarchiæ regni noſtri prædicti habeant et teneant terras ſuas et poſſeſſiones ſuas bene et in pace, libere ab omni Exactione [g] injuſta, et ab

We will and firmly command and grant that all Freemen of the whole Monarchy of our aforeſaid Kingdom may have and hold their Lands and Poſſeſſions well and in Peace, free from all unjuſt Exactions and Tallage; ſo as

NOTES.

[e] *Willielmo Domino ſuo*—not *Regi*, not the Oath of Allegiance as King, but the Oath of Fealty, from a Tenant to a Landlord, for the Lands he holds. Sull. 288.

[f] *Fideles*—this is the very technical Word of the Feudal Law for a Vaſſal. Sull. 288. Gloſſ. XV.

[g] *Exactione injuſta et ab omni tallagio*—that is, from all extraordinary hard Impoſitions and Taxes; not their ordinary Scutage or Aids. Anſwer to Petit, 38.

Notwithſtanding this Law, by which Reliefs were made certain, the Military Fees hereditary, and freed from all extraordinary Taxes, &c. William, and his Son Rufus, had introduced many ill Cuſtoms, and oppreſſed the Military Tenants to a great Degree; ſo that Hen. I. in order to ingratiate himſelf with his Subjects, granted them, on the Day of his Coronation, a Charter, by which *all ill Cuſtoms, &c.* were to be removed. This Charter, Dr. Brady thinks, was intended as a Relaxation or Abatement of the Feudal Norman Law practiſed by his Father and Brother in exacting great Reliefs, and concerning the Wardſhip of Orphans, and diſpoſing of them and Widows in Marriage; but that, at the ſame time, this Charter was an Indulgence granted to the *Norman Engliſh*, ſuch as lived in England, rather than to the ancient Natives, or *Saxon Engliſh*. Brady's Introduct. Vol. 1. p. 265.

omni

omni Tallagio; ita quod nihil ab eis exigatur vel capiatur niſi ſervicium ſuum liberum quod de jure nobis facere debent & facere tenentur; et prout ſtatutum eſt eis et illis a nobis datum et conceſſum jure hæreditario impertum per commune Conſilium totius Regni noſtri prædicti.

nothing be exacted or taken ſave their free Services, which of Right they ought and are bound to perform to us, and as it was appointed to them, and given and granted to them by us, as a perpetual Right of Inheritance by the common Council of the whole Kingdom.

L. 58.

Statuimus [a] etiam et firmiter præcipimus ut omnes Comites, et Barones, et Milites, et Servientes, [b] et univerſi liberi

We ordain alſo, and firmly command, that all Earls, and Barons, and Knights, and Servants, and all the Freemen of our

NOTES.

[a] *Statuimus*—This new Polity ſeems not to have been *impoſed* by the Conqueror, but nationally and freely *adopted* by the general Aſſembly of the whole Realm, in the ſame Manner as other Nations of Europe had before adopted it, upon the ſame Principle of Self-ſecurity. And, in particular, they had the recent Example of the French Nation before their Eyes; which had gradually ſurrendered up all its allodial or free Lands into the King's Hands, who reſtored them to the Owners as a *Beneficium* or Feud, to be held to them and ſuch of their Heirs as they previouſly nominated to the King. 2 Black. 50. See Law 52. 59.

[b] *Servientes*—And their Servants and Eſcuyers. Anſwer to Petit, 38.

According to Mr. Sullivan, theſe were "the lower Soldiers not "knighted, who had not yet got Lands, but were quartered on the "Abbeys." Sull. 289.

In our Year Books, in the Time of Edward III. the Name of *Serjeant* (the ſame with *Serviens*) is uſed for the next to Knight. As where the Court gives Direction to the four Knights to chooſe the grand Aſſiſe in a Writ of Right, *ne eſlies* (ſay they) *nul Serjeant*

homines totius regni noſtri prædicti habeant et teneant ſe ſemper bene in Armis et in equis ut decet et oportet, et quod ſint ſemper prompti et bene parati ad ſervicium ſuum integrum nobis explendum et peragendum cum ſemper opus adfuerit, ſecundum quod nobis debent de feodis [c] et tenementis ſuis de jure facere, et ſicut illis ſtatuimus per commune Concilium totius regni noſtri prædicti,

whole Kingdom aforeſaid ſhall be always fitted with Horſe and Arms as they ought to be, and always ready and well prepared to perform their whole Service to us when there ſhall be Need, according to what they ought by Law to do to us by reaſon of their Fiefs and Tenements; and as we have ordained to them by the common Council of our whole Kingdom aforeſaid; and have given and grant-

NOTES.

tant come vous poies avez Chivaliers convenient. Do not chuſe any Serjeant as long as you can find a proper Number of Knights. 22d Ed. III. 18 a.—26 Ed. III. 57. a. Seld. Tit. Hon. 2d Ed. p. 832.

So likewiſe in the Ordinances of the Parliament of the 46 Ed. III. reſpecting Knights of the Shire, *Serjeant* is placed next to Knight, "*voeſt le Roy que Chivalers & Serjantz des meulx vaues du* "*paies ſoient retournez deſore Chivalers en Parlementz.*" The King wills, that Knights and Serjeants of the moſt Subſtance in the County be from henceforth returned Knights in Parliament. Ruff. Appen. 43.

It began to grow out of Uſe about this Time, and the Title of Eſquire ſucceeded. Seld. 832.

Others are of Opinion that by *Servientes* are meant thoſe who held by Grand or Petit Serjeanty.

[c] *De Feodis et Tenementis ſuis*—for their Fees and Tenures. Anſwer to Petit, p. 39.

et

et illis dedimus et concessimus in fœdo jure [d] hæreditario.

ed to them in Fee in hereditary Right.

L. 59.

Statuimus etiam et firmiter præcipimus ut omnes liberi [e] homines totius regni nostri prædicti sint fratres conjurati ad Monarchiam nostram et ad regnum nostrum pro viribus suis et facultatibus contra inimicos pro posse suo defendendum et viriliter

We ordain also and firmly command, that all Freemen of our whole Kingdom aforesaid be sworn Brothers, manfully to preserve and defend our Monarchy or Government, and our Kingdom with all their Power, Force, and Might, against

NOTES.

[d] *Jure hæreditario*—The great Effect of this Law was to settle two Things, not expressly mentioned in the former; the first, to shew the Nature of the Service now required, Knight Service on Horseback; and the other, to ascertain to all his Tenants, Saxons as well as Normans, the Hereditary Right they had in their Lands; for if that had not been done by this Law, as now all Lands were made feudal, and their Titles to them consequently to be decided by that Law, they might otherwise be liable to a Construction, according to its Principles; that any Man, who could not shew in his Title Words of Inheritance, which the Saxons generally could not do, was but Tenant for Life. This general Law put all on the same Footing, and gave them Inheritances, as they had before, but of another Nature, the feudal one, and consequently made them subject to all its Regulations. Sull. 284. 289. 2 Black. 50. Answer to Petit, 38. See Law 55.

[e] *Liberi Homines*—The Freemen in this Law are the same as are mentioned in the 52d, 55th, and 58th Laws, and they were such as held in Military Tenure, though not knighted; for such as were, are called *Milites*, and the other *liberi Homines*, and sometimes they are taken promiscuously one for another; but they were very different from our ordinary Freeholders at this Day. Answer to Petit, p. 38, 39. Glossary, by the same Author, p. 32. See Law 52. 55. 58.

According to Sullivan, they were "the Saxon Freeholders, and the Tenants of the Church, which now was subjected to Knights Service." Sull. 289.

 servandum,

ſervandum, Pacem et Dignitatem Coronæ noſtræ integram obſervandam, et ad judicium [f] rectum et juſtitiam conſtanter omnibus modis pro poſſe ſuo ſine dolo et ſine dilatione faciendam. Hoc Decretum ſancitum eſt in Civitate *London.*

Enemies, and keep entire the Dignity and Peace of our Crown, and to give right Judgment, and conſtantly to do Juſtice by all Ways and Means, according to their Power and Ability, without Fraud or Delay. This Law was enacted in the City of *London.*

L. 63.

Hoc quoque præcipimus ut omnes habeant et teneant Legem [g] *Edwardi*

This we alſo command that all our Subjects have and enjoy the Laws of

NOTES.

[f] *Judicium rectum et Juſtitiam*—The Judgment they were to give, and the Juſtice they were to do by this Law (beſides that in their own Courts and Juriſdictions) was principally as they were Jurors or Recognitors upon Aſſize, &c.; though ſome of the greateſt of their Milites were often Sheriffs, Hundredaries, and other under Judges, and miniſterial Officers of Juſtice in the ſeveral Counties. Anſwer to Petit, p. 40. Glanville, l. 2. c. x. 11. l. 9. c. vii. 3. lib. xiii.

[g] *Legem Edwardi Regis.*—We have before ſhewn that William the Conqueror, at his Coronation, ſwore to the Obſervation of the Laws of *Edward the Confeſſor*; and with reſpect to ſuch of them as did not claſh with his Deſign of introducing the military Feudal Syſtem, he now again confirms them *in omnibus rebus*; adding thereto the above Laws and ſome others.

Regis

Regis in omnibus rebus, *adauctis* [h] *hiis* quas con-

King *Edward* in all Things; with the *Additi-*

NOTES.

[h] *Adauctis hiis*—We hope it will be no improper Conclusion of these Notes to present the Reader with the very striking View which Blackstone and Sullivan give us of the prodigious Alterations these few additional Laws of William made in the Properties of Landed Estates here, from what was their Nature and Qualities before that Time.

These Estates, in the Saxon Times, had, in general, been the absolute Properties of the Owner; they could be aliened at Pleasure, they could be devised by Will, were subject to no Exactions on the Death of the Owner, but a very moderate settled Heriot paid by the Executor. In the mean Time, on the Death of the Ancestor, the Heir entered without waiting for the Approbation of the Lord, or paying any Thing for it; and his Heir, if there was no Will, was all the Sons jointly. No Wardship or Marriage was due or exacted, if the Heir was a Minor. Now, by the Feudal Customs being introduced, no Alienation without an exorbitant Fine for a *Licence*, no Will or Testament concerning them, availed any Thing: *Aids* towards knighting his eldest Son, or marrying his eldest Daughter, not to forget the Ransom of his own Person, are become indispensable Duties. The Heir on the Death of his Ancestor, if of full Age, was plundered of the first Emoluments arising from his Inheritance, by way of *Relief* and *primer seisin*; and, if under Age, of the whole of his Estate during Infancy. And then, as Sir Thomas Smith very feelingly complains, "when he came to his own, after he "was out of *Wardship*, his Woods decayed, Houses fallen down, "Stock wasted and gone, Lands let forth and ploughed to be "barren," to make Amends, he was yet to pay Half a Year's Profits as a Fine for suing out his *Livery*; and also the Price or Value of his *Marriage*, if he refused such Wife as his Lord and Guardian had bartered for, and imposed upon him; or twice that Value if he married another Woman. Add to this, the untimely and expensive Honour of *Knighthood*, to make his Poverty more compleatly splendid. And when, by these Deductions, his Fortune was so shattered and ruined, that perhaps he was obliged to sell his Patrimony, he had not even that poor Priviledge allowed him, without paying as above an exorbitant Fine for a *Licence* of *Alienation*.

ſtituimus ad utilitatem *Anglorum*.

on of thoſe which we have appointed for the Benefit of the *Engliſh*.

NOTES.

But at length, as *Blackſtone* obſerves, we were happily freed from this complicated Slavery; and Military Tenures with all their heavy Appendages, were deſtroyed at one Blow by the Statute of 12 C. II. c. 24. and all Sorts of Tenures held of the King, or others, are turned into Free and Common Socage; ſave only Tenures in Frankalmoign, Copyholds, and the honorary Services of Grand Serjeanty.

A Statute, which, was a greater Acquiſition to the Civil Property of this Kingdom than even *Magna Charta* itſelf. Sull. 291. 2d. Black. p. 76, 77.

THE END.

www.ingramcontent.com/pod-product-compliance
Lightning Source LLC
Chambersburg PA
CBHW030254100426
42812CB00002B/436